# .Net Knowledge Book

## Web Development with Asp.Net MVC and Entity Framework

Volume 2

First Edition

Patrick Desjardins

Author: Patrick Desjardins

Self-Publishing

Email: mrdesjardins@gmail.com

WebSite: http://patrickdesjardins.com

Printed in the United States of America

Mention de dépôt legal:

Dépôt legal - Bibliothèque et Archives national du Québec, 2015

Dépôt legal - Bibliothèque et Archives national du Canada, 2015



ISBN: 978-2-9813110-2-3

## DEDICATION

I dedicate this book to my wife, Mélodie Savaria, who has been patient during the time I took to write these blog articles and hereafter this book. I also dedicate this work to my parents, who opened the path to all my realizations present and future.

# CONTENTS

| | | |
|---|---|---|
| | Acknowledgments | i |
| 1 | ADO.NET | Pg 3 |
| 2 | ASP MVC | Pg 17 |
| 3 | AUTOMAPPER | Pg 157 |
| 4 | C# | Pg 163 |
| 5 | CSS | Pg 183 |
| 6 | ENTITY FRAMEWORK | Pg 195 |
| 7 | GIT | Pg 321 |
| 8 | IIS | Pg 333 |
| 9 | JAVASCRIPT | Pg 349 |
| 10 | NO SQL, SQL, UNITY | Pg 373 |
| 11 | VISUAL STUDIO | Pg 385 |
| 12 | WEB SERVICES | Pg 421 |

# ACKNOWLEDGMENTS

I wish to thank, first and foremost, everybody who has been patient with me during this process. I wrote twice a week on my blog and the results are in this book. I owe my deepest gratitude to those who challenged me at my work, during conferences and by comments directly on my website. You have helped me to improve every day.

# 1. ADO.NET

This chapter groups every post written during 2013 and 2014 about Ado.Net. Like all chapters in this book, every article is a snapshot of a real scenario that has a high probability of happening if you are using these technologies. You will notice that every article that has been chosen to be included in this book contains the release date to identify when it was written. A permanent link is also provided that allows you to go in and read updates and comments. Feel free to go on the website to add your own comment if you wish.

## Msdtc is Unavailable Error

Release Date: 18-Mar-13
Url: http://patrickdesjardins.com/blog/?post_type=post&p=1958

**MSDTC** *is unavailable* is an error that raises when the service Distributed Transaction Coordinator is not running. To solve this issue, you have to run the service. When you boot your computer (or your server) it is normally by default with startup type to **Manual**.

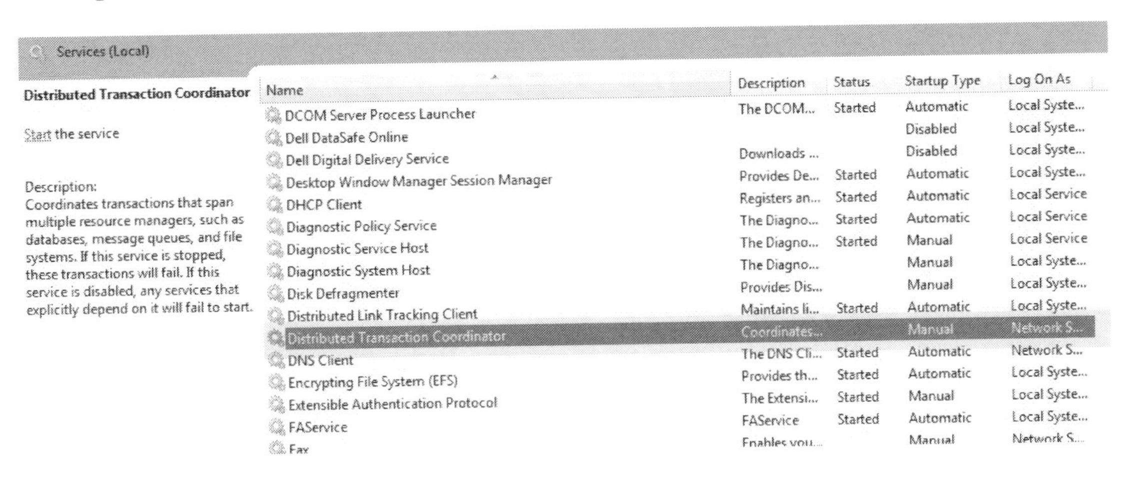


What you have to do is to select the **Automatic** startup type. To change this property, you can double click the service and in the first tab, named **General**, you can choose from a drop-down list the **Automatic** startup type.

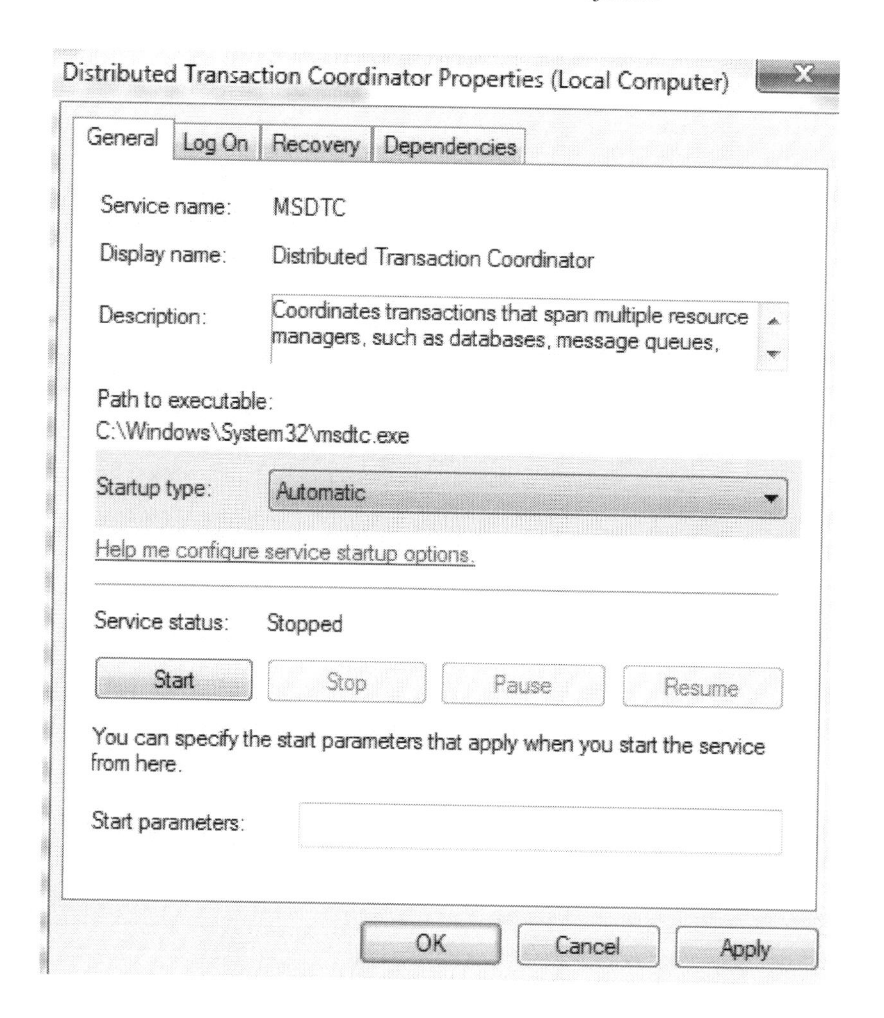


# ADO.NET DataSets in a nutshell

Release Date: 29-Jul-13
Url: http://patrickdesjardins.com/blog/?post_type=post&p=2166

Over a few years now, developers are more and more distant from **ADO.Net** with the popularity of ORM (object relational mapper). Nevertheless, it is important to take the time to remember what is used behind ORM or simply to remember that we can still use ADO.Net classes to achieve the desired behavior with a database. This article describes a disconnect object that contains information that came from a connected persistence container and/or that will be pushed to a persistence container. This is the role of the **DataSet**.

A DataSet is a snapshot of tables from your database. Once it is filled, the DataSet is not anymore connected to the database. A modification to the DataSet will not update the database tables. It does not mean that we cannot send the information back to the desired tables but it will require a new connection to the database. The DataSet is a layer of abstraction between your application data and the persistence storage. By using a DataSet, you do not know exactly if you are saving into one database or several databases, or if you are saving into an XML file.

The first property to know about DataSet is the **DataTableCollection**. This property contains the set of DataTable which can be seen as SQL table columns. The definition of the DataTable (metadata of the table) is defined by a collection of type DataColumnCollection. For data, these are located in DataRowCollection. This one is also a collection. So far, you can see a lot of similarity between DataSet properties and how SQL works. Both have tables, columns and rows.

In SQL, you can use what is called a view to manipulate the output of a table or many tables. With a DataSet, the **DataView** acts the same way by selecting what is shown. This is perfect to map data between your application and data from your persistence storage.

Usually, a DataSet is filled up with a DataAdapter which uses a **DbConnection** with **DbCommand**. They allow the DataSet to fill up and after that the connection can then be closed. The code that follows opens a connection from an SqlConnection that inherits from DbConnection and executes a select statement with an SqlDataAdapter that inherits from DbCommand.

```
var con = new SqlConnection(/*Connexion String*/);
var dataset = new DataSet();
var adapter = new SqlDataAdapter();
adapter.SelectCommand = new SqlCommand(/*Your SELECT statement*/,con)
con.Open();
adapter.Fill(dataset); //The dataset is fill up with data, it's now possible to
close the connection and use the data
con.Close();
```

The main advantage is that you are closing rapidly the connection to the database by releasing the connection to the connection pool. You should always open the connection, do your query, and close it as soon as you can. This will allow other requests to connect to the database. It is a good practice because every database has a limited amount of connections that can be accepted at the same time.

Once the connection is closed and the dataset filled up, you can manipulate the data inside **DataTableCollection**. This can be done in two different ways. The first way is to use the DataSet as a **Typed DataSet**.

```
var dataset = new DataSet();
var prop = dataset.YourEntitiesSet[0].YourProperty;
```

The second way is by using the **UnTyped DataSet**.

```
var prop = (string)dataset.Tables["YourEntitiesSet"].Rows[0]["Property"];
```

DataSet is something that you have to use if you are not using any ORM. We have not seen the complete possibilities of DataSet, like how to update back that database, but in most cases you will use the DataSet only to get data and use DbCommand to insert data to the database.

## How to handle a transaction with any ADO.Net including Entity Framework

Release Date: 01-Aug-13
Url: http://patrickdesjardins.com/blog/?post_type=post&p=2172

Transaction is handled by the namespace **System.Transactions** with **TransactionScope** or with **SqlTransaction** for DbConnection. So, there are two ways to use transaction.

The transaction scope way allows having several transactions and also being in multiple different processes. To be able to have multiple processes/threads transactions, the Microsoft Distributed Transaction Coordinator (**MSDTC**) must be enabled on the machine where the code is running. Having many transactions allows you to have transactions with different sources. That means that you can have a transaction for an SQL database and one with a complete other database. This can happen with multi-threaded applications such as a web application. This can also be required if both transactions are in imbrication. To have the main transaction passes, the imbricated commit and the main commits are required to pass. If one of the transactions fails, the rollback will be executed on all sources. As stated, this requires having MSDTC running on your server/computer. By default, ADO.Net enlists all transactions with the DbConnection. But, you could handle everything manually.

Transaction defines tree levels of trust. Partially trust uses the attribute **AllowPartiallyTrustedCallers,** removes the LinkDemand, and is used with a single application domain. DistributedTransactionPermission (DTP) that uses several transactions, and Full trust use the attribute **FullTrust** which is like DTP with durable resources.

You can use transaction implicit and explicit transaction. Explicit transaction can be defined by using the class System.Transaction.TransactionScope.

```
using (var scope = new TransactionScope())
{
    //Code here that use ADO.Net. Can be code that use Entity Framework (because it uses ADO.Net)
    //...
    scope.Complete(); //Won't abord the transaction, everything is fine. Without this call, everything rollback when the object scope is disposed
}
```

The example above displays a simple use of a transaction scope. First, you can see that we are using the keyword *using* because TransactionScope is disposable, it inherits the interface **IDisposable**. This is not required but if you do not want to use the using statement, you will need to explicitly dispose of the object. Also, you willnotice that we call **Complete()** to tell us that everything is fine. Not calling Complete would call a rollback. However, the documentation states that it is not guaranteed that calling the **Complete()** method will call a Commit of the transaction. Also, calling Complete in the nested scope has no effect on the root scope.

The last thing that you must know is that if you are using the transaction from the **DbConnection**, you can take the transaction and set it to multiple DbCommands and all DbCommands will be then linked together. Here is an example that demonstrates how to start a transaction from an SqlConnection (that inherits from DbConnection).

```
var con = new SqlConnection(/*Connection string*/);
con.Open();
var transaction = con.BeginTransaction();
var cmd1 = con.CreateCommand();
var cmd2 = con.CreateCommand();
cmd1.Transaction = transaction;
cmd2.Transaction = transaction;
cmd1.ExecuteNonQuery();
cmd2.ExecuteNonQuery();
//Later
transaction.Commit(); //or transaction.Rollback();
```

Every transaction has an **Isolation Level**. The isolation level specifies what access the transaction can reach with volatile data. The isolation is set when opening the transaction with SqlConnection.BeginTransaction method.

```
var transaction = connection.BeginTransaction(IsolationLevel.ReadCommitted);
```

Here is the official list of values. The default one is **Read Commited** which blocks the client fromwriting.

| Member name | Description |
|---|---|
| Chaos | The pending changes from more highly isolated transactions cannot be overwritten. |
| ReadCommitted | Shared locks are held while the data is being read to avoid dirty reads, but the data can be changed before the end of the transaction, resulting in non-repeatable reads or phantom data. |
| ReadUncommitted | A dirty read is possible, meaning that no shared locks are issued and no exclusive locks are honored. |
| RepeatableRead | Locks are placed on all data that is used in a query, preventing other users from updating the data. Prevents non-repeatable reads but phantom rows are still possible. |
| Serializable | A range lock is placed on the DataSet, preventing other users from updating or inserting rows into the dataset until the transaction is complete. |
| Snapshot | Reduces blocking by storing a version of data that one application can read while another is modifying the same data. Indicates that from one transaction you cannot see changes made in other transactions, even if you requery. |
| Unspecified | A different isolation level than the one specified is being used, but the level cannot be determined. When using OdbcTransaction, if you do not set IsolationLevel or you set IsolationLevel to **Unspecified**, the transaction executes according to the isolation level that is determined by the driver that is being used. |

Be careful when choosing the isolation transaction. It will affect the performance of your system if you are locking too much information for too much time. It is up to you to know for every scenario the degree of security you need.

# SQL Cache Dependency and SQL Cache Dependency Admin

Release Date: 06-Aug-13
Url: http://patrickdesjardins.com/blog/?post_type=post&p=2181

Since 2005, SQL Server can push notifications when data change. The notification of this push uses the **SQL Cache Dependency**. Before, the SQL Cache Dependency had to continually poll the database to see if data changed. Now, it is a real push. To make it work with, SQL Server you must enable **Microsoft SQL Server Service Broker**.

Once everything is installed properly (SQL Server), you must enable your database to work with a service broker.

```
ALTER DATABASE YourDatabase SET ENABLE_BROKER
GO
```

By executing this SQL statement, you may have an error like this one: "error 9772: The Service Broker in database 'YourDatabase' cannot be enabled because there is already an enabled Service Broker with the same ID." If this happens, just execute :

```
ALTER DATABASE YourDatabase SET ENABLE_BROKER WITH ROLLBACK IMMEDIATE
GO
ALTER DATABASE YourDatabase SET NEW_BROKER
GO
```

The next move is to enable notification with IIS.

```
GRANT SUBSCRIBE QUERY NOTIFICATIONS TO "TESTSERVER\ASPNET"
```

The next step is within the code. You need to set up the notification to list the database. This can be set in the global.asax

```
SqlDependency.Start(ConfigurationManager.ConnectionStrings["yourConnectionString"]
.ConnectionString);
```

You can also make it stop.

```
SqlDependency.Stop(ConfigurationManager.ConnectionStrings["yourConnectionString"].
ConnectionString);
```

In both cases, this should be set up once for your application. Here is an example.

```
string tableName = "YourTable";
string connectionString = "...";
var result = HttpContext.Current.Cache[tableName] as List<T>;

if (result == null)
{
    using (var cn = new SqlConnection(connectionString))
    {
        cn.Open();
        var cmd = new SqlCommand("SELECT * FROM ...", cn);
        cmd.Notification = null;
        cmd.NotificationAutoEnlist = true;
        SqlCacheDependencyAdmin.EnableNotifications(connectionString);
        if (!SqlCacheDependencyAdmin
            .GetTablesEnabledForNotifications(connectionString)
                .Contains(tableName))
        {
            SqlCacheDependencyAdmin
                .EnableTableForNotifications(connectionString, tableName);
        }
```

```
            var dependency = new SqlCacheDependency(cmd);
            SqlDataReader reader = cmd.ExecuteReader();
            try
            {
                while (reader.Read())
                {
                    // Load the list into result
                }
            }
            finally
            {
                // Always call Close when done reading.
                reader.Close();
            }

            HttpContext.Current.Cache.Insert(tableName, result, dependency);
        }
    }
```

As you can see, it checks if the table exists. If not, it creates a table called AspNet_SqlCacheTablesForNotification where every table name will have a row. If a value changes, the entry in this table will be removed.

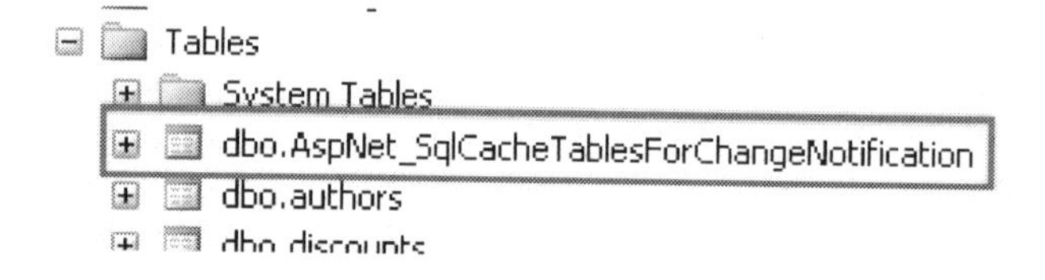


This is quite interesting for a distributed scenario where multiple sources can change the value. The SQL Server acts as a gateway where resides the information about whether the data is cached or not.

To conclude, we have seen that we can use the **SqlCacheDependencyAdmin** to enable the notification and also to create the table. We have seen that we can use the SqlCacheDependency with the cache to synchronize data between the database and the caching system. When the database changes, the cache will be flushed.

## If your notification is not triggered

I suggest that you search for a table called **sys.transmission_queue** in your database. Your notification should be stored here but was not delivered. The cause can be a lot of thing but you should try to verify if you are allowed to create the table by code, which requires being able to use the EXECUTE statement.

# SimpleMembershipProvider or SqlMembershipProvider

Release Date: 29-Jul-13
Url: http://patrickdesjardins.com/blog/?post_type=post&p=2283

I have been using for a few months in most of my projects the **SimpleMembershipProvider** instead of the old **SqlMembershipProvider**. SqlMembershipProvider has been there for over 10 years and, since Asp.Net MVC4, a new mechanism is available. This new provider comes by default with a new Asp.Net MVC project and uses the reference: WebMatrix.WebData.

The main goal of this new library is to simplify the use of a user-password application. It also gives the possibility of more options to store the information. SQL Server is still behind but you can now easily use Azure storage if desired. It also simplifies by a lot the number of tables and views required in the past by SqlMembershipProvider. Now, the tables are limited to only a few and you can customize their schema, the name of the tables, and also field names.

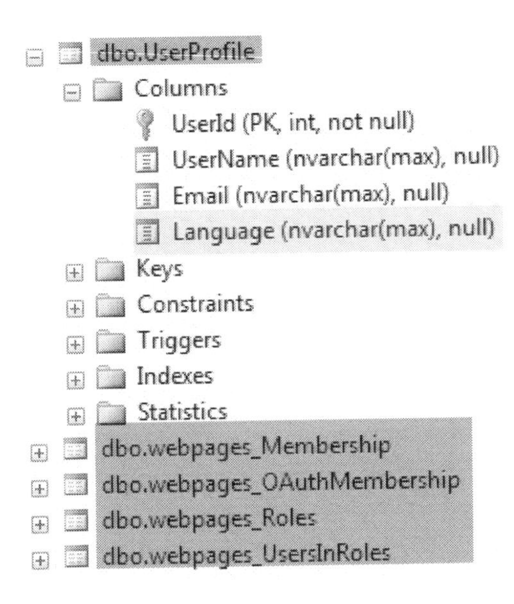


As you can see in the image above, you can add a Language field. This requires only adding a property and letting Entity Framework handle the rest.

```
[Table("UserProfile")]
public class UserProfile : ICurrentUser
{
    public UserProfile()
    {
```

```
        this.UserName = "Anonymous";
        this.Language = "en-US";
    }

    [Key]
    [DatabaseGenerated(DatabaseGeneratedOption.Identity)]
    public int UserId { get; set; }

    public string UserName { get; set; }

    public string Email { get; set; }

    public string Language { get; set; }
}
```

If you are using Entity Framework with the **migration tool**, you just need to add to your seed method one line.

```
WebSecurity.InitializeDatabaseConnection(
    "DefaultConnection",
    "UserProfile",
    "UserId",
    "UserName", autoCreateTables: true);
```

The first parameter is the Entity Framework connection string to your database; the second is the table name for the user, then the column id for the user, followed by the name that is required when we logon.

If you need to have a default role and user in your seed you can add them by using the Api.

```
protected override void Seed(DatabaseContext context)
{
  base.Seed(context);


  WebSecurity.InitializeDatabaseConnection(
  "DefaultConnection",
  "UserProfile",
  "UserId",
  "UserName", autoCreateTables: true);

  if (!Roles.RoleExists(Model.Roles.ADMINISTRATOR))
    Roles.CreateRole(Model.Roles.ADMINISTRATOR);

  if (!Roles.RoleExists(Model.Roles.NORMAL))
    Roles.CreateRole(Model.Roles.NORMAL);
```

```
  if (!WebSecurity.UserExists("123123"))
    WebSecurity.CreateUserAndAccount("123123", "123123", new {
Email="123123@123.com", Language="fr-CA"});
  if (!WebSecurity.UserExists("qweqwe"))
    WebSecurity.CreateUserAndAccount("qweqwe", "qweqwe", new { Email =
"qweqwe@qwe.com", Language = "en-US" });

  if
(!((IList<string>)Roles.GetRolesForUser("123123")).Contains(Model.Roles.ADMINISTRA
TOR))
    Roles.AddUsersToRoles(new[] { "123123", "qweqwe" }, new[] {
Model.Roles.ADMINISTRATOR });
  if
(!((IList<string>)Roles.GetRolesForUser("qweqwe")).Contains(Model.Roles.NORMAL))
    Roles.AddUsersToRoles(new[] { "qweqwe" }, new[] { Model.Roles.NORMAL });
}
```

I suggest you read further in Jon Galloway's blog article: http://tinyurl.com/cd23e6h.

## Using Intellitrace to help with debugging your .Net

Release Date: 14-Jan-14
Url: http://patrickdesjardins.com/blog/?post_type=post&p=2387

IntelliTrace is available since Visual Studio 2010 and it is available on the **Ultimate** edition only. This may be the reason why it is not very popular since a lot of developers do not have the ultimate version. Nevertheless, it is a powerful debugging tool and it has been improved slightly with the 2012 and 2013 version of Visual Studio. In short, IntelliTrace is an enhancement of the traditional breakpoint debugging, but not a replacement.

IntelliTrace allows you to have a snapshot of steps in time. This mean that if you hit a breakpoint or if you have an exception that breaks the code, IntelliTrace can show you the stack with different value that have been set. The traditional debugging allows you to modify values of variable, but IntelliTrace does not. They have different goals.

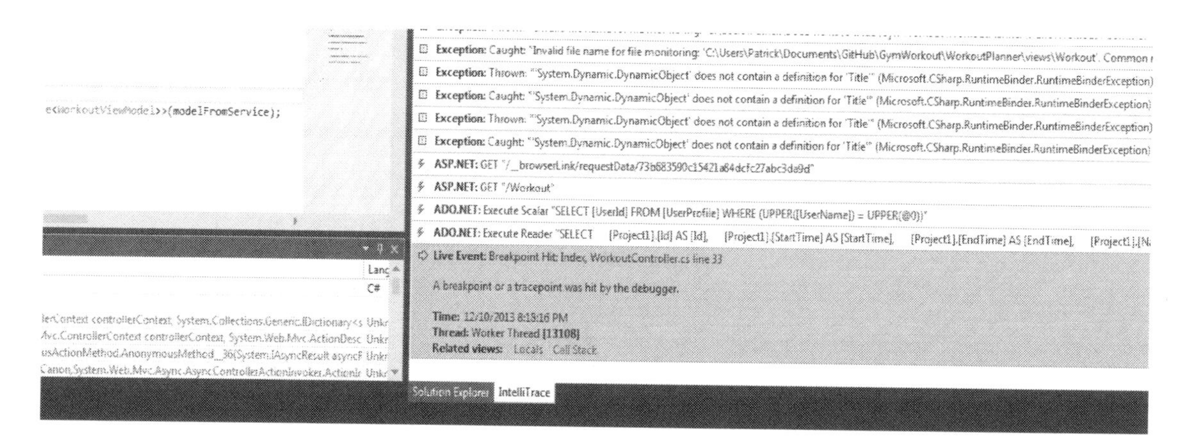


The screenshot above shows some information that you can get with a simple call to a controller. As you can see, we have information about the MVC routing and also about what SQL Query has been sent to the database. This allows you to not have to use an SQL profiler to know what is sent to the database.

```
ADO.NET: Execute Reader "SELECT     [Project1].[Id] AS [Id],     [Project1].[StartTime] AS [StartTime],     [Project1].

The command text "SELECT
    [Project1].[Id] AS [Id],
    [Project1].[StartTime] AS [StartTime],
    [Project1].[EndTime] AS [EndTime],
    [Project1].[Name] AS [Name],
    [Project1].[Goal] AS [Goal],
    [Project1].[UserId] AS [UserId],
    [Project1].[C1] AS [C1],
    [Project1].[Id1] AS [Id1],
    [Project1].[Name1] AS [Name1],
    [Project1].[Order] AS [Order],
    [Project1].[UserId1] AS [UserId1],
    [Project1].[Workout_Id] AS [Workout_Id]
    FROM ( SELECT
        [Extent1].[Id] AS [Id],
        [Extent1].[StartTime] AS [StartTime],
        [Extent1].[EndTime] AS [EndTime],
        [Extent1].[Name] AS [Name],
        [Extent1].[Goal] AS [Goal],
        [Extent1].[UserId] AS [UserId],
        [Extent2].[Id] AS [Id1],
        [Extent2].[Name] AS [Name1],
        [Extent2].[Order] AS [Order],
        [Extent2].[UserId] AS [UserId1],
        [Extent2].[Workout_Id] AS [Workout_Id],
        CASE WHEN ([Extent2].[Id] IS NULL) THEN CAST(NULL AS int) ELSE 1 END AS [C1]
        FROM  [dbo].[Workouts] AS [Extent1]
        LEFT OUTER JOIN [dbo].[WorkoutSessions] AS [Extent2] ON [Extent1].[Id] = [Extent2].[Workout_Id]
        WHERE ([Extent1].[UserId] = @p__linq__0) AND (@p__linq__0 IS NOT NULL)
    ) AS [Project1]
    ORDER BY [Project1].[Id] ASC, [Project1].[C1] ASC" was executed on connection "Data Source=.\SQLEXPRESS;Ini
Security=SSPI;MultipleActiveResultSets=True", building a SqlDataReader.

Time: 12/10/2013 8:22:17 PM
Thread: Worker Thread [14076]
Related views:   Locals   Call Stack
```

If you double click the line entry in the IntelliTrace, you see the whole detail but also the code window is going to the line where the data has been gathered. In the example above, the SQL query, the code selected the third line of the following code, the line that calls the repository.

```
public IEnumerable<Workout> GetAll()
{
    var listModel = Repository.Workout.GetAll().ToList();
    return listModel;
}
```

To enable the IntelliTrace or to change some option, go intoTools>Options>Intellitrace.

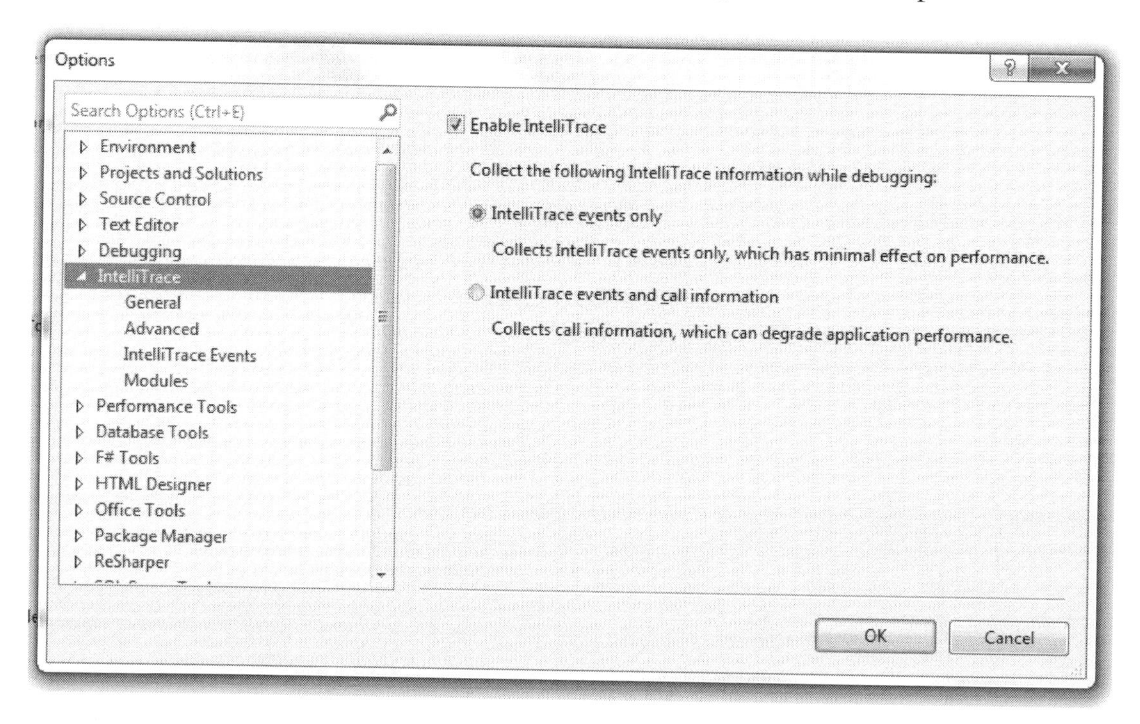


The default options allow IntelliTrace to work with events. This means that IntelliTrace has been injected in the code and records events like SQL query, http errors, exceptions, etc. It is possible to collect more information. To enable additional collection of information, in the option select *events and call*. This will slow down your debugging sessions because it injects additional code inside your code to collect information. However, richer information is recorded.

- Function name
- Values of primitive data types passed as parameters and returned value for every method
- Values of properties when they are read or changed

Call is reachable by filtering at the top of the IntelliTrace window and also from event. At the button of the event, a link "Calls" is available. If you click on it, the list of calls will be displayed. It looks a lot like the normal debugging .

# 2. ASP MVC

This chapter groups every post written during 2013 and 2014 about ASP.NET MVC. Like all chapters in this book, every article is a snapshot of a real scenario that has a high probability of happening if you are using these technologies. You will notice that every article that has been chosen to be included in this book contains the release date to identify when it was written. A permanent link is also provided that allows you to go in and read updates and comments. Feel free to go on the website to add your own comment if you wish.

## Validation with ViewModel

Release Date: 14-Jan-13
Url: http://patrickdesjardins.com/blog/?post_type=post&p=1531

This post will not explain how to do it with enterprise pattern but will focus on some solutions available to validate your Model/ViewModel with Asp.Net MVC. This article won't focus on the advantage of using **ViewModel** instead of directly using **Model** object to the view. The article will show you how to validate your view model without having to repeat yourself in several places with your validation. We want to respect the DRY concept which specifies that we should never repeat ourselves.

First of all, Asp.Net MVC will call the data annotation during the data binding and whether the class inherits from **IValidatableObject** the method **Validate**. The problem with using ViewModel is that during the binding of all the form to the ViewModel object, Asp.Net MVC executes the validation against the ViewModel and not the Model. As it should be, the validation and Data Annotation are not on the ViewModel which is bound to the controller, nor does it inherit from IValidatableObject. Also, the mapping from the View Model to the Model occurs later in the process. This means that we will need to manually call the validation to trigger the validation process which has been done to the view model.

Second, the errors which are associated with properties may not be linked directly by the model to the view model. For example, your view model may have a property FullName which concatenantes the FirstName and LastName property. During the validation process, if an error occurs on the FirstName or the LastName property, the error will be associated to those property names and not the FullName property of the ViewModel. This results in the error not being displayed around the control in the view.

There are several solutions. The easiest is to only display errors in the summary. We simply need to set **ExcludePropertyErrors** to false in the summary.

```
@Html.ValidationSummary(false)
```

By default, if no parameter is provided, the value is also false. So, you do not need to explicitly write *false*. Here is the ValidationExtensions.cs code for the two methods.

```
public static MvcHtmlString ValidationSummary(this HtmlHelper htmlHelper)
{
    return ValidationSummary(htmlHelper, false /* excludePropertyErrors */ );
}

public static MvcHtmlString ValidationSummary(this HtmlHelper htmlHelper, bool
excludePropertyErrors)
{
    return ValidationSummary(htmlHelper, excludePropertyErrors, null /* message
*/);
}
```

A second solution is to map the property from the model to the view model.

ScottGu (http://tinyurl.com/lw97hme) has a post that contains a helper class that does the job.

```
public static class ControllerExtensions
{
    public static bool TryValidateAndTranslate(this Controller controller, object
model, string prefix, object propertyMap)
    {
        return TryValidateAndTranslate(controller, model, prefix, new
RouteValueDictionary(propertyMap));
    }

    public static bool TryValidateAndTranslate(this Controller controller, object
model, string prefix, RouteValueDictionary propertyMap)
    {
    ModelMetadata metadata = ModelMetadataProviders.Current.GetMetadataForType(()
=> model, model.GetType());

    foreach (ModelValidationResult validationResult in
ModelValidator.GetModelValidator(metadata,
controller.ControllerContext).Validate(null))
    {
    var propertyName = CreatePropertyName(validationResult.MemberName, prefix,
propertyMap);
    controller.ModelState.AddModelError(propertyName, validationResult.Message);
    }

    return controller.ModelState.IsValid;
    }
```

```
    private static string CreatePropertyName(string memberName, string prefix,
RouteValueDictionary propertyMap)
    {
        string propertyName = null;
        object output = null;
        if (propertyMap.TryGetValue(memberName, out output))
            propertyName = String.Format("{0}.{1}", prefix, output.ToString());
        else
            propertyName = String.Empty;

        return propertyName;
    }
}
```

From there, you need to call the **TryValidateAndTranslate** method. The method will loop all validations associated to the object which can be a data annotation validation or a validation written inside the Validate method of **IValidatableObject**. The **ModelValidator.GetModelValidator** method is in fact used by the framework when you are using **TryValidateModel**.

The use of this method should be inside the method of the controller where the form is posted, just after the mapping from the ViewModel to the Model.

```
{//... action method
//... map view model to model
if (!this.TryValidateAndTranslate(
                modelObject,
                "ModelClassName",
                new { FirstName = "FullName", Property2 = "Property2" }))
    return View(viewModel);
}
//... else return where you want to go when everything is without error
```

If something is wrong, we display the view again with the view model; otherwise, we redirect to the list view or to any view you want where no error is found. As you can see, the last parameter lets you specify that the validation on FirstName property should be mapped to FullName. Of course, a better approach would be to set up in a central place all the mapping. The example is really just illustrative because you should try to map those properties with something like **AutoMapper** and reuse the mapping from it.

## What is the role of the Viewstart file in an Asp.Net MVC?

Release Date: 16-Jan-13
Url: http://patrickdesjardins.com/blog/?post_type=post&p=1600

Since version 3.0 of the Asp.Net MVC framework, you can use the **ViewStart** file inside the View folder. You can use it inside your area (inside the views of your area) and also have multiple ViewStart files within the View folder if your views contain a sub directory.

The ViewStart files are read by Asp.Net MVC from the root of the view folder to the deepest folder of the view that is used by the request. So, if you are using an area which has several folders for different views, you can have a ViewStart inside the "Views" folder and one inside the "Views/Folder1." Asp.Net MVC will read the ViewStart from the "Views" folder and then the one inside "Views/Folder1."

Another characteristic of the ViewStart is that it must be called "_ViewStart.cshtml". It must start with an underscore and use the .cshtml extension.

The way Asp.Net MVC reads the ViewStart file is to avoid repeating some code that must be the same between views. For example, you can define layout for the view (the master page) in one place. Instead of defining the layout at the top of each view, you can simply define a layout at the root of your views folder as file _ViewStart.cshtml and use the layout statement. Here is an example of a ViewStart file that defines the layout.

```
@{
    Layout = "~/Views/Shared/_MasterPage.cshtml";
}
```

If you need a different layout for a specific view, simply set the layout inside the view or inside a ViewStart inside the folder of the view. Since the order of reading is from the root of the Views folder to its subdirectory, this last ViewStart will set the Layout property and **override** the one defined previously.

If you are getting an exception about a cast, like the following error, it is because you are using the ViewStart outside the Views folder. You need to change the ViewStart location.

*Unable to cast object of type 'ASP._Page_Areas_Admin__ViewStart_cshtml' to type 'System.Web.WebPages.StartPage*

From there, you are limited in what you can do. But, you have access to the **ViewContext.TempData** which lets you set the variables' values. This can be interesting for future validation in further levels of ViewStart. For example, you can set something at the root of the ViewStart and redefine it later depending on some logic. Or you can add information in a list and if it is in the list in a further level perform an action.. At the end, in the Layout you could read the TempData and act in consequence.

In real life, I have once used the ViewStart with a TempData to set a JavaScript file name that needed to be loaded but not for two folders. In that ViewStart, the entry was removed. In the master page, the TempData was read and the JavaScript loaded.

```
//_ViewStart.cshtml : At the root for every views
@{
    Layout = "~/Views/Shared/_Layout.cshtml";
    ViewContext.TempData.Add("MyFileKey", @Url.Content("~/Scripts/MyFile.js"));
}

//_ViewStart.cshtml : Inside the View directory of the Area that we do not want
the JavaScript
@{
    Layout = "~/Views/Shared/_Layout.cshtml";
    ViewContext.TempData.Remove("MyFileKey");
}

//_layout.cshtml
<head>
//...

  @if(ViewContext.TempData.ContainsKey("MyFileKey"))
  {
    <script src="@ViewContext.TempData["MyFileKey"]" type="text/javascript" >
</script>
  }
//...
</head>
```

You can get more information about this at this url: http://tinyurl.com/l4v77um.

From here, you should be able to understand that the ViewStart is a way to not repeat yourself between views. You should also understand that not only the ViewStart inside the view folder of the view is executed but all ViewStart in the path of your view from the root to your view is executed.

## How to know which button submits a form to an Asp.Net MVC controller

Release Date: 04-Feb-13
Url: http://patrickdesjardins.com/blog/?post_type=post&p=1710

You may want to have multiple buttons that submit your form and do something different in a single action of your controller. So far it works this way by default but if you want to do a different action depending on which button has been used, some work needs to be done.

An example that could come up is that you want to be able to create a new entity from the view but also be able to create in batch. One button will insert the entity into the database and return into the edit mode of the newly-added entity, while a second button can simply reset the form to let you insert another new entity.

The secret is that the submit button is also an input which can have a name and a value. You simply need to have the same name and two different values.

```
<button type="submit" name="ActionSave" value="insert">Save</button>
<button type="submit" name="ActionSave" value="insertAndContinue">Save and
continue</button>
```

You can, from here, change your view model to have a property ActionSave (string) or you can go directly into the Form collection.

If you are using the **Form Collection**, the action inside your controller will look like this:

```
if (Request.Form["ActionSave"] == "insertAndContinue")
{
    // ...
}
else
{
    // ...
}
```

As you can see, you will need to define three constants — one for the command button name, one for the Save and one for the SaveAndContinue. But, this is only if you want some clean code. Otherwise, if you are not using the form collection option and instead using the ViewModel option, you need to check the value directly from the view model.

```
if (viewModel.Action == SaveAndContinue)
{
    // ...
}
```

The example above verifies the Action property of the View Model class to check if it is equal to the SaveAndContinue constant. Since the property is a string, you can have many different buttons in an action. They will all link to the same action method but with an if statement you can create a single method for each “sub-action.”

# The name model does not exist in current context with Asp.Net MVC using Area

Release Date: 06-Feb-13
Url: http://patrickdesjardins.com/blog/?post_type=post&p=1712

*The name 'model' does not exist in current context.* This is the error you can get in a view if you create the view without using an Asp.Net MVC template to create the Area first. How come the framework does not understand the command **@model**? Well, every area must have a **web.config** that will contain the definition of a specific .Net library and one of them must be the razor library to use the Razor syntax, which contains the model.

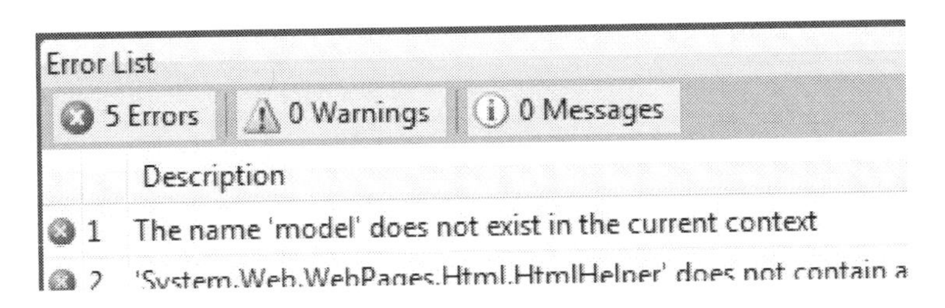


This error occurs when you create the folder without adding manually the configuration file. This is why it is always more convenient to let Visual Studio create the area. Otherwise, you can add this code in the web.config.

```
<system.web.webPages.razor>
  <host factoryType="System.Web.Mvc.MvcWebRazorHostFactory, System.Web.Mvc,
Version=3.0.0.0, Culture=neutral, PublicKeyToken=31BF3856AD364E35" />
  <pages pageBaseType="System.Web.Mvc.WebViewPage">
    <namespaces>
      <add namespace="System.Web.Mvc" />
      <add namespace="System.Web.Mvc.Ajax" />
      <add namespace="System.Web.Mvc.Html" />
      <add namespace="System.Web.Routing" />
    </namespaces>
  </pages>
</system.web.webPages.razor>
```

However, this error can be present when you use Visual Studio if the area has been created by using **"New Folder"** instead of **"New Area."** So watch which Visual Studio option you choose in the context menu.

# How to bind a collection of JavaScript items to an abstracted Asp.Net MVC collection

Release Date: 13-Feb-13
Url: http://patrickdesjardins.com/blog/?post_type=post&p=1837

Binding a JavaScript collection of items into an abstract class or interface collection is a scenario plausible in multiple business domains. Let's say that you have a collection that is built from an external service that your JavaScript needs to send back to the server. Or even simpler, let's just say that you have a JavaScript grid that when you save you take all rows of your table and send it back to the server but this one has a model which is a collection of **Interface**. How you can bind everything back together?

First, let's take some minutes to understand the mechanism. The example of a collection is simpler to understand. We have a **Model** that is bound to the **View** and the collection is **ICollection**. Having to create a table is a simple matter of looping the collection and displaying the properties needed of the interface to the UI.

For example, here is what could be the Model:

```
UIHint("MyTableTemplate")]
public readonly ICollection<IMyInterface> MyCollection;
```

The *MyTableTemplate* is an Asp.Net MVC template that simply loops the collection and displays everything inside an Html **table**, with multiple **tr** and **td**. When it is time to save everything back to the server, we need to send back the collection, which could have changed via Javascript. Rows can have been deleted, and some added. How to send back this table to the Asp.Net server? Simply by using serialization. On the submit, we need to hook the click's event and store the table serialized into a hidden field. The hidden field must have the same name of the Model property to be automatically bound by Asp.Net MVC binding. In our case, we will have a hidden field with the name "*MyCollection.*" The code below shows you how to do it generically, by having the Template using the information about the name of the property and using it for the hidden field.

```
@{
    var controlPropertyName = ViewData.TemplateInfo.HtmlFieldPrefix;
}
<input type="hidden" value="" name="@controlPropertyName" />
```

Having the same name for the hidden field and the model property lets Asp.Net MVC know where to map the information. The JavaScript invoked into the serialization is quite simple. It takes all rows and you create a JavaScript object that contains the info. The code below displays how to serialize with JavaScript two cells per row. As you can see, a "data-key" was set by the template to the row to have a unique identifier. This lets us know that this row is not new because a new row won't have any ID. The deserialization will put the default value for your key at the deserialization time.

```
var obj = [];
$('#YouTable tbody tr').each(function () {
    var tempo = {};
    tempo.PropertyKey = $(this).attr('data-key');
    tempo.Property1 = $(this).find('td').eq(0).html();
    tempo.Property2 = $(this).find('td').eq(1).html();
    obj.push(tempo);
});
$('#YourHiddenField').val(JSON.stringify(obj));
```

Now let's see what happens. Asp.Net MVC will try to bind. In fact, it should crash, and it's logical because we tried to bind to an interface. What we need to do is to create a ModelBinder and handle this specific case. Since you should know which concrete type is used for this case, when deserializing you simply need to specify to which concrete type the deserializer must instanciate.

The first step is to create a class that inherits from **IModelBinder**. This will give you the **BindModel** method. This class will be added into the tool box of Asp.Net MVC when trying to bind Http Request into the class.

```
public object BindModel(ControllerContext controllerContext, ModelBindingContext
bindingContext)
{
    var valueResult =
bindingContext.ValueProvider.GetValue(bindingContext.ModelName);
    var modelState = new ModelState { Value = valueResult };

    MyInterface actualValue = null;
    try
    {
        actualValue =
JsonConvert.DeserializeObject<MyInterface>(valueResult.AttemptedValue);
    }
    catch (FormatException e)
    {
        modelState.Errors.Add(e);
    }
    bindingContext.ModelState.Add(bindingContext.ModelName, modelState);
    return actualValue;
}
```

We also need to register the **ModelBinder** in the **Global.asax.cs** inside the **ApplicationStart** method.

```
ModelBinders.Binders.Add(typeof(IMyInterface), new MyInterfaceTypeModelBinder());
```

In the case that *IMyInterface* has some property which is interface too, you may need to specify to the deserializer to what type to map them. Here is an example.

```
public class MyInterfaceTypeModelBinder : IModelBinder
{
    public object BindModel(ControllerContext controllerContext,
ModelBindingContext bindingContext)
    {
        var valueResult = bindingContext.ValueProvider
                                        .GetValue(bindingContext.ModelName);
        var modelState = new ModelState { Value = valueResult };

        MyInterface actualValue = null;
        var settings = new JsonSerializerSettings();
        settings.Converters.Add(new MyOtherInterfaceTypeConverter());
        try
        {
            actualValue =
JsonConvert.DeserializeObject<MyInterface>(valueResult.AttemptedValue, settings);
        }
        catch (FormatException e)
        {
            modelState.Errors.Add(e);
        }
        bindingContext.ModelState.Add(bindingContext.ModelName, modelState);
        return actualValue;
    }
}
public class MyOtherInterfaceTypeConverter : JsonConverter
{
    public override bool CanConvert(Type objectType)
    {
        return (objectType == typeof(IMyOtherInterface));
    }

    public override object ReadJson(JsonReader reader, Type objectType, object
existingValue, JsonSerializer serializer)
    {
        return serializer.Deserialize<MyOtherInterfaceConcrete>(reader);
    }

    public override void WriteJson(JsonWriter writer, object value, JsonSerializer
serializer)
```

```
    {
        //... to be done if we care about serialization...
    }
}
```

From here, the model binder of Asp.Net MVC will use your model binder for your type and subtype used in the process. This whole post has used Json Newton library (http://tinyurl.com/4sza4e) for deserializing the JavaScript JSON object.

## How to add custom Data Annotation attributes to your property in Asp.Net MVC

Release Date: 22-Feb-13
Url: http://patrickdesjardins.com/blog/?post_type=post&p=1853

In many scenarios, the **ViewModel** needs to provide to the **View** some additional information. The case of having a **UIHint** attribute with the conjunction of this additional information is probably the situation most people will face at some point.

```
[DoSomething]
public MyClass MyProperty { get; set; }
```

Lets say you have a template that displays multiple data from your view model (in the example above "MyClass"). If this requires displaying something more (or less) depending on who uses it, and the view model knows this information, the only way to pass this information is by data annotation. Let's base the theory on the following example.

```
[DisableShape("Heavy")]
[UIHint("ShapeSelector")]
public Shape TopShape { get; set; }

[UIHint("ShapeSelector")]
public Shape BottomShape { get; set; }
```

The view model class has two properties which define two shapes. In both cases, the shape must be selected from a list of shapes. The difference is that one of the properties accepts only "light" shapes while the other requires a "heavy" shape. We could create two templates but we could also create a single template and allow disabling a shape. This is the case of the property "TopShape" where we will filter out all "heavy" shapes but keep everything selectable for the "BottomShape" property.

The first thing to keep in mind is that this requires changing the

**ModelMetadataProviders** of Asp.Net MVC to use a custom one. We want to be able to add multiple attributes for the whole application. This will force us to create a class from which we will inherit all our filter attributes.

```
public class CustomModelMetadataProvider : DataAnnotationsModelMetadataProvider
{
    protected override ModelMetadata CreateMetadata(
      IEnumerable<Attribute> attributes,
      Type containerType,
      Func<object> modelAccessor,
      Type modelType,
      string propertyName)
    {
        var modelMetadata = base.CreateMetadata(attributes
                    , containerType, modelAccessor, modelType, propertyName);
        attributes.OfType<MetadataAttribute>().ToList()
                    .ForEach(x => x.Process(modelMetadata));
        return modelMetadata;
    }
}
```

The custom model metadata provider code gives the possibility ofhaving multiple attributes of type **MetadataAttribute** above any of your properties.

```
public abstract class MetadataAttribute : Attribute
{
  public abstract void Process(ModelMetadata modelMetaData);
}
```

As you can see, it is simply an abstract class that lets you define a Process method which is executed in the **CreateMetadata** method. From there, you can define what parameter you want for your custom attribute. In the example we are working on, we can create a disable shape attribute that takes a string parameter. This is the filter that the selector will work against.

```
public class DisableShapeAttribute : MetadataAttribute
{
    public bool TypeShape { get; set; }
    public DisableShapeAttribute(string type)
    {
        TypeShape = type;
    }

    public DisableShapeAttribute()
    {
        TypeShape = "";
```

```
    }

    public override void Process(ModelMetadata modelMetaData)
    {
        modelMetaData.AdditionalValues.Add("DisableShape", TypeShape);
    }
}
```

The last step is to register the *CustomModelMetadataProvider* that loops every **MetadataAttribute**. This is done via the **Global.asax.cs**, inside the **Application_Start** method.

```
ModelMetadataProviders.Current = new CustomModelMetadataProvider();
```

From here you can read the attribute from your **view** or **template**. The following code illustrates how to get the attribute.

```
var attr = ViewData.ModelMetadata.AdditionalValues
                    .SingleOrDefault(x => x.Key == "DisableShape").Value;
var attrValue = attr != null && (string)attr;
```

Having access to the meta data information allows you to create a loop on the full list and to compare the type against the value found in the attribute's **Process** method. In the code above, it loops through all the metadata list's items and if it does not match the key, the *attrValue* is null.

## Asp.Net MVC 4 and logging system

Release Date: 28-Feb-13
Url: http://patrickdesjardins.com/blog/?post_type=post&p=1864

Every application must have a logging system to trace problems that occur when the system is up and running. In fact, most predictable errors should be trapped and handled already inside your code, but in real life we all know that we are not protected against every error. This is why it is important to log errors into a persistent storage like files, databases, or the event viewer of the machine.

I personally like having the log in a database or files because it is easier to access if it is on a remote machine. I found that a database is often the easiest way to get every trace because developers usually have access to the database remotely when it might not be the case for the event viewer, or for files.

Microsoft has for many years published the **Enterprise Library** (Application Block) which contains a portion that handles logging. Unfortunately, in 2013 this does not seem to be the favorite way to log even if the Enterprise Library offer a lots of flexibility. I have used many times the Enterprise Library and it works flawlessly. However, I am using more and more **ELMAH** logging (https://code.google.com/p/elmah) and really appreciate it. This is mainly because it takes five minutes to set up and it handles all unhandled errors automatically without the need of any coding.

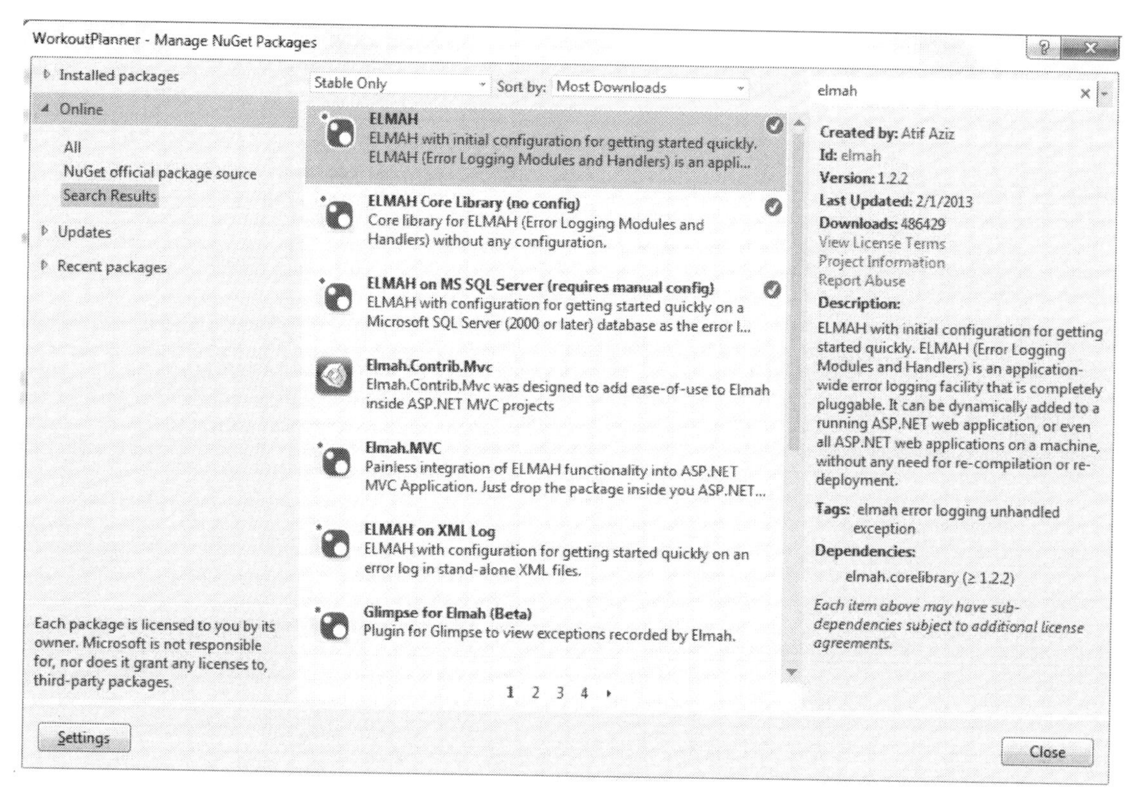


ELMAH installation could be summarized by **NuGet**. This is almost the only thing you will need to do. Open NuGet Package Manager and install ELMAH. This will add to your project the reference required and will modify the web.config. Then, if you need to store the log into your Microsoft SQL server you need to also use NuGet to download the MsSql portion.

From there, you simply need to modify the **web.config** to give a credential to the database and run a script which creates the proper table and stored procedures. The SQL scripts are available to download: https://code.google.com/p/elmah/downloads/list. You can download the script for the version of database you need. At this moment, you can download for Microsoft SQL Server, PostgreSQL, MySql, SQLite, MS Access, Oracle.

By default, you can also have access from a web page to the log stored into the database (http://yoursite/elmah.axd) if you are running it locally (this prevent users from seeing the log). If you are not using a database, every log will be stored into memory and will be flushed once the web server is restarted.

## Convert JavaScript object into Json string

Release Date: 04-Mar-13
Url: http://patrickdesjardins.com/blog/?post_type=post&p=1892

When developing JavaScript intensively at some point you may want to save the JavaScript object to your back end. To save your JavaScript object, you need to send it back to the server. Sometimes, you may be able to send the object directly by using JavaScript Ajax functionality and use the converted object with Asp.Net MVC. Other times, you may want to do it manually, sending the object into a string and deserializing into C# class.

The first approach is the simplest for a simple object where you have the same meta structure in your C# class and JavaScript object. For example, if you have a C# class that looks like this:

```
public class MyClass
{
    int a;
    int b;
}
```

You would need to send from JavaScript an object where Asp.Net MVC could map every attribute or property. It needs to have the same name.

```
var xyz = {a=1,b=2};
```

You can use JQuery to send Ajax:

```
$.ajax({
    url: 'MyController/MyAction',
    contentType: "application/json; charset=utf-8",
    type: "POST",
    data: JSON.stringify(xyz),
    dataType: "json",
    success: function (data) {
        //...
    },
    error: function () {
```

```
        //...
    }
});
```

As you can see, we pass the data using **JSON.stringify()** which sends the object serialized into a string format. The **contentType** property indicates in which format the data is sent. Meanwhile, the property **dataType** is how the data is received back (in the success, error, complete function).

When the function returns the data, it is in a string format. If the desired return is Json, like the example above by specifying that the dataType is "json", we need to deserialize the string into a JavaScript object. JQuery provides the method **jQuery.parseJSON()**. This JQuery function calls the native '**window.JSON.parse()**'; if the function doesn't exist for the browser, it falls back to the **eval** function.

```
success: function (data) {
    var obj = jQuery.parseJSON(data);
}
```

This article explains that it is possible to use JSON to transfer data from a JavaScript object with JSON to a Asp.Net action. This converts with the default model builder the JSON into an action parameter class. In a later stage, Asp.Net MVC can return an answer in JSON format and JQuery can parse it back to the string into a JSON object and be used in your JavaScript code.

# How to have a 404 error page for your Asp.Net MVC 3 or MVC 4 website

Release Date: 11-Mar-13
Url: http://patrickdesjardins.com/blog/?post_type=post&p=1871

Strangely, the question of how to create a 404 error page for your Asp.Net MVC is a question that Google does not provide many answers to. Some people suggest using a **NuGet package** that handles a 404 error; some have a solution that worked with Asp.Net MVC 1.0. But, at the end, it is just a 404 webpage. An easy task should never require a complex solution. This is why we believe the use of any NuGet package is overkill. You can use a NuGet extension to handle this but from where I am this is like using a nuclear bomb to push a nail. Instead, let's focus on what is happening and find a simple Asp.Net MVC solution. However, if you are interested in the NuGet package, here is a screenshot of the NuGet package that I am referring to.

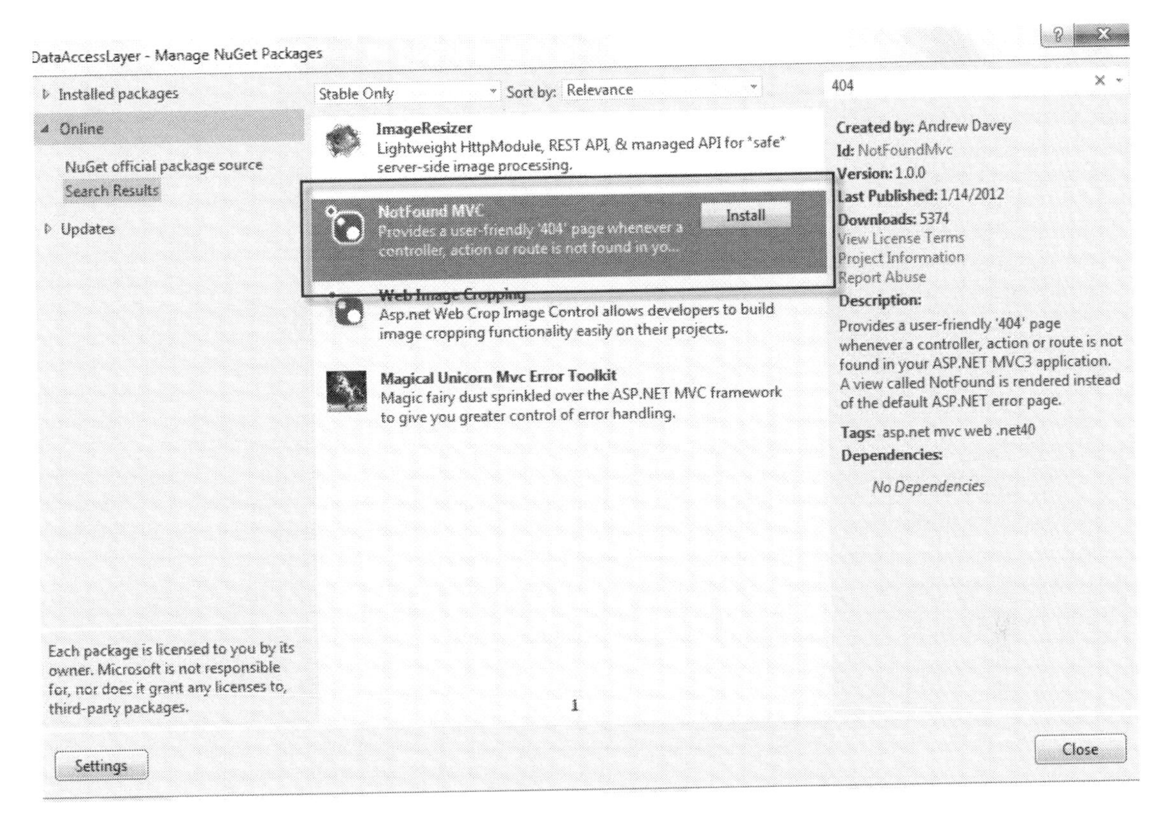


The 404 is an http status code that specifies that the server has not reach the desired page on the server. It is convenient to have this kind of page when the user enters a wrong url into the browser. The 404 page shows and tells the user that he is still on your web site but has reach a wrong destination.

First of all, if the user goes to a webpage that does not exist (a wrong controller name, or a non-existing action of your controller) you will get an error 500. The error 500 means an internal server error. I suggest you handle 404 and 500 the same way in Asp.Net MVC since we never use real pages because they are dynamically generated. Most of the time, a user will reach a control using routing which is not a real page. In both cases (http error 404 and 500), nothing is shownfrom any of your webpages and in both cases you want to alert the user of the error.

To handle the status code, I suggest that you check the http response code from the context at the end of the web request. This can be hooked in the **Global.asax.cs** file. The main advantage of this solution it that it works at the full scale of your web site. You do not need to do anything more for new controllers or new actions.

```
protected void Application_EndRequest()
```

```
{
  var statusCode = Context.Response.StatusCode;
  if (statusCode == 404 || statusCode == 500)
  {
    Response.Clear();
    var routingData = new RouteData();
    //rd.DataTokens["area"] = "AreaName"; // In case controller is in another area
    routingData.Values["controller"] = "Error";
    routingData.Values["action"] = "NotFound";
    IController c = new ErrorController();
    c.Execute(new RequestContext(new HttpContextWrapper(Context), routingData));
  }
}
```

As you can see, we clear all responses and start a brand new response by invoking the error controller that we created for 404 and 500 errors. Our new controller needs to have an action that I have called "NotFound". This action displays a view where you will be able to display a message to your visitor that will indicate that the page desired does not exist. Here is the code of the action.

```
public ActionResult NotFound()
{
  ActionResult result;

  object model = Request.Url.PathAndQuery;

  if (Request.IsAjaxRequest())
  {
    if (Request.ContentType == "application/json")
    {
      result = Json(new { Error = "Server cannot threat your request." });
    }
    else
    {
      result = PartialView(ERROR_VIEW, model);
    }
  }
  else
  {
    result = View(ERROR_VIEW, model);
  }
  return result;
}
```

This is a solution that returns the Error404 view that you can create yourself with the whole master page if the request is not Ajax. Otherwise, it returns a partial view which is still the Error404 but without the layout around it. Keep in mind that this solution expects that when you are using Ajax you have specified the content type to json and also that you handle in your Javacript the read of the property Error. If this is defined, you have to handle it.

```
$.ajax({
   type: 'POST',
   url: 'WrongPage/NotFoundPage/Blabla',
   data: JSON.stringify(jsonRequest),
   contentType: 'application/json; charset=utf-8',
   dataType: 'json',
   success: function (data, text)
   {
       //Success here
   },
   error: function (request, status, error)
   {
       if(request.status == ...)
       {
           //Read the error message from the request
       }
   }
});
```

This is how to easily handle 404/500 errors with Microsoft Asp.Net MVC framework. Of course, multiple other solutions exist. I found this one efficient, clean, and easy to create. As you can see, I have not set any logging functionality and this is because I use ELMAH (previously seen in this blog) that handles logging wrong date routing. However, this would be the perfect place to add some log information about what the request url was.

## Binding complex user template values to your Model with Asp.Net MVC

Release Date: 26-Mar-13
Url: http://patrickdesjardins.com/blog/?post_type=post&p=1927

If you have a simple class, even if it contains underlying classes, Asp.Net MVC takes care of creating all HTML input for you and it takes care to rebound everything into objects once the form is submitted back to the browser. However, if you have a custom control, called **template** in Asp.Net MVC, which lets you add sub objects with multiple properties to your main object, you will have to handle it manually.

First of all, in this type of scenario, you should use **UIHint** or **Html Helper** to generate the control itself.

```
public class MyObject
{
    public int MyObjectId { get; set; }

    [UIHint("MyTemplate")]
    public MyInnerObject YourProperty { get; set; }
}

public class MyInnerObject
{
    public int Uid { get; set; }
    public MyItems Items { get; set; }
}

public class MyItems
{
    public int Id { get; set; }
    public DateTime Date1 { get; set; }
    public DateTime Date2 { get; set; }
    public string Comment { get; set; }
}
```

The **UIHint** will generate the correct HTML output for the user. Lets say that this UIHint lets you select two dates and a comment. When you click a button, a row is added to a grid which gives the user the ability to enter the two dates and a comment. The problem is how to send back these three pieces of information to the server in a way that the user could enter several lines at the same time. The solution is to send back a collection of properties in a format that Asp.Net MVC will be able to map back to your model class.

The first thing to do is to create a hidden field in your template with the name of the property that your model has (or view model in the case where you are binding a view model to the view). This will bind the property to your template with a hidden field. This hidden field will be the transportation channel to send a collection of information that your grid contains. In our example, the name of this field should have been "YourProperty." Indeed, do not hard code that name in the template. You can use Asp.Net MVC view data info to get the bounded property name.

```
String propertyName = ViewData.TemplateInfo.HtmlFieldPrefix;
```

The second thing is to populate this hidden field. You will need to set in your save button a JavaScript that will loop through all lines and transforms all HTML inputs into a serialized Json object.

```
$(document).on('click', '#mySaveButton', function (e) {
    //1) Transform here all grid lines into the hidden field
```

```
    //2) Be sure you do not prevent default action or return false because we want to server to post normally.
});
```

This Json object will be in a string format we will insert into the hidden field. Once saved, the hidden field is sent as another normal HTML field and Asp.Net MVC will deserialize it correctly.

```
function SetHiddenField() {
    var obj = {};
    obj.Items = [];
    $('myControlThatHasAListOfItems').each(function () {
        var myObjectToSerialize = {};
        myObjectToSerialize.ID = $(this)...;
        myObjectToSerialize.Date1 = $(this)...;
        myObjectToSerialize.Date2 = $(this)...;
        myObjectToSerialize.Comment = $(this)...;
        obj.Items.push(myObjectToSerialize);
    });
    $('#MyHiddenField').val(JSON.stringify(obj));
}
```

Of course, do not create a JavaScript function hard coded like this one. You should create it in a way where you could have multiples of this custom template control in the same page without conflicting or having to edit this code in the future. In this example, the hidden field should be called "Items" and will be bound with the hidden field. Asp.Net MVC will deserialize the Json when it will be ready to bind Items. Since all properties' names match, the binding is done by magic. From here, you can use the model on your controller and save everything.

## Complex binding

In case an object cannot be deserialized by the default Asp.Net MVC model binder, a custom one is required. This is done by creating in the **Global.Asax.cs** an entry for a model binding

```
ModelBinders.Binders.Add(typeof(YourComplexClass<bool>)
                         , new YourComplexClassModelBinder());
```

and the binder. The following code has to be modified to fulfill your needs.

```
public class YourComplexClassModelBinder : IModelBinder
{
    public object BindModel(ControllerContext controllerContext, ModelBindingContext bindingContext)
```

```
    {
        var valueResult =
bindingContext.ValueProvider.GetValue(bindingContext.ModelName);
        var modelState = new ModelState
        {
            Value = valueResult
        };

        YourComplexClass<bool> actualValue = null;
        if (!string.IsNullOrWhiteSpace(valueResult.AttemptedValue))
        {
            var settings = new JsonSerializerSettings();
            settings.Converters.Add(new
                             JSonComplexConverterForYourComplexClass());
            try
            {
                actualValue = JsonConvert
                             .DeserializeObject<YourComplexClass<bool>>
                             (valueResult.AttemptedValue, settings);
            }
            catch (FormatException e)
            {
                modelState.Errors.Add(e);
            }
        }
        bindingContext.ModelState.Add(bindingContext.ModelName, modelState);
        return actualValue;
    }

    public class JSonComplexConverterForYourComplexClass : JsonConverter
    {
        public override bool CanConvert(Type objectType)
        {
            return (objectType == typeof(I_XYZ<bool>));
        }

        public override object ReadJson(JsonReader reader, Type objectType, object
existingValue, JsonSerializer serializer)
        {
            return serializer.Deserialize<XYZ>(reader);
        }

        public override void WriteJson(JsonWriter writer, object value,
JsonSerializer serializer)
        {
            throw new NotImplementedException();
        }
    }
}
```

This is often the case with an Interface that needs to be deserialized into a concrete class. In the above example, I_XYZ was the interface but when it's time to deserialize, Asp.Net MVC does not know to which type to deserialize. This is why we provide a model binder for the class that contains the property that has an I_XYZ interface and provides to Json.Net library how to read the Json for deserialization.

## Asp.Net MVC Html Helper to create link with an image

Release Date: 18-Apr-13
Url: http://patrickdesjardins.com/blog/?post_type=post&p=2010

You can use the default **Html Helper** to have a text with a url. This is most of the time sufficient but when in the scenario where you want an image to be a link, you are on your own. You could create every time a link that contains an image. But, with Asp.Net MVC, one nice way to do it would be with an Html Extension. The main reason is that you do not have to repeat the code every time. Before creating our new Html Helper, let's see the default ActionLink HTML helper that comes from Asp.Net MVC framework.

```
@Html.ActionLink("Text to display", "ActionNameHere", "ControllerNameHere"
                 , new { id = 123 }, new{@class="myClass"})
```

As you can see, this overload takes the text to display, the action name to redirect to, and the controller which belongs to the action. Then, we have the route value which in this example sends an ID to the action, and finally an HTML attribute which lets you configure the link according to some HTML attributes you desire.

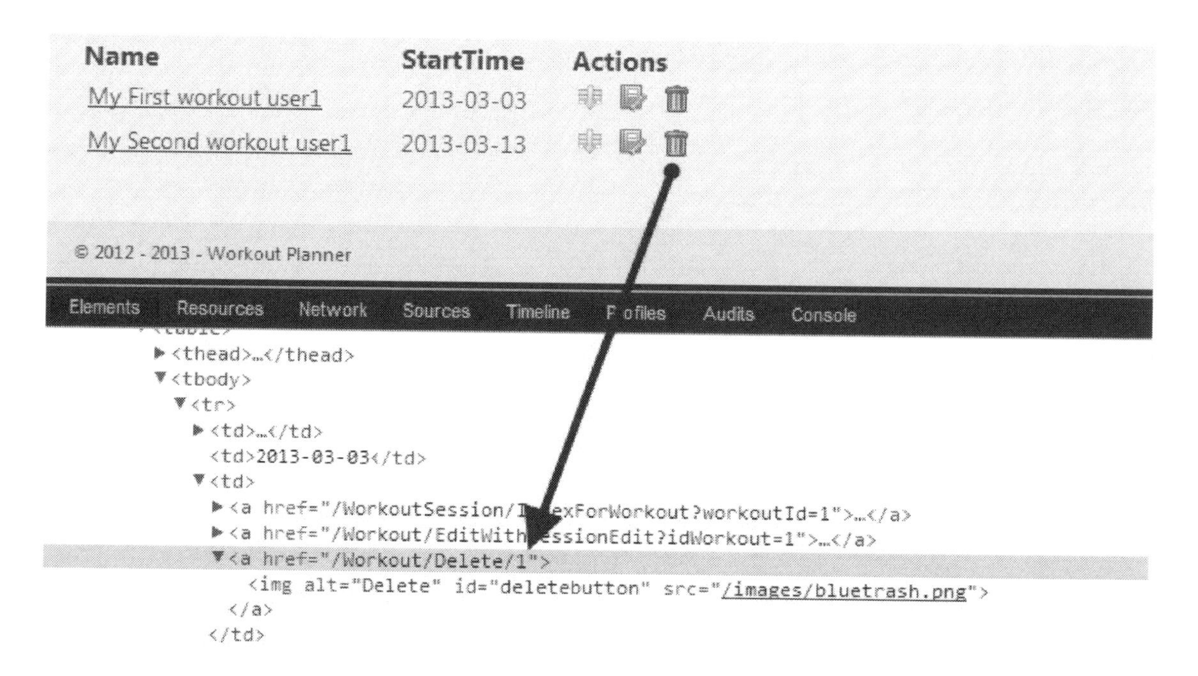


What we want to do is almost the same but adding an image. The image above shows you the expected result —an image, or icon, that is a link.

```
public MvcHtmlString ActionImage(this HtmlHelper htmlHelper,
                                 string controller,
                                 string action,
                                 object routeValues,
                                 string imagePath,
                                 string alternateText = "",
                                 object htmlAttributes = null)
{

  var anchorBuilder = new TagBuilder("a");
  var url = new UrlHelper(HtmlHelper.ViewContext.RequestContext);

  anchorBuilder.MergeAttribute("href",url.Action(action,controller,routeValues));

  var imgBuilder = new TagBuilder("img");
  imgBuilder.MergeAttribute("src", url.Content(imagePath));
  imgBuilder.MergeAttribute("alt", alternateText);

  var attributes = (IDictionary<string, object>)
                   HtmlHelper.AnonymousObjectToHtmlAttributes(htmlAttributes);
  imgBuilder.MergeAttributes(attributes);
  string imgHtml = imgBuilder.ToString(TagRenderMode.SelfClosing);

  anchorBuilder.InnerHtml = imgHtml;
```

```
  return MvcHtmlString.Create(anchorBuilder.ToString());
}
```

The first parameter lets you extend the HtmlHelper. This will let you use your new method with the @Html keyword. The next four parameters are the required parameters. The first one is the controller, then the action, the route value, and the image path. Finally, we can specify, if desired, an alternate text and additional HTML attributes.

The first part will create the link. It uses the **RequestContext** and the **UrlHelper** to create the link. In fact, it will build from the controller, the action, and the route values a url well formed from the routing schema of your Asp.Net MVC website.

The last part builds the image and adds it into the link. Finally, we merge the attribute we passed to the image. We could also do the same to have HTML attribute for the link. Here is how to HTML helper can be used.

```
@Html.ActionImage("Workout", "Delete"
                    , new { id = @workout.Id }, "/images/bluetrash.png"
                    , "Delete", new { id="deletebutton"})
```

From now on, using that line of code generates an image with an Html link. From this example, it is possible to use it to create a new Html Helper having an image and a text.

## How to create an Html Extension like ActionLink to create link only if the user has the authorization

Release Date: 08-May-13
Url: http://patrickdesjardins.com/blog/?post_type=post&p=2046

The idea to create an **Html Extension** like ActionLink to create and display a link only if the user has the authorization to the page can be very helpful. The goal here is to display the link only if the action allows the user to execute the action. This way, every user sees the link to the action that it belongs to and does not see a link to an action he cannot do.

Here is an example of the final product. The first line is the new ActionLink Html Helper and the second line is the default one. The result will be that a user that has access to the "Edit" action will see the link when others who do not have access do not see it. The second line shows everybody the link for "Details."

```
@Html.Input().ActionLink("Edit", "Edit", null, (new { id=item.Id }))
@Html.ActionLink("Details", "Details", new { id=item.Id })
```

On the controller side, you will see the Edit action with the authorization attribute.

```
[HttpGet]
[Authorize(Roles = Roles.ADMINISTRATOR)]
public ActionResult Edit(int id)
{
    //...
}
```

First of all, we need to create a class to be able to get the attribute of the action. This class is a helper that provides the possibility of reading the role from the Authorize attribute.

```
public class AttributeHelper
{
    private readonly HtmlHelper _htmlHelper;
    public AttributeHelper(HtmlHelper htmlHelper)
    {
        _htmlHelper = htmlHelper;
    }

    public IEnumerable<Attribute> GetAttributes(
                    string actionName,
                    string controllerName,
                    string method = "GET")
    {
        var controllerFactory = ControllerBuilder.Current.GetControllerFactory();
        var otherController = (ControllerBase)controllerFactory
                    .CreateController(new
                RequestContext(_htmlHelper.ViewContext.HttpContext
                                , new RouteData()), controllerName);
        var controllerDescriptor =
                new ReflectedControllerDescriptor(otherController.GetType());
        var controllerContext2 =
                new ControllerContext(new HttpContextWrapperWithHttpMethod(
                _htmlHelper.ViewContext.HttpContext.ApplicationInstance.Context
                , method)
                , new RouteData(), otherController);
        var actionDescriptor = controllerDescriptor
                            .FindAction(controllerContext2, actionName);
        var attributes = actionDescriptor.GetCustomAttributes(true)
                          .Cast<Attribute>().ToArray();
        return attributes;
    }

    private class HttpContextWrapperWithHttpMethod : HttpContextWrapper
    {
        private readonly HttpRequestBase _request;
```

```
        public HttpContextWrapperWithHttpMethod(HttpContext httpContext
                                                , string method)
            : base(httpContext)
        {
            this._request =
                new HttpRequestWrapperWithHttpMethod(httpContext.Request, method);
        }

        public override HttpRequestBase Request
        {
            get { return _request; }
        }

        private class HttpRequestWrapperWithHttpMethod : HttpRequestWrapper
        {
            private readonly string _httpMethod;

            public HttpRequestWrapperWithHttpMethod(HttpRequest httpRequest,
                                                    string httpMethod)
                : base(httpRequest)
            {
                this._httpMethod = httpMethod;
            }

            public override string HttpMethod
            {
                get { return _httpMethod; }
            }
        }
    }

}
```

If you want to use it, you must call the method and then search for the required attribute.

```
var attributeHelper = new AttributeHelper(HtmlHelper);
var att = attributeHelper.GetAttributes(actionName,
                          controllerName).OfType<AuthorizeAttribute>();
var isInRole = att.Aggregate(false, (f, g) => f |
HtmlHelper.ViewContext.HttpContext.User.IsInRole(g.Roles));
```

Line 1 instantiates the helper we created. The attribute helper gives you the possibility to get from an action of a controller the information from a specific attribute. The second line will filter to get **AuthorizedAttribute**. This can return multiple attributes so we have to use the third line to aggregate if the user is in an AuthorizedAttribute. The Html helper can now use this to display or not the link.

```
public MvcHtmlString ActionLink(string linkText
```

```
                                        , string actionName = null
                                        , string controllerName = null
                                        , object routeValues = null
                                        , object htmlAttributes=null)
{
  if (actionName == null)
  {
    actionName = HtmlHelper.ViewContext.RouteData.GetRequiredString("action");
  }
  if (controllerName == null)
  {
    controllerName =
            HtmlHelper.ViewContext.RouteData.GetRequiredString("controller");
  }
  var routeValues2 = new RouteValueDictionary(routeValues);
  var attributes = (IDictionary<string, object>)
              HtmlHelper.AnonymousObjectToHtmlAttributes(htmlAttributes);

  if (string.IsNullOrEmpty(linkText))
  {
    throw new ArgumentException("linkText");
  }
  else
  {
    var attributeHelper = new AttributeHelper(HtmlHelper);
    var att = attributeHelper
              .GetAttributes(actionName, controllerName)
              .OfType<AuthorizeAttribute>();
    var isInRole = att.Aggregate(false, (f, g) =>
          f | HtmlHelper.ViewContext.HttpContext.User.IsInRole(g.Roles));
    if (isInRole)
    {
      return MvcHtmlString.Create(HtmlHelper
              .GenerateLink(HtmlHelper.ViewContext.RequestContext
                        , HtmlHelper.RouteCollection, linkText
                        , (string)null, actionName, controllerName
                        , routeValues2, attributes));
    }
    return new MvcHtmlString("");
  }
}
```

The first two conditions are only there if the controller or action is not defined. In practice, the controller should not be used all the time because we are most of the time using an action that is inside the controller. For example, we are in the Index of a specific controller. If we want to Edit, Create, etc, all of theses action are in the controller; it does not require you to specify the controller every time. The aggregate function checks for all roles defined and if the user is in one of the roles, it returns true. When that is the case, the link is generated by using the default Asp.Net MVC url helper, otherwise, nothing is sent.

# Asp.Net MVC and the ViewData's TemplateInfo

Release Date: 15-Jun-13
Url: http://patrickdesjardins.com/blog/?post_type=post&p=1673

The **TemplateInfo** contains one interesting property which is **HtmlFieldPrefix**. This property gives the same information as the method *GetFullHtmlFieldName(string.Empty)*.

What is interesting is that from an editor template you can know the property name, which is sometimes basic if you want to build your editor or display template. This is required to be able to bind with the ModelBinder and send the information to the server once the user submits the page back to the server.

For example, if you have a special editor template for a string, you can add on your property (usually over the property of your view model or model) the **UIHint** to make a link between the property and the template. Then, in the template you could create your control.

```
@model string
@{
    var controlPropertyName = ViewData.TemplateInfo.HtmlFieldPrefix
    <input id="@controlPropertyName" name="@controlPropertyName" value="...">
    <input id="...............
}
```

Above is a short snippet that illustrates a single property. This allows several properties with the same UIHint and generates different input with different ID. You could have multiple inputs with different names and the one that will be bound will be the one that came from the ViewData.TemplateInfo. So with a single editor template you can handle multiple properties and have everything synchronized back to an Asp.Net MVC action.

Having several inputs may be something required in scenarios of multiple lists of elements that need to be selected.. For example, let's say that you have a textbox which can be loaded from a list of values. The template will contain the input with the property name to be bound later to the view model (or model) and other inputs are there only to select a possible value (via Javascript).

# Could not load file or assembly WebMatrix.WebData

Release Date: 23-Jul-13
Url: http://patrickdesjardins.com/blog/?post_type=post&p=2031

If you are creating an Asp.Net MVC website or an Asp.Net MVC Api Web Service, you may see yourself blocked on the execution with a missing file with **WebMatrix.WebData**.

*Could not load file or assembly 'WebMatrix.WebData' or one of its dependencies. The system cannot find the file specified.*

This error can be fixed by being sure that you have the WebMatrix.WebData inside your references. This assembly should be located in Asp.Net Web Page folder of Microsoft Asp.Net (c:\Program Files (x86)\Microsoft ASP.NET\ASP.NET Web Pages\v2.0\Assemblies\WebMatrix.Data.dll). The best way to get the reference is simply to click Add Reference and do a search for WebMatrix.

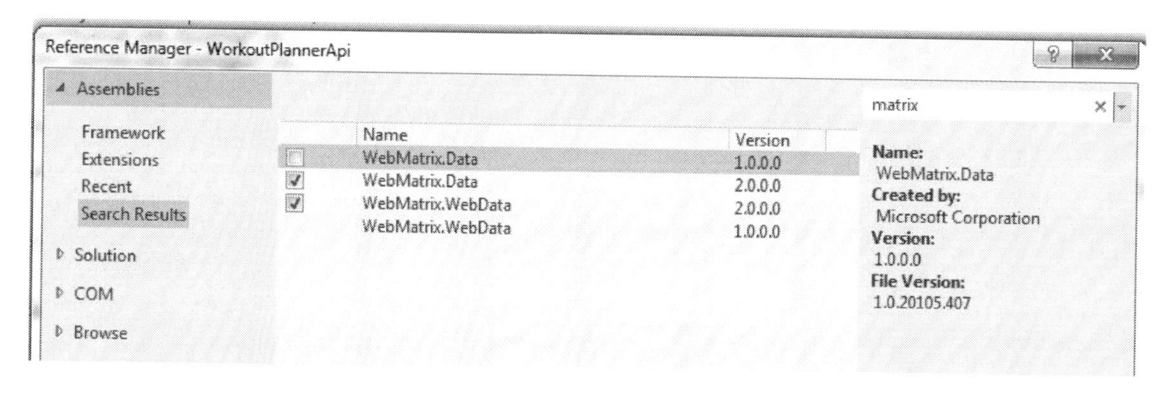


Once you are sure you have the WebMatrix DLL, be sure that this has the property "Copy Local" set to true.

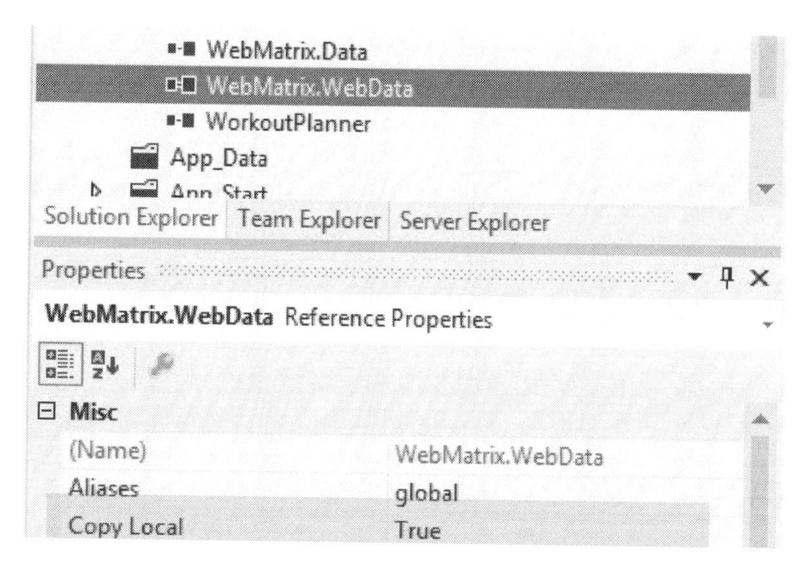

This should solve the problem of "Could not load file or assembly WebMatrix.WebData."

## How to register Area without having to specify them all in the global.asax.cs

Release Date: 12-Aug-13
Url: http://patrickdesjardins.com/blog/?post_type=post&p=2200

When you go into an existing project you have two possibilities. The first possibility is that every area is registered into the **global.asax.cs**, or with MVC 4 (and above) in the routing class that the global.asax calls. The second possibility is to use **AreaRegistration** class and have one class inherit this class per area.

The **first solution** is simple, is fast, and is suitable for a small project. (Rule of thumb: less than five areas). What you need is to add a new entry into routes.

```
protected void Application_Start()
{
    RegisterRoutes(RouteTable.Routes);
}

public static void RegisterRoutes(RouteCollection routes)
{
  routes.MapRootArea("{area}/{controller}/{action}/{id}",
          "RouteNameHere",
           new {
             area="area1",
             controller = "controller1",
             action = "action1",
             id = ""
           });
}
```

The **second solution** requires two steps. The first step is to tell the framework to auto register a specific type of class for routing, and the second step is to define one class per area for configuration purposes.

Step1: Inside Global.asax.cs

```
protected void Application_Start()
{
    AreaRegistration.RegisterAllAreas();
```

```
}
```

Step2: Inside every folder of every area you have to create a class that inherits from AreaRegistration.

```
public class MyArea_AreaRegistration : AreaRegistration
{
    public override string AreaName
    {
        get { return "MyArea"; }
    }

    public override void RegisterArea(AreaRegistrationContext context)
    {
        const string nameSpace = "MyNameSpaceForThisArea";
        const string areaName = "MyAreaName";
        const string defautlRouteUrl = areaName + "/{controller}/{action}/{id}";

        var defaultRouteValueDictionary = new RouteValueDictionary(new
        {
            action = "Index",
            id = UrlParameter.Optional
        });

        var dataTokensDictionary = new RouteValueDictionary(new
        {
            Namespaces = nameSpace,
            area = areaName,
            UseNamespaceFallback = false
        });

        context.Routes.Add(string.Format("{0}_Default", areaName)
                        , new Route(defautlRouteUrl, defaultRouteValueDictionary
                        , dataTokensDictionary, new MvcRouteHandler()));
    }
}
```

A few things are important. First, you should not copy and paste that code in all your areas. The namespace and area will change but every other line remains the same across all areas. Be smart and encapsulate the logic in a reusable place. Second, the new **MvcRouteHandler()** will most of the time be something that you will inherit from because you could set there some specification over localization. For example, you may want to have /fr/ which, if available, changes the current thread to the language specified in the url.

The override in the example above is far more complex than it should be if you do not have a custom **RouteHandler**. In fact, you could use this simple one-liner:

```
context.Routes.MapRoute("DefaultRouteForAreaXYZ"
                        , "AreaXYZ/{controller}/{action}/{id}"
                        , new {
                                  controller="Home"
                                , action="index"
                                , id= UrlParameter.Optional
                                }
                        );
```

Perhaps it is simpler, but you do not have the leverage of controlling every aspect of the routing, which is viable for projects where you do not need to parse the routing for additional features.

## Getting Started With Windows Azure

Release Date: 19-Aug-13
Url: http://patrickdesjardins.com/blog/?post_type=post&p=2236

This post shows how to transport your Asp.Net MVC to Windows **Azure**. First of all, you need to create a Windows Azure account. This can be done by going into the main website of Windows Azure. You can set up a trial account for 30 days.

We will not create a Virtual Machine, which is the ultimate control over your website (you can load any Virtual Machine), but use the **Web Sites** type of server. The creation is straightforward. You set up a name and you are up and running.

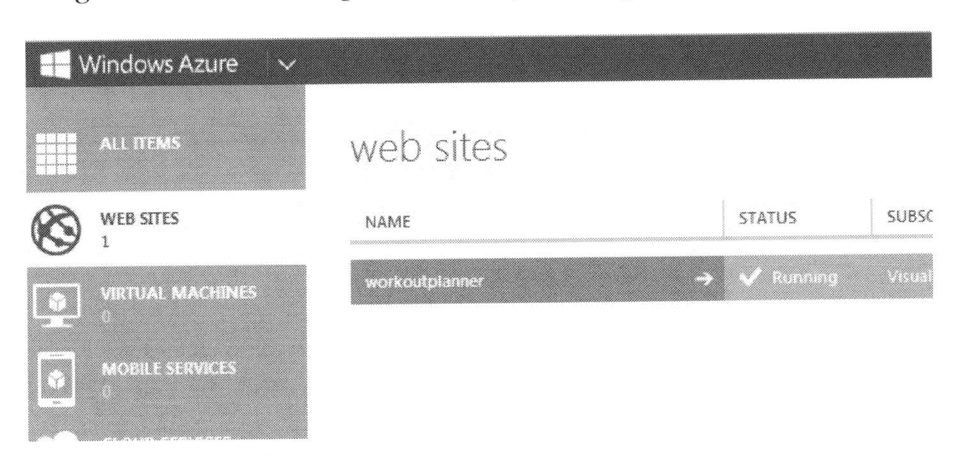


To upload your website, you have several options. One of these is to use Visual Studio with **Web Publish**. Windows Azure gives an automatically generated publishable file.

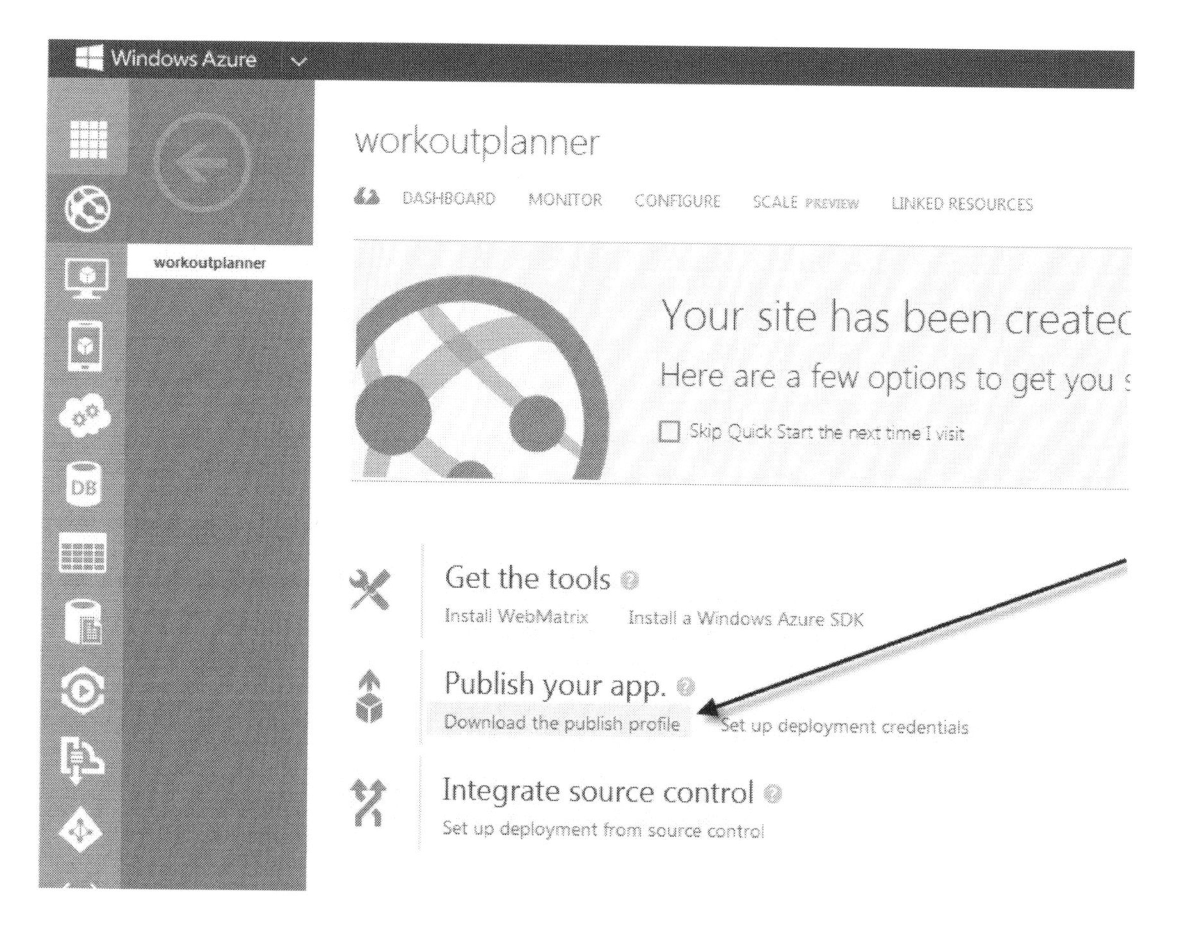


This profile can be imported inside your solution once downloaded to your development environment. Right click the **web project** and select **publish**. The first time you need to select import and select the downloaded published profile file. After the first time, you just need to select the configuration from a dropdown. The publish file is an XML file that looks like the following XML markup.

```
<publishData>
  <publishProfile profileName="workoutplanner - Web Deploy"
publishMethod="MSDeploy"
                  publishUrl="waws-prod-blu-
003.publish.azurewebsites.windows.net:443"
    msdeploySite="workoutplanner" userName="$workoutplanner" userPWD="XXX"
                  destinationAppUrl="http://workoutplanner.azurewebsites.net"
SQLServerDBConnectionString=""
                  mySQLDBConnectionString="" hostingProviderForumLink=""
controlPanelLink="http://windows.azure.com">
    <databases/>
  </publishProfile>
```

```
  <publishProfile profileName="workoutplanner - FTP" publishMethod="FTP"
                  publishUrl="ftp://waws-prod-blu-
003.ftp.azurewebsites.windows.net/site/wwwroot" ftpPassiveMode="True"
                  userName="workoutplanner\$workoutplanner" userPWD="XXX"
destinationAppUrl="http://workoutplanner.azurewebsites.net"
                  SQLServerDBConnectionString="" mySQLDBConnectionString=""
hostingProviderForumLink="" controlPanelLink="http://windows.azure.com">
    <databases/>
  </publishProfile>

</publishData>
```

The generated publish profile contain two profiles. One uses **Web Deploy** and one uses **FTP**. Azure offers these two methods while publishing. The next step is to set up a database. You can create a database with the same name you have set from your local SQL Database in your computer.

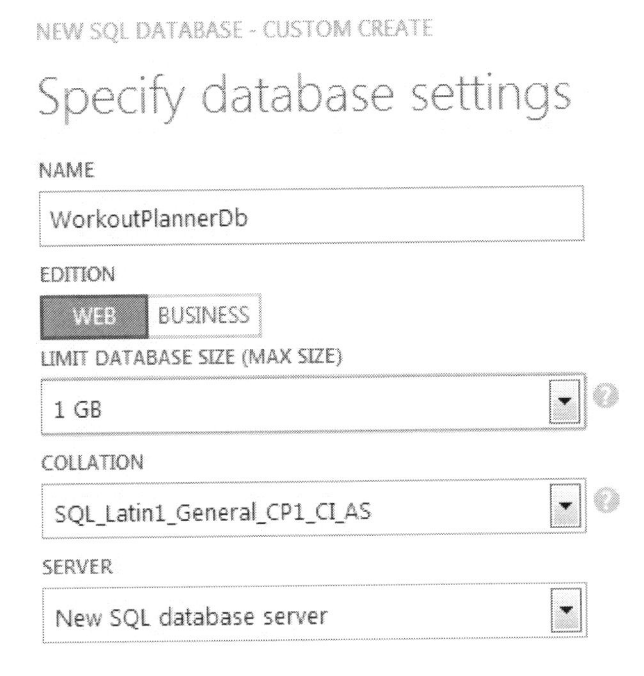


If it is your first database on Windows Azure, you will have to create a database server which will require you to create a user and password in order to connect. Next, you will have to allow your IP to be able to execute SQL Query from your computer to Windows Azure. This will let you create tables, stored procedures, views, etc.

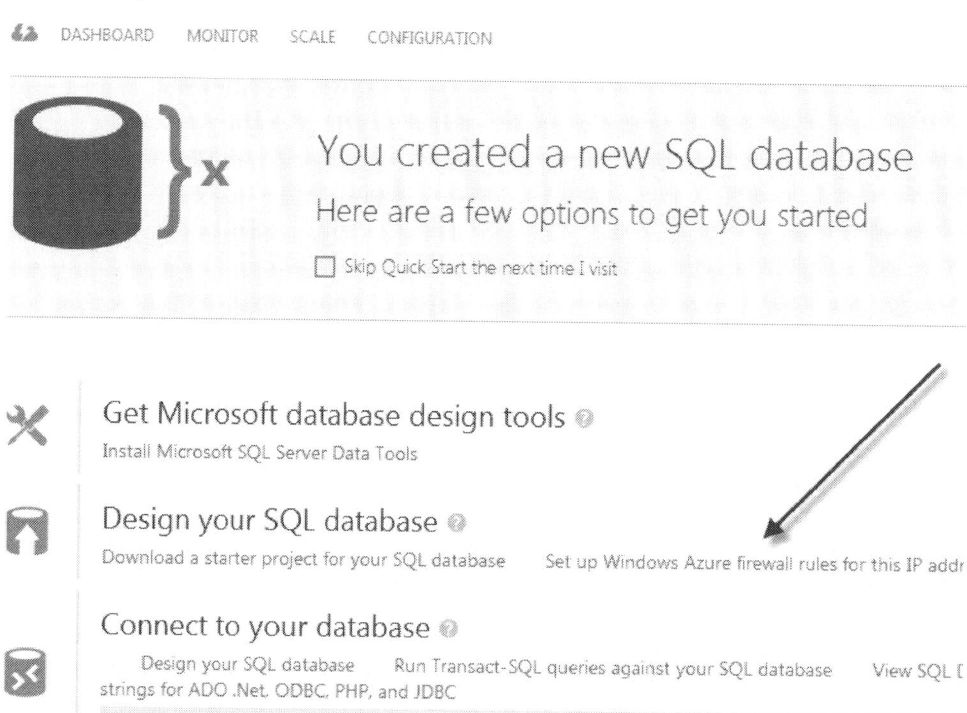


Next, open Microsoft SQL Manager and enter the server address specified inside your Database DashBoard.

Get Microsoft database design tools
Install Microsoft SQL Server Data Tools

Design your SQL database
Download a starter project for your SQL database    Set up Windows Azure firewal

Connect to your database
Design your SQL database    Run Transact-SQL queries against your SQL dat
strings for ADO .Net, ODBC, PHP, and JDBC

Server: ai8lqsptme.database.windows.net,1433

Once you can connect, it is time to take your database to Azure. I found it easier if you do not have too much data to right click your database and select Task>Generate Script and to create a Schema/Data script which will create all database tables and data. However, you might get some errors like this one :

*Msg 40514, Filegroup reference and partitioning scheme' is not supported in this version of SQL Server*

This is because you might have in your create table statement "ON [PRIMARY]" keywork which is not supported with Azure.

```
CREATE TABLE [dbo].[Exercises](
[Id] [int] IDENTITY(1,1) NOT NULL,
[Name_French] [nvarchar](max) NULL,
[Name_English] [nvarchar](max) NULL,
[Muscle_Id] [int] NULL,
CONSTRAINT [PK_dbo.Exercises] PRIMARY KEY CLUSTERED
(
[Id] ASC
)WITH (PAD_INDEX = OFF, STATISTICS_NORECOMPUTE = OFF, IGNORE_DUP_KEY = OFF,
ALLOW_ROW_LOCKS = ON, ALLOW_PAGE_LOCKS = ON) ON [PRIMARY]
) ON [PRIMARY] TEXTIMAGE_ON [PRIMARY]
```

Should become

```
[SQL highlight="9-10"]
CREATE TABLE [dbo].[Exercises](
[Id] [int] IDENTITY(1,1) NOT NULL,
[Name_French] [nvarchar](max) NULL,
[Name_English] [nvarchar](max) NULL,
[Muscle_Id] [int] NULL,
CONSTRAINT [PK_dbo.Exercises] PRIMARY KEY CLUSTERED
(
[Id] ASC
)
)
```

From there, open your solution and change the connection string to set up your new database in the Release version. This needs to have a connection string to the database you just created. With Windows Azure, it is easy because it generates for you the connection string.

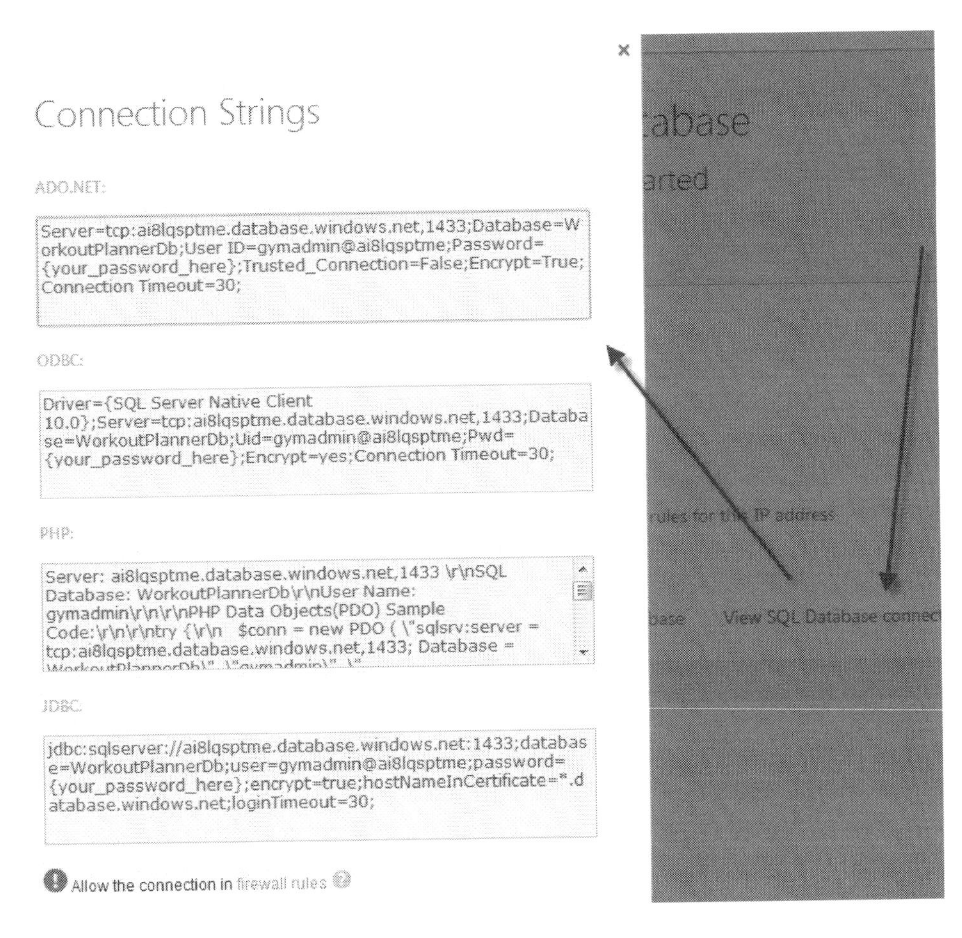


My experience was that I was getting a runtime error with the current setup. More steps were required to make the website up and running.

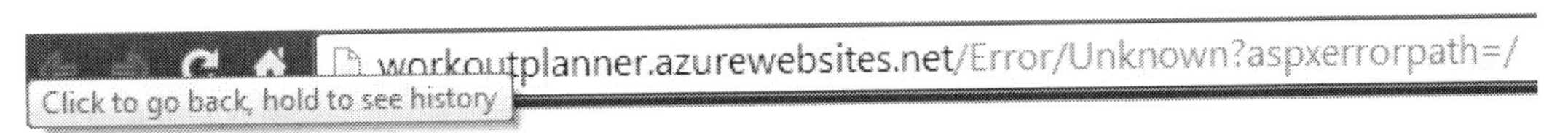


Server Error in '/' Application.

*Runtime Error*

**Description:** An exception occurred while processing your request. Additionally, another exception occurred while executing

To get the log file, you need to have an FTP account. This can be done by creating a user/password in your website dashboard. Then, click the link that will bring you to a folder where all log files are located.

re one to get started.

ı as you need for your site

0% of 1 HOUR / DAY

0% of 2.5 MINUTES / 5 MINUTES

0% of 165 MB / DAY

1% of 1024 MB

6% of 1024 MB / HOUR

quick glance

View connection strings

Download the publish profile

Reset your deployment credentials

Reset your publish profile credentials

Set up deployment from source control

STATUS
Running

VIRTUAL IP ADDRESS
No IP-based SSL binding is configured

SITE URL
http://workoutplanner.azurewebsites.net

COMPUTE MODE
Free

FTP HOST NAME
ftp://waws-prod-blu-003.ftp.azurewebsites.windows.net

FTPS HOST NAME
ftps://waws-prod-blu-003.ftp.azurewebsites.windows.net

DEPLOYMENT / FTP USER
workoutplanner\gymadmin

FTP DIAGNOSTIC LOGS
ftp://waws-prod-blu-003.ftp.azurewebsites.windows.net/LogFiles

FTPS DIAGNOSTIC LOGS
ftps://waws-prod-blu-003.ftp.azurewebsites.windows.net/LogFiles

LOCATION

If you do not see any log files, you might need to enable logs. This can be done by going to "Configuration" of the Web Sites. I have enabled Web Server Logging and Detailed Error Messages.

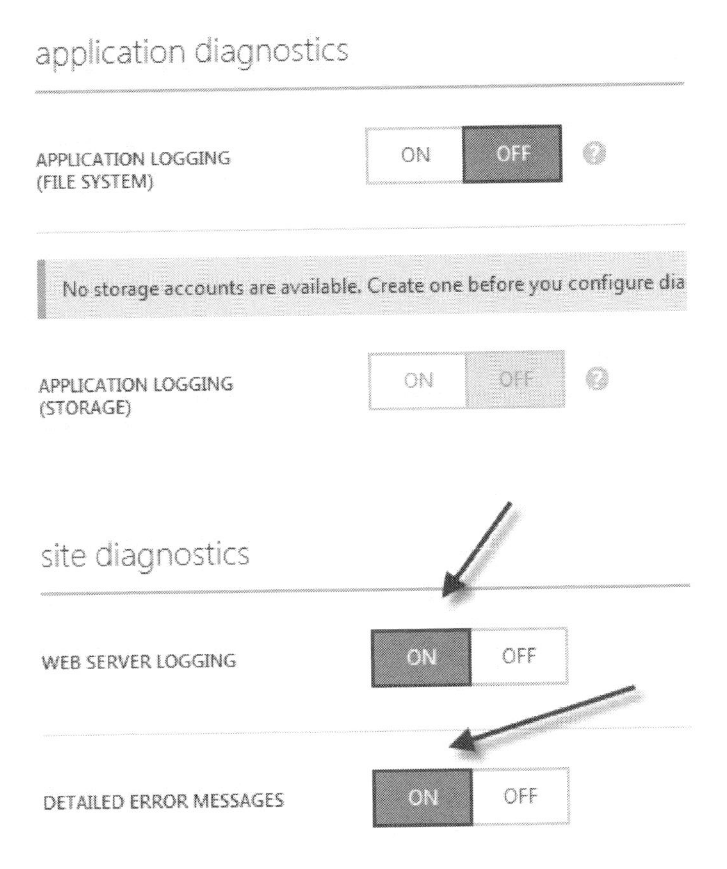


This gives us an .html file with the error. In my case, I got this message:

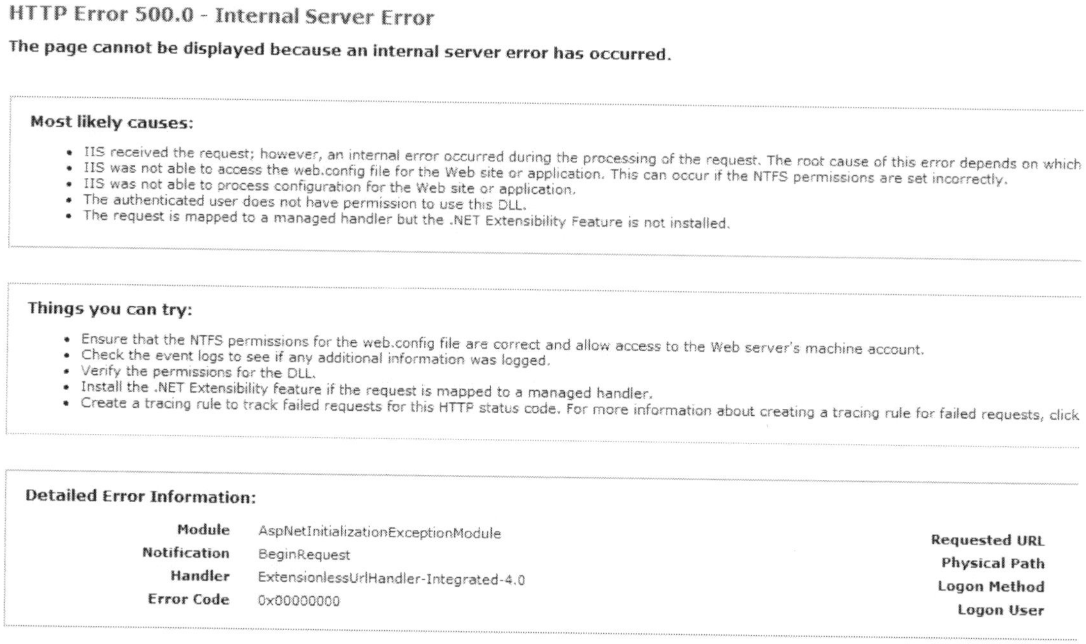

HTTP Error 500.0 - Internal Server Error

**The page cannot be displayed because an internal server error has occurred.**

**Most likely causes:**

- IIS received the request; however, an internal error occurred during the processing of the request. The root cause of this error depends on which
- IIS was not able to access the web.config file for the Web site or application. This can occur if the NTFS permissions are set incorrectly.
- IIS was not able to process configuration for the Web site or application.
- The authenticated user does not have permission to use this DLL.
- The request is mapped to a managed handler but the .NET Extensibility Feature is not installed.

**Things you can try:**

- Ensure that the NTFS permissions for the web.config file are correct and allow access to the Web server's machine account.
- Check the event logs to see if any additional information was logged.
- Verify the permissions for the DLL.
- Install the .NET Extensibility feature if the request is mapped to a managed handler.
- Create a tracing rule to track failed requests for this HTTP status code. For more information about creating a tracing rule for failed requests, click

**Detailed Error Information:**

| | | |
|---|---|---|
| **Module** | AspNetInitializationExceptionModule | **Requested URL** |
| **Notification** | BeginRequest | **Physical Path** |
| **Handler** | ExtensionlessUrlHandler-Integrated-4.0 | **Logon Method** |
| **Error Code** | 0x00000000 | **Logon User** |

Windows Azure is an interesting platform with a great interface. However, keep in mind that some changes will require you to change some of your habits in order to have everything work the way you expect it to.

# No parameterless constructor defined for this object

Release Date: 09-Sep-13
Url: http://patrickdesjardins.com/blog/?post_type=post&p=2288

A while ago I opened up a solution that was working perfectly previously. I realized that this one compiled but when I launched the browser it raised an exception :

*No parameterless constructor defined for this object*

*t*

# Server Error in '/' Application.

## *No parameterless constructor defined for this object.*

**Description:** An unhandled exception occurred during the execution of the current web request. Please review th

**Exception Details:** System.MissingMethodException: No parameterless constructor defined for this object.

**Source Error:**

Usually, this exception occurs when you are using Asp.Net MVC with Unity and this it cannot resolve the parameters of your constructor. This means that you requested a controller method but the parameters were not provided. To solve this problem, usually people that develop with Asp.Net MVC and Unity use the Unity.MVC3 (http://unitymvc3.codeplex.com/) code that lets you set the Unity dependency resolver to the framework that will resolve the controller's parameters when Asp.Net does an http request. The second option is to have a constructor without a parameter, which is often not possible.

But, in my scenario, I was using Unity.MVC3 and it was working before. The problem resided in the **Web.Config** file. Visual Studio has inserted an attribute that caused all the chaos of this exception.

The web.config has an attribute called "xmlns" with the value "http://schemas.microsoft.com/.NetConfiguration/v2.0" for the element configuration.

```
<configuration xmlns="http://schemas.microsoft.com/.NetConfiguration/v2.0">
  <configSections>
   ...
```

By removing the xmlns attribute (and its value) everything worked as before. No more exception *"No parameterless constructor defined for this object"*, no more problem. So, if you have a parameterless constructor exception when using Asp.Net MVC and Unity, check out your configuration file to be sure that this attribute is not set.

# How to use Json.Net library as the default serializer of Json in Asp.Net

Release Date: 10-Oct-13
Url: http://patrickdesjardins.com/blog/?post_type=post&p=2332

Using the default JSON serializer with Asp.Net MVC can be limited. One classic example is with **date** which returns a slashed format with an integer from the epoch number. Usually, people want a formatted date with a standard format like yyyy-MM-dd. **Json.Net** library (http://james.newtonking.com/json) handles this kind of feature. It also gives you a lot of options that I'll let you explore directly from the **Json.Net Newton King's** website.

The goal of this article is to show you how to use Json.Net library manually. This solution requires you to repeat the use of a class manually into each of your action methods every time you want to use the new serializer. This can be useful if you do not want to change at large in your system. Often, if you have a big system and you do not want to test everything, you may want to keep the new serializer for a few methods. Later, we will see how to change to default .Net serializer with the Json.Net one.

First, we need to inherit from ActionResult (or JsonResult) to have your own custom result class. This is where we will use Json.Net library.

```
public class JsonNetResult : ActionResult
{
    public Encoding ContentEncoding { get; set; }
    public string ContentType { get; set; }
    public object Data { get; set; }

    public JsonSerializerSettings SerializerSettings { get; set; }
    public Formatting Formatting { get; set; }

    public JsonNetResult(object data)
    {
        this.Data = data;
        SerializerSettings = new JsonSerializerSettings();
        Formatting = Formatting.Indented;
    }

    public override void ExecuteResult(ControllerContext context)
    {
        if (context == null)
        {
            throw new ArgumentNullException("context");
        }

        var response = context.HttpContext.Response;
        response.ContentType = !string.IsNullOrEmpty(ContentType)
                                    ? ContentType : "application/json";

        if (ContentEncoding != null)
        {
            response.ContentEncoding = ContentEncoding;
```

```
        }

        if (Data != null)
        {
            var writer = new JsonTextWriter(response.Output)
                                           { Formatting = Formatting };
            var serializer = JsonSerializer.Create(SerializerSettings);
            serializer.Serialize(writer, Data);
            writer.Flush();
        }
    }
}
```

Most of the work is at the end where we use **JsonSerializer.Create** and **.Serialize**. You could set additional default serialization settings in this class. If you want to use this class in an action method, you need to return this class.

```
public JsonResult YourMethodAction()
{
    var model = //...
    return new JsonNetResult(model);
}
```

As you see, you need to return every time a new class manually. If you do not want to do it manually and continue to use the **return Json(...)** as you are used to doing with Asp.Net MVC, you will need to override the default method. This can be easily done if you have a base controller where all your controllers inherit. In fact, you should have a base controller for many reasons.

```
public class BaseController:Controller
{
   protected internal override JsonResult Json(object data)
   {
       return new JsonNetResult(data);
   }
}
```

This creates for you the new custom serialization class and it is transparent for all your methods that need to return a Json formatted value.

## How to migrate from ASP.NET MVC 4 to ASP.NET MVC 5

Release Date: 04-Nov-13
Url: http://patrickdesjardins.com/blog/?post_type=post&p=2380

The new version of MVC (MVC 5) has been out for a few weeks. If you have Microsoft

Visual Studio 2013 and create a new web application, you will notice some improvements. First, the MVC default version is now version 5 and not version 4. This comes with a brand new Razor version which is the third one. Also, Entity Framework is now at version 6. Before going further, notice that if you are migrating to MVC5 from some older version than MVC4 then other assemblies might not be compatible. This implies more than just updating the MVC framework, but also collateral assemblies. For example, Razor version 2 does not work with MVC5.

Migrating is not an easy step to do, but if you have your MVC4 already up to date and have used NuGet for your external libraries, then the process is easier. The first step is to make sure you commit all your code to your source code repository. Preferably, label it with "Last Version MVC4". This way, if something is wrong, you will be able to go back and start from scratch.

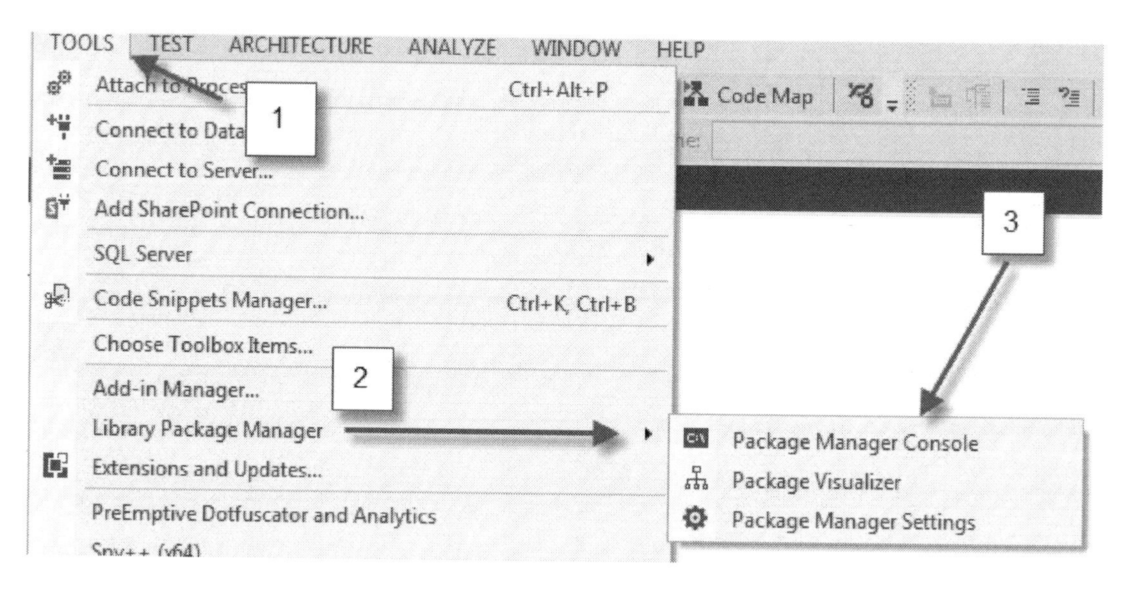


The second step is to run NuGet to update every package. This can be done with a single statement in the NuGet Console. The image above shows how to launch the package manager console. If you want to update all your packages, you can use the following command.

```
PM> Update-Package
```

This may take several minutes if you use a lot of packages. This will do about half of the job of upgrading. You will need to do this for every one of your projects that use packages from NuGet. A good practice is to have always referenced your external library with NuGet. Even if you are using the same package for some of your projects, this will not duplicate them in your *solution/packages*.

The third step is to be done in every one of your projects. I suggest you start from your web site project since it is the one that will have the most jobs to do. You can also right click the solution and manage the update for the whole solution. This will allow you to go through all the projects from one screen. Once done, open the web.config of the web project. Verify that you have Entity Framework set to version 6. The information is set inside configuration>configSections inside a section named "EntityFramework."

```
<configuration>
  <configSections>
    <section name="entityFramework"
type="System.Data.Entity.Internal.ConfigFile.EntityFrameworkSection,
EntityFramework, Version=6.0.0.0, Culture=neutral,
PublicKeyToken=b77a5c561934e089" requirePermission="false"/>
...................
```

As you can see, the version MUST be set to 6.0.0.0 and in fact it should have been modified by the NuGet update that we have done earlier. If it is not, go into your project reference and be sure that you have a reference to EntityFramework.dll.

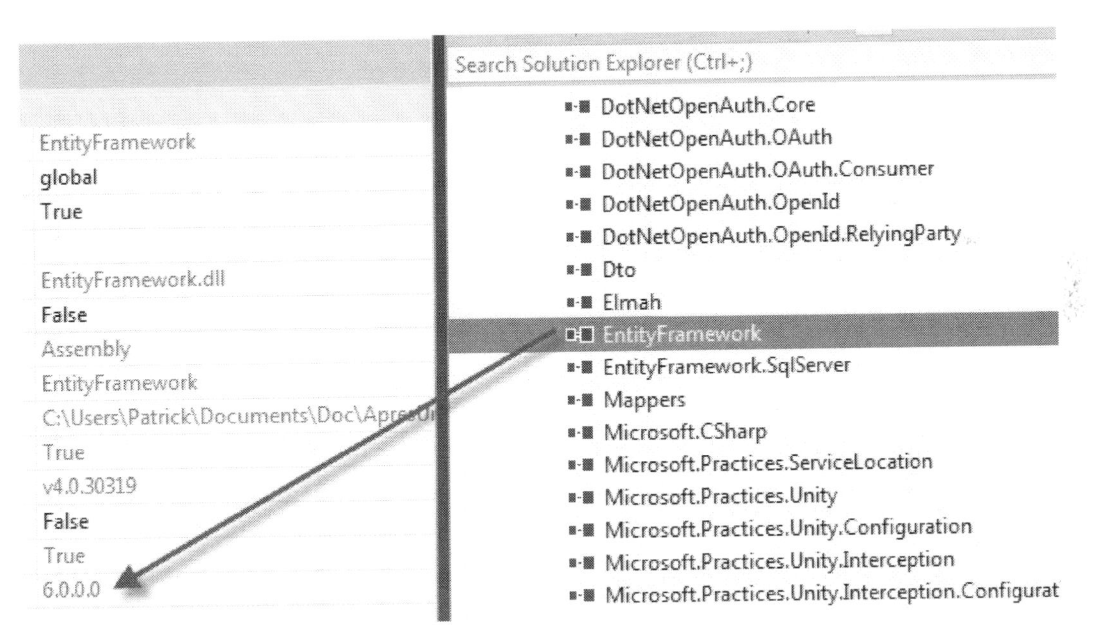


The screenshot shows you that not only is the version set to version 6.0.0.0 but that the version 6 of Entity Framework has a new dll called "EntityFramework.SqlServer." This is now required.

The next step is to go lower in your web.config to the appSetting section. You need to update the version of webpages from 2.0.0.0 to 3.0.0.0. Then, you need to set the framework to 4.5.1 (if you want to be all up to date). This can be done in the **web.config** also inside the configuration tag, under system.web:

```
<system.web>
    <compilation debug="true" targetFramework="4.5.1"/>
    <httpRuntime targetFramework="4.5.1"/>
```

Before going any further in the web.config, do not forget to open all your projects to go in the properties of the project and to select the Target Framework to 4.5.1.

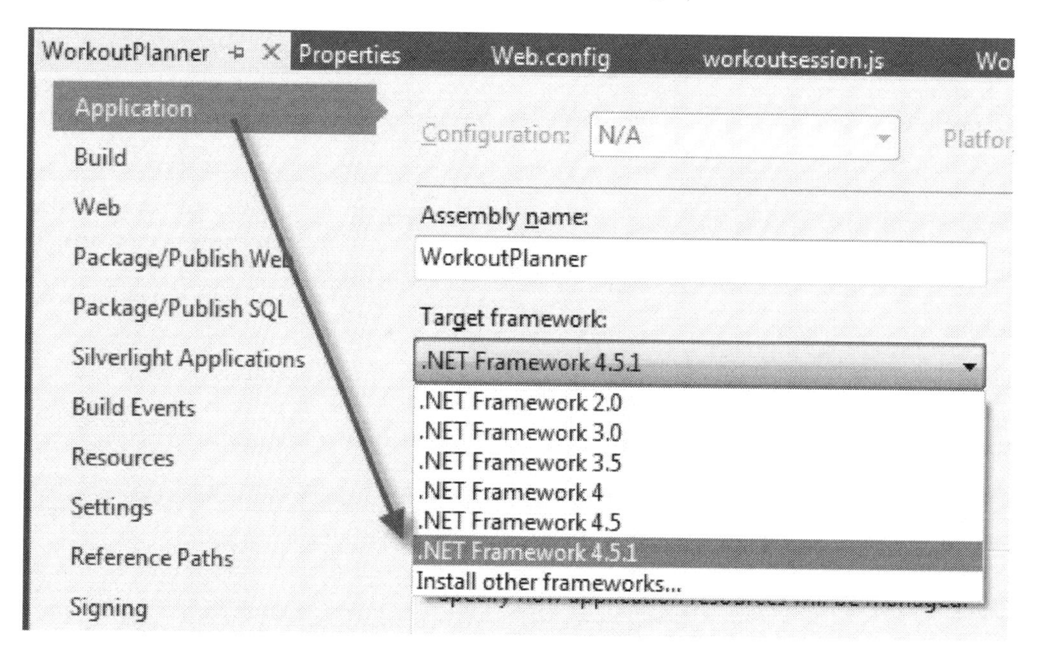


Back to the web.config, we have the runtime tag to update. Here is my runtime information; yours should be almost the same.

```
<runtime>
<assemblyBinding xmlns="urn:schemas-microsoft-com:asm.v1">
  <dependentAssembly>
    <assemblyIdentity name="WebMatrix.WebData" publicKeyToken="31BF3856AD364E35"
culture="neutral"/>
    <bindingRedirect oldVersion="0.0.0.0-3.0.0.0" newVersion="3.0.0.0"/>
  </dependentAssembly>
  <dependentAssembly>
    <assemblyIdentity name="System.Web.WebPages.Razor" publicKeyToken="31BF3856AD364E35"
culture="neutral"/>
    <bindingRedirect oldVersion="0.0.0.0-3.0.0.0" newVersion="3.0.0.0"/>
  </dependentAssembly>
  <dependentAssembly>
    <assemblyIdentity name="WebMatrix.Data" publicKeyToken="31BF3856AD364E35" culture="neutral"/>
    <bindingRedirect oldVersion="0.0.0.0-3.0.0.0" newVersion="3.0.0.0"/>
  </dependentAssembly>
  <dependentAssembly>
    <assemblyIdentity name="System.Web.Razor" publicKeyToken="31BF3856AD364E35"
culture="neutral"/>
    <bindingRedirect oldVersion="0.0.0.0-3.0.0.0" newVersion="3.0.0.0"/>
  </dependentAssembly>
  <dependentAssembly>
    <assemblyIdentity name="System.Web.Helpers" publicKeyToken="31bf3856ad364e35"/>
    <bindingRedirect oldVersion="1.0.0.0-3.0.0.0" newVersion="3.0.0.0"/>
  </dependentAssembly>
  <dependentAssembly>
    <assemblyIdentity name="System.Web.Mvc" publicKeyToken="31bf3856ad364e35"/>
    <bindingRedirect oldVersion="0.0.0.0-5.0.0.0" newVersion="5.0.0.0"/>
  </dependentAssembly>
  <dependentAssembly>
    <assemblyIdentity name="System.Web.WebPages" publicKeyToken="31bf3856ad364e35"/>
    <bindingRedirect oldVersion="1.0.0.0-3.0.0.0" newVersion="3.0.0.0"/>
  </dependentAssembly>
  <dependentAssembly>
    <assemblyIdentity name="AutoMapper" publicKeyToken="be96cd2c38ef1005" culture="neutral"/>
    <bindingRedirect oldVersion="0.0.0.0-2.2.1.0" newVersion="2.2.1.0"/>
  </dependentAssembly>
  <dependentAssembly>
    <assemblyIdentity name="WebGrease" publicKeyToken="31bf3856ad364e35" culture="neutral"/>
    <bindingRedirect oldVersion="0.0.0.0-1.5.2.14234" newVersion="1.5.2.14234"/>
  </dependentAssembly>
  <dependentAssembly>
    <assemblyIdentity name="Microsoft.Practices.Unity" publicKeyToken="31bf3856ad364e35"
culture="neutral"/>
    <bindingRedirect oldVersion="0.0.0.0-3.0.0.0" newVersion="3.0.0.0"/>
  </dependentAssembly>
  <dependentAssembly>
    <assemblyIdentity name="DotNetOpenAuth.AspNet" publicKeyToken="2780ccd10d57b246"
culture="neutral"/>
    <bindingRedirect oldVersion="0.0.0.0-4.3.0.0" newVersion="4.3.0.0"/>
  </dependentAssembly>
  <dependentAssembly>
    <assemblyIdentity name="DotNetOpenAuth.Core" publicKeyToken="2780ccd10d57b246"
culture="neutral"/>
    <bindingRedirect oldVersion="0.0.0.0-4.3.0.0" newVersion="4.3.0.0"/>
  </dependentAssembly>
  <dependentAssembly>
    <assemblyIdentity name="System.Web.Http" publicKeyToken="31bf3856ad364e35" culture="neutral"/>
    <bindingRedirect oldVersion="0.0.0.0-5.0.0.0" newVersion="5.0.0.0"/>
```

```
    </dependentAssembly>
    <dependentAssembly>
      <assemblyIdentity name="System.Net.Http.Formatting" publicKeyToken="31bf3856ad364e35"
culture="neutral"/>
      <bindingRedirect oldVersion="0.0.0.0-5.0.0.0" newVersion="5.0.0.0"/>
    </dependentAssembly>
    <dependentAssembly>
      <assemblyIdentity name="Antlr3.Runtime" publicKeyToken="eb42632606e9261f" culture="neutral"/>
      <bindingRedirect oldVersion="0.0.0.0-3.5.0.2" newVersion="3.5.0.2"/>
    </dependentAssembly>
  </assemblyBinding>
```

This tells the .Net compiler to use the new version if a reference is made to an older version. You can find information through MSDN concerning Assembly Unification.

Now, do that in all your web.config that contain similar XML elements. Once it's done, go into the view folder. This one also should contain a web.config. You need to change some version number here too. Here is one of my view folders (you can have a few because of area).

```
<?xml version="1.0"?>

<configuration>
  <configSections>
    <sectionGroup name="system.web.webPages.razor"
type="System.Web.WebPages.Razor.Configuration.RazorWebSectionGroup, System.Web.WebPages.Razor,
Version=3.0.0.0, Culture=neutral, PublicKeyToken=31BF3856AD364E35">
      <section name="host" type="System.Web.WebPages.Razor.Configuration.HostSection,
System.Web.WebPages.Razor, Version=3.0.0.0, Culture=neutral, PublicKeyToken=31BF3856AD364E35"
requirePermission="false" />
      <section name="pages" type="System.Web.WebPages.Razor.Configuration.RazorPagesSection,
System.Web.WebPages.Razor, Version=3.0.0.0, Culture=neutral, PublicKeyToken=31BF3856AD364E35"
requirePermission="false" />
    </sectionGroup>
  </configSections>

  <system.web.webPages.razor>
    <host factoryType="System.Web.Mvc.MvcWebRazorHostFactory, System.Web.Mvc, Version=5.0.0.0,
Culture=neutral, PublicKeyToken=31BF3856AD364E35" />
    <pages pageBaseType="System.Web.Mvc.WebViewPage">
      <namespaces>
        <add namespace="System.Web.Mvc" />
        <add namespace="System.Web.Mvc.Ajax" />
        <add namespace="System.Web.Mvc.Html" />
        <add namespace="System.Web.Optimization"/>
        <add namespace="System.Web.Routing" />
      </namespaces>
    </pages>
  </system.web.webPages.razor>

  <appSettings>
    <add key="webpages:Enabled" value="false" />
  </appSettings>

  <system.web>
```

```
    <httpHandlers>
      <add path="*" verb="*" type="System.Web.HttpNotFoundHandler"/>
    </httpHandlers>
    <pages
        validateRequest="false"
        pageParserFilterType="System.Web.Mvc.ViewTypeParserFilter, System.Web.Mvc,
Version=5.0.0.0, Culture=neutral, PublicKeyToken=31BF3856AD364E35"
        pageBaseType="System.Web.Mvc.ViewPage, System.Web.Mvc, Version=5.0.0.0, Culture=neutral,
PublicKeyToken=31BF3856AD364E35"
        userControlBaseType="System.Web.Mvc.ViewUserControl, System.Web.Mvc, Version=5Install-
Package -Id  Microsoft.AspNet.WebHelpers.0.0.0, Culture=neutral, PublicKeyToken=31BF3856AD364E35">
      <controls>
        <add assembly="System.Web.Mvc, Version=5.0.0.0, Culture=neutral,
PublicKeyToken=31BF3856AD364E35" namespace="System.Web.Mvc" tagPrefix="mvc" />
      </controls>
    </pages>
  </system.web>

  <system.webServer>
    <validation validateIntegratedModeConfiguration="false" />

    <handlers>
      <remove name="BlockViewHandler"/>
      <add name="BlockViewHandler" path="*" verb="*" preCondition="integratedMode"
type="System.Web.HttpNotFoundHandler" />
    </handlers>
  </system.webServer>
</configuration>
```

You have three entries to change for razor. You need to change version 2.0.0.0 to version 3.0.0.0. Also, System.Web.Mvc.MvcWebRazorHostFactory, and System.Web.Mvc need to be changed to 5.0.0.0. Then, under pages you have three other changes concerning MVC that need to be set to version 5.

The last modification that is required is to use MVC5 to open with notepad the project file of the web. Search for **ProjectTypeGuids** and remove the GUID for MVC4: {E3E379DF-F4C6-4180-9B81-6769533ABE47}.

You will not have the stuff that a brand new MV5 project has like BootStrap but this can be added later on. What you have is a project up to date with Microsoft MVC framework 5, Entity Framework 6 and using the .Net Framework 4.5.1

## Two differents approaches to save data from JavaScript to Asp.Net MVC

Release Date: 07-Nov-13
Url: http://patrickdesjardins.com/blog/?post_type=post&p=2363

There are more than **two approaches** to send data from JavaScript with Ajax to Asp.Net MVC. Today, I present you one that uses **dynamic** and one that uses **DTO** (data transfer object). The first approach is faster because it requires less code but is dynamic, which opens the door to several problems. Before anything, let's see the JavaScript that will be used by both approaches to send the information to the Asp.Net MVC controller.

```
$(document).on("click", "#btnSaveOrder", function () {
    var button = $(this);
    $(button).attr('disabled', 'disabled');
    $('.loadingAnimationfixed').show();
    var listIdOrdered = [];
    $('#sessiongrid tbody tr').each(function () {
        listIdOrdered.push($(this).attr("data-workoutsessionid"));
    });

    var toSave = {
        'OrderedWorkoutSessionList': listIdOrdered
        , 'WorkoutId': $('#Id').val()
    };

    $.ajax(
        {
            url: "/WorkoutSession/SaveWorkoutSessionOrder",
            type: "POST",
            data: JSON.stringify(toSave),
            success: function (response, status, xhr) {
                successMessage(response.Status);
            },
            error: function (XMLHttpRequest, textStatus, errorThrown) {
                if (errorThrown == "Forbidden") {
                    errorMessage("Forbidden access");
                } else {
                    errorMessage('An error occurred please retry.');
                }
            }
            , complete: function () {
                $(button).removeAttr('disabled');
                $('.loadingAnimationfixed').hide();
            }
        }
    );

    return false; //Prevent button to submit the form
});
```

The code binds with JQuery a click event to the button with the ID "*btnSaveOrder.*" We disable the button and display a loading animation division. This is so far good practice. It disallows the user from clicking twice on the button and it displays to the user what is going on. Next, we are building from the user interface a list of IDs. The situation here is that we need to save a list of IDs to the database in a specific order. The line that initializes the *tosave* variable contains a list of all IDs, which is ordered, then a variable of the current workout. So, we have an object that contains a workout ID with a list of workout session IDs that is ordered as a FIFO (first in first out) list. This object needs to be sent to the server to be saved. This is done by the JQuery Ajax method. First, we specify the URL and the method to contact the server. Second, we specify the object to send and we transform the Json into a string. Finally, we display a success message or an error message. In both cases, we enable the button and remove the animation with the complete method. From this code, we know that from the server side we need to have a POST action that is called SaveWorkoutSessionOrder, which takes a class with two properties; one is a list of integers and one is an integer.

The first approach to handle this is to go fast and to not create a class that contains a list of integers and one integer. We can do it by using the dynamic keyword. We have to deserialize the object ourself into a JSON object.

```
[HttpPost]
public JsonResult SaveWorkoutSessionOrder()
{
    dynamic json = JsonConvert.DeserializeObject(Request.Form.Get(0));

    int order = 1;
    var workout = new Workout { Id = json.WorkoutId };
    workout.Sessions = new List<WorkoutSession>();

    foreach (var id in json.OrderedWorkoutSessionList)
    {
        workout.Sessions.Add(new WorkoutSession { Id = id, Order = order++ });
    }

    try
    {
        ServiceFactory.Workout.UpdateSessionOrderOnly(workout);
    }
    catch (DataNotFoundException)
    {
        throw new HttpException((int)HttpStatusCode.Forbidden, "Cannot update the
session");
    }
    return Json(new { Status = "Saved" });
}
```

The first thing we remark on is that the method does not contain any parameter. This is because we do not allow the model binder to act but deserialize it manually inside the method. This is what the first line of the method is doing with the *JsonConvert.DeserializeObject*. We need to get the Request object and to get the first element of the form which is the one sent by JavaScript with the Ajax calls. The return value of the deserialization goes to a dynamic variable. This allows us to skip the creation of a concrete class for the list of integers and the integer. Then, we can use the variable but you do not have any IntelliSense. You need to be sure to write correctly the property name of this dynamic variable with the same name as the JavaScript prototype. If you do, everything will be fine in the execution. Nevertheless, this is not an optimal way to develop an enterprise application because of many problems. Yes, it is faster, but the cost is heavier in the long term.

As you can see, we do not have a parameter to this controller's action. Even if it is not dramatic, it is harder to unit test because it requires mocking the Request object. The second problem is with the dynamic itself. The use of dynamic weakens the entire method. The problem is that error is not detected until execution. If you are unit testing this method with a full coverage, you should not have a problem. The last problem is that we are deserializing inside the controller's action instead of delegating the process to the **Model Binder**. Every mapping between http request and controller's methods is done by the Model Binder. The cohesion of your controller is compromised and there may come a problem later on in the maintenance phase of your system.

The solution is to change the controller to take a parameter that will be deserialized by the Model Binder of Asp.Net MVC and will give us a strongly typed object. This one will be easily testable since we will be able to pass in our tests a parameter.

```
[HttpPost]
public JsonResult SaveWorkoutSessionOrder(WorkoutSessionOrder workoutSessionOrder)
{
    int order = 1;
    var workout = new Workout { Id = workoutSessionOrder.WorkoutId };
    workout.Sessions = new List<WorkoutSession>();

    foreach (var id in workoutSessionOrder.OrderedWorkoutSessionList)
    {
        workout.Sessions.Add(new WorkoutSession { Id = id, Order = order++ });
    }

    try
    {
        ServiceFactory.Workout.UpdateSessionOrderOnly(workout);
    }
    catch (DataNotFoundException)
    {
```

```
        throw new HttpException((int)HttpStatusCode.Forbidden, "Cannot update the
session");
    }
    return Json(new { Status = "Saved" });
}
```

As you can see, the first signature was changed to have a parameter. That means that we need to provide this data from the Javascript. In fact, we were sending this object previously but this time we have to specify the data type to indicate to Asp.Net MVC framework what information we are sending to deserialize. To mark the data sent to be JSON format, we need to add this line in the Ajax's call: contentType: 'application/json'.

```
$(document).on("click", "#btnSaveOrder", function () {
    var button = $(this);
    $(button).attr('disabled', 'disabled');
    $('.loadingAnimationfixed').show();
    var listIdOrdered = [];
    $('#sessiongrid tbody tr').each(function () {
        listIdOrdered.push($(this).attr("data-workoutsessionid"));
    });

    var toSave = {
        'OrderedWorkoutSessionList': listIdOrdered
        ,'WorkoutId': $('#Id').val()
    };

    $.ajax(
        {
            url: "/WorkoutSession/SaveWorkoutSessionOrder",
            type: "POST",
            data: JSON.stringify(toSave),
            contentType: 'application/json',
            success: function (response, status, xhr) {
                successMessage(response.Status);
            },
            error: function (XMLHttpRequest, textStatus, errorThrown) {
                if (errorThrown == "Forbidden") {
                    errorMessage("Forbidden access");
                } else {
                    errorMessage('An error occurred please retry.');
                }
            }
            , complete: function () {
                $(button).removeAttr('disabled');
                $('.loadingAnimationfixed').hide();
            }
        }
    );
```

That is it! Now we have seen two different approaches. The last one is the one you should use every time because it is strongly typed, easier to test and will not compile with possible errors like the one with Dynamic which will crash on execution if a typo is made.

## Asp.Net MVC error 404 The request filtering module is configured to deny a request where the query string is too long.

Release Date: 12-Nov-13
Url: http://patrickdesjardins.com/blog/?post_type=post&p=2391

If you create a new MVC projet and hit F5 to start the application by default, Visual Studio starts to execute your code. As you may know by now, Visual Studio 2013 does not have **Cassini**, the internal web server inside Visual Studio. So, **IIS Express** is quickly automatically configured and the default website starts.

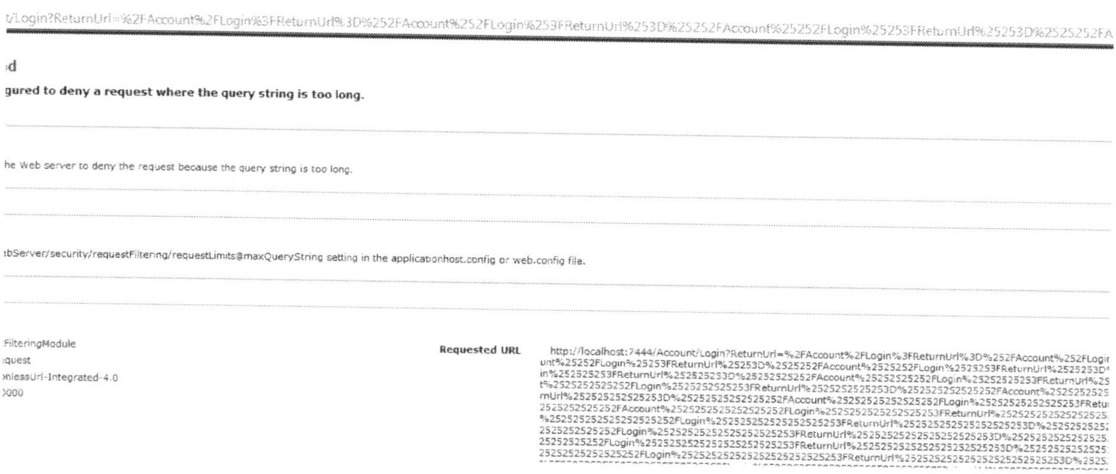

gured to deny a request where the query string is too long.

he Web server to deny the request because the query string is too long.

ebServer/security/requestFiltering/requestLimits@maxQueryString setting in the applicationhost.config or web.config file.

FilteringModule

Requested URL http://localhost:7444/Account/Login?ReturnUrl=%2FAccount%2FLogin%3FReturnUrl%3D%252FAccount%252FLogi

Unfortunately, if you do nothing, you will have an issue with the query string being too long. This is because it redirects to the login page which redirects to the login page and so on infinitely.

If you are using IIS, everything works. Personally, I am always using IIS, but I am still curious why the IIS Express, even with a brand new project, does not work. The IIS Express configuration file is located inside your document setting. By default the Windows authentication is enabled. You need to remove this and to use anonymous authentication.

# Authentication with Active Directory (AD) with Asp.Net MVC

Release Date: 25-Nov-13
Url: http://patrickdesjardins.com/blog/?post_type=post&p=2423

With Visual Studio 2013, you cannot simply choose "Intranet WebSite" to create a default website that uses **Active Directory**. Nevertheless, a wizard allows you to create it. First, select "create a new project" and select a web application.

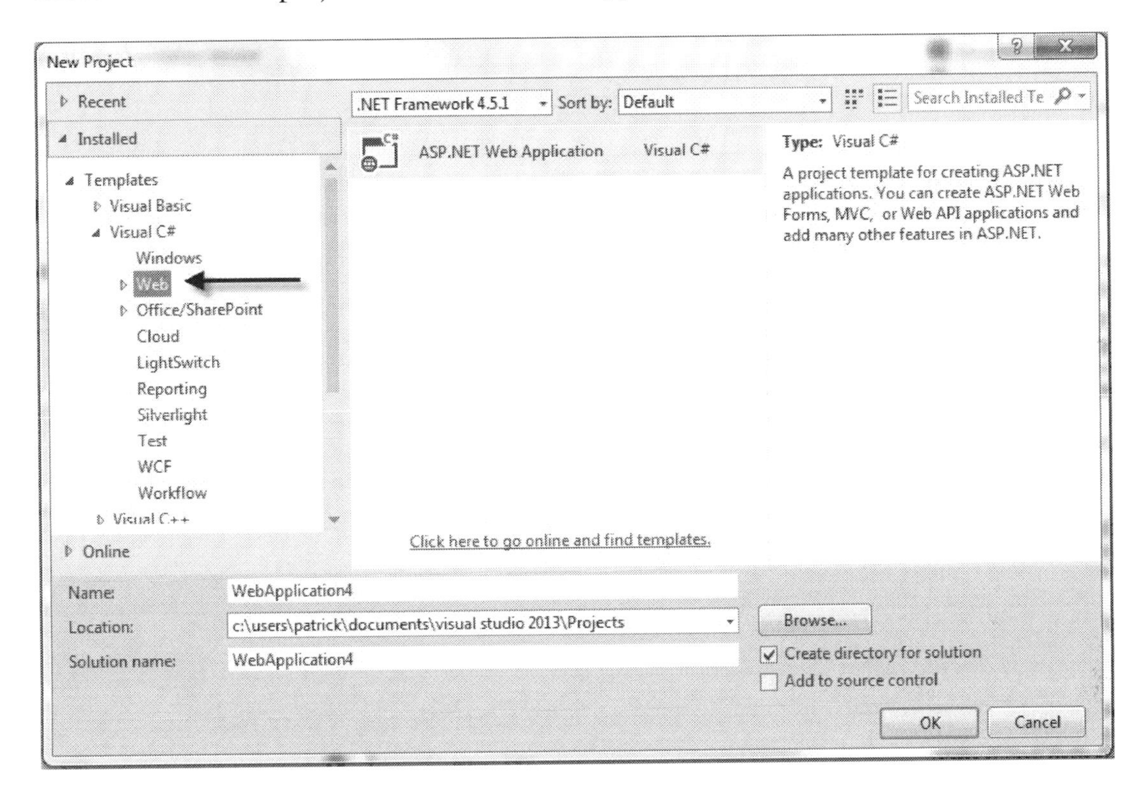


Second, you need to select MVC and click Change Authentication.

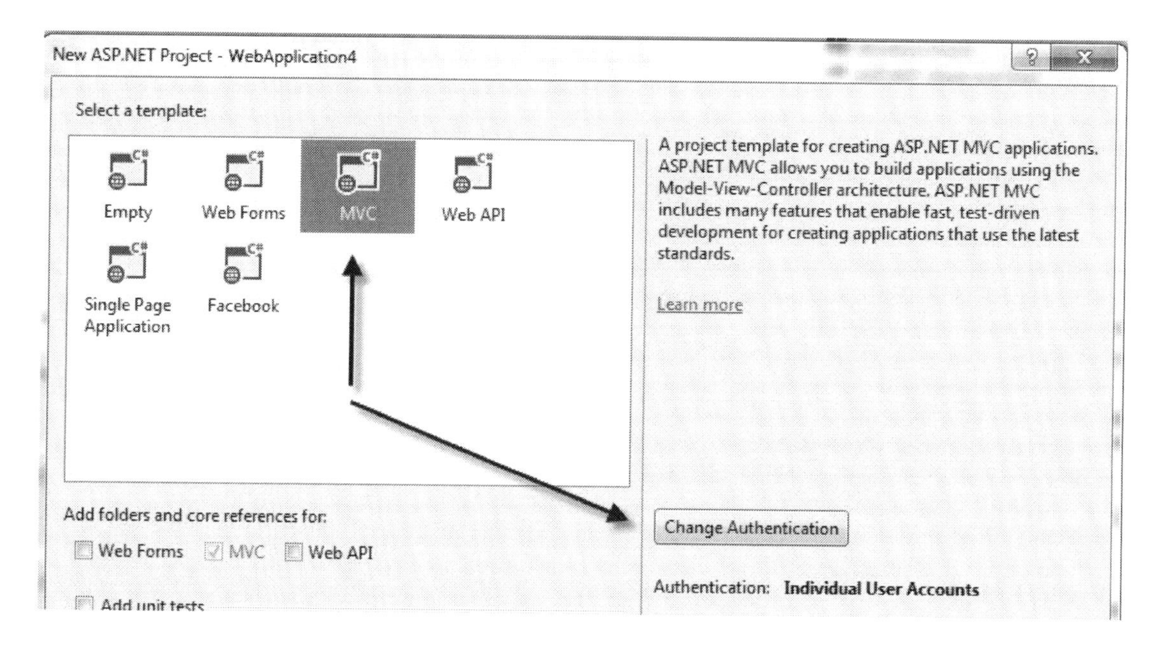


This will result in a page where you will be able to select **Organization Authentication**. Select On-Premise. This will let you specify the active directory URL.

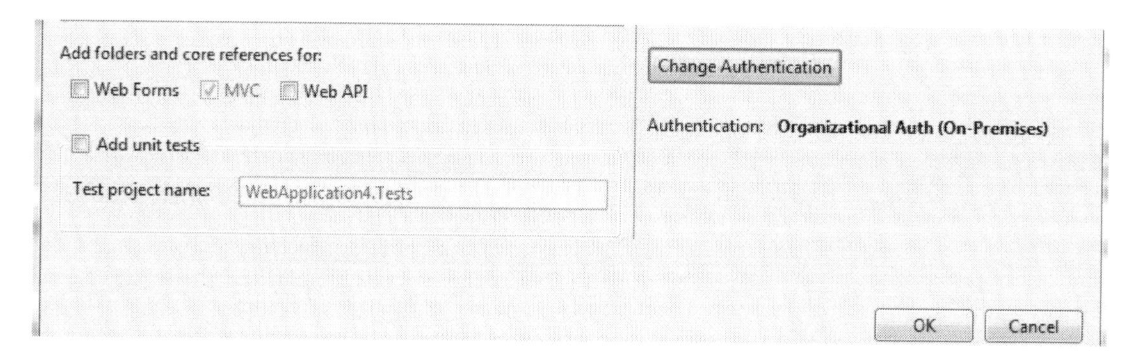


And that is it. You can also do it more manually. It is good to know because if you have to configure IIS, you will have to do some configuration yourself. First, you need to disable anonymous authentication and allow Windows authentication.

The web.config also needs to know that we use Windows authentication.

```
<system.web>
  <authentication mode="Windows" />

  <roleManager enabled="true" defaultProvider="AspNetWindowsTokenRoleProvider">
   <providers>
      <clear />
```

```
      <add
          name="AspNetWindowsTokenRoleProvider"
          type="System.Web.Security.WindowsTokenRoleProvider"
          applicationName="/" />
    </providers>
  </roleManager>
</system.web>
```

This allows the use of the **Authorize** attribute over controllers and methods.

```
[Authorize(Roles = "YOURDOMAIN\\Group1, YOURDOMAIN\\Group2")]
public ActionResult YourMethod()
{
    //...
}
```

If you want to allow the user to log in with the form instead of being automatically logged in, you need to specify a connection string in the web.config.

```
<connectionStrings>
  <add name="ADConn" connectionString="LDAP://YourConnection" />
</connectionStrings>
```

Then, you need to set up the membership provider and you are all done.

```
<membership defaultProvider="ADMembership">
  <providers>
    <add name="ADMembership"
         type="System.Web.Security.ActiveDirectoryMembershipProvider,
               System.Web,
               Version=2.0.0.0,
               Culture=neutral,
               PublicToken=b03f5f7f11d50a3a"
         connectionStringName="ADConn"
         connectionUsername="domain/user"
         connectionPassword="pwd" />
  </providers>
</membership>
```

## Asp.Net MVC localized url without having to specify the language in it

Release Date: 03-Dec-13
Url: http://patrickdesjardins.com/blog/?post_type=post&p=2429

Often we see people using for a multi-language website the option to change the language by adding a property into the session of the user which tells the server to change the culture and culture ui to something other than English. This is fine because resources files handle multiple languages if the culture is set correctly. Another way to do it is to allow the user to put the culture into the url like the following example: http://yourwebsite.com/fr-ca/controllerName/actionName. I personally dislike this approach. It has the advantage of sending a url to someone and to have it in the correct language, and this can't be done with the previous solution of allowing the user to change the language and set it to the session. But, it has the disadvantage of indicating that the language is French and still having the text in the url in English. The solution Isuggest is that if you have a public page that this should control the language with a url that is already in the desired language. You should also let the user select the language and set the client language into a session which will tell the server how to display the url. This solution gives you a good SEO url with the named url in the default language and allows the user to control the language if desired.

At the end, what we want is to have a url like this:

http://yourwebsite.com/Compte/Identification for French website and for English : http://yourwebsite.com/Account/Login

Everything starts by changing the routing. This can be done by opening the file **RouteConfig.cs** that is inside your web project under the folder App_Start.

Several things need to be done. First, we need to specify which culture will be used by your application. Then, you will have to use a custom structure to specify every controller and action with the translated values. This is required to associate every language word to an existing controller and existing action. Finally, the last step is to create a binder that will allow you to use the new mechanism to translate a route. This is an example of how the routeConfig.cs looks for a brand new Asp.Net MVC5 application with the Home and Account controller translated.

```
public class RouteConfig
{
    public static void RegisterRoutes(RouteCollection routes)
    {
        routes.IgnoreRoute("{resource}.axd/{*pathInfo}");

        var cultureEN = CultureInfo.GetCultureInfo("en-US");
        var cultureFR = CultureInfo.GetCultureInfo("fr-FR");

        var translationTables = new List<ControllerTranslation>{
        new ControllerTranslation("Home"
              , new List<Translation>{
```

```
                    new Translation(cultureEN, "Home")
                   ,new Translation(cultureFR, "Demarrer")
            }
        ,new List<ActionTranslation>{
                new ActionTranslation("About"
                , new List<Translation>{
                        new Translation(cultureEN, "About")
                    ,new Translation(cultureFR, "Infos")
                })
                , new ActionTranslation("Home"
                , new List<Translation>{
                        new Translation(cultureEN, "Home")
                    ,new Translation(cultureFR, "Demarrer")
                })
            , new ActionTranslation("Contact"
                , new List<Translation>{
                        new Translation(cultureEN, "Contact")
                    ,new Translation(cultureFR, "InformationSurLaPersonne")
                })
        })
    ,new ControllerTranslation("Account"
            ,
            new List<Translation>{
                        new Translation(cultureEN, "Account")
                    ,new Translation(cultureFR, "Compte")
            }
            ,
            new List<ActionTranslation>
            {
                new ActionTranslation("Login"
                , new List<Translation>{
                        new Translation(cultureEN, "Login")
                    ,new Translation(cultureFR, "Authentication")
                })
                ,
                new ActionTranslation("Register"
                , new List<Translation>{
                        new Translation(cultureEN, "Register")
                    ,new Translation(cultureFR, "Enregistrement")
                })

            }
    )
};

    routes.Add("LocalizedRoute", new TranslatedRoute(
        "{controller}/{action}/{id}",
        new RouteValueDictionary(new { controller = "Home"
                                    , action = "Index", id = "" }),
        translationTables,
```

```
            new MvcRouteHandler()));

        routes.MapRoute(
            name: "Default",
            url: "{controller}/{action}/{id}",
            defaults: new { controller = "Home", action = "Index"
                                    , id = UrlParameter.Optional }
        );
    }
}
```

As you can see, it can be very exhaustive to define every action of every controller. However, this configuration can be saved in a database and loaded once for the application if you desire.

We are using a lot of classes that you will need. First of all, let's define all classes that are used to structure the controllers and actions translation. I have separated all classes into four files.

```
◢ Routing
    ▷ C# ActionTranslation.cs
    ▷ C# ControllerTranslation.cs
    ▷ C# TranslateRoute.cs
    ▷ C# Translation.cs
```

```
public class ControllerTranslation
{
    public string ControllerName { get; set; }
    public List<Translation> Translation { get; set; }
    public List<ActionTranslation> ActionTranslations { get; set; }

    public ControllerTranslation(string controllerName
                                , List<Translation> translation
                                , List<ActionTranslation> actionsList)
    {
        this.ControllerName = controllerName;
        this.Translation = translation;
        this.ActionTranslations = actionsList;
    }
}
```

This is the main class that has the controller name, which is required to be able to bind the translated name for the real code name. It contains a translation list which contains for every culture the new name. This is what is used in the url. Then, it contains a list of actions. This way, we have a well-structured and logically-separated structure.

```
public class ActionTranslation
{
    public string ActionName { get; set; }
    public List<Translation> Translation { get; set; }

    public ActionTranslation(string actionName, List<Translation> translation)
    {
        this.ActionName = actionName;
        this.Translation = translation;
    }
}
```

ActionTranslation is almost the same as ControllerTranslation. The only difference is that it does not contain a list of classes.

```
public class Translation
{
    public CultureInfo CultureInfo { get; set; }
    public string TranslatedValue { get; set; }
    public Translation(CultureInfo culture, string translatedValue)
    {
        CultureInfo = culture;
        TranslatedValue = translatedValue;
    }
}
```

Finally, the Translation class contains culture information that is associated with a string that is translated into the language of the culture. Take note that you could also have an AreaTranslation that would have a Controller class list. This example is extensible for more levels of url structure without problems. For simplicity, this article concentrates its efforts for Controller and Action only. The last class is here to define a new Route. In the RouteConfig.cs class the route is defined before the default route.

```
routes.Add("LocalizedRoute", new TranslatedRoute(
              "{controller}/{action}/{id}",
              new RouteValueDictionary(new { controller = "Home", action =
"Index", id = "" }),
              translationTables,
              new MvcRouteHandler()));
```

The third parameter takes the controller list that has all actions translated. A route is a class that inherits from System.Web.Routing.Route class. This class allows you to override two important methods — RouteData GetRouteData(HttpContextBase httpContext) and VirtualPathData GetVirtualPath(RequestContext requestContext, RouteValueDictionary values). The first one is used when a request is made to the server. This means that it takes the localized words of the controller and action of the URL and translates them with your list of controllers defined previously in the RouteConfig.cs. The second one is used by Html helper to create a new link. This means it takes the real controller and action name and translates them to create a localized link for your application. This is awesome because not only is your url are in the default language but also all your links everywhere in your application are automatically translated.

```
public class TranslatedRoute : Route
{

    public List<ControllerTranslation> Controllers { get; private set; }

    public TranslatedRoute(string url, RouteValueDictionary defaults
                            , List<ControllerTranslation> controllers
                            , IRouteHandler routeHandler)
        : base(url, defaults, routeHandler)
    {
        this.Controllers = controllers;
    }

    public TranslatedRoute(string url, RouteValueDictionary defaults
                            , List<ControllerTranslation> controllers
                            , RouteValueDictionary constraints, IRouteHandler
                        routeHandler)
        : base(url, defaults, constraints, routeHandler)
    {
        this.Controllers = controllers;
    }

    /// <summary>
    /// Translate URL to route
    /// </summary>
    /// <param name="httpContext"></param>
    /// <returns></returns>
    public override RouteData GetRouteData(HttpContextBase httpContext)
    {
        RouteData routeData = base.GetRouteData(httpContext);
        if (routeData == null)
            return null;

        string controllerFromUrl = routeData.Values["controller"].ToString();
        string actionFromUrl = routeData.Values["action"].ToString();
        var controllerTranslation = this.Controllers.FirstOrDefault(d =>
d.Translation.Any(rf => rf.TranslatedValue == controllerFromUrl));
        var controllerCulture = this.Controllers
                    .SelectMany(d => d.Translation)
                    .FirstOrDefault(f => f.TranslatedValue == controllerFromUrl)
                    .CultureInfo;
        if (controllerTranslation != null)
        {
```

```
            routeData.Values["controller"] = controllerTranslation.ControllerName;
            var actionTranslation = controllerTranslation.ActionTranslations
                    .FirstOrDefault(d => d.Translation
                    .Any(rf => rf.TranslatedValue == actionFromUrl));
            if (actionTranslation != null)
            {
                routeData.Values["action"] = actionTranslation.ActionName;
            }
            System.Threading.Thread.CurrentThread.CurrentCulture =
                                                    controllerCulture;
            System.Threading.Thread.CurrentThread.CurrentUICulture =
                                                    controllerCulture;

        }
        return routeData;
    }

    /// <summary>
    /// Used in Html helper to create link
    /// </summary>
    /// <param name="requestContext"></param>
    /// <param name="values"></param>
    /// <returns></returns>
    public override VirtualPathData GetVirtualPath(RequestContext requestContext,
RouteValueDictionary values)
    {

        var requestedController = values["controller"];
        var requestedAction = values["action"];
        var controllerTranslation = this.Controllers
                          .FirstOrDefault(d => d.Translation
                          .Any(rf => rf.TranslatedValue ==
                                                  requestedController));
        var actionTranslation = controllerTranslation.ActionTranslations
                          .FirstOrDefault(d => d.Translation
                          .Any(rf => rf.TranslatedValue == requestedAction));
        var controllerTranslatedName = controllerTranslation.Translation
                          .FirstOrDefault(d => d.CultureInfo ==
                      System.Threading.Thread.CurrentThread.CurrentCulture)
                          .TranslatedValue;
        if (controllerTranslatedName != null)
            values["controller"] = controllerTranslatedName;
        var actionTranslate = controllerTranslation.ActionTranslations
                      .FirstOrDefault(d => d.Translation
                      .Any(rf => rf.TranslatedValue == requestedAction));
        if (actionTranslate != null)
        {
            var actionTranslateName = actionTranslate.Translation
                      .FirstOrDefault(d => d.CultureInfo ==
                  System.Threading.Thread.CurrentThread.CurrentCulture)
                      .TranslatedValue;
```

```
            if (actionTranslateName != null)
                values["action"] = actionTranslateName;
        }
        return base.GetVirtualPath(requestContext, values);
    }
}
```

For both methods, if we do not find the controller name or action name, it falls back to the default name. This way, nothing crashes. I have also added two lines that change the thread language. This is not required if you do not want to change the language of the whole application but it seems logical to do it. If you send a url in French, you certainly want to have the whole page use French resources.

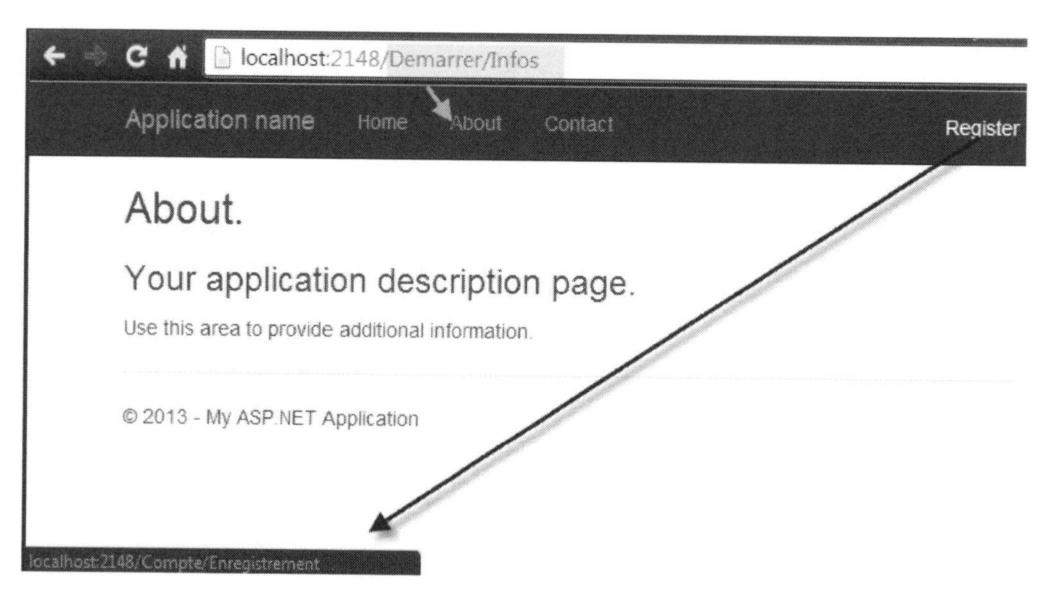


You can have the complete source code on GitHub.

## Asp.Net MVC5 with localization resource

Release Date: 06-Dec-13
Url: http://patrickdesjardins.com/blog/?post_type=post&p=2377

This post contains information to localize your Asp.Net MVC web application. I have already covered how to change the language from the url without having to use the culture code in the url. This post's goal is to detect the default language of the user's browser and to let the user select a preferred language. Never depend only on the browser language for choosing localization. I have a French keyboard since I am living in Quebec, Canada and I hate to see a website French localized by default. I want to see everything in English. I am not the only one who desires to see a specific website in a specific language and this is why you should let the user choose in which language to display your string, date and number.

Localization works by setting the current thread Culture and Culture UI with a CultureInfo class. CultureInfo can contain the region or not. So, you can have the language and the country or just the language.

```
var culture1 = new System.Globalization.CultureInfo("fr");
var culture2 = new System.Globalization.CultureInfo("fr-CA");
```

In the example above, culture1 specifies the language, French, but doesn't specify the region, which can be a problem for number and date. This is why it is always better to be region specific instead of using a neutral culture. With experience, you will see that your customers do not want the European format for currency if they live in North America. (The Euro is not the Canadian dollar!)

In an MVC application, the language is often set in the user session or cookie. It is then loaded back when one of your controllers is called. Normally, all your controllers should inherit from a base controller. This is the perfect place to set the thread culture back from the session or cookie. You can set the thread inside the **OnActionExecuting**.

```
protected override void OnActionExecuting(ActionExecutingContext filterContext)
{
      Thread.CurrentThread.CurrentUICulture
                                          = new CultureInfo(CurrentUser.Language);
      Thread.CurrentThread.CurrentCulture = new CultureInfo(CurrentUser.Language);
      //...
}
```

If you want to use by default the language set in the browser if the session is not set, it's possible. This language is set in the preference of the browser. Here are two screenshots that explain how to adjust the language for Chrome and for Internet Explorer.

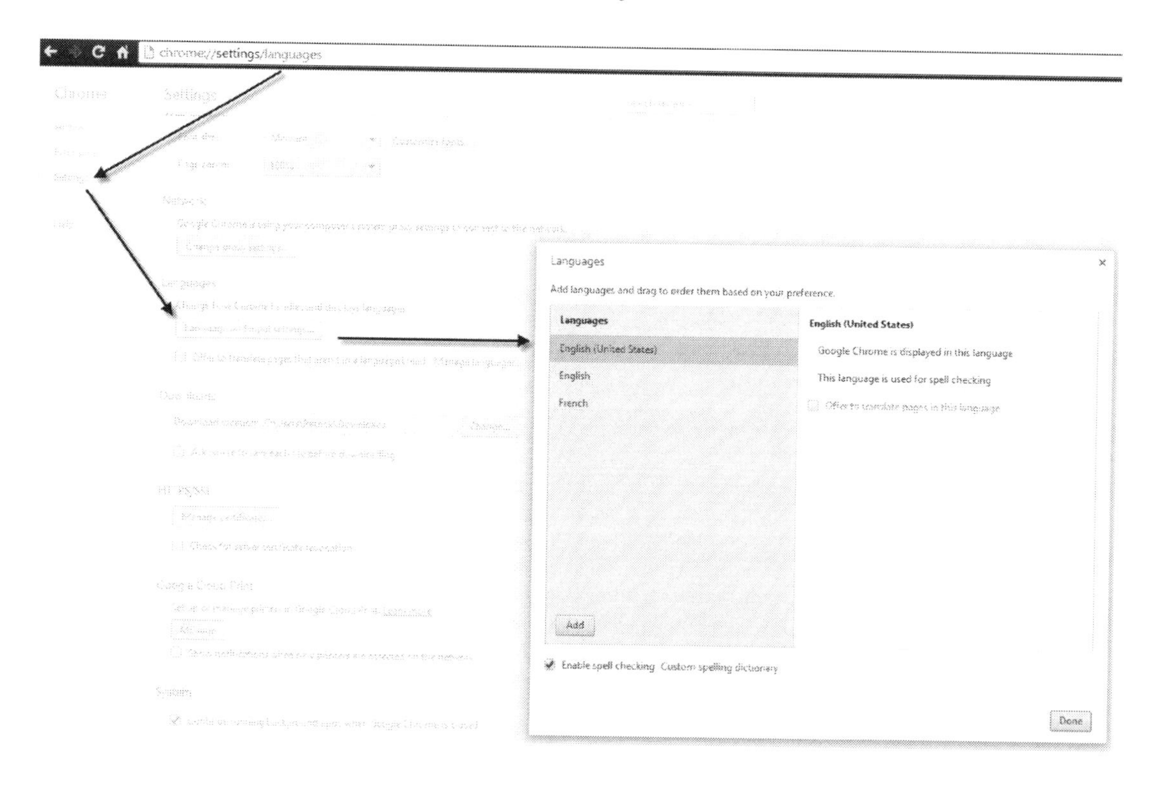
chrome://settings/languages
Languages
Add languages and drag to order them based on your preference.
Languages
English (United States)
English
French
Add
English (United States)
Google Chrome is displayed in this language
This language is used for spell checking
Enable spell checking
Custom spelling dictionary
Done

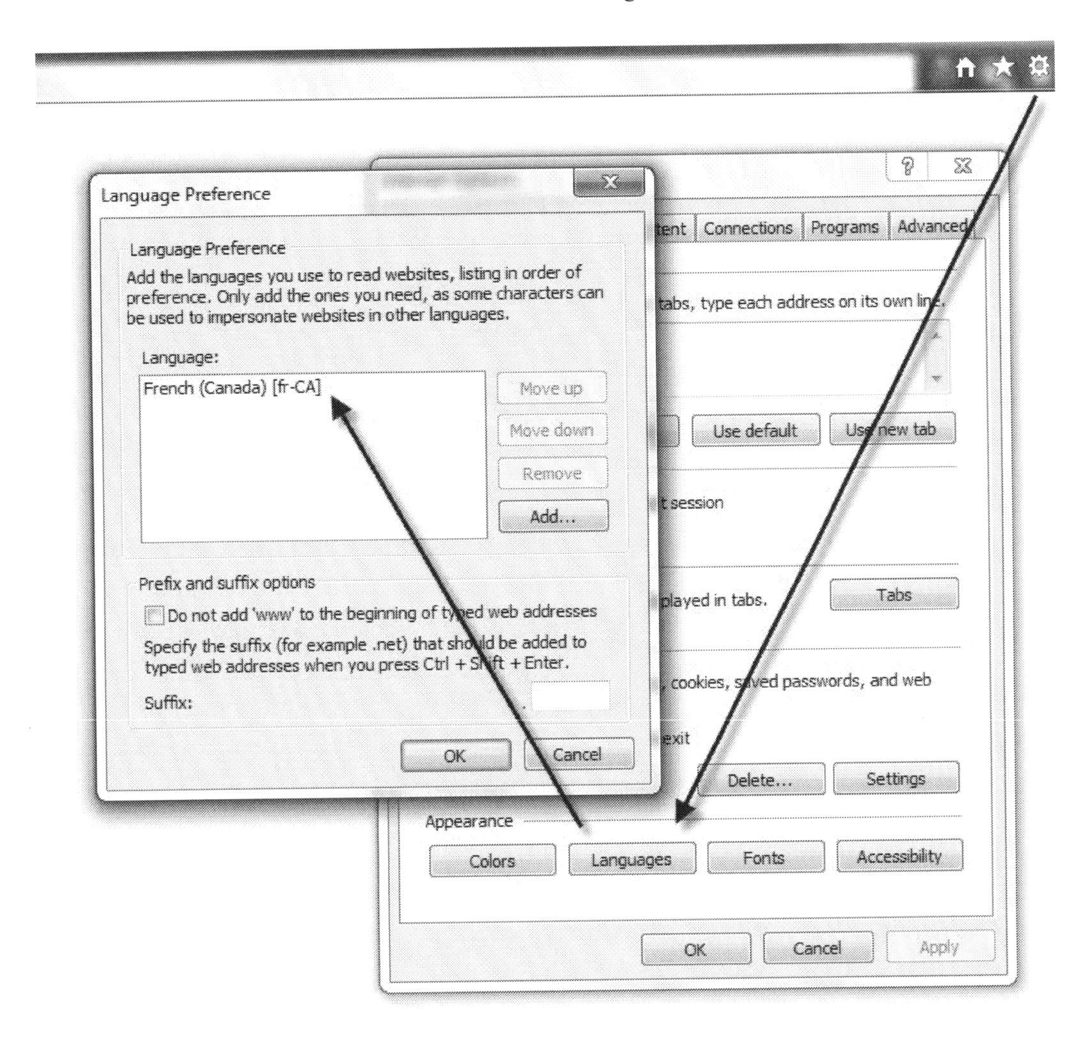


This sets the **Accept-Language** in the http header. The server receives this information, and you can read it from the Http Request header.

```
cultureName = Request.UserLanguages != null
        && Request.UserLanguages.Length > 0 ? Request.UserLanguages.First();
```

If the language is not available inside your resource file, it falls back to the localized file that doesn't have any culture. Normally, you have resource files like Message.resx, Message.en.resx, Message.fr.resx. As you can see, we do not specify the region, but we could. In fact, Asp.Net tries to take the more specific to the less specific. This is very useful because you can translate a very specific string for a specific region in Message.fr-Ca.resx without having to define every other string. When creating your resource files, set the access modifier to Public. This will allow to use your resource outside the project, which is good if you have a project for resource. This sets the build option from ResXFileCodeGenerator to PublicResXFileCodeGenerator for the custom tool to use. From here, you can use the resource inside your application by specifying the namespace and the name of the resource (without any culture) and with the key name of the resource.

```
<h1>
    @ResourcesNamespace.Titles.CreateCustomer
</h1>
```

If you do not want to type the namespace every time you can set one at the top of the file and for views you can also specify in the web.config the namespace to be added by default. Often, this is added into the web.config of the Views folder and not the whole application since the majority of times you have resources for each Views folder. If you want to add the namespace into the defaults, add your namespace under razor configuration.

```
<configuration>
  <system.web.webPages.razor>
    <host factoryType="System.Web.Mvc.MvcWebRazorHostFactory, System.Web.Mvc,
Version=5.0.0.0, Culture=neutral, PublicKeyToken=31BF3856AD364E35" />
    <pages pageBaseType="System.Web.Mvc.WebViewPage">
      <namespaces>
        <add namespace="System.Web.Mvc" />
        <add namespace="System.Web.Mvc.Ajax" />
        <add namespace="System.Web.Mvc.Html" />
        <add namespace="System.Web.Optimization"/>
        <add namespace="System.Web.Routing" />
        <add namespace="YourNamespaceHere" />
      </namespaces>
    </pages>
  </system.web.webPages.razor>
```

Finally, if you want to use the default language and then the session, here is the code you need to use inside your controller. Keep in mind that this is not what should be done if you are using what I have previously written concerning url language. This is because the url keeps the language and you do not need to check the accepted language of the browser or the session.

```
protected ICurrentUser CurrentUser
{
  get
  {
    UserSessionDTO currentUser = _sessionHandler.GetUser();
    if (currentUser != null)
    {
      UserProfile userProfile
                    =_mapperFactory.UserSessionDTO.GetModel(currentUser);
```

```
        return userProfile;
      }
      else
      {
        ICurrentUser currentUserFromProvider = _userProvider.Account;
        UserProfile fullUserProfile = _serviceFactory.Account
                        .GetByUserName(currentUserFromProvider.UserName);
        if (fullUserProfile == null)//Case of a non identified user
        {
          fullUserProfile = new UserProfile();
          fullUserProfile.Language =
                              Request.UserLanguages != null &&
                          Request.UserLanguages.Length > 0 ?
                          Request.UserLanguages.First():"en-US";
        }
        return fullUserProfile;
      }
    }
}

protected override void OnActionExecuting(ActionExecutingContext filterContext)
{
  Thread.CurrentThread.CurrentUICulture = new CultureInfo(CurrentUser.Language);
  Thread.CurrentThread.CurrentCulture = new CultureInfo(CurrentUser.Language);
  base.OnActionExecuting(filterContext);
  //....
}
```

The code above is a little bit more than necessary. It has in the base controller something that checks if the user is already logged into the session. If yes, it returns the object fully loaded. If not, which is the case for a new user who comes on your website, it uses the temporary user from the user and verifies it has a User Profile, which should be null. This creates a temporary User Profile and sets the language which is in fact the culture (I should rename this property). From the Controller.Request which is of type System.Web.HttpRequestBase, you can read the UserLanguage and take the first one defined. If none is set, I choose English from United States of America.

## Asp.Net MVC With the ValidateAntiForgeryToken For Cross Site Request Forgeries

Release Date: 02-Jan-14
Url: http://patrickdesjardins.com/blog/?post_type=post&p=2409

Cross Site Request Forgeries is also known as **CSRF**. It is a type of malicious exploit that sends commands from a user without consent to another website. CSRF exploits the trust that a site has in a user's browser. For example, a website could try to execute a form to add something to your Amazon basket! This can be limited by adding a hidden field to a form and a cookie. Both will contain the same value and when the form is submitted the hidden field is compared to the cookie value. If it's the same value, we know that the user has sent the form. If it's not, we know it's a malicious attack.

In Asp.Net MVC, ValidateAntiForgeryToken is a combination of an HTML helper (hidden field) and attribute(cookie) that allows the site to verify if the form has been created and sent by the same user. The first step is to add the HtmlHelper method @Html.AntiForgeryToken() inside the form in your view.

```
@using (Html.BeginForm())
{
    @Html.AntiForgeryToken()
    //...
```

This generates a hidden field with the name "__RequestVerificationToken" and a unique value. This is an example of the output generated:

```
<form action="/House/Create" method="post" novalidate="novalidate">
    <input name="__RequestVerificationToken" type="hidden"
value="KPyzBk0KGpjStJR96AVI38AbBujBInJNB-1XH-RwsbuifwgmxnGiF-
0R2cMHjcYBiz7yOBUnv0fZwoE2oBwiuKXalBDvsRr2RRG7nmkOsq41">
```

The code behind the HTML helper is simple. It creates an MvcHtmlString from the AntiForgery class.

```
public MvcHtmlString AntiForgeryToken()
{
   return new MvcHtmlString(AntiForgery.GetHtml().ToString());

}
```

The AntiForgery class contains the GetHtml() used in the HTML helper but also some validation of the forgery. Both use the class AntiForgeryWorker.

```
public static HtmlString GetHtml()
{
  if (HttpContext.Current == null)
     throw new ArgumentException(WebPageResources.HttpContextUnavailable);
  else
     return AntiForgery._worker.GetFormInputElement((HttpContextBase) new
HttpContextWrapper(HttpContext.Current)).ToHtmlString(TagRenderMode.SelfClosing);
```

```
}
```

The _worker that we see in the code above is of type AntiForgeryWorker. This class is about 139 lines and the core of it is the GetFormInputElement used by the GetHtml.

```
public TagBuilder GetFormInputElement(HttpContextBase httpContext)
{
    this.CheckSSLConfig(httpContext);
    AntiForgeryToken cookieTokenNoThrow = this.GetCookieTokenNoThrow(httpContext);
    AntiForgeryToken newCookieToken;
    AntiForgeryToken formToken;
    this.GetTokens(httpContext, cookieTokenNoThrow, out newCookieToken
                    , out formToken);
    if (newCookieToken != null)
        this._tokenStore.SaveCookieToken(httpContext, newCookieToken);
    if (!this._config.SuppressXFrameOptionsHeader)
        httpContext.Response.AddHeader("X-Frame-Options", "SAMEORIGIN");
    TagBuilder tagBuilder = new TagBuilder("input");
    tagBuilder.Attributes["type"] = "hidden";
    tagBuilder.Attributes["name"] = this._config.FormFieldName;
    tagBuilder.Attributes["value"] = this._serializer.Serialize(formToken);
    return tagBuilder;
}
```

This is interesting to see how the value is generated. As we can see, it is using the serializer to serialize the form token. The form token is buildbt inside the class TokenValidator that take ssome property of the Identity. I will not go deeper because it goes a little beyond the scope of this article. Just remember that the token is unique for the user. However, the GetFormInputElement code above is also important for something else. The token store role is to create the cookie which also setthe token.

```
public void SaveCookieToken(HttpContextBase httpContext, AntiForgeryToken token)
{
    HttpCookie cookie = new HttpCookie(this._config.CookieName
                              , this._serializer.Serialize(token))
    {
        HttpOnly = true
    };
    if (this._config.RequireSSL)
        cookie.Secure = true;
    httpContext.Response.Cookies.Set(cookie);
}
```

The way the **ValidateAntiForgeryToken** attribute works is by checking to see that the cookie and hidden form field left by the Html.AntiForgeryToken() Html Helper essentially exist and that they match. If they do not exist or match, it throws an

HttpAntiForgeryException.

```
[HttpPost]
[ValidateAntiForgeryToken]
0 references
public ActionResult Create(FormCollection collection)
{
    try
    {
        // TODO: Add insert logic here
```

The attribute does have a **ValidateAntiForgeryTokenAttribute** method that calls the AntiForgery class. I have previously mentioned that it has the method not only to get the input but also for validation. Here is where it's used.

```
public ValidateAntiForgeryTokenAttribute()
      : this(new Action(AntiForgery.Validate))
{
}
```

This method goes through several methods of the framework to end at the ValidateTokens(…) methods that look like the code below.

```
public void ValidateTokens(HttpContextBase httpContext, IIdentity identity,
AntiForgeryToken sessionToken, AntiForgeryToken fieldToken)
{
    if (sessionToken == null)
        throw
HttpAntiForgeryException.CreateCookieMissingException(this._config.CookieName);
    if (fieldToken == null)
        throw HttpAntiForgeryException
              .CreateFormFieldMissingException(this._config.FormFieldName);
    if (!sessionToken.IsSessionToken || fieldToken.IsSessionToken)
        throw HttpAntiForgeryException
              .CreateTokensSwappedException(this._config.CookieName,
         this._config.FormFieldName);
    if (!object.Equals((object) sessionToken.SecurityToken, (object)
fieldToken.SecurityToken))
        throw HttpAntiForgeryException
              .CreateSecurityTokenMismatchException();
    string str = string.Empty;
    BinaryBlob binaryBlob = (BinaryBlob) null;
    if (identity != null && identity.IsAuthenticated)
    {
    binaryBlob = this._claimUidExtractor.ExtractClaimUid(identity);
    if (binaryBlob == null)
         str = identity.Name ?? string.Empty;
```

```
    }
    bool flag = str.StartsWith("http://", StringComparison.OrdinalIgnoreCase)
          || str.StartsWith("https://", StringComparison.OrdinalIgnoreCase);
    if (!string.Equals(fieldToken.Username, str, flag
          ? StringComparison.Ordinal : StringComparison.OrdinalIgnoreCase))
        throw HttpAntiForgeryException
              .CreateUsernameMismatchException(fieldToken.Username, str);
    if (!object.Equals((object) fieldToken.ClaimUid, (object) binaryBlob))
        throw HttpAntiForgeryException
              .CreateClaimUidMismatchException();
    if (this._config.AdditionalDataProvider != null
          && !this._config.AdditionalDataProvider
          .ValidateAdditionalData(httpContext, fieldToken.AdditionalData))
        throw HttpAntiForgeryException.CreateAdditionalDataCheckFailedException();
}
```

What interests us is all possible exceptions that are thrown. You can see that it can raise the **HttpAntiForgeryException** for several cases, like if the cookie is missing, which is the case for Cross Site Request Forgeries, or if the form does not have the hidden field, or if there is a token mismatch between the cookie and the form.

All the complexity of the mechanism is hidden by the Asp.Net MVC framework. At the end, you only need to remember to add the HTML helper to your form and to add the attribute to the action of your controller that receives the form inputs.

# When to use IsCustomErrorEnabled with Asp.Net MVC

Release Date: 10-Jan-14
Url: http://patrickdesjardins.com/blog/?post_type=post&p=2411

If you are using Asp.Net MVC, your should have a **BaseController** that every controller of your project inherits. In this base controller, your should override the method OnException.

```
protected override void OnException(ExceptionContext filterContext)
{
    //1) Write log here
    //2) Redirect from the yellow screen of death to a custom nice error page
}
```

At least, this is what it should have. The step 1) has nothing to do with the **ExceptionContext.HttpContext.IsCustomErrorEnabled**. The second step, yes. In fact, when you are developing, the yellow screen is very informative.

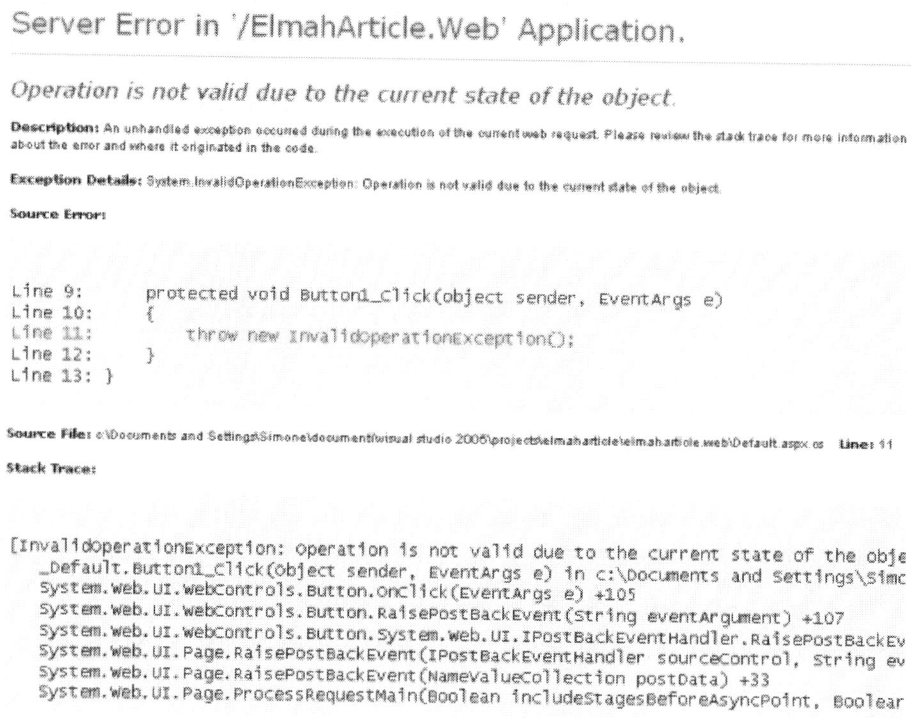

Server Error in '/ElmahArticle.Web' Application.

*Operation is not valid due to the current state of the object.*

**Description:** An unhandled exception occurred during the execution of the current web request. Please review the stack trace for more information about the error and where it originated in the code.

**Exception Details:** System.InvalidOperationException: Operation is not valid due to the current state of the object.

**Source Error:**

```
Line 9:      protected void Button1_Click(object sender, EventArgs e)
Line 10:     {
Line 11:         throw new InvalidOperationException();
Line 12:     }
Line 13: }
```

**Source File:** c:\Documents and Settings\Simone\documenti\visual studio 2005\projects\elmaharticle\elmaharticle.web\Default.aspx.cs **Line:** 11

**Stack Trace:**

```
[InvalidOperationException: Operation is not valid due to the current state of the obje
   _Default.Button1_Click(Object sender, EventArgs e) in c:\Documents and Settings\Simc
   System.Web.UI.WebControls.Button.OnClick(EventArgs e) +105
   System.Web.UI.WebControls.Button.RaisePostBackEvent(String eventArgument) +107
   System.Web.UI.WebControls.Button.System.Web.UI.IPostBackEventHandler.RaisePostBackEv
   System.Web.UI.Page.RaisePostBackEvent(IPostBackEventHandler sourceControl, String ev
   System.Web.UI.Page.RaisePostBackEvent(NameValueCollection postData) +33
   System.Web.UI.Page.ProcessRequestMain(Boolean includeStagesBeforeAsyncPoint, Boolear
```

This is why it can be interesting to not keep it with the default one. Having this screen is quite harsh for a user that goes into your side. However, it contains information valuable for you when debugging.

```
protected override void OnException(ExceptionContext filterContext)
{
  if (filterContext.HttpContext.IsCustomErrorEnabled)
  {
     filterContext.ExceptionHandled = true;
     this.View("YourErrorPage").ExecuteResult(this.ControllerContext);
  }
}
```

**IsCustomErrorEnabled** is true when in the web.config the **customerror** is set to true. It is false when it is set to false. When the value is set to **remoteonly**, it is also true but only when executing on localhost (127.0.0.1) and false when not. It is interesting to get the default webpage with all the information to debug. It is possible to use this variable, with the IsCustomErrorEnabled, and to leverage it inside your base controller, like with the **OnException** in the above example.

# Migrating Asp.Net MemberShip to Asp.Net MVC Identity for authentication

Release Date: 27-Jan-14
Url: http://patrickdesjardins.com/blog/?post_type=post&p=2591

I was using WebMatrix with the Gym Workout project (https://github.com/MrDesjardins/GymWorkout). But, it was not a clean way to handle authentication. It was in the middle of the old membership with a new flavor. However, since Microsoft is going with the new One Asp.Net Owin Identity framework which allows claims but also to be dissociated from Microsoft SQL Server, that makes it more appealing. It is also on the frame of OWIN, so we have almost all positive features without the negative parts. Finally, Identity does have aclean way to have a custom field to extend the default username/password attribute. It is clean because it creates specific columns for each field. So, if you have an existing Asp.Net MVC, how do you upgrade to the Identity framework for authentication? This is what I will explain in this Identity tutorial.

First, some libraries are required.

- Microsoft.AspNet.Identity.EntityFramework
- Microsoft.AspNet.Identity.Core
- Microsoft.AspNet.Identity.OWIN

These can be found by using NuGet with the following command:

```
PM> Install-Package Microsoft.AspNet.Identity.Core
PM> Install-Package Microsoft.AspNet.Identity.Owin
PM> Install-Package Microsoft.AspNet.Identity.EntityFramework
PM> Install-Package Microsoft.Owin.Host.SystemWeb
```

The next step is to get rid of everything concerning the user which is in its own class called for the project "UserProfile." Instead, I created a new class called "ApplicationUser" which inherits from the default one of Identity framework. I removed the WebUserProvider because now it will use Entity Framework to get user information. Providers are not required and everything will go with the service layer to the data access layer to the database with Entity Framework (EF). The AccountModel (in fact the view model) still exists, which allows our custom fields like Role, Language and Email in the view. Everything is bound to the model class ApplicationUser.

```
public class ApplicationUser : IdentityUser, ICurrentUser
{
    public ApplicationUser()
    {
        Email = "";
```

```
        Language = "";
    }
    public string UserId
    {
        get { return base.Id; }
        set { }
    }
    public string Email { get; set; }
    public string Language { get; set; }

}
```

Even if the ApplicationUser inherits from IdentityUser which has an ID property, the ICurrentUser that we had previously used the UserId property. This is why it is defined in ApplicationUser and links to the IdentityUser. The only thing that we will do later is to ignore this property so as to not have the data inside the database. We also need to create an ApplicationUserService that contacts the Data Access Layer.

A major change concerns the ServiceFactory class which has every entity's service classes. Since the Account comes from the database and we do not want to go to the database every time one of the entities requires something related to the user to be logged, they need to share the same account. This requires a change in the constructor that is going to take in its constructor the IUserProvider which has a property Account. This is passed to every service constructor.

```
public class ServiceFactory : IServiceFactory
{
    private IUserProvider _userProvider;
    #region Implementation of IServiceFactory

    public IAccountService Account { get; private set; }
    public IMuscleService Muscle { get; private set; }
    public IWorkoutService Workout { get; private set; }
    public IWorkoutSessionService WorkoutSession { get; private set; }
    public IWorkoutSessionExerciseService WorkoutSessionExercise { get; private
set; }

    public IExerciseService Exercise { get; private set; }

    #endregion

    public ServiceFactory(IRepositoryFactory repositoryFactory
            , IMapperFactory mapperFactory, IUserProvider userProvider)
    {
        _userProvider = userProvider;
        var account = _userProvider.Account;
        Account = new ApplicationUserService(repositoryFactory, mapperFactory);
```

```
        Muscle = new MuscleService(repositoryFactory, mapperFactory, account);
        Workout = new WorkoutService(repositoryFactory, mapperFactory, account);
        WorkoutSession = new WorkoutSessionService(repositoryFactory
                                    , mapperFactory, account);
        WorkoutSessionExercise = new
         WorkoutSessionExerciseService(repositoryFactory, mapperFactory, account);
        Exercise = new ExerciseService(repositoryFactory, mapperFactory
                                        , Muscle, account);
    }
}
```

Entities inherit from BaseService.

```
public abstract class BaseService
{
    public BaseService(IRepositoryFactory repositoryFactory
                        , IMapperFactory mapperFactory, ICurrentUser user)
    {
        Repository = repositoryFactory;
        Mapper = mapperFactory;
        Repository.SetUser(user);
    }

    protected IRepositoryFactory Repository { get; private set; }
    protected IMapperFactory Mapper { get; private set; }
}
```

When the service is initialized, it uses the injected Repository to set the user that is also injected. Since the ServiceFactory calls the Account once, one call is made to the database. After that, it only sets the object to the repository, which could be used later.

The concept of IUserProvider remains. This is because we will use a *WebUserProvider* for the Asp.Net MVC and a *WebServiceUserProvider*.

The Global.asax.cs file changes because it does not use anymore the AuthConfig.RegisterAuth() because the Identity with OWIN does have a Startup page in the App folder.

```
public partial class Startup
{
    // For more information on configuring authentication, please visit
http://go.microsoft.com/fwlink/?LinkId=301864
    public void ConfigureAuth(IAppBuilder app)
    {
        // Enable the application to use a cookie to store information for the
signed in user
        app.UseCookieAuthentication(new CookieAuthenticationOptions
```

```
        {
            AuthenticationType = DefaultAuthenticationTypes.ApplicationCookie,
            LoginPath = new PathString("/Account/Login")
        });
        // Use a cookie to temporarily store information about a user logging in
with a third party login provider
        app.UseExternalSignInCookie(DefaultAuthenticationTypes.ExternalCookie);
    }
}
```

This also requires registering the Startup class with another Startup class that is used as a bootstrapper for the OWIN container.

```
using Owin;

[assembly: OwinStartup(typeof(WorkoutPlanner.Startup))]
namespace WorkoutPlanner
{
    public partial class Startup
    {
        public void Configuration(IAppBuilder app)
        {
            ConfigureAuth(app);
        }
    }
  }
```

Notice the assembly instruction that tells which class is used for OwinStartup. It uses two classes but could use one. The only benefit of splitting the class in two is to have one startup entry and the code to configure somewhere else. This could later unclutter the booting class.

The migration changes also. The Seed method does not use WebSecurity to initialize a default user. It uses the ApplicationUser class with the UserStore and UserManager class that uses Entity Framework to work with the database.

To create the database with all Identity classes and all the business classes, the migration command in the package console is required.

```
update-database -ConfigurationTypeName "Configuration"
```

This works because the Configuration class inherits from *DbMigrationsConfigurations* which allows the migration tool to be executed. It takes the database context to be used. In our case, it's the one that contains all entities of the application.

```
public class Configuration : DbMigrationsConfiguration<DatabaseContext>
{
```

```
    public Configuration()
    {
        base.AutomaticMigrationsEnabled = true;
    }

    protected override void Seed(DatabaseContext context)
    {
        var userStore = new UserStore<ApplicationUser>(context);
        var manager = new UserManager<ApplicationUser>(userStore);

        var role = new IdentityUserRole {
                    Role = new IdentityRole(Model.Roles.ADMINISTRATOR) };
        var user = new ApplicationUser() {
                    UserName = "123123", Email = 123123@123.com
                                  , Language = "en-US" };
        user.Roles.Add(role);
        IdentityResult result = manager.Create(user, "123123");

        var role2 = new IdentityUserRole {
                        Role = new IdentityRole(Model.Roles.NORMAL) };
        var user2 = new ApplicationUser() { UserName = "qweqwe"
                    , Email = "qweqwe@qweqwe.com", Language = "fr-CA" };
        user.Roles.Add(role2);
        IdentityResult result2 = manager.Create(user2, "qweqwe");

        var muscles = new[]{new Muscle { Id = 1, Name = new LocalizedString
                                { French = "Cou", English = "Neck" } },
            new Muscle { Id = 2, Name = new LocalizedString
                                { French = "Épaule", English = "Shoulder" } }
            };


        context.Set<Muscle>().AddOrUpdateRange(muscles);
        //... and so on...
        base.Seed(context);
     }
}
```

When working with Asp.Net Identity one key is to have your database context class inherit from IdentityDbContext and not directly from DbContext. Otherwise, you will get keys that are not defined for IdentityUserLogin, IdentityUserRole, IdentityUserLogins and IdentityUserRoles.

```
DataAccessLayer.Database.IdentityUserLogin: : EntityType 'IdentityUserLogin' has
no key defined. Define the key for this EntityType.
DataAccessLayer.Database.IdentityUserRole: : EntityType 'IdentityUserRole' has no
key defined. Define the key for this EntityType.
```

```
IdentityUserLogins: EntityType: EntitySet 'IdentityUserLogins' is based on type
'IdentityUserLogin' that has no keys defined.
IdentityUserRoles: EntityType: EntitySet 'IdentityUserRoles' is based on type
'IdentityUserRole' that has no keys defined.
```

```
   public      class      DatabaseContext      :IdentityDbContext<ApplicationUser>,
IDatabaseContext
```

Migrating from **Asp.Net Membership** to **Identity** is not something that can be done for the first time in under a few hours. In fact, it took me around 12 hours to figure out that I had to inherit from **IdentityDbContext** and to solve several seeding problems. Also, having to use Entity Framework changed a little bit how to use the user information. Nevertheless, the time is not exponential since it concerns only users and roles entities. I believe that it should take less than a day for someone who has all the information.

# Handling Creation and Edition Screen with EditorFor

Release Date: 11-Feb-14
Url: http://patrickdesjardins.com/blog/?post_type=post&p=2625

Creation and Edition screen share a lot of similar information. The view is the same but changes if it has a read only screen. Nevertheless, the create and edit view should share the same cshtml to limit future modifications like adding a field or modifying existing fields. It is possible to have the Creation.cshtml and Edition.cshtml use the same partial class. The code below shows how it can be done.

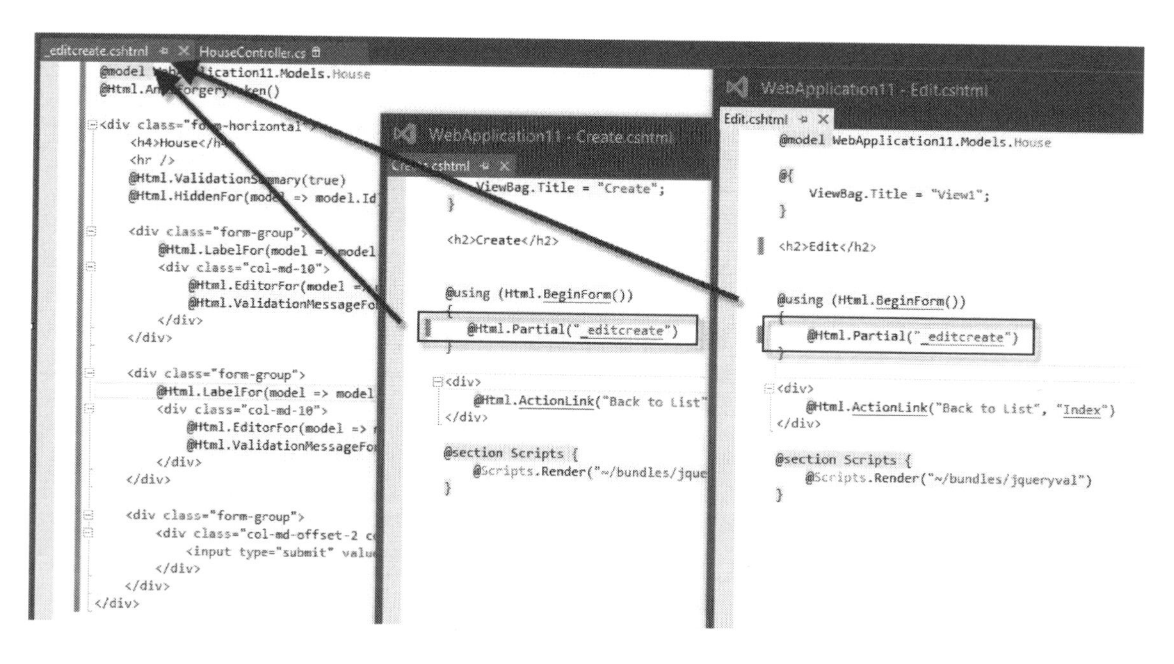

One way to do it is to use the html helper **EditorForModel**. Often, EditorFor and DisplayFor are used for individual input control but this can be used also for regrouping them. So, the **EditorForModel** is used to share between edition and creation the same group of edition control, and inside the **EditorTemplates** you have a file name that has the model (or view model if you are using view model) used by the controller. Inside the editor templates of the model you can use EditorFor to leverage the dynamic of editor template for controls.

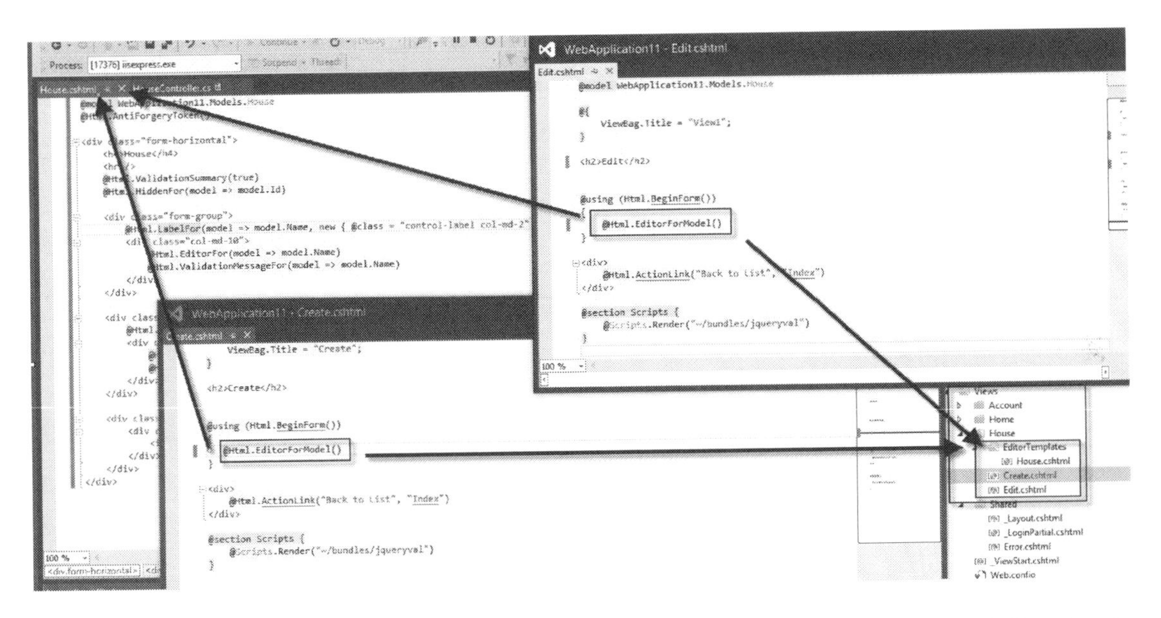


The forms are not shared because they generate the HTML by the controller that has called them. For example, the edition form generates the action with the controller and action name as shown below.

```
<form action="/House/Edit/1" method="post">
```

## How to create your own Asp.Net MVC Html Helper namespace

Release Date: 20-Feb-14
Url: http://patrickdesjardins.com/blog/?post_type=post&p=2612

Html helper allows you to have reusable code around your application for Html creation. For example, the Html helper for a textbox creates an Html Input of type text. It allows you to set the name and the value from the model. Html helpers are a must to use with Asp.Net MVC.

At some point, custom helpers are required to be developed in-house for specific needs. A simple approach is to simply create an extension method to the HTML helper. Here is a small example of creating an Html helper. The Html helper is an extension to the HtmlHelper class.

```
public static class MyHtmlHelpers
{
    public static MvcHtmlString OutputName(this HtmlHelper helper, string name)
    {
        return new MvcHtmlString(string.Format("<h1>{0}</h1>", name));
    }
}
```

This can be used in views this way:

```
@Html.OutputName("Patrick")
```

The problem with this approach is that it becomes harder and harder with time to know which Html Helper are from Asp.Net MVC and which ones are custom ones. It also becomes cumbersome to not have namespace inside the helpers.

This problem brings us to this blog post, where we will put all custom Html helpers into a specific method inside the HtmlHelper. What we want is to create segmentation of all Html Helpers. The following code is the result of what we want to create. Inside the HtmlHelper class, we will inject a method that will be our namespaces. We could set all our inputs controllers into Input and divide with other "namespaces" other Html input. To be short, we will create only the input one in this blog post and only for the creation of a select list. As you will see, we will create a non-generic Helper, like in the code below, but also the generic one. This will give us the possibility of using a Lambda expression to specify which properties to use instead of specifying it with a string.

```
@Html.Input().SelectorFor("MyPropertyName", new[] { "Item1", "Item2" })
@Html.Image()... //And so on.
```

First, we need to inject the method for our namespaces.

```
public static class HtmlHelperNameSpaces
{
    public static HelperExtensionInputFactory Input(this HtmlHelper helper)
    {
        return new HelperExtensionInputFactory(helper);
    }

    public static HelperExtensionInputFactory<TModel> Input<TModel>(
                                                this HtmlHelper<TModel> helper)
```

```
    {
        return new HelperExtensionInputFactory<TModel>(helper);
    }
}
```

In the code above, we see that we have two Input methods. One takes an HtmlHelper and the other one a generic HtmlHelper. We can have more methods for more "namespaces". The same logic applies. We need to take the HtmlHelper as the first parameter to create the extension. Then, we need to return the Html Helper that has the code.

```
/// <summary>
/// Generic
/// </summary>
public class HelperExtensionInputFactory<TModel> : HelperExtensionInputFactory
{
    private HtmlHelper<TModel> HtmlHelper { get; set; }

    public HelperExtensionInputFactory(HtmlHelper<TModel> htmlHelper)
        : base(htmlHelper)
    {
        HtmlHelper = htmlHelper;
    }

    public MvcHtmlString SelectorFor<TValue>(
            Expression<Func<TModel, TValue>> property, IEnumerable<string> items)
    {
        var meta = ModelMetadata.FromLambdaExpression(property
                                                    , this.HtmlHelper.ViewData);
        string fullPropertyName = HtmlHelper.ViewContext.ViewData.TemplateInfo
            .GetFullHtmlFieldName(ExpressionHelper.GetExpressionText(property));

        var selectBuilder = new TagBuilder("select");
        selectBuilder.MergeAttribute("name", fullPropertyName);
        selectBuilder.MergeAttribute("id", fullPropertyName);
        selectBuilder.MergeAttribute("class", "selector");

        foreach (var item in items)
        {
            var optionBuilder = new TagBuilder("option");
            optionBuilder.MergeAttribute("value", item);
            optionBuilder.SetInnerText(item);
            selectBuilder.InnerHtml += optionBuilder.ToString();
        }
        return new MvcHtmlString(selectBuilder.ToString());
    }
}
```

```
/// <summary>
/// Non-Generic
/// </summary>
public class HelperExtensionInputFactory
{
    private HtmlHelper HtmlHelper { get; set; }

    public HelperExtensionInputFactory(HtmlHelper htmlHelper)
    {
        this.HtmlHelper = htmlHelper;
    }

    public MvcHtmlString SelectorFor(string fullPropertyName
                                            , IEnumerable<string> items)
    {

        var selectBuilder = new TagBuilder("select");
        selectBuilder.MergeAttribute("name", fullPropertyName);
        selectBuilder.MergeAttribute("id", fullPropertyName);
        selectBuilder.MergeAttribute("class", "selector");

        foreach (var item in items)
        {
            var optionBuilder = new TagBuilder("option");
            optionBuilder.MergeAttribute("value", item);
            optionBuilder.SetInnerText(item);
            selectBuilder.InnerHtml += optionBuilder.ToString();
        }
        return new MvcHtmlString(selectBuilder.ToString());
    }
}
```

The generic version inherits fromthe non-generic. Both take the **HtmlHelper** in parameters. This allows us to use anything from the Html helper. The Html helper gives information about the ViewContext and it gives you the possibility of using another Html Helper within your Html Helper.

The code in this blog post creates an Html Select input for a property passed in parameters and fills everything from a list of strings. It could be better to have a distinction between caption and value but that is not the goal of this blog post. We could also reuse a lot of codes between both…nevertheless, the interesting part is how everything is bound together. As you can see, only the HtmlHelperNameSpaces is static. Everything underneath is concrete. It also provides the possibility of having generic and non-generic helpers. Finally, we can have several namespaces by adding two methods every time to the HtmlHelperNameSpaces class.

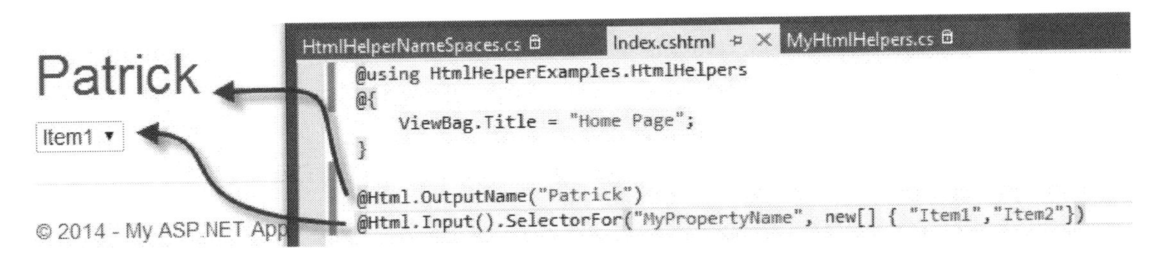


Here is a screen shot of the code explained above. It is clear that the second one uses our "namespace" which groups all our custom Html helpers. You can find the source code of namespace HtmlHelper at GitHub (https://github.com/MrDesjardins/HtmlHelperExamples).

## Asp.Net MVC Custom Data Annotation

Release Date: 25-Feb-14
Url: http://patrickdesjardins.com/blog/?post_type=post&p=2660

Asp.Net MVC Data Annotation is a powerful way to have business logic reusable over all your projects. Some exist by default in the **System.ComponentModel.DataAnnotations** namespace. Among the most-used Data Annotations is the Required and StringLength attribute.

Data Annotation is used by Asp.Net MVC **Data Binder** that converts Html input values back into your model. During this process, it calls every validation from Data Annotation. In fact, it uses the **IValidatableObject** interface so that you can even have your model inherit to have validation inside a method if you want.

At some point, you may have some validations that are repeated across multiple classes. This is the case for required fields. Instead of validating with an IF statement in the Validate method provided by IValidatableObject or having your setter check the value of the property, an alternative is the Data Annotation. It has the advantage of being productive for you because you just need to add the attribute over the property and the validation is done. It can also be unit tested once and you can be sure that, for every property that uses it, it is executed. Another point for Data Annotation is the possibility to easily have JavaScript doing the same thing for you. This means that with a single Data Annotation you can have client side and server side validation.

Before going any further in the theory, let's create a small project with a simple model class in which the custom Data Annotation is used.

```
public class MyClass
{
    [PrimeNumberOnly]
    [Display(Name = "Prime Number")]
    public int PrimeNumber { get; set; }
    public DateTime StartDate { get; set; }
    public DateTime EndDate { get; set; }
}
```

This is the model class. I have created the *PrimeNumberOnly* attribute which is a custom Data Annotation. I used the Display attribute because I will use this instead of the property name in the custom Data Annotation for error. But this is not required. If it is not declared, the property name is used.

The controller is very simple. It checks for the **ModelState** to see if it has an error; if yes, it displays back the form, otherwise it redirects to the list of my class.

```
[HttpPost]
public ActionResult Create(MyClass myClass)
{
    if (ModelState.IsValid)
    {
        return RedirectToAction("Index");
    }
    else
    {
        return View();
    }
}
```

Here comes what is interesting — the custom Data Annotation.

```
public class PrimeNumberOnly : ValidationAttribute
{
    protected override ValidationResult IsValid(object value
                                               , ValidationContext validationContext)
    {
        if (value != null)
        {
            int valueInteger;
            if (int.TryParse(value.ToString(), out valueInteger))
            {
                if (IsPrime(valueInteger))
                {
                    return ValidationResult.Success;
                }
                else
                {
```

```
                return new ValidationResult(string.Concat(
                 validationContext.DisplayName, " is not a prime number"));
            }
        }
        else
        {
            return new ValidationResult(string.Concat(
                    validationContext.DisplayName, " must be an integer"));
        }
    }
    return ValidationResult.Success;
}

private bool IsPrime(int number)
{
    //...
}
}
```

The custom validation class must inherit from a specific class to be handled by Asp.Net MVC. It must inherit from **ValidationAttribute**. This is the base class for a Data Annotation attribute. It is totally all right to inherit from an existing Data Annotation, too, like the Required attribute. This can be interesting if you are going to enhance an existing Data Annotation. But this is not our case since we want to block non-prime numbers.

This interface lets you override a method named **IsValid** that takes two parameters. The first one is the value non-typed. The second is information about the context. The property name, the instance of the the class being validated, is also available and the pretty name, too (the one that uses the display attribute). The IsValid must return Validation.Success if everything is fine. However, if something is wrong, it must return a **ValidationResult** object. The ValidationResult accepts a message that will be used by Asp.Net MVC to acknowledge. It is also possible to mark not only the property that is being tested but to mark other properties of the class with ValidationResult with the same error.

Create

MyClass

Prime Number 10 Prime Number is not a prime number

If you want to pass the *ErrorMessage* to the attribute, you can. By default, it uses the

*FormatErrorMessage* method that takes the property name. So, if you pass a custom error with a {0} the parameter is a substitute. In the code above, the property display name is used and replaced in the error message.

```
return new ValidationResult(base.FormatErrorMessage
                                        (validationContext.DisplayName));
```

If you want to add the member name you have to supply a second parameter.

```
return new ValidationResultbase.FormatErrorMessage
        (validationContext.DisplayName,new []{ validationContext.MemberName}));
```

If you want to have multiple parameters like having numbers or property names to show, it is possible to combine resource files and formatting. To do so, do not use *FormatErrorMessage* but use the *ErrorMessageString* and do the formatting yourself.

```
return new ValidationResult(string.Format(this.ErrorMessageString
        ,"One", "Two", DateToBeAfter), new[] { validationContext.MemberName);
```

So far, half of the job is done because if we erase the number and type a valid entry, the error will not go away before the form is submitted again. This is normal; we have coded only the server-side aspect of the Data Annotation. A second interface is required to be inherited to have client-side validation. This time, it is named **IClientValidatable**. This interface comes from the System.Web.Mvc interface. This means that if you are using View Model, do not inherit the model from this attribute but from the view model. Otherwise, you are mixing back-end classes and front-end classes. For the purpose of this exercise, I am mapping directly the model class to the view, which means that it is acceptable to have my model class inherit from *System.Web.Mvc.IClientValidatable*. Please, do not copy and paste that if you are developing a serious application.

The **IClientValidatable** interface comes with the **GetClientValidationRules** method. This gives us the possibility to extend the HTML generated for a property. When Asp.Net MVC generates the input, it can add an additional data- tag. These tags are required for the client side. They are called unobtrusive since it adds information to the Html input without attaching the Javascript. This means that we have a third step to do which will be to tell JavaScript to use those added attributes. But first, why add **data-** to our Html input that has the custom Data Annotation? It is required for several reasons. First, if the logic is in error, we need an error message. It cannot be hard coded into the JavaScript because this message can be localized. Adding a data- tag with the error message gives you the possibility to get the message and to expose it to your user if the error occurs. Second, you can add additional information to the Html input by an attribute like value to be used in the JavaScript validation. Here is an example.

```
public class PrimeNumberOnly : ValidationAttribute, IClientValidatable
{
    protected override ValidationResult IsValid(object value, ValidationContext validationContext)
    {
        //...
    }

    private bool IsPrime(int number)
    {
        //...
    }

    public IEnumerable<ModelClientValidationRule>
       GetClientValidationRules(ModelMetadata metadata, ControllerContext context)
    {
        var rule = new ModelClientValidationRule
        {
            ValidationType = "primenumber",
            ErrorMessage = FormatErrorMessage(metadata.GetDisplayName()),

        };

        //This is not required. For the purpose of showing how to pass information to the JavaScript I will set two values.
        rule.ValidationParameters.Add("primenumberparam1", "Value1");
        rule.ValidationParameters.Add("primenumberparam2", "Value2");

        yield return rule;
    }
}
```

In the example above, we are setting a single rule with a validation message (the ErrorMessage) that is set to the *data-val-primenumber*. I also added two lines that add validation parameters. In a real situation, this can be a dynamic value to be checked during the JavaScript method that will validate the input. For checking if a number is a prime number, no parameter is required.

Keep in mind that you cannot use a capital letter in the ValidationType or you will have a yellow screen of death with this message:

*Validation type names in unobtrusive client validation rules must consist of only lowercase letters. Invalid name: "primeNumber", client rule type: System.Web.Mvc.ModelClientValidationRule.*

The result of the Html is:

```
<div class="col-md-10">
    <input class="text-box single-line"
           data-val="true"
           data-val-number="The field Prime Number must be a number."
           data-val-primenumber="The field Prime Number is invalid."
           data-val-primenumber-primenumberparam1="Value1"
           data-val-primenumber-primenumberparam2="Value2"
           data-val-required="The Prime Number field is required."
           id="PrimeNumber"
           name="PrimeNumber"
           type="number" value="">
    <span class="field-validation-valid"
          data-valmsg-for="PrimeNumber"
          data-valmsg-replace="true">
    </span>
</div>
```

This also needs to have some libraries installed and referenced in your Html page.

```
<script src="~/Scripts/jquery.validate.js"></script>
<script src="~/Scripts/jquery.validate.unobtrusive.js"></script>
<script src="~/Scripts/PrimeNumberOnlyValidation.js"></script>
```

You may need to add with NuGet the **unobstructive.js**.

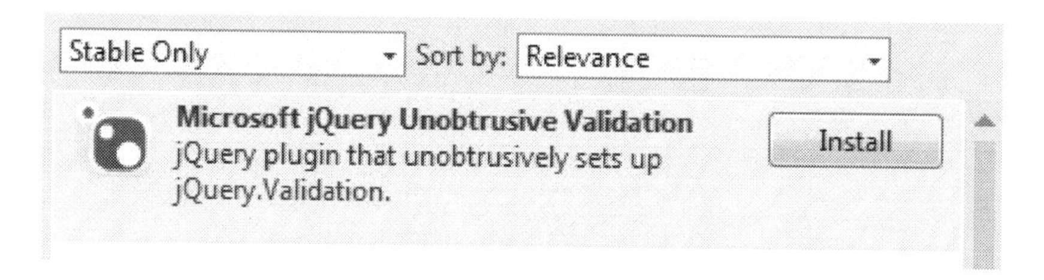


The **validate.js** must be before the **unobstructive.js** file. The PrimeNumberOnlyValidation.js file contains the validation in Javascript. It is required to be configured once; then you just need to have the script added to your file. Here is the complete file:

```
$.validator.addMethod("primenumber", function (value, element, params) {
    if (value) {
        if (value == 1)
            return false;
        if (value == 2)
            return false;

        for (var i = 3; i < value; i = i + 2) {
            if (value % i == 0) return false;
```

```
        }
    }
    return true;
});

$.validator.unobtrusive.adapters.add('primenumber'
    , ['primenumberparam1', 'primenumberparam2']
    , function (options) {
        options.rules["primenumber"] = {
            primenumberparam1: options.params.primenumberparam1,
            primenumberparam2: options.params.primenumberparam2
        };
        options.messages["primenumber"] = options.message;
    }
    );
```

The first statement registers the method to be called when the validation is triggered. It is the same algorithm to check a prime number in JavaScript as in C#. If it returns false, then the error message specified in the C# code is shown. This is possible because the error message is inside the data tag of the input. The tag is "data-val-primenumber.".b The second adds an adapter to JQuery validator. The first parameter is the name of the validator. It is the same name as the method. Then, you specify the parameter set in C#. Finally, an anonymous function transfers the value of each parameter from C# to the JQuery validation plugin. It does the hook between the HTML attribute data- generated from C# to Javascript.

If you are getting a problem with the plugin, verify that you have all JavaScript loaded in the good sequence. To test the plugin, you have to hit the button save. By default, JQuery Validator does not validate *onblur* but when the form is submitted. Finally, you can get the whole project code in GitHub (https://github.com/MrDesjardins/TestingDataAnnotationProject ).

# Enterprise Asp.Net MVC Part 8: Asp.Net cache before repository

Release Date: 27-Feb-14
Url: http://patrickdesjardins.com/blog/?post_type=post&p=2680

At some point in the life of your software, its performance can become an issue. If you have optimized your queries or your Entity Framework configurations, then the next step is to think about keeping some data in memory or in an external cache. This has the advantage of having the data already available for you in a fast access.

Changing your code for caching requires changes on your infrastructure classes and interface because we want to have something flexible and not tightly bound to Asp.Net since this will be used in the **Data Access Layer**. Having your caching in the data access allows this change to not have any repercussions into the rest of the layers like the front-end layers and the business logic layer.

```
public interface ICacheConfiguration
{
    bool IsActivate();
}
```

The first code creation concerns the interface to configure the cache. So far, to keep it simple, only one property is set, named "IsActivate." It is about whether the cache is activated or not. A caching system must always have the possibility to be deactivated. The reason is so that if your data becomes not what you expect you can turn off the cache and use the main persistence. If the problem is solved, then it means that the problem is the cache. Otherwise, the problem is with the persistence or the logic that used the data.

```
public interface ICacheProvider
{
    void Set<T>(T objectToCache) where T : ICachableModel;
    void Set(string key, Object objectToCache);
    T Get<T>(T key) where T : ICachableModel;
    object Get(string key);
    object Delete(string key);
    T Delete<T>(T objectTodelete) where T : ICachableModel;
    bool IsInCache(string key);
    bool IsInCache<T>(T objectToVerify) where T : ICachableModel;
}
```

This second new interface allows you to have something in front of the technology used. You can have a memory cache, an external caching system, or an Azure cache behind this interface.

```
public interface ICachableModel
{
    string GetCacheKey();
}
```

Most of the methods are defined twice. One uses a string key, and the other uses an **ICachableModel**. This interface allows the model class to have its logic to build its unique key.

```
public class MemoryCache : ICacheProvider
{
    private readonly ObjectCache cache;
```

```
private readonly CacheItemPolicy defaultPolicy;
private readonly ICacheConfiguration configuration;

public MemoryCache(ICacheConfiguration configuration)
{
    this.configuration = configuration;
    this.cache = new System.Runtime.Caching.MemoryCache(
        Constants.Configurations.CacheNameConfiguration);
    this.defaultPolicy = new CacheItemPolicy();
}

public void Set<T>(T objectToCache) where T : ICachableModel
{
    if (configuration.IsActivate())
    {
        cache.Set(objectToCache.GetCacheKey(), objectToCache, defaultPolicy);
    }
}

public void Set(string key, object objectToCache)
{
    if (configuration.IsActivate())
    {
        cache.Set(key, objectToCache, defaultPolicy);
    }
}

public T Get<T>(T objectToCache) where T : ICachableModel
{
    if (configuration.IsActivate())
    {
        return (T)cache.Get(objectToCache.GetCacheKey());
    }
    else
    {
        return default(T);
    }
}

public object Get(string key)
{
    if (configuration.IsActivate())
    {
        return cache.Get(key);
    }
    else
    {
        return null;
    }
}
```

```
    public object Delete(string key)
    {
        if (configuration.IsActivate())
        {
            return cache.Remove(key);
        }
        else
        {
            return null;
        }
    }

    public T Delete<T>(T objectTodelete) where T : ICachableModel
    {
        if (configuration.IsActivate())
        {
            return (T)cache.Remove(objectTodelete.GetCacheKey());
        }
        else
        {
            return default(T);
        }
    }

    public bool IsInCache(string key)
    {
        if (configuration.IsActivate())
        {
            return cache.Contains(key);
        }
        else
        {
            return false;
        }
    }

    public bool IsInCache<T>(T objectToVerify) where T : ICachableModel
    {
        if (configuration.IsActivate())
        {
            return cache.Contains(objectToVerify.GetCacheKey());
        }
        else
        {
            return false;
        }
    }
}
```

This implementation uses the **System.Runtime.Caching.** as you can see, it also uses the configuration to disable the cache. This way to proceed does not affect any of the caller code. In fact, all methods return the default value when the cache does not find the value. This should tell the caller to continue with the default persistence strategy.

The caller should be in the Services classes if you have followed the previous post about Enterprise Asp.Net MVC application.

```
var cacheResult = (YouEntity)this.cache.Get("YouUniqueKey123");
if (cacheResult == null)
{
  var repositoryResult = yourRepository.GetYourEntity();
  this.cache.Set("YouUniqueKey123", repositoryResult);
  return repositoryResult;
}
else
{
  return cacheResult;
}
```

This creates a simple architecture for caching. It has the flexibility to use the concrete cache you want and to have high cohesive classes. Configurations could have additional information about how many times the entity must stay in cache, or the information about external caches like which IP or PORT to use for MemCached, for example.

# Asp.Net MVC Login with email instead of UserName with Identity

Release Date: 04-Mar-14
Url: http://patrickdesjardins.com/blog/?post_type=post&p=2686

I found it very strange that it is not a simple task to log in with an email in Asp.Net MVC. You cannot simply decide what property is the identifier. Asp.Net MVC decides for you that it is the UserName property. Here is the IdentityUser class from Microsoft.AspNet.Identity.EntityFramework.

```
namespace Microsoft.AspNet.Identity.EntityFramework
{
    public class IdentityUser : IUser
    {
        public virtual string Id { get; set; }
        public virtual string UserName { get; set; }
        public virtual string PasswordHash { get; set; }
```

```
        public virtual string SecurityStamp { get; set; }
        public virtual ICollection<IdentityUserRole> Roles { get; private set; }
        public virtual ICollection<IdentityUserClaim> Claims { get; private set; }
        public virtual ICollection<IdentityUserLogin> Logins { get; private set; }
        public IdentityUser()
        {
            this.Id = Guid.NewGuid().ToString();
            this.Claims = (ICollection<IdentityUserClaim>)
                                            new List<IdentityUserClaim>();
            this.Roles = (ICollection<IdentityUserRole>)
                                            new List<IdentityUserRole>();
            this.Logins = (ICollection<IdentityUserLogin>)
                                            new List<IdentityUserLogin>();
        }
        public IdentityUser(string userName) : this()
        {
            this.UserName = userName;
        }
    }
}
```

The first step to use email is to add an email property to this class. Microsoft Identity team has not sealed the class, so it is possible to inherit from it and add your own property. This will extend what we can do with Identity.

```
public class ApplicationUser : IdentityUser
{
    public string Email { get; set; }
}
```

That is it for the model. Entity Framework uses this class instead of the default one if you define your DbContext with a special class.

```
public class MainDbContext : IdentityDbContext<ApplicationUser>{//...}
```

That is what is required. This creates in the background a DbSet of your class that inherits from IdentityUser. I have called mine ApplicationUser, but you can use whatever you prefer. **IdentityDbContext** overrides OnModelCreating. This is important so that if you inherit from it you call the base class to still have all the configuration provided by the **IdentityDbContext**. To be more detailed, the OnModelCreating associates the custom class to the AspNetUsers table. It does plenty of other things, but what concerns us right now is this. From here, if you instruct Entity Framework to build your database, you should see in the database your field in Identity table.

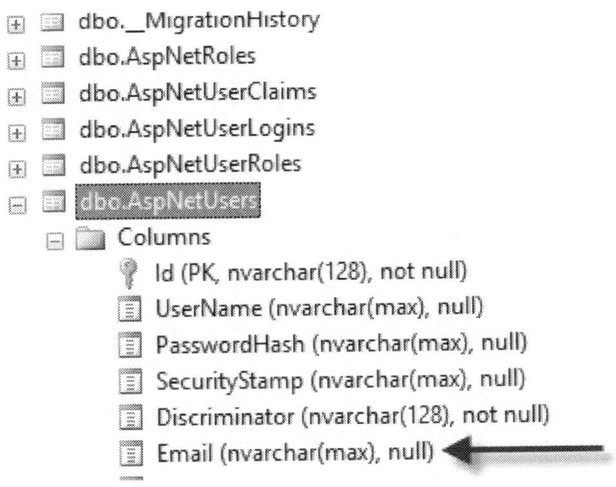

dbo._MigrationHistory
dbo.AspNetRoles
dbo.AspNetUserClaims
dbo.AspNetUserLogins
dbo.AspNetUserRoles
dbo.AspNetUsers
Columns
Id (PK, nvarchar(128), not null)
UserName (nvarchar(max), null)
PasswordHash (nvarchar(max), null)
SecurityStamp (nvarchar(max), null)
Discriminator (nvarchar(128), not null)
Email (nvarchar(max), null)

The next step is to change the View Model and the View. The View Model for the registration uses a UserName property. We can remove this and add one for Email.

```
public class RegisterViewModel
{
    [Required]
    [StringLength(100
                , ErrorMessage = "The {0} must be at least {2} characters long."
                , MinimumLength = 6)]
    [DataType(DataType.Password)]
    [Display(Name = "Password")]
    public string Password { get; set; }

    [DataType(DataType.Password)]
    [Display(Name = "Confirm password")]
    [Compare("Password"
        , ErrorMessage = "The password and confirmation password do not match.")]
    public string ConfirmPassword { get; set; }

    [Required]
    [Display(Name = "Email")]
    [DataType(DataType.EmailAddress)]
    public string Email { get; set; }
  }
```

This is the place where you can add additional data annotation to have more validation. Then, we need to change the view that uses the Register View Model. We need to remove the username form group to add a new one for email.

```
<div class="form-group">
    @Html.LabelFor(m => m.Email, new { @class = "col-md-2 control-label" })
```

```
    <div class="col-md-10">
        @Html.TextBoxFor(m => m.Email, new { @class = "form-control" })
    </div>
</div>
```

The last step is to change the controller to do something with the email and username. Since **Identity** still uses the username and password combination,we have to trick the system.

First of all, we need to generate a username from the email. It is not possible to use the email directly because it has some invalid characters like @. You can have a small method that transforms the user name.

```
public string GenerateUserName(string email)
{
    return email.Replace("@", "").Replace(".", "").Replace("-", "");
}
```

From here, you can create a new ApplicationUser and assign your generated user name into the property. The next code remains the same by calling the UserManager.

Second, we need to modify the login because the user will enter an email and you need to transform it to a username. The login ViewModel needs to be changed.

```
public class LoginViewModel
{

    [Required]
    [DataType(DataType.EmailAddress)]
    [Display(Name = "Email")]
    public string Email { get; set; }

    [Required]
    [DataType(DataType.Password)]
    [Display(Name = "Password")]
    public string Password { get; set; }

    [Display(Name = "Remember me?")]
    public bool RememberMe { get; set; }
}
```

The view also changes by not having input for a username but for an email. This is the same way we have done it for the registration page. I will not put the code here, to keep it simple.

Finally, the controller must be changed too. Not a lot of things need to be changed but since we ask for an email and the system uses a username we must convert it.

```
var user = await userService.FindAsync(GenerateUserName(model.Email)
                                        , model.Password);
```

In conclusion, it requires some manipulation but it is not difficult. It would be cleaner not to manipulate the UserName property but it is still not a nightmare to proceed.

## Concerning the username

The algorithm that generates the username is not strong. Collision can occur if you have the concatenation this way. This is not a huge deal since it will fail to save in the database but still a better way is to have something unique. To save a character like @ as part of a username, the framework allows you to configure the UserManager to have not just alphanumeric characters.

```
public UserManager(IMainDbContext dbContext)
{
  var dbMainContext = dbContext.GetDbContext();
  this.userManager = new UserManager<ApplicationUser>
                   (new UserStore<ApplicationUser>(dbMainContext));

  //Allow to have email in the username
  this.userManager.UserValidator = new UserValidator<ApplicationUser>
                                   (this.userManager)
  {
    AllowOnlyAlphanumericUserNames = false
  };
}
```

As you can see, you can set a new **UserValidator** and set the **AllowOnlyAlphanumericUserNames** to false. This is way better because you can use the full email for the username. Manipulating the string is not an excellent solution because you can fall way more easily into a scenario of duplicates which would raise exceptions.

# Asp.Net MVC Model Validation

Release Date: 06-Mar-14
Url: http://patrickdesjardins.com/blog/?post_type=post&p=2709

I have played around with **Data Annotation** and **IValidatableObject** interface. They are the two officials ways to validate your model with Asp.Net MVC framework. The Data

Annotation and the **Validate** method of the interface **IValidatableObject** are used when the model binding is executing during the post from the web page to the controller and also when saving with Entity Framework. It is also possible to manually execute the validation.

The problem I have encountered was during the unit test. If you do unit tests you will see that if something is wrong with Data Annotation the Validate method is not even called. The reason behind this behavior is that Data Annotation is for light validation like if a field is required. If this is not required, then it does not make sense to go to the Validate method because it will fail further validations. This is quite true but not interesting if you want to have all possibles errors of the object.

Another issue that I had with Data Annotation is that if you do have annotation in a property of your first model class, then they are not validated. A small test can show this behavior. See the following code.

```
[TestClass]
public class UnitTest1
{
    [TestMethod]
    public void TestMethod2()
    {
        var s = new Annot1();
        var results = s.Validate();
        Assert.AreEqual(2, results.Count());
    }
}

public class Annot1 : BaseClass2
{
    public Annot1()
    {
        Annot1Property3 = new Annot2();
    }

    public string Annot1Property1 { get; set; }
    public string Annot1Property2 { get; set; }
    public Annot2 Annot1Property3 { get; set; }

}

public class Annot2 : BaseClass2
{
    [Required]
    public string Annot2Property1 { get; set; }
    [Required]
    public string Annot2Property2 { get; set; }
```

```
}

public abstract class BaseClass2
{
    public IEnumerable<ValidationResult> Validate()
    {
        var results = new List<ValidationResult>();
        var validationContext = new ValidationContext(this, null, null);
        Validator.TryValidateObject(this, validationContext, results, true);
        return results;
    }
}
```

This test fails because we expect to have two validation errors from the class Annot2. However, the two required fields are not calculated into the validation.

How can you have validation from Data Annotation from every inheritance level and have at the same time every validate method executed, even if the field is not there? You need to create your own **Validate** method that will call the **TryValidateObject** on every inheritance level. Here is an example that shows how to use the base model class that has a validate method. It has the advantage that we can call the validate at each level of inheritance but also just call the base class which will go deeper to validate everything.

```
public abstract class BaseClass
{
    public IEnumerable<ValidationResult> Validate()
    {
        var results = new List<ValidationResult>();
        var validationContext = new ValidationContext(this, null, null);
        Validator.TryValidateObject(this, validationContext, results, true);
        var r = new List<ValidationResult>(results);

        if (this is IValidatableObject)
        {
            IEnumerable<ValidationResult> errors =
             (this as IValidatableObject).Validate(new ValidationContext(this));
            r.AddRange(errors);
        }
        var childrenResults = ValidateChildren();
        r.AddRange(childrenResults);
        return r;
    }

    public abstract IEnumerable<ValidationResult> ValidateChildren();

}
```

```
public class Class1 : BaseClass, IValidatableObject
{
    public Class1()
    {
        Property1 = new Class2();
    }
    public Class2 Property1 { get; set; }
    [Required]
    public string AString1 { get; set; }
    public IEnumerable<ValidationResult> Validate
                            (ValidationContext validationContext)
    {
        return new[] { new ValidationResult("Error from class1") };
    }

    public override IEnumerable<ValidationResult> ValidateChildren()
    {
        var r = new List<ValidationResult>();
        var childrenResult = Property1.Validate();
        r.AddRange(childrenResult);
        return r;
    }
}

public class Class2 : BaseClass, IValidatableObject
{
    public Class2()
    {
        Property2 = new Class3();
    }
    public Class3 Property2 { get; set; }
    [Required]
    public string AString2 { get; set; }
    public IEnumerable<ValidationResult> Validate
                            (ValidationContext validationContext)
    {
        yield return new ValidationResult("Error from class2");
    }

    public override IEnumerable<ValidationResult> ValidateChildren()
    {
        var r = new List<ValidationResult>();
        var childrenResult = Property2.Validate();
        r.AddRange(childrenResult);
        return r;
    }
}

public class Class3 : BaseClass
```

```
{
    [Required]
    public string AString3 { get; set; }

    public override IEnumerable<ValidationResult> ValidateChildren()
    {
        return new List<ValidationResult>();
    }
}

[TestClass]
public class UnitTest1
{
    [TestMethod]
    public void TestMethod1()
    {
        var s = new Class1();
        var results = s.Validate();
        Assert.AreEqual(5, results.Count());
    }
}
```

This works. You can call the validate directly to Class3 and have one validation result. But the main objective is to call the validation on Class1. Class1 has a property that uses Class2 and this one has Class3. Three levels deep! The code is not clean because it has some repetition but the problem is solved. Every ValidateChildren calls all properties that have a class that must be validated. It accumulates all validation results and returns them. The validate method explicitly calls the Validate method so even if the Data Annotation has an error, it is executed. You can find all unit test code in this GitHub Repository (https://github.com/MrDesjardins/ValidationProject).

## Asp.Net Bind Attribute for your Controller

Release Date: 11-Mar-14
Url: http://patrickdesjardins.com/blog/?post_type=post&p=2641

Asp.Net MVC gives you the possibility of controlling the flow of information between Html Form and .Net Controller. It is possible to have model classes that are bound to Html Forms but without desiring them to be sent back from forms.

A simple case can be that we have a user model class that has an *IsAdmin* property. The user class can be bound to an Html form, and instead of having an *EditorFor* for this property, a simple *DisplayFor* is set. A hacker could create a hidden field inside the form with the name *IsAdmin* and send "True." Once the form is submitted, the *IsAdmin* will be bound because the Model Binding maps every form name field to properties of the class. Asp.Net

MVC lets you specify which properties are allowed to be bound from a form or which properties should never be read from the Html form. This is also called whitelisting properties or blacklisting properties.

To demonstrate this feature, I created a simple model class that has five properties which can be nullable. These properties are all bound to an Html Form. For the purpose of this exercise, they are all bound to text boxes. In fact, as mentioned, some could not have been bound to an editable control or someone could forge the post later on. The first example sends all properties back to the controller, and the controller sets all information into a view bag and shows again the view. The view should be filled up with the view bag information.

Here are all the steps:

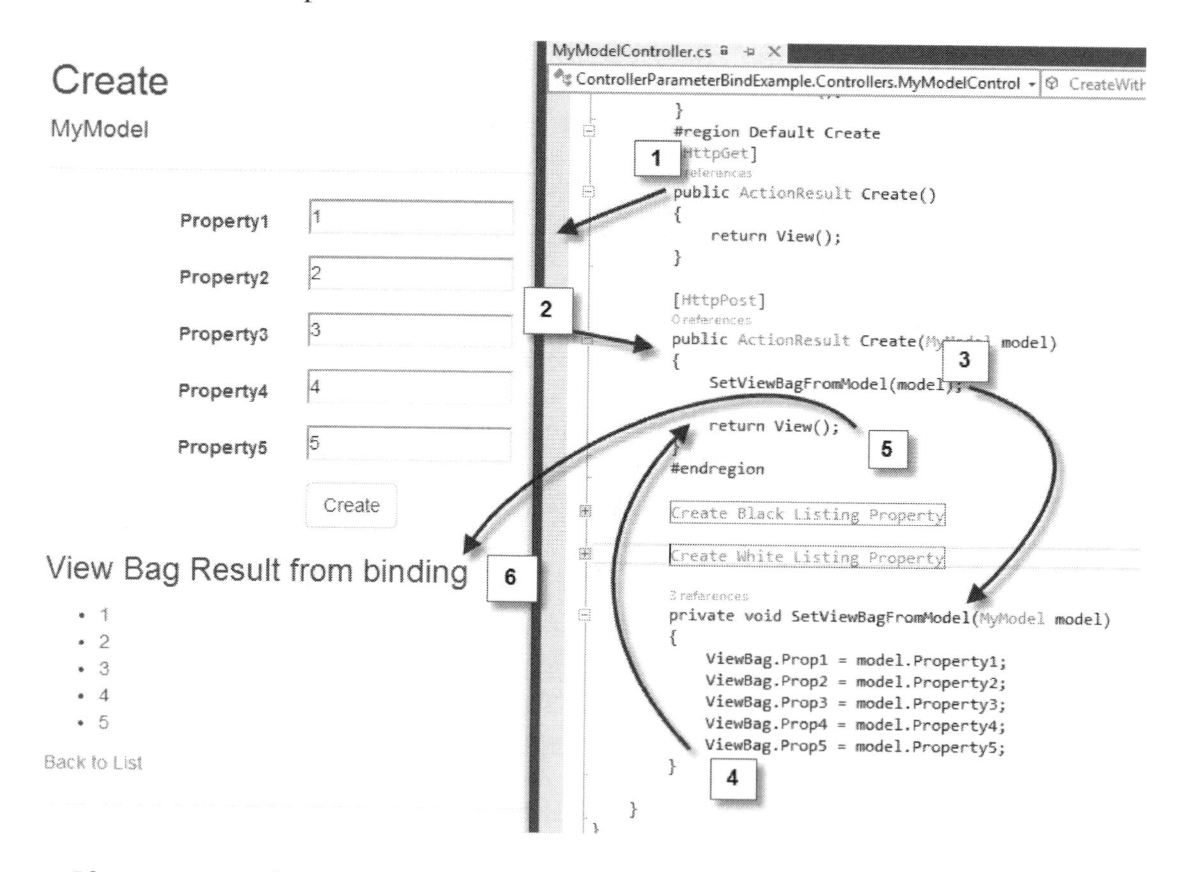


If property1 and property2 should not be bound from the form, we need to blacklist them. To tell the Asp.Net MVC Model Binding to not use properties, the attribute **Bind** must be used with the property **Exclude**. This phenomenon is shown in the following screenshot. You can see that the property 1 and property 2 are not inside the view bag. The reason is that the model binder does not set the value to the model which kept the value to the default one. Since the model is nullable int for all properties, the default value remain NULL.

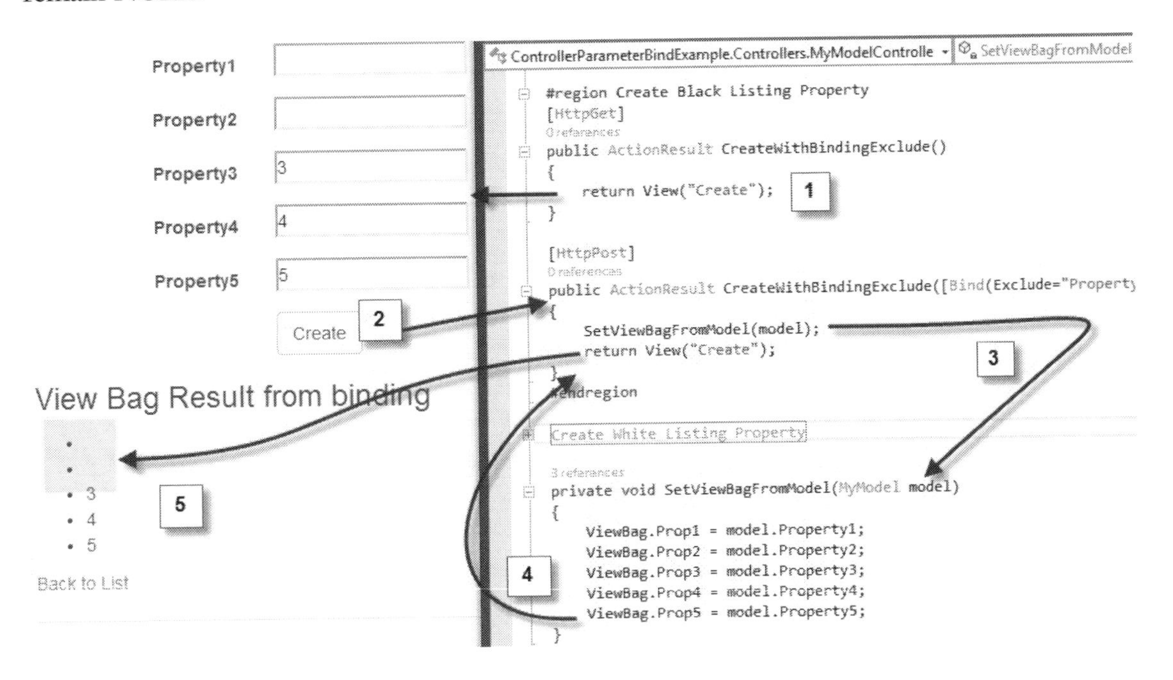


Finally, another scenario is available to whitelist properties. This option is interesting if you do have a lot of properties to exclude. Instead of having to specify a lot of properties in the exclude field, you just need to specify a few in the **Include** field.

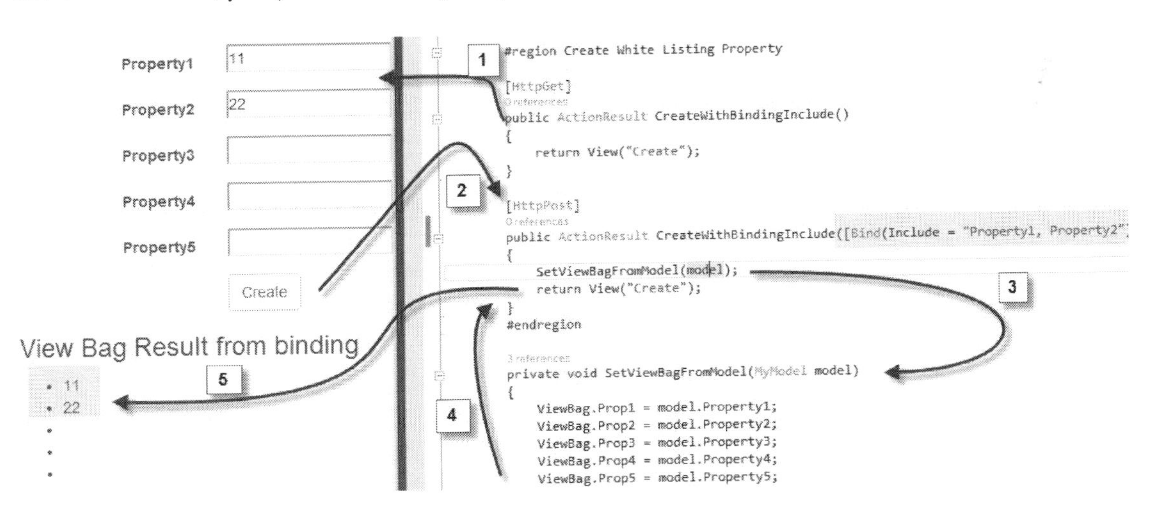


You can see everything discussed in this blog post by downloading my Asp.Net MVC Bind project (https://github.com/MrDesjardins/ControllerParameterBindExample).

# Asp.Net MVC, how to simplify your testing with contextual class

Release Date: 29-Mar-14
Url: http://patrickdesjardins.com/blog/?post_type=post&p=2692

A good practice is to inject a **running context** class and a class that has information about the current user. This can be injected by your favorite injector of control container. I like dividing one for the running context and one for the current user. The first one gets information about the running context and uses the second one. In fact, the running context has many advantages. It allows you to easily separate from any of your code all information about how to get the user and also about the time. The time issue can become a nightmare if you are using directly DateTime.Now all over the place in your code. The problem is that you may have different time zones and you may want to hide the logic that handles it. This is often the case if you have severs around the world. It is also the simplest way to unit test. If you want to test something about the current date, using the running context to set the "current time" is easier. It allows you to test all different paths. Here is an example in code of both interfaces.

```
public interface IRunningContext
{
    ClaimsPrincipal GetUser();
    string GetUserId();
    string GetUserDisplayName();
    DateTime GetCurrentTime();
    string GetDomainNameWithPort();
}

public interface ICurrentUserInformation
{
    string GetCurrentUserName();
    string GetCurrentUserId();
    string GetCurrentEmail();
    ClaimsPrincipal GetUser();
}
```

The concrete representation of these interfaces could be one for Http that uses the HttpContext for the user and the current DateTime for the time.

```
public class HttpContextCurrentUserInformation : ICurrentUserInformation
{
    public string GetCurrentUserName()
    {
        return HttpContext.Current.User.Identity.Name;
    }
```

```
    public string GetCurrentUserId()
    {
        return HttpContext.Current.User.Identity.GetUserId();
    }

    public string GetCurrentEmail()
    {
        return "";
    }

    public ClaimsPrincipal GetUser()
    {
        IAuthenticationManager auth =
                    HttpContext.Current.GetOwinContext().Authentication;
        ClaimsPrincipal u = auth.User;
        return u;
    }
}

public class HttpRunningContext : IRunningContext
{
    private readonly ICurrentUserInformation currentUserInformation;

    public HttpRunningContext(ICurrentUserInformation principal)
    {
        currentUserInformation = principal;
    }

    public ClaimsPrincipal GetUser()
    {
        return currentUserInformation.GetUser();
    }

    public string GetUserId()
    {
        return currentUserInformation.GetCurrentUserId();
    }

    public string GetUserDisplayName()
    {
        return currentUserInformation.GetCurrentUserName();
    }

    public DateTime GetCurrentTime()
    {
        return DateTime.Now;
    }

    public string GetDomainNameWithPort()
```

```
    {
        var stringDomain = HttpContext.Current.Request.Url.Authority;
        return stringDomain;
    }
}
```

Having these interfaces allows you to easily mock them when unit tests require. You can have in your code initialization something that sets up your running context. Here is a code with **Moq** Mocking Framework.

```
protected Mock<IRunningContext> runningContext; //...

[TestInitialize]
public void InitializeBetweenTest()
{
    runningContext = new Mock<IRunningContext>();
    runningContext.Setup(d => d.GetCurrentTime())
                         .Returns(new DateTime(2014, 03, 02));
    runningContext.Setup(d => d.GetUserId())
                         .Returns(ApplicationUser.SYSTEM_TEST_USER_ID);
}
```

With few lines of code, you can mock. It also gives a great advantage in organizing information about the context of the situation like the time, current user, etc.

# Inline Razor Helper instead of Html Helper for your Asp.Net MVC WebSite

Release Date: 08-Apr-14
Url: http://patrickdesjardins.com/blog/?post_type=post&p=3409

In Asp.Net MVC you have two ways to create code that can be reusable within your page, or editor template, or display template. Asp.Net MVC calls these reusable mechanisms Helpers. You can create **Html Helper** or **Razor Helper**. They are both generating Html but in a different way. The first one is independent of any rendering engine, while the second one uses only Razor. One comes with several helpers already created for you, like Html.ActionLink, Html.LabelFor, Html.EditorFor while the second one does not have any developed for you. However, the second one can use the first one. This is not true the other way around.

Let's see the first one, Html Helper. It is more popular than the other one. It is coded in C# (of VB.Net) and is in fact an extension to HtmlHelper. You just have to create a static class with a static method that extends System.Web.Mvc.HtmlHelper. Here is a small example.

```
namespace TestHtmlHelper.HtmlHelper
{
    public static class MyCustomHtmlHelper
    {
        public static MvcHtmlString MyFirstHelper(
                                        this System.Web.Mvc.HtmlHelper htmlHelper)
        {
            return new MvcHtmlString("Test");
        }
    }
}
```

If you want to use this extension, you just have to use the @Html keyword in any of your views or templates.

```
@using TestHtmlHelper.HtmlHelper<div>@Html.MyFirstHelper()</div>
```

This will render:

```
<div>Test</div>
```

This is not impressive, but in fact these helpers can be very useful when you specify a property, like for @Html.TextBoxFor(model=>model.MyDate). This can use reflection to get the display name which can be added in the helper to create a label to add or to check the type to render something depending on the property type. It goes beyond just outputting static Html.

Let's create a simple Html Helper that takes a object in parameter where we can specify which property to display. We will do something simple that sets the name of the property into a header tag and its value inside a paragraph.

```
public static class MyCustomHtmlHelper
{
    public static MvcHtmlString MyFirstHelper
                    (this System.Web.Mvc.HtmlHelper htmlHelper)
    {
        return new MvcHtmlString("Test");
    }

    public static MvcHtmlString YourGenericHelperFor<TModel, TProperty>
    (this HtmlHelper htmlHelper, Expression<Func<TModel, TProperty>> expression)
    {
        ModelMetadata metadata =
            ModelMetadata.FromLambdaExpression(expression, htmlHelper.ViewData);
        var propertyName = metadata.PropertyName;
```

```
        var value = metadata.Model;
        return new MvcHtmlString
                (string.Format("<h1>{0}</h1><p>{1}</p>", propertyName, value));
    }
}
```

As you can see, the Html Helper does not know how the model class is made. It just knows that it takes by parameter an expression where we will get by reflection the property and its value. The use of this method is like the TextBoxFor Html helper.

```
@model TestHtmlHelper.Models.MyModel
@using TestHtmlHelper.HtmlHelper
<div>@Html.MyFirstHelper()</div>
<div>@Html.TextBoxFor(d => d.Name)</div>
<div>@Html.YourGenericHelperFor(d => d.Name)</div>
```

The result is previsible, as you can see:

```
<div>Test</div>
<div><input id="Name" type="text" name="Name" value="This is a test name" /></div>
<div><h1>Name</h1>This is a test name</div>
```

Before going into the Razor Html Helper, you can see that inside the Html Helper I am concatenating strings to have my end result. This is only possible in a simple scenario. Otherwise, it becomes a mess. This is why you can use Html classes to help you render your output. In fact, the Html Helper we just created should be coded this way:

```
public static MvcHtmlString YourGenericHelperPropertyConstructedFor
                        <TModel, TProperty>(this HtmlHelper htmlHelper
                        , Expression<Func<TModel, TProperty>> expression)
{
    //Get values
    var metadata = ModelMetadata
                        .FromLambdaExpression(expression, htmlHelper.ViewData);
    var propertyName = metadata.PropertyName;
    var value = metadata.Model;
    //Html Construction
    var header = new TagBuilder("h1") {InnerHtml = propertyName};
    var paragraph = new TagBuilder("p") {InnerHtml = value.ToString()};
    return new MvcHtmlString(header.ToString() + paragraph);
}
```

Of course, at first look we can see no problem. But, this is just two tags. Imagine nested Html elements with Html attributes. Imagine having a lot of classes, inputs, and styles. This can become a huge method of several dozens of lines. Of course, the Html rendering is also not simple but it is always more readable than having a huge amount of classes that call each of them. This is why the next approach is very interesting.

Creating inline razor helper can be done directly into any .cshtml file but it does not have the ability to be reusable, which is not something useful. This is why it is possible to store them into that App_Code. To create an app code, you have to right click the project and add an existing asp.net folder.

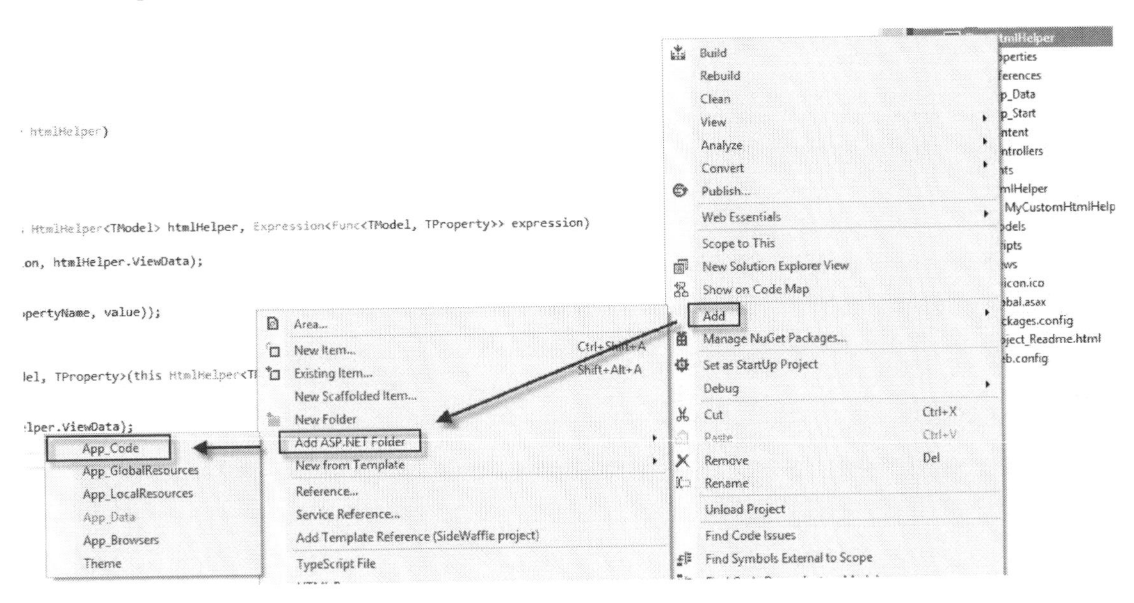


From there, you can add your .cshtml that can have several Razor helpers. The use is simple. You have to use the @ followed by the file name inside the App_Code followed by the name of the helper.

```
<div>    @RazorInlineHelper.MyFirstRazorHelper()</div>
```

The file looks like this:

```
@helper MyFirstRazorHelper()
{    <p>Test Razor</p>}
```

We can have parameters link Html Helper. If we try to reproduce the previous method from the Html helper into Razor Helper the file would look like this.

```
@helper MyFirstRazorHelper()
{
    <p>Test Razor</p>
}
```

```
@helper YourGenericHelperFor(string propertyName, string value)
{
    <h1>@propertyName</h1><p>@value</p>
}

@helper YourGenericHelperPropertyConstructedFor(string propertyName, string value)
{
    <h1>@propertyName</h1><p>@value</p>
}
```

We can see that it is not possible to use a Lambda expression to get attribute value or to get value. You have to pass them as a parameter. For example, the YourGenericHelperFor was changed to get two strings, one for the property name and one for the value. The use looks like this:

```
<div>
    @RazorInlineHelper.MyFirstRazorHelper()
</div>
<div>
    @Html.TextBoxFor(d => d.Name)
</div>
    <div>
    @RazorInlineHelper.YourGenericHelperFor(@Html.DisplayNameFor(d=>d.Name)
                    .ToString(), @Model.Name)
</div>
<div>
    @RazorInlineHelper.YourGenericHelperPropertyConstructedFor(@Html
                        .DisplayNameFor(d => d.Name).ToString(), @Model.Name)
</div>
```

One other limitation is the use of an existing Html helper. StackOverFlow has a solution to create an Html Helper that does some trick to access the Html helper of the page. Here is one solution:

```
public static HtmlHelper<object> GetPageHelper(this
                                  System.Web.WebPages.Html.HtmlHelper html)
{
    return ((System.Web.Mvc.WebViewPage)WebPageContext.Current.Page).Html;
}
```

It is possible from there to use it inside your Helper @Html. I added the whole post code into https://github.com/MrDesjardins/TestHtmlHelper for you to play around with the code. Have fun using **Html helper** and **Razor Helper**. Keep in mind that Helper does not do as much as Html Helper but can in the end be a lot easier to maintain.

# Asp.Net Editor Template with BootStrap for Currency Field

Release Date: 10-Apr-14
Url: http://patrickdesjardins.com/blog/?post_type=post&p=2717

If you are developing an application that requires using money, this money must be in a currency. So, every time you have to select an amount of money, you have to select the currency too. A design pattern is to have a class that represents the money instead of using a decimal directly. For example.

```
public class Contest
{
    public Money InitialCapital { get; set; }
}

public class Money
{
    public Money()
    {
        Currency = CurrencyType.Canada;
    }

    public decimal Value { get; set; }
    public int CurrencyTypeId
    {
        get { return this.Currency.Id; }
        set { this.Currency = CurrencyType.GetFromId(value); }
    }
    /// <summary>
    /// This is ignored by EntityFramework
    /// </summary>
    public CurrencyType Currency { get; set; }
}
```

This code uses the pattern **Value Object** for all currencies. This is why it has additional code that you may not need. In fact, what is important is that the Money class has the money itself inside the Value property and then the currency inside CurrencyType property.

From there, you have a **View Model** that is different. This is a good example of why having a view model is important. The view model will have the whole list of existing and possible currencies that the user can choose from. This is not the type of information that you should have in your model since the model should represent the reality. The view model should look this way:

```
public class ContestViewModel
```

```
{
    [UIHint("SelectorForMoneyViewModel")]
    public SelectorForMoneyViewModel InitialCapital { get; set; }
}
```

The SelectorForMoneyViewModel is a simple class that has the Money and the list of available currencies.

```
public class SelectorForMoneyViewModel
{
    public MoneyViewModel Current { get; set; }

    public List<SelectorItem> AvailableCurrencies { get; set; }

    public SelectorForMoneyViewModel()
    {
        this.Current = new MoneyViewModel();
        this.AvailableCurrencies = new List<SelectorItem>();
    }
}
```

From there, the **Editor Template** can use this list and put the whole list into the currency dropdown. The result should look like the following picture. The first image is the control when not open and the second picture when the user clicked the currency field.

Close:

Open:

This is possible with the use of **BootStrap** but can be reproduced without it. I am using BootStrap because it is available by default with Asp.Net MVC since version 5.

```
@model ViewModel.Selectors.Implementations.Money.SelectorForMoneyViewModel

<div class="input-group">
    @Html.EditorFor(viewModel => viewModel.Current.Value)
    @Html.HiddenFor(viewModel => viewModel.Current.Currency.Id)
    <div class="input-group-btn">
        <button type="button" class="btn btn-default dropdown-toggle"
                data-toggle="dropdown">@Model.Current.Currency.DisplayText<span
            class="caret"></span></button>
        <ul class="dropdown-menu pull-right">
            @foreach (var currency in Model.AvailableCurrencies)
            {
                <li><a href="#"
                    data-id="@currency.Id">@currency.DisplayText</a></li>
            }
        </ul>
    </div><!-- /btn-group -->
</div><!-- /input-group -->
```

First of all, we need to set up a hidden field to set the value of the selected currency. This would require some JavaScript to set from the the dropdown value into the hidden field that will be sent to the server. The first EditorFirst is important because it shows the value. The rest of the code is the dropdown that is set at the right of the textbox with the decimal value.

Here is the JavaScript that must be used for every page that has the component.

```
//For each link that is inside a FORM when used as DropDown-Menu Item we want to
be able
//to click an element and set this one as the visual one. We also set the value of
the selected
//item into the hidden field of the selected dropdown to have this value pushed to
the server.
$('form').on('click', '.dropdown-menu>li>a',
    function () {
        return dropdownMenuLinkAction($(this));
    }
);

//@description: Dropdown menu for a choice
//@param link: a link that must be under the dropdown-menu
function dropdownMenuLinkAction(link) {
    //Current link information
    var htmlLink = $(link);
    var clickedId = htmlLink.attr('data-id');
    var clickedDisplayName = htmlLink.html();
    var controlContainer = htmlLink.closest('.input-group');
    //Change the hidden field (should only have one)
```

```
        controlContainer.find(':hidden').each(
            function () {
                $(this).val(clickedId);
            }
        );
        //Change the visual of the dropdown (should only have one)
        controlContainer.find('.dropdown-toggle').each(
            function () {
                var htmlDropDown = $(this);
                var currentFullHtml = htmlDropDown.html();
                var toRemove = htmlDropDown.text();
                var toWriteBack = currentFullHtml.replace(toRemove, "");
                htmlDropDown.html(clickedDisplayName + " " + toWriteBack);
            }
        );
        $(this).dropdown("toggle"); //Close the menu once clicked
        return false;
}
```

It attaches to every form that has a dropdown an action that is linked to each option of the dropdown. This action takes the information set into the HTML attribute data-id and moves it into the HTML hidden field. The second part is to update the dropdown label to display the selected currency to the control when this box is closed.

# How to make an Asp.Net MVC HtmlHelper that uses generic work with Razor

Release Date: 17-Apr-14
Url: http://patrickdesjardins.com/blog/?post_type=post&p=3438

If you create an Html Helper with Asp.Net MVC that takes a generic type, you may stumble into a problem when using it. An error concerning compilation of the page when executing raises, with a yellow screen of death.

*An exception of type 'System.Web.HttpCompileException' occurred in System.Web.dll but was not handled in user code Compiler Error Message: CS1502: The best overloaded method match for 'System.Web.WebPages.WebPageExecutingBase.Write(System.Web.WebPages.HelperResult)' has some invalid arguments*

This code is the result of simply calling this line:

```
@Html.Test<ContestListItemViewModel>() //Does not work
```

The Html Helper is very simple.

```
public static MvcHtmlString Test<TEntityType>(this HtmlHelper htmlHelper)
{
        return new MvcHtmlString("<p>Test</P>");
}
```

To make it work, you have to have it inside a Razor statement like this:

```
@{
    var x = Html.Test<ContestListItemViewModel>();
    @Html.Raw(x);
}
```

The problem is it is not very clean. However, it is possible to fix this with a single line statement if you wrap the Html Helper within parentheses.

```
@(Html.Test<ContestListItemViewModel>())
```

How come? Well, Razor becomes confused if it has to render the result with Html or with a C# variable because of the *ContestListItemViewModel* that is interpreted as Html. Adding parentheses helps Razor to generate the Html output and removes the confusion, which removes the error.

## How to use Asp.Net DisplayFor or EditorFor within a loop

Release Date: 22-Apr-14
Url: http://patrickdesjardins.com/blog/?post_type=post&p=3441

You can use the Html Helper to use the template system of Asp.Net MVC. You can have @Html.DisplayFor and @Html.EditorFor. The first one is to display the information into a read only control and the latter is the control that allows you to modify the value. Both take as a parameter a Lambda expression of the view Model. Without going into too much detail about where DisplayFor or the EditorFor take their file, just remember that it searches for a folder **EditorTemplates** or **DisplayTemplates** in the directory where the view uses one of these helpers first and then it goes to check for Views>Shared>DisplayTemplates or EditorTemplates.

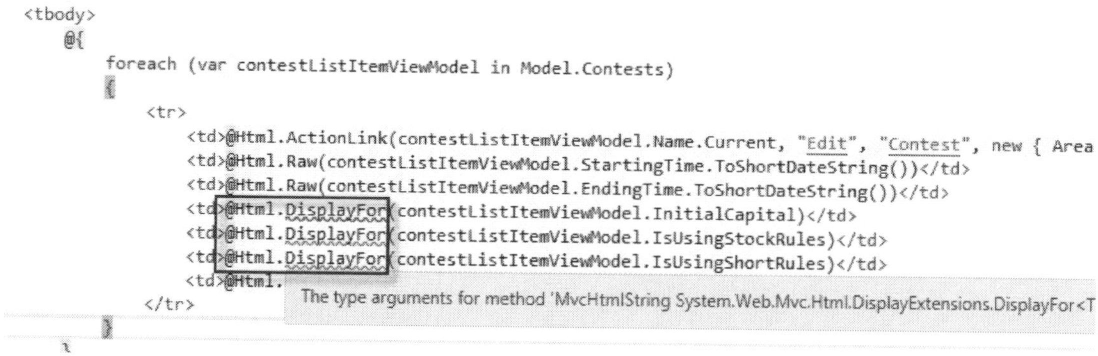

```
<tbody>
    @{
        foreach (var contestListItemViewModel in Model.Contests)
        {
            <tr>
                <td>@Html.ActionLink(contestListItemViewModel.Name.Current, "Edit", "Contest", new { Area
                <td>@Html.Raw(contestListItemViewModel.StartingTime.ToShortDateString())</td>
                <td>@Html.Raw(contestListItemViewModel.EndingTime.ToShortDateString())</td>
                <td>@Html.DisplayFor(contestListItemViewModel.InitialCapital)</td>
                <td>@Html.DisplayFor(contestListItemViewModel.IsUsingStockRules)</td>
                <td>@Html.DisplayFor(contestListItemViewModel.IsUsingShortRules)</td>
                <td>@Html.
            </tr>       The type arguments for method 'MvcHtmlString System.Web.Mvc.Html.DisplayExtensions.DisplayFor<T
        }
    }
```

But what if you want to use one of these two methods within a loop to show the value of a collection inside your model? This collection is from another type of the model and you cannot select from the Lambda expression items within a collection but only a property of the model. The trick is to use Lambda for the current page model but not using any of the property. Instead, simply choose the variable you want to use the template item.

```
<tbody>
    @{
        foreach (var contestListItemViewModel in Model.Contests)
        {
            <tr>
                <td>@Html.ActionLink(contestListItemViewModel.Name.Current,
"Edit", "Contest", new { Area = Constants.Areas.ADMINISTRATOR
                , id = contestListItemViewModel.Id }, null)</td>
                <td>@Html.DisplayFor(d =>
            contestListItemViewModel.StartingTime.ToShortDateString())</td>
                <td>@Html.DisplayFor(d =>
    contestListItemViewModel.EndingTime.ToShortDateString())</td>
                <td>@Html.DisplayFor(d =>
            contestListItemViewModel.InitialCapital)</td>
                <td>@Html.DisplayFor(d =>
            contestListItemViewModel.IsUsingStockRules)</td>
                <td>@Html.DisplayFor(d =>
            contestListItemViewModel.IsUsingShortRules)</td>
                <td>@Html.DisplayFor(d =>
            contestListItemViewModel.IsUsingOptionRules)</td>
            </tr>
        }
    }
</tbody>
```

As you can see, the code in this example is inside a foreach and I can use the DisplayFor Html Helper. The variable for the expression is "d" but I do not use the "d" variable. Instead, I am using the variable that is populated by the foreach "contestListItemviewModel." This is the simplest way to use the powerful reusable template system within a loop in Asp.Net MVC.

## Integer DisplayTemplates, EditorTemplates and Nullable Value

Release Date: 10-Jun-14
Url: http://patrickdesjardins.com/blog/?post_type=post&p=3535

You can define templates in the **DisplayTemplates** and **EditorTemplates**. If you define one template for integer you can have an error saying that the model item requires a string.

*The model item passed into the dictionary is of type 'System.Int32', but this dictionary requires a model item of type 'System.String'*

This error occurs if you name the template **int.cshtml** or **integer.cshtml**. Even if you have defined the *@model int* or *@model int?*.

The solution is to name the file **Int32.cshtml**. CLR type names are used and not C# alias.

Another important detail to remember is that if you want to have **integer** and **nullable integer** you can only do it within one template. So, always define the type with its nullable type. For example, the integer should be in the file Int32.cshtml and the template could be something like this (for DisplayTemplate):

```
@model int?
@if (Model.HasValue)
{
    @Html.Raw(Model)
}
else
{
    @:-
}
```

## Asp.Net MVC @: vs text tag vs Html.Raw

Release Date: 03-Jul-14
Url: http://patrickdesjardins.com/blog/?post_type=post&p=3578

Asp.Net MVC offers several ways to output Html from a Razor page, also know as a .cshtml page or the view.

The first way is to use the syntax shortcut **@:**. This indicates to MVC that the rest of the line is a content block. The advantage of this way to output is that Visual Studio handles closing and opening tags and will continue to work by showing you if a closing tag is missing. The disadvantage is that you cannot use this for an Html tag that is over multiple lines.

The second way is the tag. Very similar to the shortcut syntax but this time it goes on several lines.

```
<text>
    This is super to output something like the date : @DateTime.Now
</text>
```

Finally, you can use the Html Helper **.Raw**. You have to remember that the helper returns an HtmlString. This requires you to use the @ before the Html Helper. Otherwise, the method will return the value but nothing will be rendered.

```
@Html.Raw("<div>It works</div>")
Html.Raw("<div>This does not work</div>")
```

If you are within a multi-statement block @{...} and you want to output Html then you have all three choices. The first one is the **@:** and the second one is the Html Helper **Raw**.

```
<div class="row">
@{
    foreach (var contest in Model.SubscribedContests)
    {
        if (iSubScribe != 0 && iSubScribe % itemPerColumnSubScribe == 0)
        {
            @Html.Raw("</div>");
            @:</div>
        }
    }
}
</div>
```

As you can see, the two closing divisions are legal. Both solutions output the div html tag. You cannot use directly the HTML because it expects to have C# code because we are between a @{ } tag. Visual Studio will not be able to resolve the Html.

The third choice is with the text.

```
@{
    <text>
        <p>It is @DateTime.Now</p>
    </text>
}
```

It is very flexible and easy to output Html, use variables, and to mix multi-statement blocks inside Razor.

## Asp.Net MVC : Having one form and multiple submit buttons

Release Date: 06-Aug-14
Url: http://patrickdesjardins.com/blog/?post_type=post&p=3546

Imagine the case that you have a form that you *Save* but that you could *Save and Continue*. Or a Form that you can *Save* or *Delete*. Both in the same form. You want to be able to do two actions with a single form. This possible scenario can be handled with Asp.Net MVC very easily.

First of all, you proceed as usual in Razor by creating your form and adding inside it all input boxes.

Second, you add inside the form your two buttons. However, you set a value for your buttons and a name that must be the same for all your buttons. Having your buttons with the same name will trigger the browser to send the one that is active. If you are pressing the first button, the value of this first button is sent.

```
<input type="submit" name="action" value="Save" />
<input type="submit" name="action" value="Save and Continue" />
<!-- OR -->
<button type="submit" name="action" value="save">Save</button>
<button type="submit" name="action" value="saveAndContinue">Save and
Continue</button>
```

Using button over input has the advantage to let you set a value that does not change of the localized string that is displayed on the screen.

The third step is on the server side. The controller's action must read the value and make a decision.

```
public ActionResult Register(string action, YourViewModel viewModel)
{
    if (button == "save")
```

```
    {
    }
    //...
}
```

This can be improved by using a constant between the Controller and the View. This way, you do not have strings that are different if someone changes the name of the button.

## Why is RouteData Null in my Asp.Net Mvc Controller?

Release Date: 13-Aug-14
Url: http://patrickdesjardins.com/blog/?post_type=post&p=3610

This article explains how to not have the **RouteData** null in the controller. If you have your own implementation of Controller and you use base.RouteData you may have a special surprise. Sometimes it can be null.

```
public class BaseController : Controller
{
    public BaseController()
    {
        var routeData = base.RouteData;// This can be wrong
    }
}
```

The problem is that the routing may have not yet been analyzed by the controller. This is why you must not use the RouteData in the controller. The place to be sure that this is set is in **OnActionExecuting**. MSDN explains that the RouteData is not defined before being called by **Initialize**. This Initialize method is private and is called by Asp.Net

```
public class BaseController : Controller
{
    public BaseController()
    {

    }
    protected override void OnActionExecuting
                            (ActionExecutingContext filterContext)
    {
        base.OnActionExecuting(filterContext);
        var routeData = base.RouteData;
    }
}
```

After calling the base.OnActionExecution(...) you can call the RouteData.

# Asp.Net MVC OnActionExecuting To Redirect Action

Release Date: 21-Aug-14
Url: http://patrickdesjardins.com/blog/?post_type=post&p=3662

Asp.Net MVC allows you to catch an Http Request by overriding the **OnActionExecuting** and make a decision before executing the desired Controller-Action method. This can be interesting in the case where you want to verify something and if this validation is wrong to redirect the user.

A small use case could be that your user has to be part of a team/contest/group and if the user is not, then we redirect to a message. Instead of having in all your actions a validation to see if the user belongs to the group, it is simpler and less repetitive to have in your controller the *OnActionExecuting* overrided.

Here is an example in .Net.

```
protected override void OnActionExecuting(ActionExecutingContext filterContext)
{
  base.OnActionExecuting(filterContext);
  if (this.RouteData != null
        && this.RouteData.Values
            .ContainsKey(Constants.RoutePortionName.ACTIVE_CURRENT_CONTEST_ID))
  {
    var success = SetCurrentActivePortefolioByContestId(
                  Convert.ToInt32(this.RouteData
                  .Values[Constants.RoutePortionName.ACTIVE_CURRENT_CONTEST_ID]));
    if (!success)//This is the case when the user does not belong to the contest
but try to do an action on the contest
      filterContext.Result = new RedirectToRouteResult(
        new RouteValueDictionary {
                { Constants.AREA, Constants.Areas.ERRORS },
                { Constants.CONTROLLER, "UserError" },
                { Constants.ACTION, "InvalidContest" }
        });
    }
  }
  else
  {
    this.CurrentActivePortefolio = null;
  }
}
```

First, we call the base class to continue to normal behavior of the execution but after we do the logic. The first condition statement verifies that in the URL we have the Contest ID defined. If yes, than we are trying to execute an action on the Contest (which is a group or a team or anything you want). If it is set, we need to verify if the user belongs to this group. This is done by calling the method **SetCurrentActivePortefolioByContestId**. This method calls the database with the ID of the Contest and the ID of the User. If the database returns an entry from the database this means that you have a match and we do not redirect. Otherwise, we redirect. This is where something must be done more than just calling **RedirectToAction**. In fact, we have to change the current execution context values. As you may have seen, the **OnActionExecution** has a single parameter. This parameter has a **Result** property that can be defined with the Area, Controller and Action you desired. In the example, this is where we redirect the user into the Errors area.

## Asp.Net MVC Routing With Custom User Information In URL

Release Date: 26-Aug-14
Url: http://patrickdesjardins.com/blog/?post_type=post&p=3665

Having a clean URL is something very important. It is easier for the user to understand the navigability. It is easier to bookmark or to directly go into a page from the URL. It is also interesting to pass information directly into the URL instead of accumulating data in a session or into the database. For example, let's say that your user can perform an action into a specified group or team. Instead of letting your user click the group and set this in the session you can use the URL. Why? Because the session will die and you will have to redirect the user to a specific URL to allow him to select the group again and it is not interesting in the point of view of a URL that will be missing information.

These are wrong urls:

```
http://yourwebsite/Contest/Orders/New
http://yourwebsite/Contest/Orders/Edit
http://yourwebsite/Contest/Transactions/List
```

These are good urls:

```
http://yourwebsite/Contest/1/Orders/New
http://yourwebsite/Contest/1/Orders/100/Edit
http://yourwebsite/Contest/1/Transactions/List
```

The second group of URLs is better because it is clear that we are creating Order for Contest number 1. It is also clear that we are editing order #100 of the contest number 1. Finally, it is clear and easy to share the Transaction list for contest number 1 too.

How do we handle an informative URL in Asp.Net MVC? With routing! It is also very simple to define a URL for a specific area. In the cases we have seen so far, everything is in the Contest area. To define those URLs, we have to open the **ContestAreaRegistration.cs**. Asp.Net MVC when creating in the Area generated in the Area folder a Registration file.

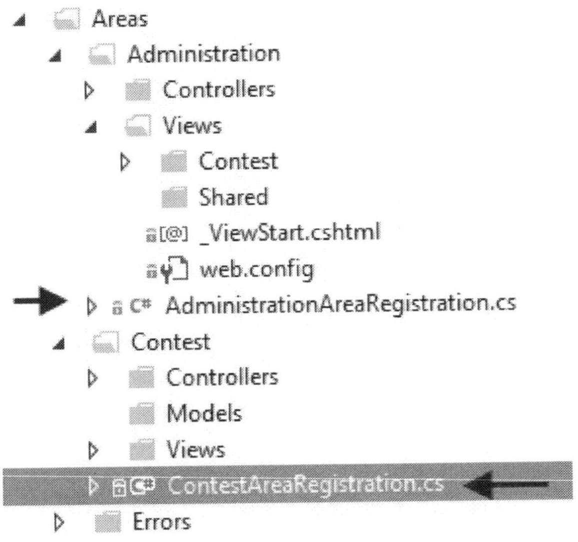

- Areas
  - Administration
    - Controllers
    - Views
      - Contest
      - Shared
      - _ViewStart.cshtml
      - web.config
    - AdministrationAreaRegistration.cs
  - Contest
    - Controllers
    - Models
    - Views
    - ContestAreaRegistration.cs
  - Errors

```
public class ContestAreaRegistration : AreaRegistration
{
    public override string AreaName
    {
        get
        {
            return Constants.Areas.CONTEST;
        }
    }

    public override void RegisterArea(AreaRegistrationContext context)
    {
        AddContestRelatedRoute(context);
        AddDefaultContestRoute(context);
    }
    private static void AddContestRelatedRoute(AreaRegistrationContext context)
    {
        var defaultValue = new List<KeyValuePair<string, object>>
            {
              new KeyValuePair<string, object>("action", "Index")
            , new KeyValuePair<string,
            object>(Constants.RoutePortionName.ACTIVE_CURRENT_CONTEST_ID,
            UrlParameter.Optional)
        , new KeyValuePair<string, object>("id", UrlParameter.Optional) };
```

```
        var constraints = new List<KeyValuePair<string, object>> {
            new KeyValuePair<string,
              object>(Constants.RoutePortionName.ACTIVE_CURRENT_CONTEST_ID, @"\d+")
};
        dynamic defaultValueObject =
                        ListPropertiesToAnonymousObject.Convert(defaultValue);
        dynamic constraintsObject =
                       ListPropertiesToAnonymousObject.Convert(constraints);
        context.MapRoute(Constants.Areas.CONTEST + "_contest_activated"
                       , Constants.Areas.CONTEST + "/{" +
                   Constants.RoutePortionName.ACTIVE_CURRENT_CONTEST_ID +
                   "}/{controller}/{action}/{id}", defaultValueObject,
                   constraintsObject);
    }
    private static void AddDefaultContestRoute(AreaRegistrationContext context)
    {
        context.MapRoute(Constants.Areas.CONTEST + "_default",
                         Constants.Areas.CONTEST + "/{controller}/{action}/{id}"
                        , new { action = "Index", id = UrlParameter.Optional });
    }
}
```

This is the whole class, what interests us is the **AddContestRelatedRoute** method. This method adds the possibility of inserting the contest ID inside the URL.

```
private static void AddContestRelatedRoute(AreaRegistrationContext context)
{
    var defaultValue = new List<KeyValuePair<string, object>> {
        new KeyValuePair<string, object>("action", "Index")
                , new KeyValuePair<string,
                object>(Constants.RoutePortionName.ACTIVE_CURRENT_CONTEST_ID,
                UrlParameter.Optional)
        , new KeyValuePair<string, object>("id", UrlParameter.Optional) };
    var constraints = new List<KeyValuePair<string, object>> {
            new KeyValuePair<string,
            object>(Constants.RoutePortionName.ACTIVE_CURRENT_CONTEST_ID, @"\d+")
    };
    dynamic defaultValueObject =
ListPropertiesToAnonymousObject.Convert(defaultValue);
    dynamic constraintsObject =
ListPropertiesToAnonymousObject.Convert(constraints);
    context.MapRoute(Constants.Areas.CONTEST + "_contest_activated"
                    , Constants.Areas.CONTEST + "/{" +
Constants.RoutePortionName.ACTIVE_CURRENT_CONTEST_ID +
"}/{controller}/{action}/{id}"
                    , defaultValueObject, constraintsObject);
}
```

The first line specifies the default action, the default route contest ID, and the ID. We can add constraints, like in this example we add that we want a number for the current contest. The choice of having a List and KeyValuePair is to use a constant for the name of the routing section. This allows us to reuse the constant to get from the URL in the controller.

```
this.RouteData.Values[Constants.RoutePortionName.ACTIVE_CURRENT_CONTEST_ID]
```

The first dynamic keyword creates from the List the anonymous object required by the MapRoute method. It is the same from the constraint.

```
public static class ListPropertiesToAnonymousObject
{
    public static ExpandoObject Convert
                (IEnumerable<KeyValuePair<string, object>> keyValues)
    {
        var expendo = new ExpandoObject();
        var expendoCollection = (ICollection<KeyValuePair<string
                                                , object>>)expendo;

        foreach (var kvp in keyValues)
        {
            expendoCollection.Add(kvp);
        }
        return expendo;
    }
}
```

The last line of the method uses the two anonymous objects created from the List of KeyValuePair.

```
context.MapRoute(Constants.Areas.CONTEST + "_contest_activated"
        , Constants.Areas.CONTEST + "/{" +
            Constants.RoutePortionName.ACTIVE_CURRENT_CONTEST_ID +
        "}/{controller}/{action}/{id}"
        , defaultValueObject
        , constraintsObject);
```

This is where the URL pattern is defined. The first part is the Area, followed by the ID of the contest. The constant is used to match the default values, and the constraints in the second part. The third part is the controller name, the fourth part is the action and the optional ID.

You can add as many mappings as you want for your route. It is also possible to set them globally in the **RouteConfig.cs** file located in the **App_Start** folder.

Finally, a pretty URL in Asp.Net MVC is very straightforward and does not require a lot of knowledge of URL Rewrite like it would have required with PHP and Apache, for example. It comes by default and extending them is a breeze.

# Asp.Net MVC EditorTemplate and DisplayTemplate with HtmlAttributes On Custom Template

Release Date: 02-Sep-14
Url: http://patrickdesjardins.com/blog/?post_type=post&p=3677

The **EditorTemplate** and the **DisplayTemplate** can be used with the HtmlHelper EditorFor and DisplayFor. It is also possible to pass in a second parameter custom HTML attributes. This is very interesting if you need to add style class.

```
@Html.EditorFor(d => d.PriceLimit
                , new { htmlAttributes = new
                  { @class = "col-md-8 order-price-money-limit" } })
```

The example above calls the EditorFor on the *PriceLimit* property. The Html helper second parameter, an anonymous object, sets htmlAttributes. This is also an anonymous object that sets two classes. One class is for BootStrap and the second is a custom one. If you have defined that the *PriceLimit* must use a custom homemade template, then you may want to gather this information and use it on the HTML element you desire. For example, this is the custom editor template:

```
<div ?????????>
    @Html.EditorFor(viewModel => viewModel.Current.Value)
    @Html.HiddenFor(viewModel => viewModel.Current.Currency.Id)
</div>
```

As you can see, the first line would benefit from the HTML attributes passed by the EditorFor to set up some attributes, like setting the class. The task would have been easy if we only wanted to pass the HTML attribute to a TextBoxFor, or any existing defined Html helper. The reason is you could simply set the **viewdata** back to the second parameter. However, if you are in the scenario where you want to use the HTML attributes for any HTML element, then some code must be written. Also, we need to think about the possibility that the custom editor template (or display template) may want to have HTML attributes by default and just be enhanced by the HTML attributes passed by the Html Helper.

```
<div class="constant-class-always-there ????" ?????????>
    @Html.EditorFor(viewModel => viewModel.Current.Value)
    @Html.HiddenFor(viewModel => viewModel.Current.Currency.Id)
</div>
```

The first task is to handle the case where we may want to have default attributes. The code that is following this paragraph is set at the top of the Editor Template. In this example, we want to be sure that the class "input-group" is set. Whatever is passed on from the Html Helper EditorFor, we want to have this class set.

```
@{
    object htmlAttributes = null;
    if (Html.ViewData.ContainsKey("htmlAttributes"))
    {
        htmlAttributes =
                 Html.Custom()
                .RenderHtmlAttributes(ViewData["htmlAttributes"]
                                      , new { @class = "input-group" });
    }
    else
    {
        htmlAttributes = Html.Custom()
                         .RenderHtmlAttributes(new { @class = "input-group" });
    }
}
```

The *if* statement checks if the EditorFor HTML helper contains any HTML attributes, and if that is the case, then it adds it to the EditorFor HTML attributes; otherwise, it just sets it without taking care of the view data passed by the HTML helper. Something may have caught your attention: the **RenderHtmlAttributes** method. This is a custom HTML helper that takes one or multiple objects and creates an **MvcHtmlString** to be used in your Razor code. The end result would look like this:

```
@{
    object htmlAttributes = null;
    if (Html.ViewData.ContainsKey("htmlAttributes"))
    {
        htmlAttributes = Html.Custom().RenderHtmlAttributes
                (ViewData["htmlAttributes"], new { @class = "input-group" });
    }
    else
    {
        htmlAttributes = Html.Custom()
                         .RenderHtmlAttributes(new { @class = "input-group" });
    }
}
<div @htmlAttributes>
```

```
    @Html.EditorFor(viewModel => viewModel.Current.Value)
    @Html.HiddenFor(viewModel => viewModel.Current.Currency.Id)
</div>
```

The RenderHtmlAttributes loops all HTML attributes objects and extend each of them to create a final **RouteValueDictionary**. Finally, it creates a string.

```
public MvcHtmlString RenderHtmlAttributes(params object[] htmlAttributes)
{
  var finalRouteValue = new RouteValueDictionary();
  foreach (var htmlAttribute in htmlAttributes)
  {
    var routeValue = new RouteValueDictionary(htmlAttribute);
    finalRouteValue = finalRouteValue.Extend(routeValue);
  }
  var htmlAttributesString = String.Join(" "
            , finalRouteValue.Keys.Select(key => String.Format("{0}=\"{1}\""
                , key, this.htmlHelper.Encode(finalRouteValue[key]))));
  return MvcHtmlString.Create(htmlAttributesString);
}
```

The heavy lifting in handling if one HTML attribute object contains a key that has already been defined, or not, to handle the merge is done in the **Extend** method. For example, if two HTML attributes define the key "class" than we want to merge both values to have in the final result a single "class" key with both class values defined. The extend method code is like below.

```
public static RouteValueDictionary Extend(this RouteValueDictionary destination
                                 , IEnumerable<KeyValuePair<string, object>> source)
{
  foreach (var srcElement in source.ToList())
  {
    if (destination.ContainsKey(srcElement.Key))
    {
      destination[srcElement.Key] += " " + srcElement.Value;
    }
    else
    {
      destination[srcElement.Key] = srcElement.Value;
    }

  }
  return destination;
}
```

Here are two unit tests. The first one has two different keys. The end result is that both keys are not merged together. The second test has two route values with the same key, each of them with different values. The result is that both values are in the first object.

```
[TestClass]
public class RouteExtensionsTest
{
    [TestMethod]
    public void
GivenTwoRouteValueDictionary_WhenBothDoesNotContainSameKey_ThenValueAreNotMerged()
    {
        // Arrange
        var valueObject1 = new RouteValueDictionary { { "key1", "value1" } };
        var valueObject2 = new RouteValueDictionary { { "key2", "value2" } };

        // Act
        valueObject1.Extend(valueObject2);

        // Assert
        Assert.AreEqual("value1", valueObject1["key1"].ToString());
    }

    [TestMethod]
    public void
GivenTwoRouteValueDictionary_WhenBothContainSameKey_ThenValueAreMerged()
    {
        // Arrange
        var valueObject1 = new RouteValueDictionary { { "key1", "value1" } };
        var valueObject2 = new RouteValueDictionary { { "key1", "value2" } };

        // Act
        valueObject1.Extend(valueObject2);

        // Assert
        Assert.AreEqual("value1 value2", valueObject1["key1"].ToString());
    }
}
```

It requires some effort to work with Editor Template and Display Template when you want to go beyond basic functionalities. However, it is possible to extend everything with some Html Helper and Extension methods.

# Modify the Html Output of any of your Pages Before Rendering

Release Date: 04-Nov-14
Url: http://patrickdesjardins.com/blog/?post_type=post&p=3784

In some situations, you may want to alter the HTML output that the Asp.Net MVC renders. An interesting case is that you may have several user controls that inject directly into the HTML some JavaScript or CSS. To keep your page loading fast, you want to have everything at the bottom of the Html. Of course, other ways exist, but one can let Asp.Net MVC render everthing. One solution is, just before sending back to the client the Html output in the response, to remove all those JavaScript and CSS tags out of the Html markup and then add them all at the bottom of the Html. This article describes how to modify the Asp.Net MVC default rendering pipeline to inject your own hook that will be placed between the end of the Asp.Net MVC rendering engine and the sending of it to the client. It will also explain how to have this option in an atomic scenario of only allowing this alteration for a specific action up to all requests.

The first class to create is the class that will play with the content produced. I created a small filter called *MyCustomStream* that removes all Script tags and replaces them with a comment and then adds all Script tags removed before the closing Html tag. This way, all scripts are set at the end of the page.

```
public class MyCustomStream : Stream
{
    private readonly Stream filter;


    public MyCustomStream(Stream filter)
    {
        this.filter = filter;
    }

    public override void Write(byte[] buffer, int offset, int count)
    {
        var allScripts = new StringBuilder();
        string wholeHtmlDocument = Encoding.UTF8.GetString(buffer, offset, count);
        var regex = new Regex(@"<script[^>]*>(?<script>([^<]|<[^/])*)</script>"
                        , RegexOptions.IgnoreCase | RegexOptions.Multiline);
        //Remove all Script Tag
        wholeHtmlDocument = regex.Replace(wholeHtmlDocument
             , m => {
                        allScripts.Append(m.Groups["script"].Value);
                        return "<!-- Removed Script -->";
                        });

        //Put all Script at the end
        if (allScripts.Length > 0)
        {
            wholeHtmlDocument = wholeHtmlDocument.Replace("</html>"
                        , "<script type='text/javascript'>" +
                    allScripts.ToString() + "</script></html>");
```

```
    }
    buffer = Encoding.UTF8.GetBytes(wholeHtmlDocument);
    this.filter.Write(buffer, 0, buffer.Length);
}

public override void Flush()
{
    this.filter.Flush();
}

public override long Seek(long offset, SeekOrigin origin)
{
    return this.filter.Seek(offset, origin);
}

public override void SetLength(long value)
{
    this.filter.SetLength(value);
}

public override int Read(byte[] buffer, int offset, int count)
{
    return this.filter.Read(buffer, offset, count);
}

public override bool CanRead
{
    get { return this.filter.CanRead; }
}

public override bool CanSeek
{
    get { return this.filter.CanSeek; }
}

public override bool CanWrite
{
    get { return this.filter.CanWrite; }
}

public override long Length
{
    get { return this.filter.Length; }
}

public override long Position
{
    get { return this.filter.Position; }
    set { this.filter.Position = value; }
}
```

```
}
```

To make it work for controllers or actions, you must create an **attribute**. When the action is executed and has the attribute (or if the controller of the action has the attribute) the filter is applied.

```
public class MyCustomAttribute: ActionFilterAttribute
{
    public override void OnActionExecuted(ActionExecutedContextfilterContext)
    {
        var response = filterContext.HttpContext.Response;

        if (response.ContentType == "text/html") {
            response.Filter = new
                 MyCustomStream(filterContext.HttpContext.Response.Filter);
        }

    }
}
```

You can also set it to all your controllers by setting the attribute to the **Global.Asax.cs**

```
protected void Application_Start()
{
    GlobalFilters.Filters.Add(new MyCustomAttribute());
}
```

But, so far something is wrong. The filter is called multiple times because the stream is output in chunks of several bytes. Since we are playing with the Html, we must replace HTML elements when the whole document is loaded. This requires us to modify a little bit the implementation above. The filter's class must have a buffer. We will append all chunks into our buffer and when this one is full, we will initiate our transformation in this buffer and use this memory buffer to output into the filter stream.

The first step is to have a **Stream** to buffer. I choose to use the **MemoryStream** because it has a method like ToArray() that simplifies our life when it is time to read the whole buffer. The **Flush** method needs modification to accumulate all bytes of the page before hooking the filter and writing back the modified buffer.

```
public class MyCustomStream : Stream
{

    private readonly Stream filter;
    private readonly MemoryStream cacheStream = new MemoryStream();

    public MyCustomStream(Stream filter)
```

```
    {
        this.filter = filter;
    }

    public override void Write(byte[] buffer, int offset, int count)
    {
        cacheStream.Write(buffer, 0, count);
    }

    public override void Flush()
    {
        if (cacheStream.Length > 0)
        {
            var allScripts = new StringBuilder();
            string wholeHtmlDocument =
Encoding.UTF8.GetString(cacheStream.ToArray(), 0, (int)cacheStream.Length);
            var regex = new
             Regex(@"<script[^>]*>(?<script>([^<]|<[^/])*)</script>"
                , RegexOptions.IgnoreCase | RegexOptions.Multiline);
            //Remove all Script Tag
            wholeHtmlDocument = regex.Replace(wholeHtmlDocument
                , m => {
                        allScripts.Append(m.Groups[0].Value);
                        return "<!-- Removed Script -->";
                        });

            //Put all Script at the end
            if (allScripts.Length > 0)
            {
                wholeHtmlDocument = wholeHtmlDocument.Replace("</html>"
                            , "<script type='text/javascript'>" +
                        allScripts.ToString() + "</script></html>");
            }
            var buffer = Encoding.UTF8.GetBytes(wholeHtmlDocument);
            this.filter.Write(buffer, 0, buffer.Length);
            cacheStream.SetLength(0);
        }
        this.filter.Flush();
    }

    public override long Seek(long offset, SeekOrigin origin)
    {
        return this.filter.Seek(offset, origin);
    }

    public override void SetLength(long value)
    {
        this.filter.SetLength(value);
    }
```

```
    public override int Read(byte[] buffer, int offset, int count)
    {
        return this.filter.Read(buffer, offset, count);
    }

    public override bool CanRead
    {
        get { return this.filter.CanRead; }
    }

    public override bool CanSeek
    {
        get { return this.filter.CanSeek; }
    }

    public override bool CanWrite
    {
        get { return this.filter.CanWrite; }
    }

    public override long Length
    {
        get { return this.filter.Length; }
    }

    public override long Position
    {
        get { return this.filter.Position; }
        set { this.filter.Position = value; }
    }
}
```

You can put whatever you want inside the if statement of the **Flush** method. In my case, I removed all scripts of the file, replaced them with a comment and finally put all scripts at the end of the file, just before the closing Html tag.

```
52     <div class="col-md-4">
53         <h2>Get more libraries</h2>
54         <p>NuGet is a free Visual Studio extension that makes it easy to add, remove, and update libra
55         <p><a class="btn btn-default" href="http://go.microsoft.com/fwlink/?LinkId=301866">Learn more
56     </div>
57     <!-- Removed Script -->
58     <div class="col-md-4">
59         <h2>Web Hosting</h2>
60         <p>You can easily find a web hosting company that offers the right mix of features and price f
61         <p><a class="btn btn-default" href="http://go.microsoft.com/fwlink/?LinkId=301867">Learn more
62     </div>
63     <!-- Removed Script -->
64 </div>
65         <hr />
66         <footer>
67             <p>&copy; 2014 - My ASP.NET Application</p>
68         </footer>
69     </div>
70
71     <!-- Removed Script -->
72
73     <!-- Removed Script -->
74
75
76
77 <!-- Visual Studio Browser Link -->
78 <!-- Removed Script -->
79 <!-- Removed Script -->
80 <!-- End Browser Link -->
81
82 </body>
83 <script type='text/javascript'><script src="/bundles/modernizr?v=wBEWDufH_8Md-Pbioxomt90vm6tJN2Pyy9u9z
   v=FVs3ACwOLIVInrAl5sdzR2jrCDmVOWFbZMY6g6Q0ulE1"></script><script src="/bundles/bootstrap?v=2Fz3B0iizV2
84     {"appName":"Chrome","requestId":"d2d6172627514fd18741ef84ab148ecf"}
85 </script><script type="text/javascript" src="http://localhost:34911/6dee62ac88aa4b7e8d76fb3c0e32c288/b
```

The result can be seen if you show the source in any browser. This method is efficient but at the cost that we are playing with the output result and indeed add some overhead in the rendering pipeline. This kind of filter must be used only in specific cases where it is the only way to accomplish a transformation. The cases of JavaScript or CSS are two cases where it is logical to do if you are developing in an older oriented way where "control/component/usercontrol" inject their own JavaScript and CSS. However, in a new system you should not rely on this kind of replacement. It tends to develop a bad habit to throw code everywhere without checking the consequences. It also adds some performance penalty by having to pass through all the code instead of initially setting the coe at the right place. This can be efficiently done by using **section** with ASP.net MVC. Finally, this kind of replacement can cause problems because of dependencies. In this small example, nothing really is changed, but in a bigger code base some JavaScript may need to be before specific Html elements or have dependencies to other JavaScript files. Moving with an automatic process may require more code than the one shown in this article.

You can find the source code of this example in GitHub (https://github.com/MrDesjardins/FilterExample).

# 3. AUTOMAPPER

This chapter groups every post written during 2013 and 2014 about AutoMapper. Like all chapters in this book, every article is a snapshot of a real scenario that has a high probability of happening if you are using these technologies. You will notice that every article that has been chosen to be included in this book contains the release date to identify when it was written. A permanent link is also provided that allows you to go in and read updates and comments. Feel free to go on the website to add your own comment if you wish.

## Automapper Ignore vs UseDestinationValue, what is the difference?

Release Date: 17-May-13
Url: http://patrickdesjardins.com/blog/?post_type=post&p=2062

Automapper gives you a big leverage when it's time to take the value from one object into another object. Sometimes, value must not be transferred. This can be the case for a class that does not have the property or for a class that has some logic that will do the proper instanciation later.

Automapper gives the property **Ignore** which tells the mapper to not take the value of a property. Ignore not also ignores the mapping for the property but will also ignore the mapping of all inner properties. What does it mean? In fact, if the property is not a primitive type but in another class, then if you are using ignore the class properties won't be mapped.

But, if you have a scenario where you must not map the property but map all inner properties then you should use **UseDestinationValue**.

To conclude, the **Ignore** method will not map any property, includingthe inner property of the property defined to be ignored. **UseDestinationValue** will not map the property. It keeps the reference of the property but will map only the value. It's the same with collection. The reference of the collection stays the same while the object inside it is mapped.

## Automapper binds automatically property of property by concatenating property name

Release Date: 14-Nov-13

Url: http://patrickdesjardins.com/blog/?post_type=post&p=2397

This title has a lot of "properties," I know. Today, I will show you with a simple unit test that **Automapper** binds properties' properties automatically with the name. For example, a class that has a property called *User* that has behind its class a property called *FirstName* and *LastName*, will auto-bind to *MyMappedClass.UserFirstName* and *MyMappedClass.UserLastName*.

```
[TestClass]
public class UnitTest1
{
    public class ClassA
    {
        public ClassA()
        {
            this.PropertyA = new ClassAB();
        }

        public ClassAB PropertyA { get; set; }
    }

    public class ClassAB
    {
        public int Id { get; set; }
        public string Suffixe { get; set; }
        public string NotTheSame { get; set; }
    }

    public class ClassB
    {
        public int PropertyAId { get; set; }
        public string PropertyASuffixe { get; set; }
        public string NotReallyTheSame { get; set; }
    }

    [TestMethod]
    public void TestMethod1()
    {
        var c = new ClassA();
        c.PropertyA.Id = 123;
        Mapper.CreateMap<ClassA, ClassB>();
        var mapped = Mapper.Map<ClassA, ClassB>(c);
        Assert.AreEqual(c.PropertyA.Id, mapped.PropertyAId);
        Assert.AreEqual(c.PropertyA.Suffixe, mapped.PropertyASuffixe);
        Assert.IsNull(mapped.NotReallyTheSame);
    }

}
```

The code above shows you this reality. The ClassA is mapped to ClassB. Class A does not specify any Automapper configuration, just a single **CreateMap** without options. Nevertheless, Automapper is bright enough to bind ID and Suffix from ClassA to ClassB. This is because the names of those properties are present in the mapped ClassB class with the concatenation of the two properties' names.

## Using AutoMapper to Map Abstract Classes

Release Date: 20-Mar-14
Url: http://patrickdesjardins.com/blog/?post_type=post&p=3395

**AutoMapper** lets you map your object from one class to another class. It works fine until you want to map from a class to an **abstract** class. The reason is that **AutoMapper** instantiates the desired class type and, since an abstract class cannot be instantiated, will crash.

```
//Mapping
Mapper.CreateMap<SelectorItem, OrderType>();
//Use the mapping
var model = AutoMapper.Mapper.Map<SelectorItem, OrderType>(viewModel);
```

The code creates the map from SelectorItem that is a normal class and OrderType that is an abstract class. The use of this map will not work. To fix this problem the mapping configuration must be changed to specify to **AutoMapper** how to instantiate the OrderType class, the abstract class.

```
Mapper.CreateMap<SelectorItem, OrderType>().ConstructUsing(OrderTypeCreator);
```

The mapping requires the use of the **ConstructUsing** method that has two signatures.

```
IMappingExpression<TSource, TDestination> ConstructUsing
                                   (Func<TSource, TDestination> ctor);
IMappingExpression<TSource, TDestination> ConstructUsing
                            (Func<ResolutionContext, TDestination> ctor);
```

The first one is easy to use. It takes a method that has the source which is the class we start with and returns a destination class that is the abstract class.

```
private OrderType OrderTypeCreator(SelectorItem arg)
{
    return OrderType.GetFromId(arg.Id);
}
```

This example takes from the concrete class the ID and uses a factory to return the correct concrete class that inherits from the abstract OrderType class. This way, we have AutoMapper that can map to an abstract Class without problem.

## AutoMapper and constructor with parameters

Release Date: 06-May-14
Url: http://patrickdesjardins.com/blog/?post_type=post&p=3465

In some uses you are forced to have classes that have **constructor with parameters**. This is more rare if you are using Entity Framework (EF) because it requires a parameterless constructor. However, if the scenario occurs, remember that **AutoMapper** does not have this constraint. In fact, you can have a private parameterless constructor for Entity Framework (EF) and force the use of a public constructor with parameters when using it in your code.

First of all, during the mapping configuration, you must use **ConstructUsingServiceLocator** method.

```
Mapper.CreateMap<ContestEditableViewModel, Model.Entities.Contest.Contest>()
                                            .ConstructUsingServiceLocator();
```

This instructs AutoMapper to check for the option **ConstructServicesUsing** method that can be provided during the mapping instruction.

Second, when you are using AutoMapper to map between classes, you must specify every parameter.

```
var model = AutoMapper.Mapper.Map<ContestEditableViewModel,
                                  Model.Entities.Contest.Contest>
        (viewModel, options=>
                options.ConstructServicesUsing(t=>new
                        Model.Entities.Contest.Contest(yourFirstParameter,
                        yourSecondParameter, /*and so on*/)
                ));
```

This way, you can have classes that have parameters and control how to provide them values. Of course, another way is to instanciate your class into the object before mapping.

```
var contest = new Contest(param1, param2);
Mapper.Map(sourceViewModel, contest);
```

# 4. C#

This chapter groups every post written during 2013 and 2014 about AutoMapper. Like all chapters in this book, every article is a snapshot of a real scenario that has a high probability of happening if you are using these technologies. You will notice that every article that has been chosen to be included in this book contains the release date to identify when it was written. A permanent link is also provided that allows you to go in and read updates and comments. Feel free to go on the website to add your own comment if you wish.

## Linq Aggregate to concatenate string with a comma

Release Date: 01-Apr-13
Url: http://patrickdesjardins.com/blog/?post_type=post&p=1982

If you have an array that you want to flatten into a string with a comma between each entry, you could use **Linq** with a one-liner delegate to reach this goal.

```
string flatten = inputs.Aggregate((current, next) =>
                                    string.Format("{0}, {1}", current, next));
```

This is quite powerful as you can see; you do not have to do validation to know if you have reached the last entry to not add a trailing comma. Without Linq and the aggregate function, you would have to loop and to verify this condition.

```
string flatten = string.Empty;
for (int i = 0; i < inputs.Length; i++)
{
    if (i != (i.Length - 1))
    {
        flatten += str + ", ";
    }
    else
    {
        flatten += str;
    }
}
```

I do not know about you, but I found it easier to read the **Aggregate** method than the second snippet of code. Of course, this example could have been done with a simple String.Join to join a list with a string between every element. This is just for a simple example of the Aggregate function which could been more than just concatenating a string.

# How to display a list by category with Linq and Grouping

Release Date: 03-Apr-13
Url: http://patrickdesjardins.com/blog/?post_type=post&p=1916

If you are using Asp.Net MVC, you could have a set of entities which are going to be mapped from your model to your view model. Here is a sample of a situation where we have an exercise that is related to a muscle. It is a **1** to **n** relationship where the exercise is linked to a single muscle, but the muscle could be trained by many exercises.

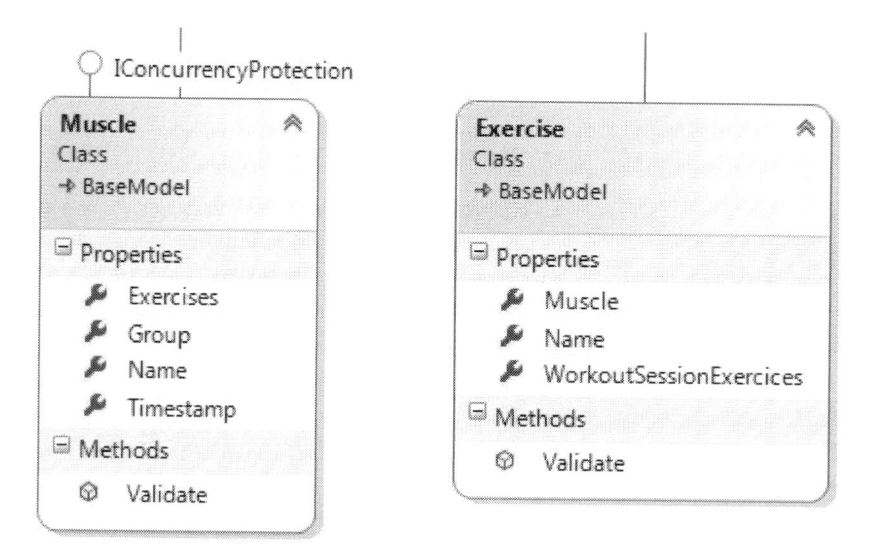


As you can see, the mapping between the view model and the model is simple. The side showing the exercise, where only one instance of muscle could be attached, is merged into the view model of the exercise. This one is called *ExerciseViewModel* in the following class diagram.

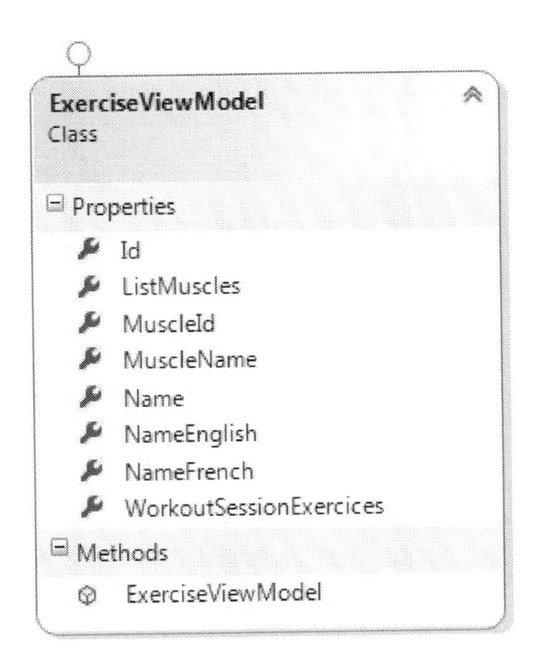


So, if you want to display a list of exercises you can get the whole list by getting from your database context the list of exercises. Here is the partial view that gets a list of ExerciseViewModel and displays a list of all exercises inside an Html list.

```
@model IEnumerable<ViewModels.ExerciseViewModel>
<ul class="exercises-container-source">
    @foreach (var exercise in Model)
    {
        <li data-exercise-id="@exercise.Id">
            <span class="exerciseName">@exercise.Name</span>
        </li>
    }
</ul>
```

Let's say that now you want to display exercises by their muscle group. This is not a problem from the class point of view because the *ExerciseViewModel* contains directly the *MuscleId* and *MuscleName*.

The "old school" way to do it would be to sort the collection by the exercise name, then loop through the collection and every time the muscle group changes, write the muscle name.

```
<ul class="exercises-container-source">
    int lastId = -1;
```

```
    @foreach (var exercise in Model.OrderBy(d=>d.MuscleId))
    {
      if(lastId != exerciseMuscleId)
      {
        if(lastId != -1)
        {
            </ul>
        }
        <h3>@exercise.MuscleName</h3>
        <ul class="exercises-container-source">
        lastId = exerciseMuscleId;
      }
        <li data-exercise-id="@exercise.Id">
            <span class="exerciseName">@exercise.Name</span>
        </li>
    }
</ul>
```

This kind of code is not particularly great and invokes some logic to understand it correctly. First, we have to change the last muscle ID into a variable and change its value depending on a comparison. Second, we have to handle the creation of the Html tag "UL" because a header tag (h3) cannot be inserted between "UL" tags. This means that we need to open and close the "UL" tag every time we have an exercise.

With **Linq and Grouping** we can simplify by a lot this whole process. The main advantage of the next methodology is that without modifying any back-end classes the view page will be cleaner and easier to understand.

```
@model IEnumerable<ViewModels.ExerciseViewModel>
@model IEnumerable<ViewModels.ExerciseViewModel>
@foreach (var exerciseGroup in Model.GroupBy(d =>
                                new { Id = d.MuscleId, Name = d.MuscleName }))
{
    <h3>@exerciseGroup.Key.Name</h3>
    <ul class="exercises-container-source">
        @foreach (var exercise in exerciseGroup)
        {
            <li data-exercise-id="@exercise.Id">
                <span class="exerciseName">@exercise.Name</span>
            </li>
        }
    </ul>
}
```

Here you go. No more integer to know that last exercise, no more weird handling of the "UL." It's very clear, so the maintainability of the code is easier. As you can see, we first group every exercise by *MuscleId* and *MuscleName*. We need to have both because we want to show the name. As you can see, we also display the name which is part of the key. With Visual Studio 2010 and 2012, your anonymous type will be handled by Microsoft Intellisense and you will see that your Key's property has the *Id* and the *Name* properties. After displaying the muscle name, you just need to loop through the collection of exercises and display the exercise name.

I hope that you will be able to use the Linq Grouping functionality in you application more often because it can greatly help a simple task to be cleaner.

## C# two dimensional array with double bracket and with single bracket

Release Date: 16-Oct-13
Url: http://patrickdesjardins.com/blog/?post_type=post&p=2340

With Microsoft .Net and C# it is possible to have multiple dimensions array in two different ways. One uses a **double bracket** and one uses a single bracket with a **comma**.

```
int [][] myDoubleArray = new int[100][];
int [,] mySingleArrayActingAsTwoDimensional = new int[100,100];
```

The first example is in fact an array of an array. You can have multiple dimensions for your second dimension. It is called a **jagged array**.

```
int [][] myDoubleArray = new int[100][];
myDoubleArray[0] = new int[5];
myDoubleArray[1] = new int[10];
myDoubleArray[2] = new int[50];
myDoubleArray[...] = new int[...];
```

This leads to the possibility of having a variable that is not uniform in its size. It can, but it does not mean it is a perfect rectangle. The second way to make a multiple dimensional array is by using the comma. This forces the size to be defined for both dimensions and to be the same for each row. It is also not possible to get a row-like array of array because it is based on an index.

```
int [,] mySingleArrayActingAsTwoDimensional = new int[100,100];
mySingleArrayActingAsTwoDimensional[50] = ... // CRASH!!!
mySingleArrayActingAsTwoDimensional[50,0] = 1;
```

For the jagged array to loop through all items, we must check for each array. This is required to get its size because it can change.

```
for (int i = 0; i < myDoubleArray.Length; i++)
{
    for (int j = 0; j < myDoubleArray[i].Length; j++)
    {
        myDoubleArray[i][j] = i * j;
    }
}
```

For a rectangle array, it is not required and we can just check the first item length.

```
for (int i = 0; i < mySingleArrayActingAsTwoDimensional.GetLength(0); i++)
{
    for (int j = 0; j < mySingleArrayActingAsTwoDimensional.GetLength(1); j++)
    {
        mySingleArrayActingAsTwoDimensional[i, j] = i * j;
    }
}
```

Finally, you can create a **jagged array** with a short nomenclature.

```
var jaggedArrayTwoDimension = { new int[5], new int[10], new int[] { 1, 2, 3, 4,
5, 6, 7, 8, 9, 10 } };
```

The last example creates an array of two dimensions. In three rows, the first one has five integers, the second has 10 integers and the last row has 10 integers. The first two rows are integer not defined and the last row has integer defined from 1 to 10.

# Implicit Implementation of Interface vs Explicit Implementation of Interface

Release Date: 22-Oct-13
Url: http://patrickdesjardins.com/blog/?post_type=post&p=2217

What is the difference between implicit and explicit interface?

```
class Program
{
    static void Main(string[] args)
    {
    }
}
```

```
public class Interface : IInterface
{
}

interface IInterface
{
    void Method1();

}
```

Implement interface 'IInterface'

Explicitly implement interface 'IInterface'

**Implicit** interface allows access to the method without having to cast the object to the interface type while **explicit** interface requires you to cast your object to the interface. Why would you want to have explicit interface? Because if you have several methods from different interfaces with the same signature, the only way to call the good method is to do it explicitly.

Here is an example of an implicit interface:

```
public class Interface : IInterface
{
    public void Method1()
    {
        throw new NotImplementedException();
    }
}
```

Here is an example of an explicit interface:

```
public class Interface : IInterface
{
    public void IInterface.Method1()
    {
        throw new NotImplementedException();
    }
}
```

And you can use both at the same time:

```
public class Interface : IInterface
{
    void Method1()
    {
        throw new NotImplementedException();
    }

    void IInterface.Method1()
    {
        throw new NotImplementedException();
    }
}
```

Let's examine the following code:

```
class Program
{
    static void Main(string[] args)
    {
        var x = new Interface();
        x.Method1();
        Console.ReadLine();
    }
}

public class Interface : IInterface, IInterfaceWithSameMethodSignature
{
    public void Method1()
    {
        Console.WriteLine("IInterface:Method1 Implicit");
    }

    void IInterface.Method1()
    {
        Console.WriteLine("IInterface:Method1");
    }

    void IInterfaceWithSameMethodSignature.Method1()
    {
        Console.WriteLine("IInterfaceWithSameMethodSignature:Method1");
    }
}

interface IInterface
{
    void Method1();
}
```

```
interface IInterfaceWithSameMethodSignature
{
    void Method1();
}
```

As you can see, the Main method has a variable named 'x'. If we check the IntelliSense we see only the first Method1() of the Interface class. The reason is that we pass through the implicit method. If we want to use the explicit Method of the IInterface we need to cast 'x'.

```
Interface x = new Interface();
x.Method1();    //Implicit prints: "IInterface:Method1 Implicit"
((IInterface)x).Method1();    //Explicit 1 prints: "IInterface:Method1"
((IInterfaceWithSameMethodSignature)x).Method1();    //Explicit 2 prints:
"IInterfaceWithSameMethodSignature:Method1"
```

This is handy because it disambiguates which methods to be called. This can be handy if the object is passed to a method that requires the interface in a parameter. This one is cast when passed by parameters.

```
class Program
{
    static void Main(string[] args)
    {
        var x = new Interface();
        Method(x);

        Console.ReadLine();
    }

    static void Method(IInterfaceWithSameMethodSignature expl)
    {
        expl.Method1();
    }
}
```

The Interface class is used with the *x* object. This is passed to a method that requires the interface *IInterfaceWithSameMethodSignature*. When *Method1* is called, the one of *IInterfaceWithSameMethodSignature* is called —the explicit method.

# ImmutableList and the namespace System.Collections.Immutable

Release Date: 24-Oct-13
Url: http://patrickdesjardins.com/blog/?post_type=post&p=2359

An immutable list has the property of being not modifiable after its creation. String is immutable because each time you change its value a new instance is created. If you want to have the same behavior with a list, you need to use an immutable list.

The creation of an **ImmutableArray** can be from a method or from another list. But first, you need to use **NuGet** to download the package. You also need to use .Net Framework 4.5.

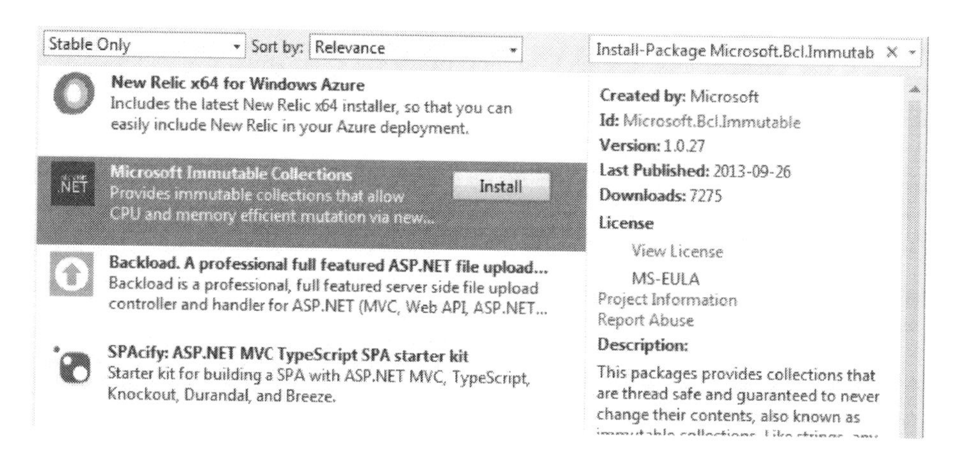


or with the package console with this line:

```
Install-Package Microsoft.Bcl.Immutable
```

The code:

```
using System.Collections.Immutable;

ImmutableList<int> array = ImmutableList.Create<int>(100, 101, 300);
List<int> myList = new List<int> { 100, 101, 300 };
ImmutableList<int> array2 = ImmutableList.ToImmutableList<int>(myList);
```

As you can see, you need to use the namespace **System.Collections.Immutable**. The namespace contains more than only ImmutableList, but also contains an ImmutableDictionary, ImmutableQueue, ImmutableSet and ImmutableStack.

- System.Collections.Immutable
  - { } System.Collections.Immutable
    - IImmutableDictionary<TKey,TValue>
    - IImmutableList<T>
    - IImmutableQueue<T>
    - IImmutableSet<T>
    - IImmutableStack<T>

# How to quickly initialize a C# Dictionary in one line

Release Date: 15-Apr-14
Url: http://patrickdesjardins.com/blog/?post_type=post&p=3445

I stumbled into a situation where I had to fill up a dictionary but desired not to use the .Add method. The case appears to be frequent if you are using Help Helper of Asp.Net MVC. The reason is that if you want to add an HTML attribute by Html Helper then you have to provide a dictionary of key values that represents the attribute name and attribute value. Here is a class that represents a simple scenario.

```
public class ColumnHeader
{
    public IDictionary<string, string> Attributes { get; set; }
}
```

If you want to initialize the property, then you can use new but also double the curly braces.

```
var col = new ColumnHeader {
                Attributes = new Dictionary<string, string>
                    {
                            { "attribute1", "value1" }
} };
```

This is an example of how to add a single value into the dictionary. As you can see, we have a first curly brace to initialize the property itself and then we have the double curly brace that initializes the dictionary and the key value. If we wanted to initialize two items, we could by adding a comma after the curly brace for the key value.

```
var col = new ColumnHeader {
                Attributes = new Dictionary<string, string>
                    {
```

```
{ "attribute1", "value1" }, { "attribute2", "value2" } } };
```

Nothing more to be said. Initializing a dictionary with C# without having to initialize it with the empty constructor and then adding individually every key value is very straightforward.

## Converting anonymous objects to Dictionary<string, string>

Release Date: 12-Jun-14
Url: http://patrickdesjardins.com/blog/?post_type=post&p=3470

Some Asp.Net MVC Html Helpers have the possibility to add **anonymous object** as a parameter to assign key value. This is the case for HtmlAttributes parameter. If you want to create your own Html Helper or simply have the possibility of using an anonymous object, you may stumble into the case that you need to **enumerate keys and values**.

```
public string Url(string action, string controller
                                    , string area = null, object routeValues = null)
{
    //Code here
}
```

The code above is an example. You may want to have a method that generates a url from some parameters. The last parameter named *routeValues* is of type object. This one is created to be used for an anonymous object.

```
Url("action", "controller", "area", new {Id = "123", Name="This is my name"});
```

The Url's method can then loop through all the properties. Something that can help you is to create an anonymous method for an object that converts everything into an **IDictionary** where it will be easy to manipulate keys (property name) and values.

```
public static class ObjectExtensions
{
    public static IDictionary<string, object> AsDictionary(this object source
                    , BindingFlags bindingAttr = BindingFlags.DeclaredOnly
                    | BindingFlags.Public | BindingFlags.Instance)
    {
        return source.GetType().GetProperties(bindingAttr).ToDictionary
        (
            propInfo => propInfo.Name,
            propInfo => propInfo.GetValue(source, null)
        );
    }
```

```
}
```

It uses reflection to get all properties and from these properties gets all values. Here is a unit test for the **AsDictionary** extension method.

```
[TestClass]
public class ObjectExtensionsTest
{
    [TestMethod]
    public void GivenAnObject_WhenThisOneHasMultipleProperties_ThenDictionary()
    {
        // Arrange
        var objectToConvert = new { Id = "Test", Name = "Test2" };

        // Act
        var dictionary = objectToConvert.AsDictionary();

        // Assert
        Assert.AreEqual(2, dictionary.Keys.Count);
        Assert.AreEqual(objectToConvert.Id, dictionary["Id"]);
        Assert.AreEqual(objectToConvert.Name, dictionary["Name"]);
    }
}
```

# C# Constructor Should not Call Virtual Method

Release Date: 28-Sep-14
Url: http://patrickdesjardins.com/blog/?post_type=post&p=3484

Instantiating an object calls, obviously, the controller of the class. In the case that the class inherits from a second class, the base constructor is called before the code inside the derived class. The order of the calls can be shown very easily by printing to the console every time the constructor is called.

```
class Program
{
    static void Main(string[] args)
    {
        var classA = new ClassA();
        Console.ReadLine();
    }
}

public class ClassA : ClassB
{
    public ClassA()
    {
```

```
        Console.WriteLine("ClassA Constructor");
    }
}
public class ClassB
{
    public ClassB()
    {
        Console.WriteLine("ClassB Constructor");
    }

}
```

```
0 references
class Program
{
    0 references
    static void Main(string[] args)
    {
        var classA = new ClassA();
        Console.ReadLine();
    }
}

2 references
public class ClassA:ClassB
{
    1 reference
    public ClassA()
    {
        Console.WriteLine("ClassA Constructor");
    }
}
2 references
public class ClassB
{
    0 references
    public ClassB()
    {
        Console.WriteLine("ClassB Constructor");
    }
}
```

```
file:///C:/Users/desjp/Doc
ClassB Constructor
ClassA Constructor
```

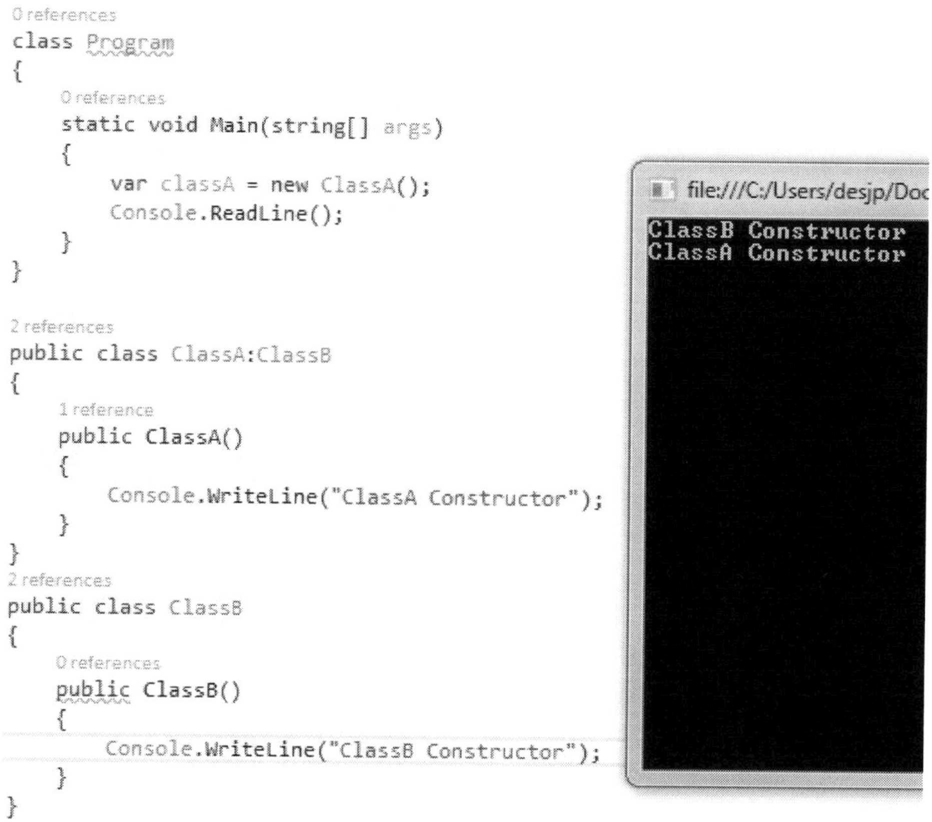

Having a virtual method allows the derived class to override the method. If the base class calls the method, this one call, if overrided, calls the one in the derived class. This means that if you are instantiating value in the derived class this one will not have the data instantiated yet. This can produce unexpected errors like having null reference or working with a set of data that is not initialized with the desired value. The problem is that in the lifetime of the class, this could be inherited, which would create new unexpected scenarios for where the virtual method is defined.

We can transform the previous code into this scenario. For example, let's create a new virtual method where we return a string. In the derived class, we will return the name of the current process. In the base class, we return a simple string. The derived class must instantiate the *Process* object to get information about the current process. This has been instantiated in the constructor. Since it will be called after the base constructor is done with its initialization and since the base constructor calls the virtual method, this one will crash. The error occurs because the base class calls the method that is overriden. The override is executed. It uses a variable that is not yet instanciated.

```
public class ClassA : ClassB
{
    private Process currentProcess;
    public ClassA()
    {
        Console.WriteLine("ClassA Constructor");
        currentProcess = Process.GetCurrentProcess();
    }

    public override string TestMethod()
    {
        return currentProcess.ProcessName;
    }
}
public class ClassB
{
    public ClassB()
    {
        Console.WriteLine("ClassB Constructor");
        TestMethod();
    }

    public virtual string TestMethod()
    {
        return "Test";
    }
}
```

The result is that the *TestMethod* from the base class calls the *TestMethod* of the derived class and crashes at the *currentProcess* line.

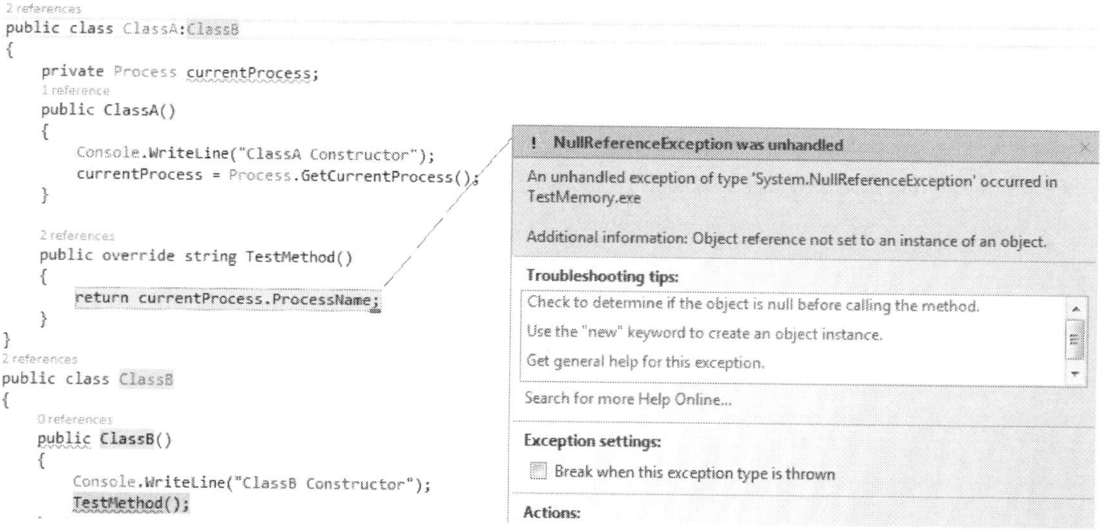

```
2 references
public class ClassA:ClassB
{
    private Process currentProcess;
    1 reference
    public ClassA()
    {
        Console.WriteLine("ClassA Constructor");
        currentProcess = Process.GetCurrentProcess();
    }

    2 references
    public override string TestMethod()
    {
        return currentProcess.ProcessName;
    }
}
2 references
public class ClassB
{
    0 references
    public ClassB()
    {
        Console.WriteLine("ClassB Constructor");
        TestMethod();
```

! NullReferenceException was unhandled

An unhandled exception of type 'System.NullReferenceException' occurred in TestMemory.exe

Additional information: Object reference not set to an instance of an object.

Troubleshooting tips:

Check to determine if the object is null before calling the method.

Use the "new" keyword to create an object instance.

Get general help for this exception.

Search for more Help Online...

Exception settings:

Break when this exception type is thrown

Actions:

A simple way to solve this issue is to seal the class. However, on the other hand, sealing limits the possibility of expanding your class and it forces you to not have a virtual method in this sealed class. Or, you can limit the calls of virtual methods inside the constructor.

# C# Using Statement Inside or Outside the Class Namespace

Release Date: 10-Nov-14
Url: http://patrickdesjardins.com/blog/?post_type=post&p=3798

.Net works with libraries that you can reference in the project and then use in any code file. The keyword **using** is the one to use inside the C# file to be able to use classes from an external library or a different namespace from the one the code bselongs in the file. Of course, if you do not want to use the using statement, you can when using a class from another namespace specify the name with the whole namespace path.
For example:

```
var x = new OtherLibrary.OtherNameSpace.Xyz.TheClass();
```

Having the whole namespace in the code can become cumbersome. This is why the **using** statement exists. By default, using is at the top of the file.

```
using System;
namespace MyNameSpace
{

    public class MyClass
```

```
    {
        //...
    }
}
```

But this could also be different by having the *System* namespace directly inside the namespace.

```
namespace MyNameSpace
{
    using System;
    public class MyClass
    {
        //...
    }
}
```

But what is the difference? The difference is the priority of how the .Net will use external dependencies. The priority is to the **using** inside the namespace and then to the one of the file. This is why having the using inside the namespace can be safer in that you can be sure that no other library can hijack a namespace and break your code. For example, you could create a class named Math, and still be in your namespace and having this one be used instead of System.Math. But, to remove this possibility, if you set *using System;* inside your namespace then you are sure to have the real Math class be used (or to have a conflict during compilation file if both are explicitly marked with using).

A rule of thumb is to set the using inside your namespace, this way you have less chance of having a behavior that you do not expect.

## KeyValuePair does not return NULL with Linq to Object SingleOrDefault Method

Release Date: 24-Nov-14
Url: http://patrickdesjardins.com/blog/?post_type=post&p=3828

If you have a list of **key value pair** and you are searching for something that might not be there, you may want to use **SingleOrDefault**, or **FirstOrDefault** to get this element. If it does not exist, you may think that the Linq to object returns null but in fact, it returns the default value which is a new instance of KeyValuePair class.

```
var kvp1 = new KeyValuePair<string, string>("a", "b");
var kvp2 = new KeyValuePair<string, string>("c", "d");
```

```
var list = new List<KeyValuePair<string, string>> {kvp1, kvp2};
var value = list.SingleOrDefault(d => d.Key == "notfound").Value;
```

The code above returns from **SingleOrDefault** a new **KeyValuePair** object with the Key and the Value to NULL. The return of the Linq is not NULL. In fact, this is the case in any of your classes that you search and that this is not found.

```
var kvp3 = new MyKeyValuePair {Key = "a", Value = "b"};
var kvp4 = new MyKeyValuePair {Key = "c", Value = "d"};
var list2 = new List<MyKeyValuePair> { kvp3, kvp4 };
var value2 = list.SingleOrDefault(d => d.Key == "notfound").Value;

public class MyKeyValuePair
{
    public string Key { get; set; }
    public string Value { get; set; }
}
```

The result is that value2 is an **Exception** and this is because **SingleOrDefault** has returned NULL. How come? It returns the default value that has the name of the method specified. So, if we verify the default value of a class we will get an empty object, right? Wrong! We are getting a NULL.

```
var defaultIs = default(MyKeyValuePair); //This return null!
```

If we check the source code of SingleOrDefault, we realize that it uses the exact same default method.

```
public static TSource SingleOrDefault<TSource>(this IEnumerable<TSource> source,
Func<TSource, bool> predicate)
{
    if (source == null) throw Error.ArgumentNull("source");
    if (predicate == null) throw Error.ArgumentNull("predicate");
    TSource result = default(TSource);
    long count = 0;
    foreach (TSource element in source) {
    if (predicate(element)) {
        result = element;
        checked { count++; }
    }
    }
    switch (count) {
    case 0: return default(TSource);
    case 1: return result;
    }
    throw Error.MoreThanOneMatch();
}
```

**KeyValuePair** class, or should I say the KeyValuePair **struct** default is different. The reason is that the default value of a structure is not the same as a class. It returns a new structure and not null. The mystery is now resolved. For your information, you cannot define your "default value" for your classes. Here is something interesting from MSDN.

*The solution is to use the default keyword, which will return null for reference types and zero for numeric value types. For structs, it will return each member of the struct initialized to zero or null depending on whether they are value or reference type.*

# System.IO.Path.GetFullPath

Release Date: 11-Dec-14
Url: http://patrickdesjardins.com/blog/?post_type=post&p=3870

Migrating Asp.Net Mem you manipulate paths and files with System.IO.Path which is better than trying to handle everything by string. Great! You are using *Path.Combine("c:\data\","file.txt")* and everything is fine. You have understood that combining path and file are way easier with Path.Combine. It handles for you every slash, so you do not have to handle string with substring and indexof. However, the dream stops brutally the day you have something with a relative path that goes to the parent folder. For example, the line below crashes.

```
Path.Combine(@"c:\data\","..\file.txt");
```

Having double dot returns the the c: drive in the example above, but combine will not do it for you. This is why you need to use **Path.GetFullPath**.

```
Path.GetFullPath(@"c:\data\..\file.txt");
```

This will clean the path and output *c:\file.txt.*

The conclusion is that file path manipulation must still use the *System.IO.Path* but different methods should be used depending on the case you are encountering.

# C# Allow External Library To Access Internal Visibility

Release Date: 19-Dec-14
Url: http://patrickdesjardins.com/blog/?post_type=post&p=3539

I am not a fan of what I will show you here but it can be a life saver someday in your career.

What I will show you is how to access an internal type from an external library. You have read it correctly. Even if the goal of internal visibility is to hide the type to be used outside the assembly, it is possible since framework 2.0 to create an exception by naming which assembly/library can use the internal type.

Why would we want that? Well, a simple case could be that you want to unit test some internal classes and that you are doing all your unit tests in a unit test project. This one needs to access the internal type and you must use a special attribute to allow that. Another case would be that you have the getter public but the setter internal. If you want a specific assembly to be able to write and no other one then you can use this attribute. This forces you to have only one way to set information into your property.

The attribute is set anywhere in the code of your assembly. It can be at the top of a class or in AssemblyInfo file. Even if it is at the top of a class, remember that it allows access to the complete assembly. This is why it is a better approach to set the attribute in the AssemblyInfo file.

```
[assembly: InternalsVisibleTo("MyBusinessAssembly")]
[assembly: InternalsVisibleTo("MyOtherBusinessRelatedAssembly")]
[assembly: InternalsVisibleTo("MyUnitTestProjectName")]
```

If you are using a signed DLL, then you will need to use the **sn.exe** command line tool. This can be used directly in the **Visual Studio Command Prompt**. It will produce a public token that can be used in the InternalsVisibleTo attribute.

```
sn -Tp c:\yourpath\toyourdll\abc.dll
```

```
[assembly:InternalsVisibleTo("MyBusinessAssembly,
            PublicKey=000000000001111111111122222222222.....")]
[assembly:InternalsVisibleTo("MyOtherBusinessRelatedAssembly,
            PublicKey=000000000001111111111122222222222.....")]
[assembly:InternalsVisibleTo("MyUnitTestProjectName,
            PublicKey=000000000001111111111122222222222.....")]
```

# 5. CSS

This chapter groups every post written during 2013 and 2014 about CSS. Like all chapters in this book, every article is a snapshot of a real scenario that has a high probability of happening if you are using these technologies. You will notice that every article that has been chosen to be included in this book contains the release date to identify when it was written. A permanent link is also provided that allows you to go in and read updates and comments. Feel free to go on the website to add your own comment if you wish.

## How to make a div/span at the bottom right of a div with CSS

Release Date: 28-Jan-13
Url: http://patrickdesjardins.com/blog/?post_type=post&p=1692

You need to set the parent container to **relative**. When the position is relative, everything that will be under the container with the position to **absolute** will be absolute to the relative parent.

```
.parent
{
  position: relative;
}

.child
{
 position: absolute;
 bottom: 0;
 right:0;
}
```

From here, if you create a child inside the parent container, the child will be at the bottom of the parent.

```
<div class="parent">
    <p>This is the parent container</p>
    <br /><br /><br />
    <p>This is the parent container</p>
    <br /><br /><br />
    <br /><br /><br />
    <span class="child">Last line at the bottom</span>
</div>
```

An absolute div (or any other element) is relative to the first **relative** parent. In case no element has been marked something else than **static** (like to relative) then the first element will be used, which is the Html element.

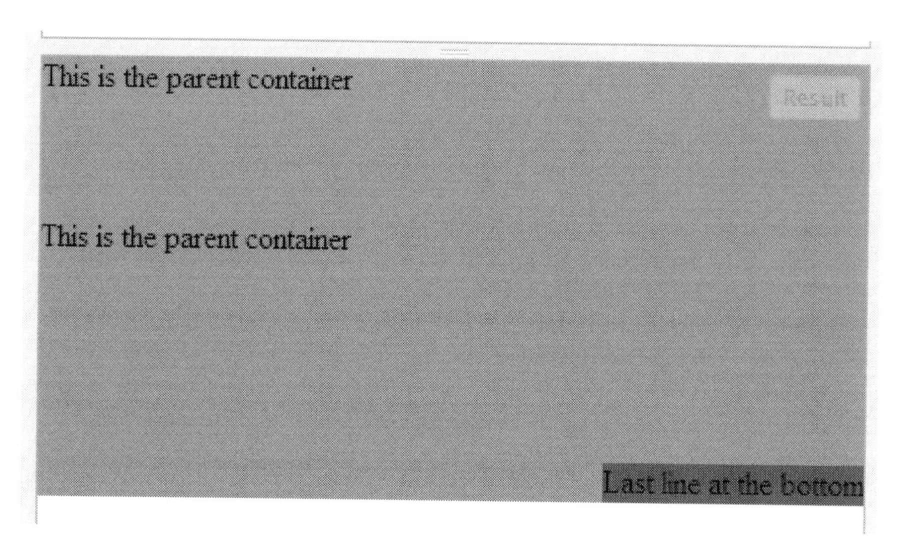


You can see the result in action with JSFiddle: http://jsfiddle.net/KA6YE/

# Having a menu at the top of the screen with inner anchor

Release Date: 24-Jun-13
Url: http://patrickdesjardins.com/blog/?post_type=post&p=1747

If you want to have a menu that will change what is selected depending on where you are on the screen, this can be done. First, you need to define your menu. Second, you need to have an anchor inside your webpage. This is done by setting ID to some element of your page. The example below has set ID to three links. We could have set the ID to H1 tag also.

```
<ul id="top-menu">
    <li class="active">
        <a href="#">Home</a>
    </li>
    <li>
        <a href="#header1">Header 1</a>
    </li>
    <li>
        <a href="#header2">Header 2</a>
    </li>
    <li>
        <a href="#header3">Header 3</a>
```

```
    </li>
</ul>

<a id="header1">This is my header 1</a>
<p>Text here ...</p>
<a id="header2">This is my header 2</a>
<p>Text here ...</p>
<a id="header3">This is my header 3</a>
<p>Text here ...</p>
```

The next step is to write some JavaScript code that will use the scroll position to know what is the active anchor. The JavaScript will also verify if a link is clicked.

```
var lastId,
    topMenu = $("#top-menu"),
    topMenuHeight = topMenu.outerHeight()+15,
    // All list items
    menuItems = topMenu.find("a"),
    // Anchors corresponding to menu items
    scrollItems = menuItems.map(function(){
        var item = $($(this).attr("href"));
        if (item.length) { return item; }
    });

// Bind click handler to menu items
// so we can get a fancy scroll animation
menuItems.click(function(e){
    var href = $(this).attr("href"),
        offsetTop = href === "#" ? 0 : $(href).offset().top-topMenuHeight+1;
    $('html, body').stop().animate({
        scrollTop: offsetTop
    }, 300);
    e.preventDefault();
});

// Bind to scroll
$(window).scroll(function(){
    // Get container scroll position
    var fromTop = $(this).scrollTop()+topMenuHeight;

    // Get id of current scroll item
    var cur = scrollItems.map(function(){
        if ($(this).offset().top < fromTop)
            return this;
    });
    // Get the id of the current element
    cur = cur[cur.length-1];
    var id = cur && cur.length ? cur[0].id : "";
```

```
    if (lastId !== id) {
        lastId = id;
        // Set/remove active class
        menuItems
          .parent().removeClass("active")
          .end().filter("[href=#"+id+"]").parent().addClass("active");
    }
});
```

Finally, the last step is to set the CSS to have a fixed menu that will stay at the top of the screen.

```
body {
    height: 6000px;
}

#top-menu {
    position: fixed;
    z-index: 1;
    background: white;
    left: 0;
    right: 0;
    top: 0;
}

#top-menu li {
    float: left;
}

#top-menu a {
    display: block;
    padding: 5px 25px 7px 25px;
    -webkit-transition: 1s all ease;
    -moz-transition: 1s all ease;
    transition: 1s all ease;
    border-top: 3px solid white;
    color: #666;
    text-decoration: none;
}

#top-menu a:hover {
    color: #000;
}

#top-menu li.active a {
    border-top: 3px solid #333;
    color: #333;
    font-weight: bold;
}
```

```
#header1{
    position: absolute;
    top: 400px;
}

#header2{
    position: absolute;
    top: 800px;
}

#header3{
    position: absolute;
    top: 1200px;
}
```

Here is an example; the code is pretty much the same as here. I have adapted the code here for this blog. The credit goes to the person who has posted it on JsFiddle: http://jsfiddle.net/mekwall/up4nu/. If you want to have an existing website that uses that technique, you can go see http://letsmake.github.com/bettertogether/ which uses this type of menu and effect.

# How to flip a div with JQuery and CSS3 animation

Release Date: 11-Jul-13
Url: http://patrickdesjardins.com/blog/?post_type=post&p=1884

If you are curious about what we will discuss in this blog post, you can visit JsFiddle for the code and an example of how to flip a div with CSS3 and some Javascript. First of all, here is the Html markup which defines two divisions which are each a side. Both sides contain a text. When using the button, it goes from one div to the other with an animation that flips the division. The goal is to simulate that the user clicked somewhere and we go behind a div.

```
<section id="zone">
    <div class="recto">
        Patrick
    </div>
    <div class="verso" style="display:none">
        Desjardins
    </div>
    <button id="btnFlip">Flip</button>
</section>
```

The second step is to define a style to all those Html markups. It also defines the animation that we use to make it look like we were flipping the div to go behind it.

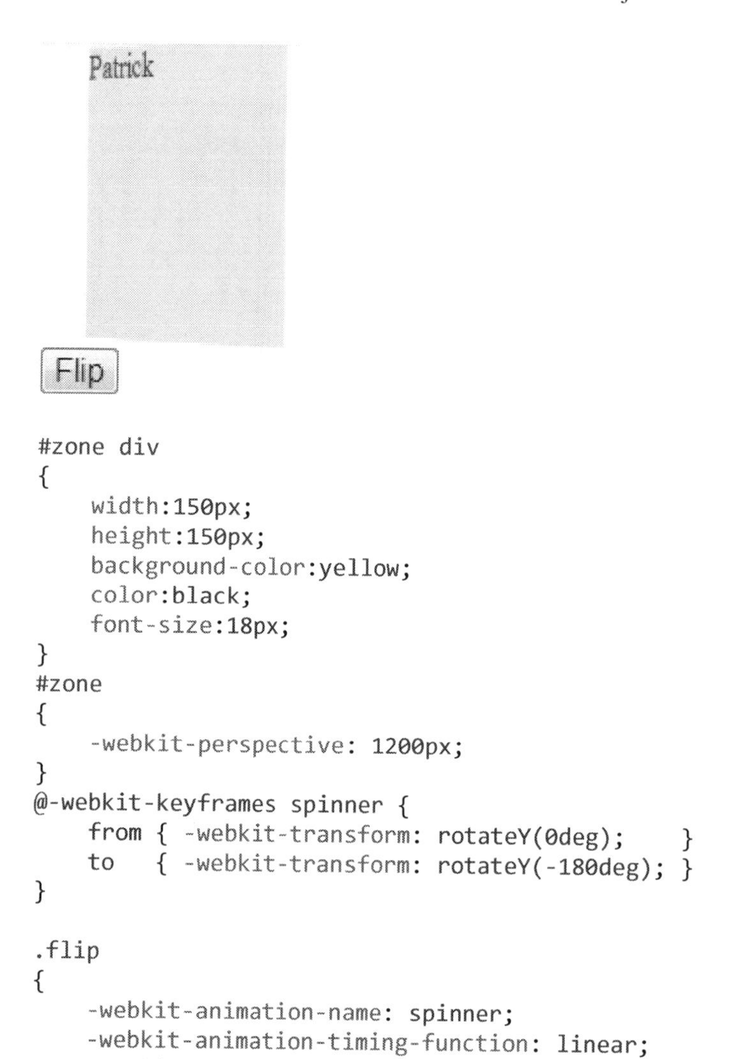


```
#zone div
{
    width:150px;
    height:150px;
    background-color:yellow;
    color:black;
    font-size:18px;
}
#zone
{
    -webkit-perspective: 1200px;
}
@-webkit-keyframes spinner {
    from { -webkit-transform: rotateY(0deg);    }
    to   { -webkit-transform: rotateY(-180deg); }
}

.flip
{
    -webkit-animation-name: spinner;
    -webkit-animation-timing-function: linear;
    -webkit-animation-iteration-count: 1;
    -webkit-animation-duration: 1s;
    -webkit-transform-style: preserve-3d;
    -webkit-transform-origin:50% 50%;
}
```

The first selector (*#zone div*) defines the final state of both divisions. This is required because we want to be able to flip something similar. Also, we will be able to flip back to the original state. Nonetheless, we define a perspective for the zone which will create during the animation a sense of depth. Finally, we specify animation key frames which do a 3D transformation by using the CSS3 feature called rotateY. This will create a flip at the Y axis. Also, the class "flip" is defined which specifies where the rotation occurs (in the middle of the div) and also the duration, which is 1 second in this example.

The last step is to define the action of the button. This action could have been placed directly onto the div but to not mix concepts here, we will attach a click event to a button.

```
$(document).on("click", "#btnFlip", function flipDiv() {
    $('#zone div:hidden').removeClass('flip')
    $('#zone div:visible').addClass('flip')
    .delay(600)
    .fadeOut(300, function () { $('#zone div:not(.flip)').fadeIn(300); });
});
```

What we aredoing here is that we remove from the hidden div the "flip" class and add it to the other division. This lest us havea continual movement of the class "flip" between the front and the back.

## Flipping a div (part 2)

Release Date: 15-Jul-13
Url: http://patrickdesjardins.com/blog/?post_type=post&p=1898

In a previous post, we have discussed how to flip a division. However, JavaScript was involved with CSS3 while only CSS3 could have been enough. For the curious, here is the code/JsFiddle (most of the code is not from me, but I cannot find the source).

First of all, the Html structure changes a little with two divisions with the same class ("side") within two divisions. One is the card container and the second is card. The card will be the one animated while the card container acts as a placeholder.

```
<div class="card-container">
    <div class="card">
        <div class="side"><img src="thisisanimage.png" /></div>
        <div class="side back">This is some text</div>
    </div>
</div>
```

As for the CSS, the perspective is also set to have a thirdd look of depth. This is what the card-container is for.

After, the card is assigned to have a transition of 1 second. Nothing is triggered until the card has a transformation applied, which is the case with the next CSS statement.

```
.card-container {
    -webkit-perspective: 600;
    margin-bottom: 20px;
```

```
    position: relative;
    width: 150px;
}

.card {
    position: absolute;
    -webkit-transform-style: preserve-3d;
    -webkit-transition: all 1s ease-in-out;
    width: 100%;
}
.card:hover {
    -webkit-transform: rotateY(180deg);
}
.card .side {
    -webkit-backface-visibility: hidden;
    position: absolute;
    width: 100%;
}
.card .back {
    color: #404853;
    font-size: 14px;
    font-weight: bold;
    line-height: 150px;
    text-align: center;
    -webkit-transform: rotateY(180deg);
    background-color:yellow;
}
```

The ":hover" statement raises the transition to be executed (with the 1 second time). As you may have noticed, the use of "backface-visibility" lets the rendering not display the back of the div but instead display the other division which rotates at the same time. This creates the illusion that we are seeing the back of the division, but in fact, we are showing the other division. This is possible because of the position set to absolute. This puts both divisions over each other.

## Modifying BootStrap Tab Control for Extra Small Device

Release Date: 27-Mar-14
Url: http://patrickdesjardins.com/blog/?post_type=post&p=3402

If you are using **BootStrap** and the **Tab** control you may have a weird rendering for Extra Small Device (under 768 pixels).

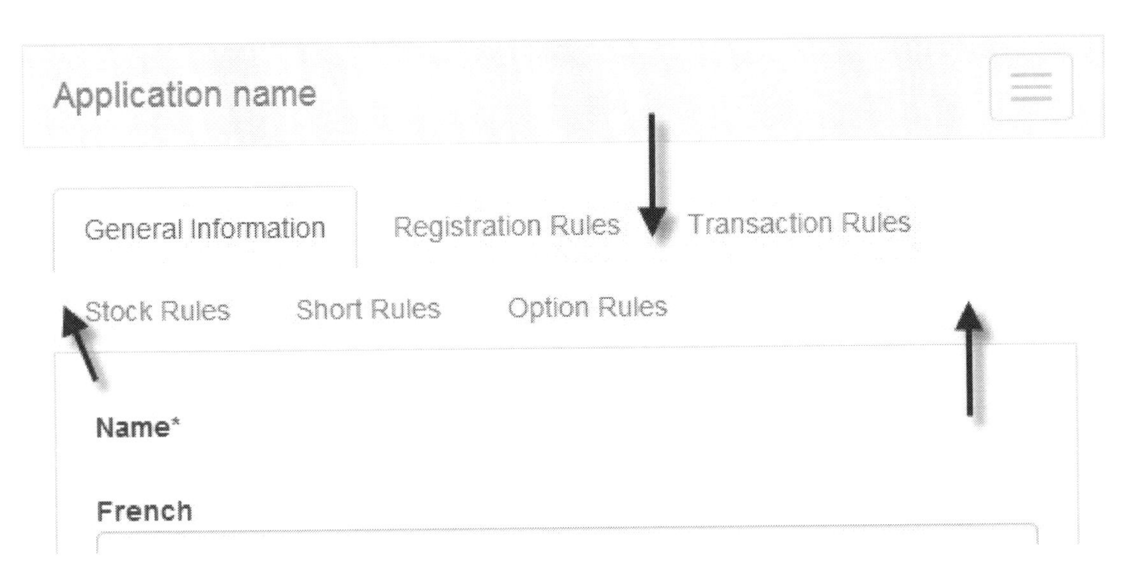


To fix this, it is possible for you to add this code. It removes the borders and removes the background.

```
/*For smaller device, tab control should not appear*/
@media (max-width: 767px) {
    .nav-tabs > li {
        float:none;
        border:1px solid #dddddd;
    }
    .nav-tabs > li.active > a{
        border:none;
    }
    .nav > li > a:hover, .nav > li > a:focus,
    .nav > li > a:hover, .nav > li > a:focus,
    .nav-tabs > li.active > a, .nav-tabs > li.active > a:hover, .nav-tabs >
li.active > a:focus
     {
        background:none;
        border:none;
    }

}
```

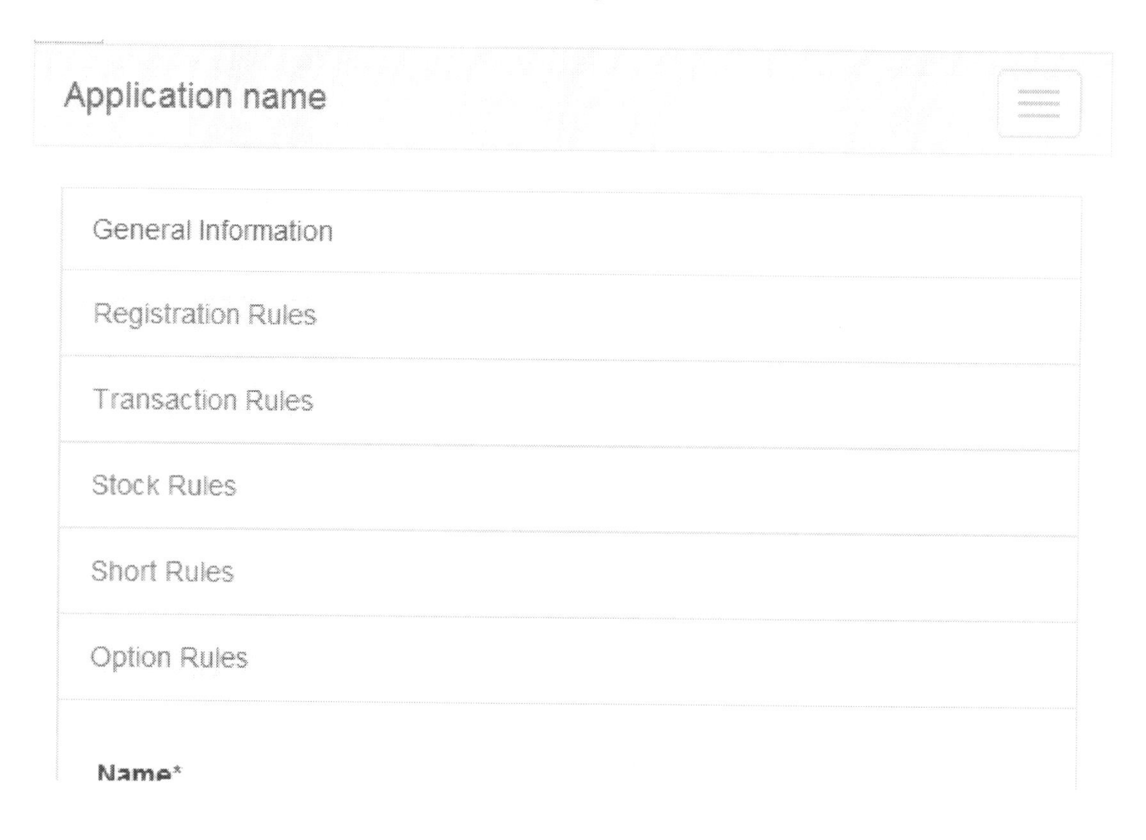


The end result is much better than the default behavior and the solution is simple and clean. I hope that it helps someone.

# JQuery Calendar And Input-Group Of BootStrap Problem With Z-Order

Release Date: 28-Aug-14
Url: http://patrickdesjardins.com/blog/?post_type=post&p=3672

BootStrap has a class named **input-group** that allows you to have an input box with a button before or after. The problem is that it sets all inputs with a z-index to 2. JQuery Calendar is bound to control, like input box. If you have multiple rows of input, and if one of them is bound to JQuery Calendar, the result is having a calendar behind a text box.

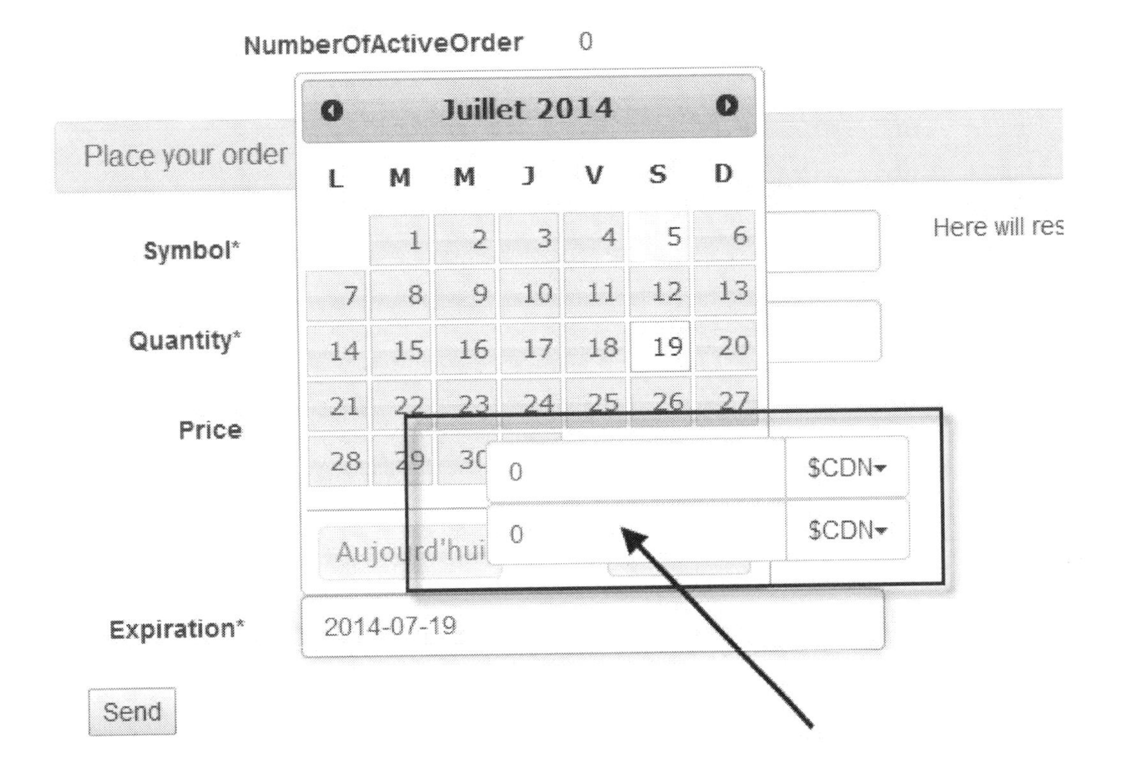


To fix this issue, we need to set JQuery Calendar over the z-index, over 2. This is a rare occasion where the !important keyword is mandatory.

```
/*Fix a bug with BootStrap that set input within input-group with a z-order to 2.
   This makes the JQuery Calendar appear behind the input box*/
.ui-datepicker{ z-index: 3 !important;}
```

There is no need to have the z-index with a huge value.

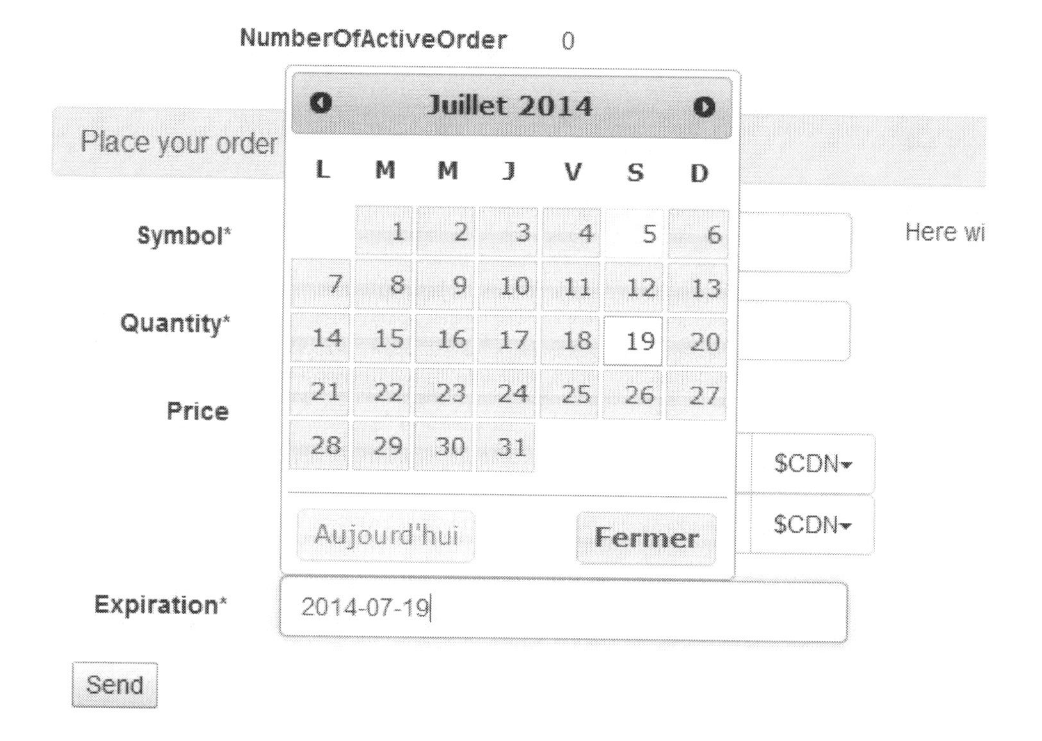


The fix is simple and short and was easy to find. The trick was to check with any browser developer tool and verify the div of the calendar to figure out the z-index.

# 6. ENTITY FRAMEWORK

This chapter groups every post written during 2013 and 2014 about Entity Framework. Like all chapters in this book, every article is a snapshot of a real scenario that has a high probability of happening if you are using these technologies. You will notice that every article that has been chosen to be included in this book contains the release date to identify when it was written. A permanent link is also provided that allows you to go in and read updates and comments. Feel free to go on the website to add your own comment if you wish.

## How to rebuild the database from Entities with Membership table

Release Date: 09-Jan-13
Url: http://patrickdesjardins.com/blog/?post_type=post&p=1546

If you are using Entity Framework with **membership**, you may come into situations where you need to rebuild your database because you are changing your models. In that case you want to also have the membership tables back when you are rebuilding your database. Here is a way to do it.

First of all, you need to open the **Package Manager Console**. This console opens a console where you will be able to write commands to the Entity Framework Migration Tools.

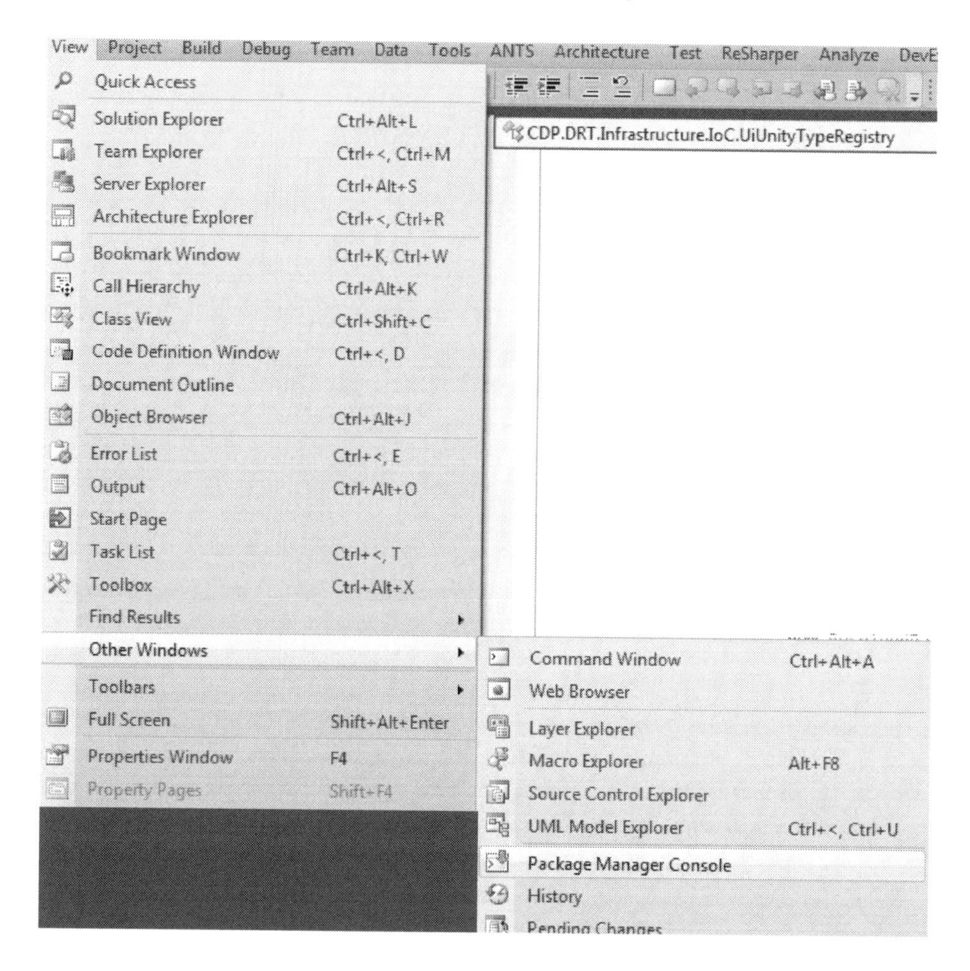


The primary command to be used is **Update-Database**. In fact, I always prefer to use "Update-Database -Verbose -Force"

The verbose option lets you see all operations that are done which can be helpful in case of a problem. The force drops all tables instead of altering them. This can be useful in situations where the structure changes a lot.

# The object cannot be deleted because it was not found in the ObjectStateManager

Release Date: 15-Feb-13
Url: http://patrickdesjardins.com/blog/?post_type=post&p=1844

The object cannot be deleted because it was not found in the ObjectStateManager. This message means that the entity is not attached to the database context (**DbContext**). You need to attach first the entity to the **IDbSet** of the **DbContext**. From here, you can remove the entity.

```
if (!_set.Local.Contains(entity))
{
    _set.Attach(entity);
}
_set.Remove(entity);
```

That is it! We check if the entity is already attached. If it is, then we do not need to do anything. Otherwise, we attach. Attaching will take the primary key of the entity and delete this it even if it is not fully loaded. The code above could be in a *Remove* method.

## Entity Framework and the error The DELETE statement conflicted with the REFERENCE constraint.

Release Date: 19-Feb-13
Url: http://patrickdesjardins.com/blog/?post_type=post&p=1846

Entity Framework can raise an error concerning a conflict with reference when deleting an entity. One of these errors is the following one.

*The DELETE statement conflicted with the REFERENCE constraint.*

To solve this issue we need to **delete cascade** instead of a simple remove. We have seen in a previous post how to use delete in cascade with Entity Framework. In short, you have to specify the many side to the other side (required or optional) and then specify the delete cascade statement with the true parameter.

```
...HasMany(e => e.ParentDetails)
   .WithOptional(s => s.Parent)
   .WillCascadeOnDelete(true);
```

## Using IDbSetExtensions.AddOrUpdate with Migration Tool fail

Release Date: 25-Feb-13
Url: http://patrickdesjardins.com/blog/?post_type=post&p=1857

Using **IDbSetExtensions.AddOrUpdate** with Migration Tool fail if you are using a custom **IDbSet**.

*Unable to call public, instance method AddOrUpdate on derived IDbSet type 'DataAccessLayer.Database.FilteredDbSet`1[Model.Workout]'. Method not found.*

The exception above is raised when using *PM> update-database -verbose -force*. The class **FilteredDbSet** inherits **IDbSet** and should be able to use the method **AddOrUpdate** which is pretty useful when seeding data. But the exception raises and the reason is that it tries to get the method definition with a parameter. If we decompile the code, we can see inside the else statement the second line that calls from the *type* variable the *GetMethod*.

```
public static void AddOrUpdate<TEntity>(this IDbSet<TEntity> set
                        , params TEntity[] entities) where TEntity : class
{
  RuntimeFailureMethods.Requires(set != null, (string) null, "set != null");
  RuntimeFailureMethods.Requires(entities != null, (string) null, "entities !=
null");

  DbSet<TEntity> set1 = set as DbSet<TEntity>;
  if (set1 != null)
  {
    InternalSet<TEntity> internalSet = (InternalSet<TEntity>) set1.InternalSet;
    IDbSetExtensions.AddOrUpdate<TEntity>(set1
                    , IDbSetExtensions.GetKeyProperties<TEntity>(typeof (TEntity),
                    internalSet), entities);
  }
  else
  {
    Type type = set.GetType();
    MethodInfo method = type.GetMethod("AddOrUpdate", new Type[1]
    {
      typeof (TEntity[])
    });
    if (method == (MethodInfo) null)
      throw
System.Data.Entity.Resources.Error.UnableToDispatchAddOrUpdate((object) type);
    method.Invoke((object) set, (object[]) new TEntity[1][]
    {
      entities
    });
  }
}
```

Instead, we will call the **GetMethod** without the second parameter and create our own

AddOrUpdate method.

```
public static void AddOrUpdate<TEntity>(this IDbSet<TEntity> set
                                , params TEntity[] entities) where TEntity : class
{
  var set1 = set as DbSet<TEntity>;
  if (set1 != null)
  {
    System.Data.Entity.Migrations.IDbSetExtensions.AddOrUpdate(set,entities);
  }
  else
  {
    Type type = set.GetType();
    MethodInfo method = type.GetMethod("AddOrUpdate");

    if (method == null)
      throw new Exception("");
    var data = new object[entities.Length];
    for (int i = 0; i < entities.Length; i++)
    {
      data[i] = entities[i];
    }
    method.Invoke(set, data);
  }
}
```

Also, you can see that we call Invoke by passing a single array of an object. This is required to be able to call the method correctly. The trick is to create the extension and to use it instead of **IDbSetExtension** and you will be able to call the method without any exception.

## How to save multiple entities in inheritance at the same time with Entity Framework 5.0

Release Date: 06-Mar-13
Url: http://patrickdesjardins.com/blog/?post_type=post&p=1904

Not every page should be CRUD. In the case of our enterprise example (previous post), a software that handles workout exercise, we had first created a CRUD application. So, the user had to create the workout in one page, then go into another one to create sessions and then another to associate every exercise into a session. In fact, for every session of exercise the user had to go into a page, associate it with an existing exercise and then go back to the list and do it again and again. So, if you create a new workout with five sessions (for every day of the week) you have to go to seven pages for every exercise. That means that if we have 10 exercises per training we had to go into 57 pages! With the proposed solution to handle all exercises in the same page we only have one page to go to. Here is the database to inform you concerning the schema before going with Entity Framework to save multiple objects at the same time.

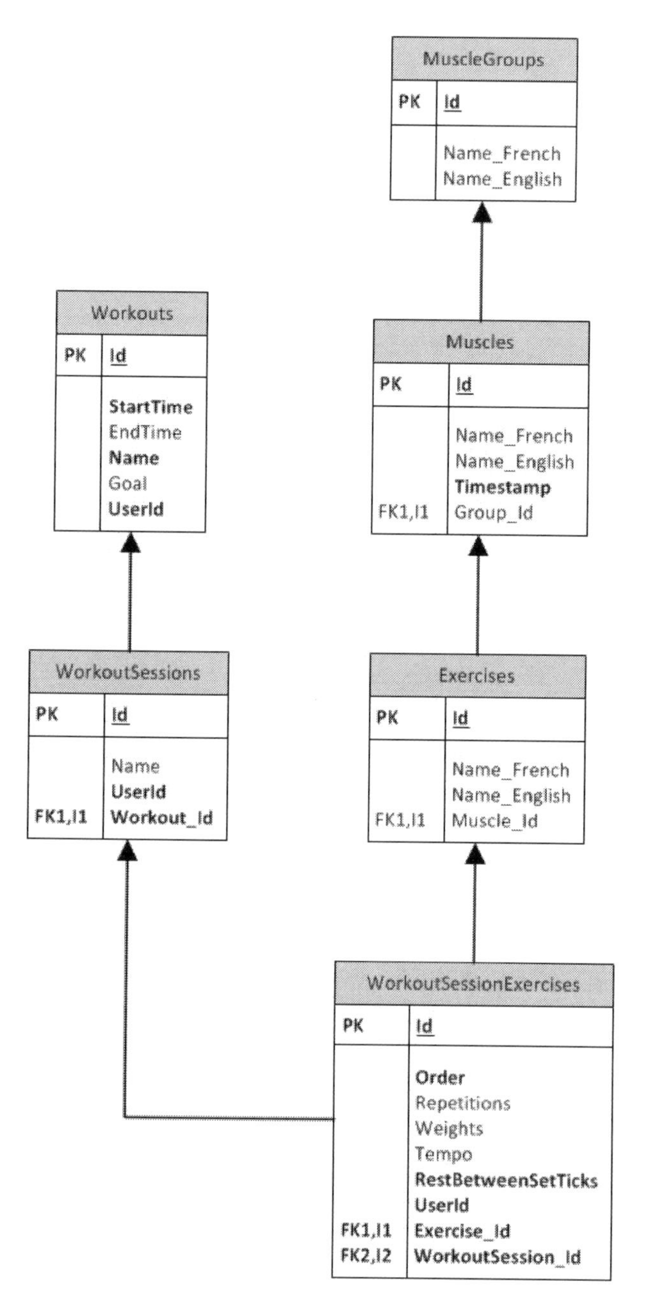

I am not displaying the whole code for creating a Workout from A to Z but concentrated on the goal of this article, which is saving multiple entities. The entity we want to save is the one called "Workout" and we want to save the sessions and the exercises within the same page. We won't create a new exercise from this page, or a muscle or a group of muscles. But, we will use them.

The first step is to get from the form all information. I am not explaining in detail here because there are multiple ways to do it. Let's say that our Model is fully loaded. When I say Model, it is the Workout class loaded with WorkoutSessions and WorkoutSessionExercises. It does not mean that those objects have all scalar properties loaded. For example, we may have only the exercises ID and not the name of this one. In fact, you shouldn't have everything loaded because the form should not let you edit exercise name. So, we only pass from the form to the controller information concerning the unique identifier (in our case IDs) and some other information like the Order of the exercise (see the class WorkoutSessionExercises).

From there, the saving process starts. The controller should call the service layer, which calls the repository. The big work starts right here. The first thing to do is to set up a transaction scope. The main reason is that we need to delete exercises that the user might have removed when at another time we want to add new exercises. We should remove all unused exercises first and then add everything. Otherwise, it will not able to differentiate in the data context which one is removed, and which one is added. The use of transaction scope creates a protection if something goes wrong in the later stage that nothing will be deleted. The transaction scope used is the same one that was used in the past with **Ado.Net**, in fact, Entity Framework uses Ado.Net behind it, and it is not a problem to still use it. Watch out! You will need to have **MSDTC** service running because multiple connections to the database will be created.

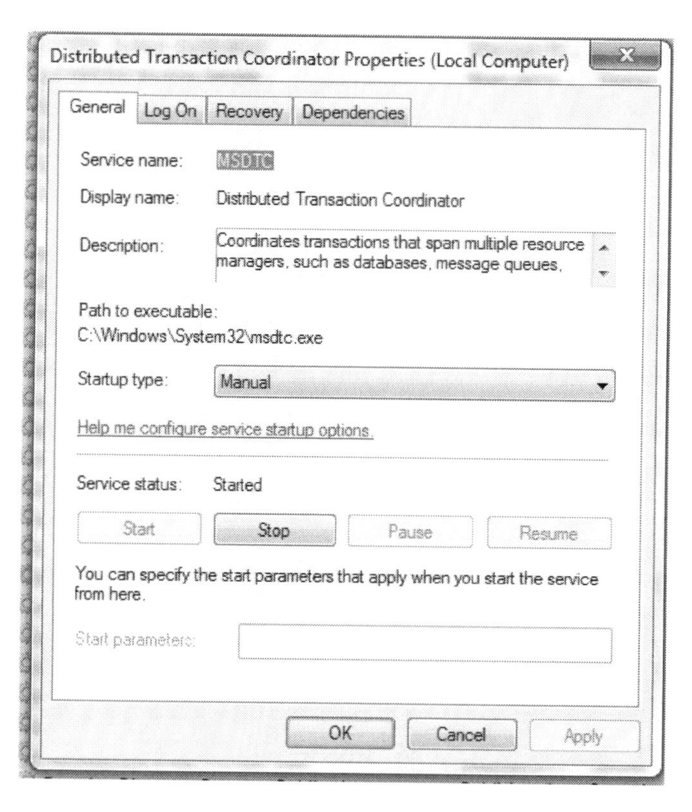


```
public int Update(Workout entity)
{
  using (var scope = new TransactionScope())
  {
    // Remove

    // Insert
    scope.Complete();
  }
}
```

This is how the code should be — a transaction that is before and after the remove instruction and insert intruction. In our case, the code looks like this:

```
public int Update(Workout entity)
{
  int count = -1;
  using (base.DatabaseContext.RemoveValidation())
  {
    using (var scope = new TransactionScope())
    {
      RemoveWorkoutSessionExercisesNotUsedAnymore(entity);
```

```
      SetupWorkoutForRepository(entity);
      DatabaseContext.UpdateOwnable(entity);
      var ent = DatabaseContext.SetOwnable<Workout>()
                          .Local.SingleOrDefault(d => d.Id == entity.Id);
      DatabaseContext.Entry(ent).CurrentValues.SetValues(entity);
      count = DatabaseContext.SaveChanges();
      scope.Complete();
    }
  }
  return count;

}
```

As you can see, a few things are added. First, the DatabaseContext is using a *USING* with RemoveValidation method. This is a custom method that removes temporarily all validations by Entity Framework. The code calls *ValidateOnSaveEnabled* and sets it to false and puts it back to true once the scope of the using is over. This is not a requirement for you, but I left it there for the reason that you may have to do it. The justification is quite simple. When you are saving from partial data that contain only the primary key (ID) and you attach these you may have some error stating that some required field isn't provided. If you tell Entity Framework not to check the validation, you won't have this trouble.

Second, you see that we call *RemoveWorkoutSessionExercisesNotUsedAnymore*(…) followed by *SetupWorkoutForRepository*(…). The *Remove* function does a query to the database to get the list of existing entities and compares with the one provided by the form (from the web page). All entities that were there and that are not anymore are removed.

```
private void RemoveWorkoutSessionExercisesNotUsedAnymore(Workout entity)
{
  var listWorkoutSessionExerciseThatStillRemain =
entity.Sessions.SelectMany(d=>d.WorkoutSessionExercises).Select(d=>d.Id).ToArray()
;
  var workoutSessionExerciseFromDatabase =
DatabaseContext.SetOwnable<WorkoutSessionExercise>()
    .Where(d=>!listWorkoutSessionExerciseThatStillRemain.Contains(d.Id)
                && d.WorkoutSession.Workout.Id == entity.Id)
    ;
  foreach (var sessionExercise in workoutSessionExerciseFromDatabase)
  {
    DatabaseContext.SetOwnable<WorkoutSessionExercise>().Remove(sessionExercise);
  }
  DatabaseContext.SaveChanges();
}
```

The code is good for a new and a modified Workout entity. In the case of a new entity, the list of workout session exercises from the database will be empty and nothing will be removed. In the case of a modified Workout that contains workout session exercises, those are removed if they are not found in the list of IDs that the user uses. At the end, we call SaveChange() which commits the delete statement to the SQL Server. Of course, since we are in a transaction, nothing will be really committed yet.

Third, the *SetupWorkoutForRepository* is called. This method is the heart of the work for modifying an entity with multiple children objects. Once the setup is done, the database is saved and the transaction is completed. At this final moment, every delete and insert is commited to the SQL Server Database.

Let's take a look at the setup method which prepares the model class to be saved by Entity Framework.

```
private void SetupWorkoutForRepository(Workout entity)
{
  if (entity.Sessions != null)
  {
    foreach (var workoutSession in entity.Sessions)
    {
      if (workoutSession.WorkoutSessionExercises != null)
      {
        foreach (var workoutSessionExercise in
workoutSession.WorkoutSessionExercises)
        {
          if (workoutSessionExercise.Exercise != null)
          {
            if (workoutSessionExercise.Exercise.Id == BaseModel.NOT_INITIALIZED)
            {
              workoutSessionExercise.Exercise = null; //Should never go there
            }
            else
            {
              if (DatabaseContext.Set<Exercise>().Local
                         .All(e => e.Id != workoutSessionExercise.Exercise.Id))
              {
                workoutSessionExercise.Exercise = DatabaseContext.Set<Exercise>()
                                          .Attach(workoutSessionExercise.Exercise);
              }
              else
              {
                workoutSessionExercise.Exercise =
DatabaseContext.Set<Exercise>().Local.Single(e => e.Id ==
                                               workoutSessionExercise.Exercise.Id);
              }
            }
          }

          if (workoutSessionExercise.Id == BaseModel.NOT_INITIALIZED)
```

```
          {
            //New workout session exercise
            DatabaseContext.SetOwnable<WorkoutSessionExercise>()
                                                   .Add(workoutSessionExercise);
          }
          else
          {
            if (DatabaseContext.Set<WorkoutSessionExercise>().Local
                                    .All(e => e.Id != workoutSessionExercise.Id))
            {
              DatabaseContext.SetOwnable<WorkoutSessionExercise>()
                                                   .Attach(workoutSessionExercise);
            }
          }
        }

        if (workoutSession.Id == BaseModel.NOT_INITIALIZED)
        {
            DatabaseContext.SetOwnable<WorkoutSession>().Add(workoutSession);
        }
        else
        {
          var dbEntry = DatabaseContext.SetOwnable<WorkoutSession>().Local
                               .SingleOrDefault(e => e.Id == workoutSession.Id);
          if (dbEntry==null)
          {
            dbEntry = DatabaseContext.SetOwnable<WorkoutSession>()
                                                   .Attach(workoutSession);
          }
        }

        foreach (var workoutSessionExercise in
workoutSession.WorkoutSessionExercises)
        {
          workoutSessionExercise.WorkoutSession =
                              DatabaseContext.SetOwnable<WorkoutSession>()
                             .Local.SingleOrDefault(d=>d.Id == workoutSession.Id);
        }
      }
    }
  }
}
```

I will go through the whole method because almost all possibles cases are treated. First, a Workout contains a list of sessions. Most of the time, this collection will not be null and we will start looping through them. The same mechanism is executed for the WorkoutSessionExercises collection. Since, in our case, exercises aren't deleted or modified directly into this screen, we have some cases simplified. This is why we know that the exercise cannot be null. But, we know that the user can set an exercise to a session. Two scenarios occur. The first one is that it is the first time we use this exercise. If that is the case, then we need to set Entity Framework an attached object that will represent the exercise. This is done with the line

```
workoutSessionExercise.Exercise = DatabaseContext.Set<Exercise>()
                                        .Attach(workoutSessionExercise.Exercise);
```

The second one is when the exercise has already been used. So, it has already been attached or has been added. We use the Local property to get the instance of the entity from Entity Framework and this gives us the certitude that we are working on the same Exercise.

```
workoutSessionExercise.Exercise = DatabaseContext.Set<Exercise>().Local
                   .Single(e => e.Id == workoutSessionExercise.Exercise.Id);
```

At the end, we do the same for the workout session exercise. Why do we do exercise first and then do the exercise session? Because attaching or adding the exercise session would result in attaching their sub property which is not what we want because we want to control whether or not we attach the entity. We want to control what is attached and added and this is why we need to attach stuff from the bottom up.

Also, you may want to save some properties and not everything. In that case you can select the property and indicate if it has changed or not.

```
DatabaseContext.Entry(dbEntry).Property(d => d.Name).IsModified = false;
```

This is an example that we could have set for the WorkoutSession if we wanted not to change the WorkoutSession name.

To conclude, it is possible to save multiple objects that are composed within a single Entity Framework data context. This approach is not without negative effect. You will soon realize that it requires some time to code every attachment correctly and depending on how your objects are composed and how you use Entity Framework (with or without ID for each foreign key, with or without loading the full graph) your configuration will change.

# Using a FilteredDbSet with Entity Framework to have dynamic Filtering

Release Date: 20-Mar-13
Url: http://patrickdesjardins.com/blog/?post_type=post&p=2019

If you are using an application that requires having your user own data and not let other see or edit it, you need to specify to each of your entities a user ID to whom the entity belongs. All my entities that belong to a user inherit from **IUserOwnable**. This interface forces the entity to have a UserId.

```
public interface IUserOwnable
{
    int UserId { get; set; }
}
```

From here, when I want to get the list of entities of my users I just need to specify in the where clause the logged user ID and Entity Framework get me all entities that belong to this user. The following example shows you how to get all workouts from the logged user.

```
public override IQueryable<Workout> GetAll()
{
    return DatabaseContext.Set<Workout>().Where(e=>e.UserId == loggedUserId);
}
```

The problem is that you need to set the UserId every time. This can lead to a problem of security if a developer forgets to add the condition. It's also a pain to repeat this code everywhere. This is why a better way to do it is to have a **FilteredDbSet** which will automatically add this condition. Here is the FilteredDbSet class.

```
using System;
using System.Collections;
using System.ComponentModel;
using System.Linq;
using System.Linq.Expressions;

public class FilteredDbSet<TEntity> : IDbSet<TEntity>, IOrderedQueryable<TEntity>,
IListSource where TEntity : class
{
    private readonly DbSet<TEntity> _set;
    private readonly Action<TEntity> _initializeEntity;
    private readonly Expression<Func<TEntity, bool>> _filter;

    public FilteredDbSet(DbContext context, Expression<Func<TEntity, bool>>
filter, Action<TEntity> initializeEntity)
        : this(context.Set<TEntity>(), filter, initializeEntity)
    {
    }

    public IQueryable<TEntity> Include(string path)
    {
        return _set.Include(path).Where(_filter).AsQueryable();
    }
```

```
    private FilteredDbSet(DbSet<TEntity> set, Expression<Func<TEntity, bool>>
filter, Action<TEntity> initializeEntity)
    {
        _set = set;
        _filter = filter;
        _initializeEntity = initializeEntity;
    }

    public IQueryable<TEntity> Unfiltered()
    {
        return _set;
    }

    public TEntity Add(TEntity entity)
    {
        DoInitializeEntity(entity);
        return _set.Add(entity);
    }
    public void AddOrUpdate(TEntity entity)
    {
        DoInitializeEntity(entity);
        _set.AddOrUpdate(entity);
    }
    public TEntity Attach(TEntity entity)
    {
        DoInitializeEntity(entity);
        return _set.Attach(entity);
    }

    public TDerivedEntity Create<TDerivedEntity>() where TDerivedEntity : class,
TEntity
    {
        var entity = _set.Create<TDerivedEntity>();
        DoInitializeEntity(entity);
        return entity;
    }

    public TEntity Create()
    {
        var entity = _set.Create();
        DoInitializeEntity(entity);
        return entity;
    }

    public TEntity Find(params object[] keyValues)
    {
        var entity = _set.Find(keyValues);
        if (entity == null)
            return null;
```

```
    return entity;
}

public TEntity Remove(TEntity entity)
{
    if (!_set.Local.Contains(entity))
    {
        _set.Attach(entity);
    }
    return _set.Remove(entity);
}


public ObservableCollection<TEntity> Local
{
    get { return _set.Local; }
}

IEnumerator<TEntity> IEnumerable<TEntity>.GetEnumerator()
{
    return _set.Where(_filter).GetEnumerator();
}

IEnumerator IEnumerable.GetEnumerator()
{
    return _set.Where(_filter).GetEnumerator();
}

Type IQueryable.ElementType
{
    get { return typeof(TEntity); }
}

Expression IQueryable.Expression
{
    get
    {
        return _set.Where(_filter).Expression;
    }
}

IQueryProvider IQueryable.Provider
{
    get
    {
        return _set.AsQueryable().Provider;
    }
}
```

```
    bool IListSource.ContainsListCollection
    {
        get { return false; }
    }

    IList IListSource.GetList()
    {
        throw new InvalidOperationException();
    }

    void DoInitializeEntity(TEntity entity)
    {
        if (_initializeEntity != null)
            _initializeEntity(entity);
    }

    public DbSqlQuery<TEntity> SqlQuery(string sql, params object[] parameters)
    {
        return _set.SqlQuery(sql, parameters);
    }
}
```

From here, you just need to call the **DbSet** that is filtered instead of the default one.

```
public override IQueryable<Workout> GetAll()
{
    return DatabaseContext.SetOwnable<Workout>();
}
```

Of course, the DatabaseContext is your class that inherited from DbContext. The SetOwnable method will call the FilteredDbSet.

```
public IDbSet<TEntity> SetOwnable<TEntity>() where TEntity : class, IUserOwnable
{
    return new FilteredDbSet<TEntity>(this, entity => entity.UserId ==
                                        CurrentUser.UserId
                                    , entity => entity.UserId = CurrentUser.UserId);
}
```

As you can see, we create a **FilteredDbSet** and assign the user ID with the CurrentUser, which is the logged user.

# AsNoTracking() to force your data context to get everything from the database

Release Date: 28-Mar-13
Url: http://patrickdesjardins.com/blog/?post_type=post&p=1974

You can specify Entity Framework to get everything back from the database instead of using what has been already loaded from the database. A use case would be that you attach an entity from the web form and you save everything. You may return the view from the entity loaded but this will not get the full object if it has been attached previously.

```
public Workout Get(int id)
{
    return DatabaseContext
            .SetOwnable<Workout>()
            .Include(x => x.Sessions)
            .Include("Sessions.WorkoutSessionExercises")
            .Include("Sessions.WorkoutSessionExercises.Exercise")
            .AsNoTracking()
            .Single(c => c.Id == id);
}
```

With the addition of **AsNoTracking**, the information does not come from the local storage of the database context but from the database every time.

# SQL Tracing without having SQL Server Tools

Release Date: 11-Apr-13
Url: http://patrickdesjardins.com/blog/?post_type=post&p=1999

It is always a good idea to be able to see what is happening behind when you are using ORM, like Entity Framework. If you have the possibility to get the full-blown **SQL Server** with tools, than you have the **SQL Profiler** that can tell you every query executed. Unfortunately, if you are using the SQL Express Edition, you won't have the SQL Profiler available.

However, you still can get thoses queries output into a log file with the SQL Express edition. First of all, be sure to stop the SQL Express Service. This can be done by going into the Services.msc

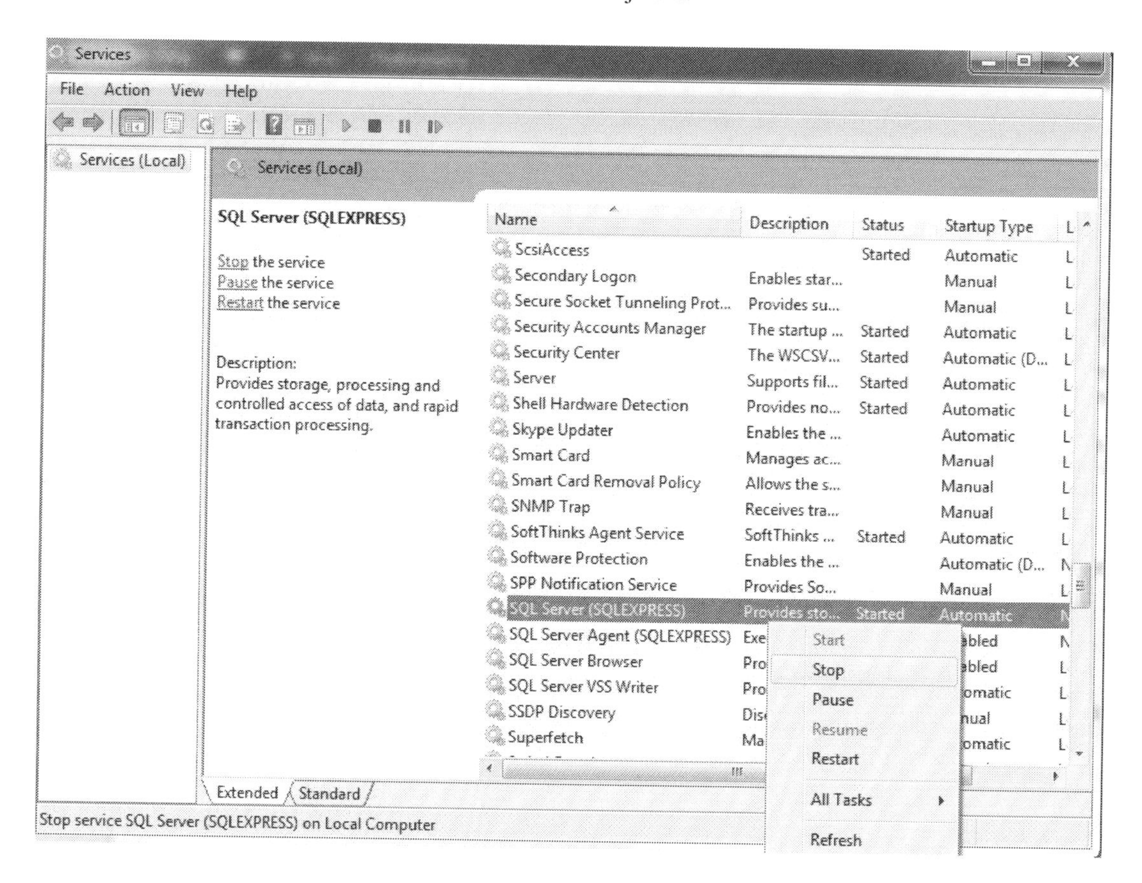


Or you can use the command prompt with the command "net stop" with the parameter of the service which should be "MSSQL$SqlExpress." Of course, this must be done with administrator privileges.It would look like this:

```
Administrator: C:\Windows\System32\cmd.exe

Microsoft Windows [Version 6.1.7601]
Copyright (c) 2009 Microsoft Corporation.  All rights reserved.

C:\Windows\system32>net stop MSSQL$SqlExpress
The SQL Server (SQLEXPRESS) service is stopping.
The SQL Server (SQLEXPRESS) service was stopped successfully.
```

To enable the service to run again, but this time with the log, we need to start the SQL Service with the flag "/T4032".

```
net start MSSQL$SQLEXPRESS /T4032
```

The last thing to do is open the **SQL Server Management Studio** and execute the following command:

```
dbcc traceon(3605, -1)
```

From here, you just need to consult the log file. With SQL Server 2012 Express edition on a Windows 7 OS, you will find the log file here:

*C:\Program Files\Microsoft SQL Server\MSSQL11.SQLEXPRESS\MSSQL\Log*

## How to update a specific field of your entity with a generic method and Entity Framework

Release Date: 16-Apr-13
Url: http://patrickdesjardins.com/blog/?post_type=post&p=2006

If you are using **Entity Framework** with a repository layer which has the basic method like Get, Update, Insert (or Add) and Delete you are already in a good position. But what if you want to update a single property without having to load the whole entity from the database? If you have only the primary key (ID) of your entity and the value of the property you want to update, you may want to simply update the field with a where clause with the ID. In SQL, we would create the following query.

```
update [dbo].[WorkoutSessions]
set [Name] = 'New Name',
    [Order] = 1
where ([Id] = 123)
```

With **Entity Framework**, you could create a single method like "UpdateNameAndOrder" but this would end up with a lot of update methods if you needed to have partial update among many properties. A better approach would be to specify which properties we want to update.

```
public int Update(T entity, Expression<Func<T, object>>[] properties)
{
  DatabaseContext.Entry(entity).State = EntityState.Unchanged;
  foreach (var property in properties)
  {
    var propertyName = ExpressionHelper.GetExpressionText(property);
    DatabaseContext.Entry(entity).Property(propertyName).IsModified = true;
  }
  return DatabaseContext.SaveChangesWithoutValidation();
}
```

The code above is in the **BaseRepository** class of the project described in the "Enterprise project" (http://tinyurl.com/nzcwv5y). As you can see, it takes as its second parameter an **expression of a function**. This will let us use this method by specifying in a Lambda expression which property to update.

```
...Update(Model, d=>d.Name);
//or
...Update(Model, d=>d.Name, d=>d.SecondProperty, d=>d.AndSoOn);
```

As you can see, the Update method first line changed the state to **Unchanged**. We could have usied Attach of the IDbSet but since in the Enterprise project we have special sets, a way to simply go directly to the DbSet of the current database context is to go directly to the **Entry**. Next, we loop all properties chosen. Inside the loop, we are using a **System.Web.Mvc** namespace. We could have used the code of **GetExpressionText** without having to use this namespace. Here is the code if you do not want a reference to this dll.

```
public static string GetExpressionText(LambdaExpression expression)
{
  Stack<string> stack = new Stack<string>();
  Expression expression1 = expression.Body;
  while (expression1 != null)
  {
    if (expression1.NodeType == ExpressionType.Call)
    {
      MethodCallExpression methodCallExpression =
                                      (MethodCallExpression) expression1;
      if (ExpressionHelper.IsSingleArgumentIndexer(
                                      (Expression) methodCallExpression))
      {
stack.Push(ExpressionHelper.GetIndexerInvocation(Enumerable.Single<Expression>(
          (IEnumerable<Expression>) methodCallExpression.Arguments),
        Enumerable.ToArray<ParameterExpression>((IEnumerable<ParameterExpression>)
        expression.Parameters)));
        expression1 = methodCallExpression.Object;
      }
      else
        break;
    }
    else if (expression1.NodeType == ExpressionType.ArrayIndex)
    {
      BinaryExpression binaryExpression = (BinaryExpression) expression1;
      stack.Push(ExpressionHelper.GetIndexerInvocation(
                      binaryExpression.Right,
                Enumerable.ToArray<ParameterExpression>((IEnumerable<Parameter
                Expression>) expression.Parameters)));
      expression1 = binaryExpression.Left;
    }
```

```
    else if (expression1.NodeType == ExpressionType.MemberAccess)
    {
      MemberExpression memberExpression = (MemberExpression) expression1;
      stack.Push("." + memberExpression.Member.Name);
      expression1 = memberExpression.Expression;
    }
    else if (expression1.NodeType == ExpressionType.Parameter)
    {
      stack.Push(string.Empty);
      expression1 = (Expression) null;
    }
    else
      break;
  }
  if (stack.Count > 0 && string.Equals(stack.Peek(), ".model"
                                        , StringComparison.OrdinalIgnoreCase))

    stack.Pop();
  if (stack.Count <= 0)
    return string.Empty;
  return Enumerable.Aggregate<string>((IEnumerable<string>) stack
                    , (Func<string, string, string>) ((left, right) => left +
                right)).TrimStart(new char[1]
  {
    '.'
  });
}
```

What it does is take from the lambda the name of the property selected. The last thing the update method is doing is saving without executing the validation on the entity. This is required since not the whole entity is loaded. Some properties required might not be loaded which would result in validation exception. To be honest, an improvement would be to execute the validation for the updated property, but for the sake of simplicity we will stay smaller.

To conclude, it is possible to update an entity in a generic way without having to preload the object or update all its properties.

## How to include correctly a property within a collection when using Entity Framework code first

Release Date: 10-May-13
Url: http://patrickdesjardins.com/blog/?post_type=post&p=2052

I have several examples (http://tinyurl.com/ovzthap) in this website that include a string with the property when it is a property inside a collection of my main entity. Here is one example:

```
return DatabaseContext
            .SetOwnable<Workout>()
            .Include(x => x.Sessions)
            .Include("Sessions.WorkoutSessionExercises")
            .Include("Sessions.WorkoutSessionExercises.Exercise")
            .Single(c => c.Id == id);
```

At least, this example uses the property for the Sessions. But why did I write with a string for the two others included? Because Sessions is a collection which doesn't let me link to one of its properties. Instead, it links me to a list of properties of the collection. This is quite logical if we think about it. However, I still have the problem of using a string which will lead in the maintenance phase to some possible problem when refactoring. Renaming a property does not change the string. This is why it would be better to specify the property of the collection. This can be done by using the Linq method "**Select**".

```
return DatabaseContext
            .SetOwnable<Workout>()
            .Include(x => x.Sessions)
            .Include(x => x.Sessions
                     .Select(d=>d.WorkoutSessionExercises))
            .Include(x => x.Sessions.Select(d=>d.WorkoutSessionExercises
                     .Select(g=>g.Exercise)))
            .Single(c => c.Id == id);
```

As you can see, we load the collection Sessions, then we load the collection WorkoutSessionExercise which is inside every Session. Finally, we load every Exercise that is a property without being a collection. This example shows you that even multiple collections deep you can still avoid using a string to specify what to include and what not.

## Validation failed for one or more entities. See EntityValidationErrors property for more details.

Release Date: 13-May-13
Url: http://patrickdesjardins.com/blog/?post_type=post&p=2057

The problem with the error "Validation failed for one or more entities. See 'EntityValidationErrors' property for more details." is that you cannot go inside it. In fact, you need to cast this one into **DbEntityValidationException** to be able to see inner errors.

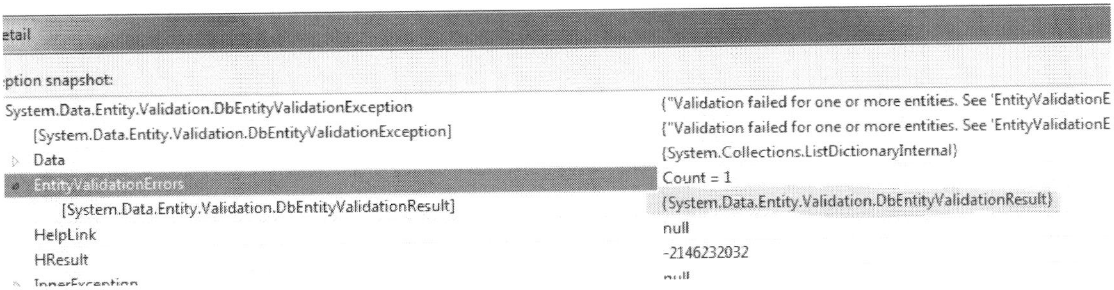

etail

ption snapshot:

| | |
|---|---|
| System.Data.Entity.Validation.DbEntityValidationException | {"Validation failed for one or more entities. See 'EntityValidationE |
| [System.Data.Entity.Validation.DbEntityValidationException] | {"Validation failed for one or more entities. See 'EntityValidationE |
| Data | {System.Collections.ListDictionaryInternal} |
| EntityValidationErrors | Count = 1 |
| [System.Data.Entity.Validation.DbEntityValidationResult] | {System.Data.Entity.Validation.DbEntityValidationResult} |
| HelpLink | null |
| HResult | -2146232032 |

To see the exception details, you need to open the watch window, or the immediate window and type this line :

```
((System.Data.Entity.Validation.DbEntityValidationException)$exception).EntityVali
dationErrors
```

From here, you will be able to see which entities are problematic and also what inner validation errors have been thrown.

## Entity Framework context operations in perspective with their entry states

Release Date: 27-May-13
Url: http://patrickdesjardins.com/blog/?post_type=post&p=2080

When manipulating data with Entity Framework and the context, you are changing the state of the entity. For example, if you insert a new entity, the state will be changed to *Added*. This article shows you all context operations that change the entity state and will show you that you can do what most of the operations do by simply changing manually the state of the entity. Before going deeper with the operations, lets see all states. You can get the list of states by going into **EntityState** class of System.Data.

```
namespace System.Data
{
  [BindableType(IsBindable = false)]
  [Flags]
  public enum EntityState
  {
    Detached = 1,
    Unchanged = 2,
    Added = 4,
    Deleted = 8,
    Modified = 16,
  }
}
```

The **Detached** state is when an object is not yet attached to Entity Framework's context. By default, if you create a new instance of a class, this one is not attached. Another way to be detached is when you delete an entity. This will be deleted from the database by Entity Framework but the object reference remains in your code andwill be back to detached. Having said that, moving back to detached does not delete the entity but does not make Entity Framework know about it. We could also manually set the entry to detached to have this one not tracked.

```
var category = context.Categories.Find(id);
context.Categories.Remove(category);
context.SaveChanges(); // Will delete and set category as detached
//Is the same as
var category = context.Categories.Find(id);
context.Entry(category).State = EntityState.Detached;
context.SaveChanges(); // Will do nothing in the database because it's detached
and it would required to be "Deleted" to be deleted.
```

The example above calls **Remove** to delete the entity. When deleting the state goes from **Added** to **Delete** to **Detached**. So both codes below are doing the same thing, deleting the entity from the database.

```
var category = context.Categories.Find(id);
context.Categories.Remove(category);
context.SaveChanges();
//Is the same as
var category = context.Categories.Find(id);
context.Entry(category).State = EntityState.Deleted;
context.SaveChanges();
```

The **Unchanged** state occurs when the entity is tracked by Entity Framework's context but has not changed yet. You can have this state if you use the method Attach() or if you change the state with Entry().

```
var category = new Category { Id = 123 };
context.Categories.Attach(category);
context.SaveChanges();
//Is the same as
var category = new Category { Id = 123 };
context.Entry(category).State = EntityState.Unchanged;
context.SaveChanges();
```

The **Added** state is a synonym for insertion. When a new entity is added to the context, it will be inserted into the database. In Entity Framework words, it is called **Added**. This can be done by using the **Add** method or by changing the state to **EntityState.Added**.

```
var category = new Category { Id = 123 };
context.Categories.Add(category);
context.SaveChanges();
//Is the same as
var category = new Category { Id = 123 };
context.Entry(category).State = EntityState.Added;
context.SaveChanges();
```

Finally, it can be **Modified**. This state will do an update to the property that has been changed. Once the update has been done by calling **SaveChanges**, the state comes back to attached.

```
var category = context.Categories.Find(id); //State is to attached
context.Categories.Update(category); //State is now updated
context.SaveChanges(); //State is now attached
//Is the same as
var category = context.Categories.Find(id); //State is to attached
context.Entry(category).State = EntityState.Modified; //State is now updated
context.SaveChanges(); //State is now attached
```

Without going into much detail, you can handle the modified state by using "**ApplyCurrentValues**". This will check the object passed by parameter and if changes are found will mark those properties with the new value and with the **Modified** state.

```
var category = context.Categories.Attach(new Category { ID =
categoryThatCameFromUserForm.ID });
context.Categories.ApplyCurrentValues(categoryThatCameFromUserForm);
context.SaveChanges(); //State is now attached
```

We could also specify manually which property could have been changed with the Entry method.

```
var category = context.Categories.Attach(new Category { ID =
categoryThatCameFromUserForm.ID });
context.Entry(category).Property(d => d.Name).IsModified = true;
context.SaveChanges(); //State is now attached
```

To conclude, it is possible to handle Entity Framework's entities with several approaches. The first method, with operation, is perfect for simple cases, whereas the second method, with state, gives you further control over what is modified and creates an abstract level over Entity Framework if required. For example, you could easily add some code that checks if the Id is Null or not, and if it's null changes the state to Added, otherwise sets the state to Modified.

# How to rename complex type to not have the prefix of the class name

Release Date: 13-Jun-13
Url: http://patrickdesjardins.com/blog/?post_type=post&p=1901

Entity Framework has a standard with the naming of columns. This is also the case with complex types, which will be added to every table where complex types are used by entities. By default, Entity Framework will concatenate the name of the complex type with an underscore and the name of the property. If you prefer not having the complex type name, you can simply specify the column name you desire.

```
modelBuilder
        .ComplexType<Audit>()
        .Property(type => type.CreatedBy)
        .HasColumnName("CreatedBy");
```

In the database, instead of having a field with "Audit_CreatedBy," you will have only "CreatedBy." This may be useful in some situations, but by experience it's easier to do the mapping between complex types when you **keep** the prefix. It is up to you, and your coding/database standard, to figure out if it is appropriate or not.

# How can I run an update on specific properties for detached objects?

Release Date: 19-Jun-13
Url: http://patrickdesjardins.com/blog/?post_type=post&p=1888

In some scenarios you will want to update a specific property but not others. This can be for security reasons or for performance reasons. In either case, the goal is to update only a specific property of your entity. In Entity Framework, this can be done by specifying to the database context (dbcontext) the property status. Each property does have an **IsModified** property that can be set to true or false.

```
context.Entry(yourObject).Property(u => u.YourProperty).IsModified = true;
```

Of course, if your object is from view, this is not known by Entity Framework's database context and will require attaching it first.

```
using (var entities = new MyDbContext())
{
```

```
    var entity = new YourEntity { Id = id, Name = "Test" };
    entities.YourEntities.Attach(entity);
    entities.Entry(entity).Property(e => e.Name).IsModified = true;
    entities.SaveChanges();
}
```

This will save *YourEntity* entity but only change the Name property. This is quite useful in scenarios where you do not want the user to hack a web form to add properties that you don't want to be read by Entity Framework. By specifying which property is modified, you tell Entity Framework to generate the SQL with only the "Set" for them. For example:

```
UPDATE YourEntitySET Name = "Test"WHERE Id = 123;
```

Finally, you may want to close the automatic validation if you are using the validation mechanism. This can be done by setting the **ValidateOnSaveEnabled** to false.

```
entities.Configuration.ValidateOnSaveEnabled = false;
```

The reason is that since not all the objects are loaded, you may have some validations on field that should be required that are not done at this time. To temporarily disable the validation, use **ValidateOnSaveEnabled**. Of course, set it back to true once the save changes is done.

## Entity Framework and conversion of a datetime2

Release Date: 22-Jun-13
Url: http://patrickdesjardins.com/blog/?post_type=post&p=2117

Have you ever gotten a conversion error when saving an entity with Entity Framework? Even with Entity Framework 5.0, you may receive the following error message that the value is out of rabge.

*The conversion of a datetime2 data type to a datetime data type resulted in an out-of-range value.\r\nThe statement has been terminated.*

This is the case if you have a date time set to 0001-01-01 because it is out of range for SQL Server (even with SQL Server 2008 R2). In fact, SQL Server dates can have dates only after the year 1753.

The solution to this problem is to set a property date or to make nullable this field in the database and into your entity. This way, you could set it to null if the date is not set. Otherwise, you can use, instead of of 0001-01-01, another date that has a "not set date" which is over 1753-01-01.

## Validation failed for one or more entities. See EntityValidationErrors property for more details.

Release Date: 02-Jul-13
Url: http://patrickdesjardins.com/blog/?post_type=post&p=1890

With EF4.1, EF4.3 and EF5.0 you may have an Entity Validation Error and you may not know how to get the details of the error. Entity Framework encapsulates the error into a class named **DbEntityValidationException** which is not casted in the debugger.

*Validation failed for one or more entities. See 'EntityValidationErrors' property for more details.*

To be able to get the information, you can add to your **Watch Panel** (inside Visual Studio) or into the **Immediate Panel** or **Quick Watch** the following line when the error occurs:

```
((System.Data.Entity.Validation.DbEntityValidationException)$exception).EntityVali
dationErrors
```

From here, you will be able to get which entity is in error and what is the error. A Data Annotation error or validation error will be clearly written inside the DbEntityValidationException.

## How to load hierarchical structure with recursive with Entity Framework 5

Release Date: 22-Aug-13
Url: http://patrickdesjardins.com/blog/?post_type=post&p=2257

Loading a hierarchical structure can be done in different ways. Here are two ways to handle data structure that is recursive. Let's define the scenario we want to parse. The structure we want to parse is hierarchical; it looks like a tree. A main parent node with children which can have entities and/or have itself a parent node to start a sub-tree. Also, let's say that children cannot contain a parent that is already used somewhere else in the tree. This will remove the possibility of having infinite recursion.

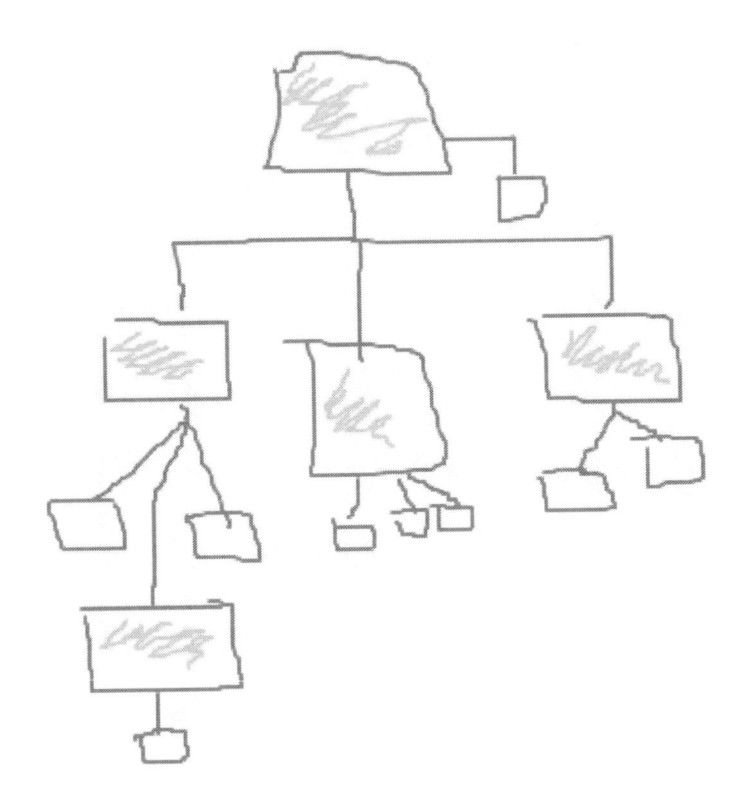

In the graphic above, you can see that we have two types of container. One is bigger than the other . In fact, the bigger one is a node that can have either children of a specific entity, which cannot contain any other structural entity, or can contain another bigger container which contains a list of children. So, since we do not know how the tree is structured, it is not possible to use eager loading as we do normally by including the property desired.

```
_context.Parent
    .Include(d => d.OtherProperty)
    .Include(d => d.Children)
    .Include(d => d.Children.Select(dd=>dd.OtherProperty)
    .Include(d => d.Children.Select(dd=>dd.Children)
    .Include(d => d.Children.Select(dd=>dd.OtherProperty........) //We cannot
proceed this way because we do not know how many level
    .Include(d => d.Children.Select(dd=>dd.Children.......)//We cannot proceed
this way because we do not know how many level
    .Single(p => p.ID == id);
```

This gives us the option of loading the Children, if this one has children, and then load it the way we just loaded the parent since every child becomes a parent. This requires a recursive method. The problem is that it works, but every load will create a new parent. We need to map every value to the first parent to have at the end a single hierarchical tree. Here is how we can do it with **eager loading**. We need to load every property and set it back to the object that we have received in order to, at the end, have a tree fully loaded.

```
private Parent RecursiveLoad(Guid id)
{
    var ParentFromDatabase = _context.Parent
        .Include(d => d.Children)
        .Include(d => d.Children.Select(dd => dd.OtherProperty))
        .Single(p => p.ID == id);

    foreach (var child in ParentFromDatabase.Children)
    {
        var childNotLoaded = child;
        var childFullyLoaded = _context.Child
            .Include(d => d.Parent)
            .Include(d => d.OtherProperty)
            .Single(d => d.ID == childNotLoaded.ID);

        child.OtherProperty = childFullyLoaded.OtherProperty;   //Require to set
back the value because we want by reference to have everything in the tree
        child.Parent = RecursiveLoad(childFullyLoaded.Parent.ID); //Require to set
back the value because we want by reference to have everything in the tree
    }
    return ParentFromDatabase;
}
```

But we can do better with **explicit loading**. One of the positive characteristics of explicit loading is that it loads itself. You do not need to map the loaded object to the existing one, it has already been loaded into it. Here is the version with explicit loading:

```
private Parent RecursiveLoad(Parent parent)
{
    var ParentFromDatabase = _context.Entry(parent)
    .Collection(d => d.Children);//Children are loaded, we can loop them now

    foreach (var child in parent.Children)
    {
        _context.Entry(child).Reference(d => d.OtherProperty).Load();
        RecursiveLoad(child);
    }
    return ParentFromDatabase;
}
```

This has the advantage of removing every mapping since the object is loaded itself by entity framework. Still, this kind of loading comes with a price. If we have 40 leaves in the tree, this means that every of them will be loaded by the database which results to 40 SQL queries. One approach that can reduce the number of requests is to have the ID (int or

Guid) inside the object, and from there you can check if it has a value. This will reduce the number of calls to the database at the amount of parent only (not final leaves, which returns 0 elements). Still, the amount is huge, and for a large application a custom solution with a view returning a bunch of data and parsed manually may be a good solution. Nevertheless, if you need to save the tree, you could end up with a problem which you do not have when having the whole structure loaded by Entity Framework.

# Mapping navigation property to a different name of the database foreign key (Entity Framework 5)

Release Date: 29-Aug-13
Url: http://patrickdesjardins.com/blog/?post_type=post&p=2254

In some rare cases you may have to map an entity to a column which does not have the same name. Let's take a simple exemple of an entity *Muscle* which has many *Exercises*. A single *exercise* is related to a single required *muscle*.

```
modelBuilder
    .Entity<Exercise>()
    .HasRequired(b => b.Muscle)
    .WithMany(m => m.ExerciseRelated)
    .IsIndependent()
    .Map(p=>p.MapKey(m => m.MuscleID, "Muscle_ID");
```

In the example above, you can see that *Exercise* marks its *Muscle* property to be required and sets the *Muscle* entity to have multiple *Exercises*. If you want to not have both sides link to each other, you can set the **WithMany** parameter to nothing, which would mean that only *Exercise* has a *Muscle* association, and not *Muscle* to *Exercises*.

The next keywork in the Linq statement is **IsIndependent** which specifies to Entity Framework that the foreign key is not the one you expect and that you will map to another name. But, this keywork does not exist anymore with Entity Framework 5.

*Consolidation of IsIndependent in the Code First relationship API. When configuring relationships in Feature CTP5 the IsIndependent method was used to identify that the relationship did not have a foreign key property exposed in the object model. This is now done by calling the* ***Map*** *method.* ***HasForeignKey*** *is still used for relationships where the foreign key property is exposed in the object model.*

So this is the code above with Entity Framework 5:

```
modelBuilder
    .Entity<Exercise>()
    .HasRequired(b => b.Muscle)
    .WithMany(m => m.ExerciseRelated)
    .Map(p => p.MapKey("Muscle___ID"));
```

So instead of using the default navigation name which should have been "Muscle_ID" (Entity name + primary key with underscore between), Entity Framework will use "Muscle___ID". Beware of the **HasColumnName** property which is for property name. That is not the same as MapKey. The HasColumnName is not for association but for property. The **MapKey** keyword shines for association only when there is **HasColumnName** for property.

```
modelBuilder
    .Entity<Exercise>()
    .Property(x => x.Muscle)
  .HasColumnName("MuscleX");
```

## What is the difference between MapKey and HasForeignKey?

Release Date: 18-Sep-13
Url: http://patrickdesjardins.com/blog/?post_type=post&p=2292

You can define association **1 to many** and define the relationship with both code snippets below. One is defined with a string, the other one with a property. **HasRequired** with association defined by string looks like the below code.

```
this.HasRequired(a => a.Property1)
    .WithMany()
    .Map(a => a.MapKey("MyFK"));
```

**HasRequired** with association defined by property looks like this:

```
this.HasRequired(a => a.Property1)
    .WithMany()
    .HasForeignKey(a => a.MyFK);
```

Both mappings create exactly the same database schema with a non nullable foreign key. The configuration that maps with the **MapKey** method is used when you do not want to have the foreign key as a property in your entity class. This is called **Independent Association**. The mapping with **HasForeignKey** is when the foreign key is a property in the entity. This type is called **Foreign Key Association.** You can use the one you want. Personally, I prefer to use the **HasForeignKey** because it is strongly mapped and if the property name is refactored I am sure that the property will follow. However, this goes beyond just a preference for strongly map.

**Independent association** is interesting if your model is purely object oriented and does not have anything related to Entity Framework. Pure Poco class is where associations are only defined by property. However, this is more complex when it is time to handle associations with Entity Framework. The main reason is that you have to load the property or attach it if it exists. On the other hand, Foreign key association requires just setting the ID of the property without loading or attaching the existing relation when working with Entity Framework. This is why using **Foreign Key Association** is simpler. You have the property but for each association property you have also a property that defines the key of this property. One to many association can be Independent or Foreign key association while many to many can only be a Foreign Key association.

# How to bind SQL View to an Entity Framework object

Release Date: 07-Oct-13
Url: http://patrickdesjardins.com/blog/?post_type=post&p=2294

If you do not want to create an Entity and to configure it with the ToTable() to the name of your view, you can use a direct method from the context to call the database and bind the result into a class.Here is how to do it with the ToTable method:

```
public class WorkoutConfiguration : EntityTypeConfiguration<Workout>
{
    public WorkoutConfiguration()
    {
        base.ToTable("dbo", "ViewNameHere");
        base.HasMany(d => d.Sessions)
            .WithRequired(d=>d.Workout)
            .WillCascadeOnDelete(true);
    }
}
```

Here is how to do it with a direct SQL statement:

```
var workouts = _dbContext.Database.SqlQuery<Workout>("select * from dbo.Workout");
```

The SqlQuery acts the same with the binding of value as with Entity Framework. Every field is mapped with the corresponding method. You can use the **AS** statement to change the return value of some fields to be the same name of your methods.

```
var workouts = _dbContext.Database.SqlQuery<Workout>("select id as ID, name as
nameFR from dbo.Workout");
```

At first, the last solution seems to be faster and fine, but consider the first one if you are using table or view because it is better. It is better because you do not have to handle a string with an SQL query. If the database changes, you will not notice any problem until the query is executed. It is more a workaround than a good "enterprise" solution. But, the last one can be a good compromise if you need to use a stored procedure. Nevertheless, always ask yourself in the long term what will be the repercussions of your choice.

# How to set up Entity Framework Code first to have only one side 0 to 1 relationship

Release Date: 29-Oct-13
Url: http://patrickdesjardins.com/blog/?post_type=post&p=2367

Let's say you have an entity that can have a relation to a second entity but not every time. This is a 0..1 to 1 or 0..1 to many relationship. In this example, the scenario is that we have one entity that has a relation to a second entity. The second entity does not have any reference to the first one. At first, we may think that this code below works.

```
modelBuilder
    .Entity<EntityOne>()
    .HasOptional(d => d.EntityTwo)
    .WithOptionalDependent();
```

The **WithOptionalDependent** tells EF (Entity Framework) that *EntityOne* is the one of the two entities that holds the reference which is optional as stated with the **HasOptional** property. No! This raises an error that tells us that it cannot find the *EntityTwo_ID* key. This is problematic because in the scenario we are talking about the foreign key has a special name. So, we have to configure the foreign key. Of course, if your FK is named *EntityTwo_ID* then you are all fine.

```
modelBuilder
    .Entity<EntityOne>()
    .HasOptional(d => d.EntityTwo)
    .WithOptionalDependent()
    .Map(d => d.MapKey("EntityTwoID");
```

The **HasForeignKey** is not available from **WithOptionalDependent**, but with **Map** we can set up the foreign key name. Unfortunately, this does not work either. The error is an invalid column name. From here, we can realize that the **MapKey** is used by the principal entity and not the dependent.

Still, we want to have a 0..1 relation. How can we set up this optional relationship with Entity Framework without having on the other side the property mapped to the other entity? We need to use **HasOptional** and treat the whole situation not as 0..1 to 1 but 0..1 to many.

```
modelBuilder
    .Entity<EntityOne>()
    .HasOptional(d => d.EntityTwo)
    .WithMany()
    .HasForeignKey(d => d.EntityTwoID);
```

To make it work, we use **WithMany** without specifying the other side property (since we do not have it) and we use **HasForeignKey** to specify the correct foreign key. And that is it! It works!

# Entity Framework SELECT VALUE Q with ESQL, why?

Release Date: 18-Nov-13
Url: http://patrickdesjardins.com/blog/?post_type=post&p=2417

When you are using Entity Framework and want to pass a query string manually, you have to use SELECT VALUE XXX FROM. But why? This is a good question and often we see SELECT VALUE Q FROM, so why Q? In fact, it can be anything but must be a single word. ESQL allows you to select with a row wrapper or without. When using VALUE, it adds a wrapper which creates a return of a materialized data record. Entity Framework handles this materialized data record to bind the result into a context object. Without the VALUE, you do not have any wrapper and you get back a set of rows.

Here is an example with SELECT VALUE. We receive a strongly typed set of objects.

```
string queryString = "SELECT VALUE q from table1.attr1 as q";
ObjectQuery<T> query = context.CreateQuery<T>(queryString);
```

You can also specify which field you return if you do not want every field.

```
string queryString = "SELECT VALUE row (q.Field1 as Field1, q.Field2 as Field2)
                      from table1.attr1 as q)";
ObjectQuery<T> query = context.CreateQuery<T>(queryString);
```

This time, the keyword **row** is required because it's a reserved keyword by ESQL. **Row** constructs an anonymous value. The following example returns a set of rows. As you can see, we have a **DbDataRecord**.

```
string queryString = "SELECT q table1.attr1 as q";
ObjectQuery<DbDataRecord> query = context.CreateQuery<DbDataRecord>(queryString);
```

Most of the time, you will use the SELECT VALUE q FROM … The use of ESQL must be as low as you can because it opens a door to have SQL Query inside your code, which the ORM is there to abstract. Nevertheless, sometimes, for optimization, ESQL is perfect.

# Entity Framework Inheritance

Release Date: 10-Dec-13
Url: http://patrickdesjardins.com/blog/?post_type=post&p=179

Business logic can have model classes that inherit another class. The data of the instanced class and the inherited class might be saved in the database when the Object Context is saved. Entity framework lets you choose the strategy you desire to save them into the database. Three strategies are available : TPH, TPT and TPC inheritance.

## Table per hierarchy (TPH) Inheritance Mapping Strategy

This is the simplest strategy. It takes all properties of the base class and all properties of the inherited class and merges them into a single table. This means if 10 classes inherit a single class, all properties of these 10 classes plus the properties of the inheritance one will be merged into one table. For example, you have three classes, two sub-classes that inherit a single base class.

```
public class Book
{
    public string ISBN { get; set; }
    public int PageCount { get; set; }
}

public class Magazine : Book
{
    public string MagazineProperty { get; set; }
}

public class Encyclopedia:Book
{
    public string EncyclopediaProperty { get; set; }
}
```

The class diagram of these three classes is the following:

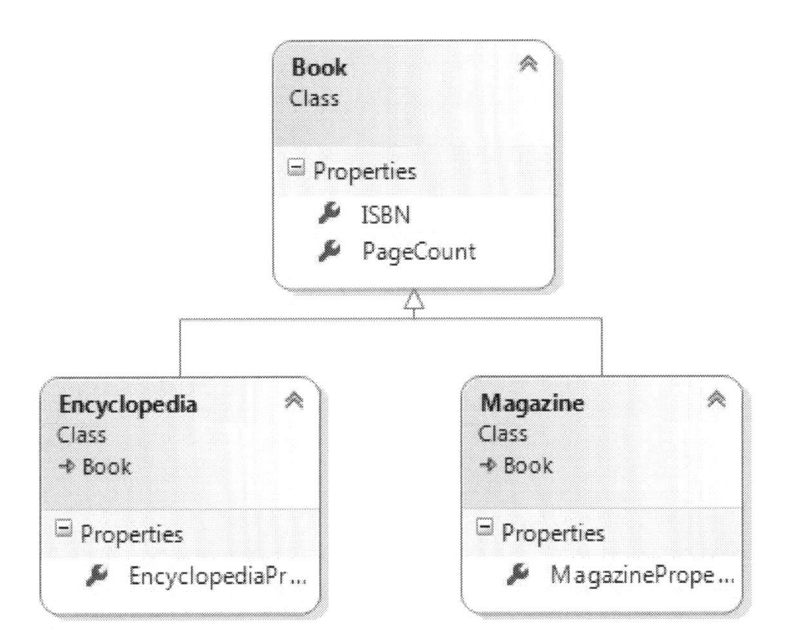


This will result in a single table with all properties nullable which are from a subclass. To create a short test, simply add these three classes to a .Net project. Then, you need to set up the database context.

```
public class TestContext:DbContext
{
    public TestContext()
        : base("TestContext")
    {

    }
    public DbSet<Magazine> Magazines { get; set; }
    public DbSet<Encyclopedia> Encyclopedia { get; set; }


    protected override void OnModelCreating(DbModelBuilder modelBuilder)
    {
        modelBuilder.Conventions.Remove<PluralizingTableNameConvention>();
        modelBuilder.Entity<Book>().HasKey(d => d.ISBN);

    }
}
```

Do not forget to add Entity Framework with NuGet and set up the web.config with a good connection string. To get entity framework you can do a search inside NuGet manager or in the package console.

```
-    Menu Project > Manage NuGet Packages
-    Select the Online tab
-    Select the EntityFramework package
-    Click Install
```

Or

```
PM> install-package entityframework
```

The configuration file should have a config section (which is added from NuGet) and the connection string to be set up to the SQL instance you have and the database you want to use.

```
<configuration>
  <configSections>
    <section name="entityFramework"
             type="System.Data.Entity.Internal.ConfigFile.EntityFrameworkSection
                   , EntityFramework, Version=6.0.0.0, Culture=neutral,
               PublicKeyToken=b77a5c561934e089" requirePermission="false" />
  </configSections>
  <connectionStrings>
    <add name="TestContext"
         connectionString="Data Source=PATRICK-I7\SQLEXPRESS
               ;Initial Catalog=TestContextDatabase;Integrated Security=SSPI;"
         providerName="System.Data.SqlClient"/>
  </connectionStrings>
...
```

This is the most basic setup possible; we simply set the primary key to the base class. We do not set anything for sub-classes. Then, we need to let Entity Framework create the database. For that, just instanciate the dbcontext and do something to the query. We could also generate the database with the migration tool but, for simplicity, let's just add a new Encyclopedia in the main method.

```
using (var context = new DataAccessLayer.TestContext())
{
    context.Encyclopedia.Add(new Models.Encyclopedia { ISBN = "123" });
    context.SaveChanges();
}
```

Here is how the table looks:

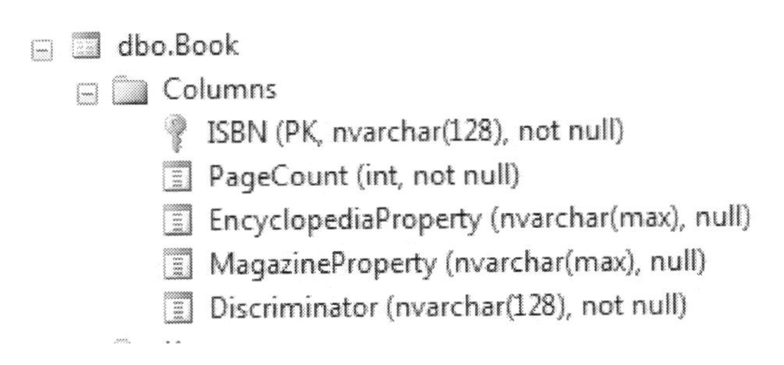


In fact, the table has an additional value which is a discriminator. This column is used by Entity Framework to know which subclass is required to be instanced. It is possible to edit the string, but by default it is the class name.

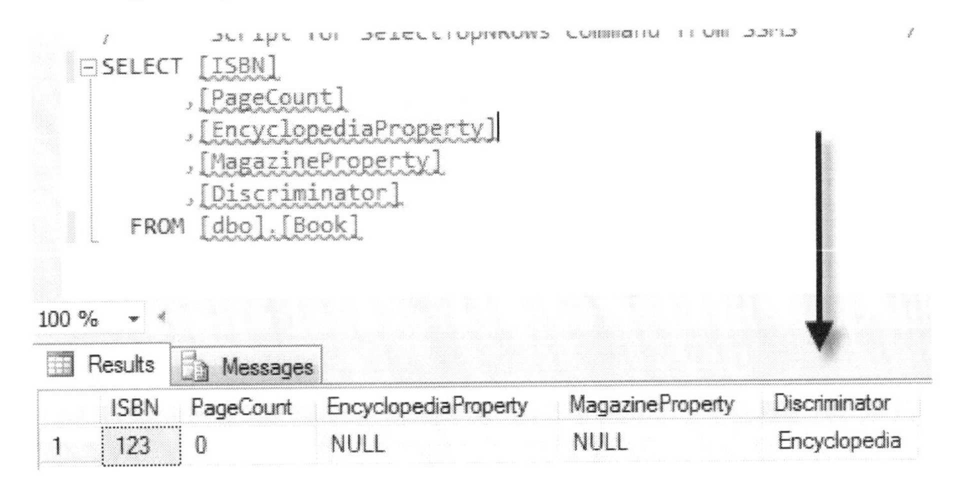


This mapping strategy is good for performance and simplicity. It is also the default used by Entity Framework.

## Table per type (TPT) Inheritance Mapping Strategy

All types are mapped to their own table. This produces a normalized database, while TPH doesn't. For the same example as above, with TPH, the database would have three tables.

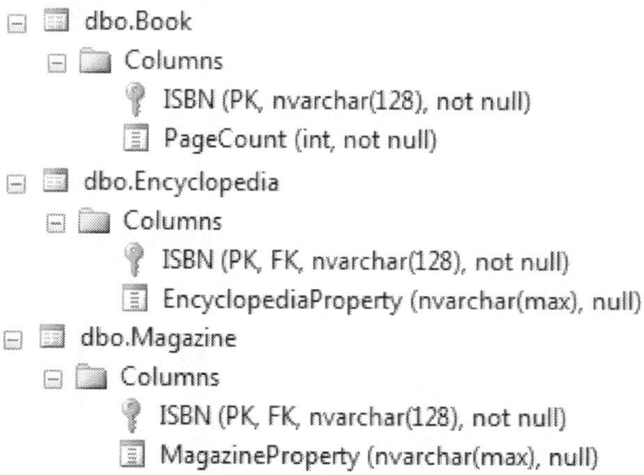

```
dbo.Book
    Columns
        ISBN (PK, nvarchar(128), not null)
        PageCount (int, not null)
dbo.Encyclopedia
    Columns
        ISBN (PK, FK, nvarchar(128), not null)
        EncyclopediaProperty (nvarchar(max), null)
dbo.Magazine
    Columns
        ISBN (PK, FK, nvarchar(128), not null)
        MagazineProperty (nvarchar(max), null)
```

Entity Framework performs more inner joins to be able to know which table to use for a subclass when information is gathered from the database. This result is less useful than the previous approach. Nevertheless, tables are cleaner because they don't have a huge amount of nullable properties.

To configure table per type (TPT) it requires setting the table for the subclass.

```
public class TestContext : DbContext
{
    public TestContext()
        : base("TestContext")
    {
    }

    public DbSet<Book> Book { get; set; }
    public DbSet<Magazine> Magazines { get; set; }
    public DbSet<Encyclopedia> Encyclopedia { get; set; }

    protected override void OnModelCreating(DbModelBuilder modelBuilder)
    {
        modelBuilder.Conventions.Remove<PluralizingTableNameConvention>();
        modelBuilder.Entity<Magazine>().ToTable("Magazine");
        modelBuilder.Entity<Encyclopedia>().ToTable("Encyclopedia");
        modelBuilder.Entity<Book>().ToTable("Book").HasKey(d => d.ISBN);
    }
}
```

If we delete the database and run again the code, the database is created with two tables.

## Table per concrete type (TPC) Inheritance Mapping Strategy

Table per concrete type, also know as TPC, creates a single class per subclass. Every property of the inherited class is set into each of the subclass tables. This leads to a duplicated structure. If you have two classes that inherit one class, the inherited field will be inside the two tables.

```
dbo.Encyclopedia
    Columns
        ISBN (PK, nvarchar(128), not null)
        EncyclopediaProperty (nvarchar(max), null)
        PageCount (int, not null)
dbo.Magazine
    Columns
        ISBN (PK, nvarchar(128), not null)
        MagazineProperty (nvarchar(max), null)
        PageCount (int, not null)
```

As you can see in the example above, the ISBN and PageCount are repeated in both of the subclasses' tables. You can also notice that there is no table for the base class. The reason is that all fields of the base are already in all subclasses.

The configuration is more complex.

```
public class TestContext:DbContext
{
    public TestContext()
        : base("TestContext")
    {

    }
    public DbSet<Magazine> Magazines { get; set; }
    public DbSet<Encyclopedia> Encyclopedia { get; set; }


    protected override void OnModelCreating(DbModelBuilder modelBuilder)
    {
        modelBuilder.Conventions.Remove<PluralizingTableNameConvention>();
        modelBuilder.Entity<Magazine>().Map(m =>
        {
            m.MapInheritedProperties();
            m.ToTable("Magazine");
        });
```

```
        modelBuilder.Entity<Encyclopedia>().Map(m =>
        {
            m.MapInheritedProperties();
            m.ToTable("Encyclopedia");
        });
        modelBuilder.Entity<Magazine>().HasKey(d => d.ISBN);
        modelBuilder.Entity<Encyclopedia>().HasKey(d => d.ISBN);
    }
}
```

The code generated in SQL is complex. It has a subquery with union to know from which table to take its data. This result in bad performance for a heavy inheritance model. TPC is good for deep inheritance, TPH is good for a small entity with not a lot of property and TPT is good for a small inheritance level with many properties. Personally, I lean toward TPT most of the time. Having a normalized database is important in most enterprises and performance is not that bad if the inheritance is only one level.

## Entity Framework and the Unit of Work pattern

Release Date: 16-Dec-13
Url: http://patrickdesjardins.com/blog/?post_type=post&p=2214

This article is a summary of how to make use of a unit of work with Entity Framework. First of all, Entity Framework is a unit of work by itself. You can do multiple inserts, updates and deletes and it is not until a **SaveChanges** that everything is committed to the SQL Server. The problem is that you may want to have multiple repositories. This means that if you want to be under the same transaction, you want to share the save DbContext. Here comes the unit of work, a pattern that shares the DbContext. The reference of DbContext is shared across repositories, which is interesting because if we want to be domain driven we can share the DbContext between repositories of the same domain. It's also interesting for unit testing. The reason is that the unit of work has an interface which can be easily mocked.

I have seen an article on Asp.Net website concerning Entity Framework and the unit of work pattern but I believe it's wrong. I prefer the one of Julie Lerman in her Pluralsight video. The main reason is that the one of Asp.Net includes the repository inside the unit of work and the DbContext. The one of Julie Lerman only contains the DbContext and the unit of work is passed through every repository of the domain.

Here is the representation of all the layers that we would like with the unit of work.

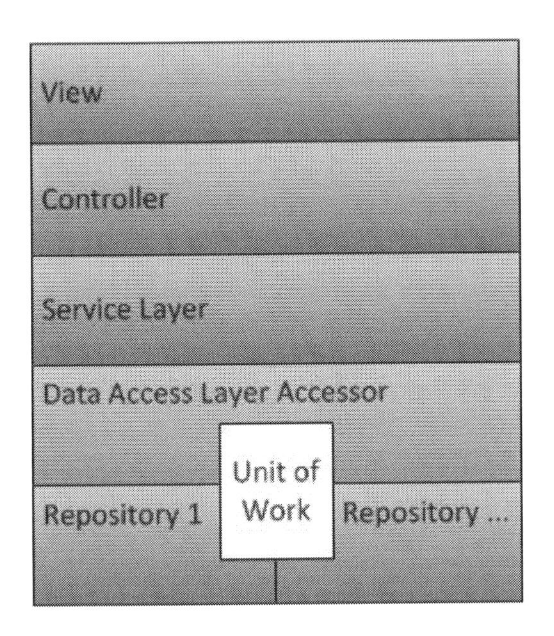


As you can see, the controller should contact the service layer where all queries are from databases, access to caching services and web services are executed. For the database part, we contact the data access layer accessor, which is an abstraction for the unit of work and repositories. This allows every developer who uses repositories to abstract the need to create the unit of work and to pass it through constructors. The accessor does have a reference to repositories and to the unit of work.

This article explains how to create a layered approach that has a controller, a service layer, a data access layer accessor with repositories and unit of work with a simple set of entities. I already wrote an article for repository and entity framework. This was another simpler way to design the repository. Previously, a facade was passing the DbContext to all repositories, which created the same behavior as the unit of work pattern. However, the unit of work is more elaborate and allows a unit test easily and allows you to reuse a repository in several DbContexts if required. Having the possibility to create several DbContexts and to share them by domain (for domain driven design) is important for big software. It increases the performance of the database context by having a limited number of entities to handle. So, the previous way to handle a repository is perfect if you have under 50 entities. This is a rule of thumb and it depends on many factors. If you have a lot of entities and you can draw specific domains, the approach of unit of work in this post is preferable. As you will see, a lot more classes will be needed and this is not a small detail to consider before going this way.

## Creating the entities, the database context and the tables

First of all, let's create entities and a simple context that we will call directly from the controller. This should never have been done in enterprise but it will allow us to migrate the code from a simple basic code to a more heavily-layered application.

```
public class Animal
{
    public int Id { get; set; }
    public string Name { get; set; }

    public virtual ICollection<Animal> Enemies { get; set; }
    public virtual ICollection<Animal> EnemyOf { get; set; }
}

public class Cat : Animal
{
    public int NumberOfMustache { get; set; }
    public int RemainingLife{get;set;}
}

public class Dog : Animal
{
    public string Type { get; set; }
}
```

We have two classes, one for Cat and one for Dog. Both inherit from Animal class. These are very simple classes because we want to focus on the unit of work and not on complex classes. The next step is to create the database context. The first step is to get Entity Framework. This can be done by using NuGet with the interface ("Manage NuGet Package") or with a command line:

```
PM> install-package entityframework
```

Then, we need to inherit from DbContext and set up web.config to have a connection string for the database. The web.config looks like this:

```
<configuration>
  <configSections>
    <section name="entityFramework"
type="System.Data.Entity.Internal.ConfigFile.EntityFrameworkSection,
EntityFramework, Version=6.0.0.0, Culture=neutral,
PublicKeyToken=b77a5c561934e089" requirePermission="false" />
  </configSections>
  <connectionStrings>
    <add name="EntityConnectionString" connectionString="Data Source=PATRICK-
I7\SQLEXPRESS;Initial Catalog=UnitOfWork;Integrated Security=SSPI;"
```

```
        providerName="System.Data.SqlClient" />
  </connectionStrings>
```

The first step is that we have a new configSection for Entity Framework. This has been added automatically. The line that is required to be added manually is the connection string. The last step is to configure the entity. Since we are simplifying the whole application for the purpose of the unit of work, the model class will be directly the entity. Some may want in an enterprise application to have an additional layer not share entity classes with the model.

```
public class AllDomainContext:DbContext
{
    public AllDomainContext():base("EntityConnectionString")
    {
    }

    protected override void OnModelCreating(DbModelBuilder modelBuilder)
    {
        base.OnModelCreating(modelBuilder);

        //Table per type configuration
        modelBuilder.Entity<Dog>().ToTable("Animals");
        modelBuilder.Entity<Dog>().ToTable("Dogs");
        modelBuilder.Entity<Cat>().ToTable("Cats");

        //Primary keys configuration
        modelBuilder.Entity<Animal>().HasKey(k => k.Id);

        modelBuilder.Entity<Animal>()
            .HasMany(entity => entity.Enemies)
            .WithMany(d => d.EnemyOf)
            .Map(d => d.ToTable("Animals_Enemies_Association")
                    .MapLeftKey("AnimalId")
                    .MapRightKey("EnemyId"));

    }
}
```

The configuration has something special for the *Enemies* list because I did not want to handle the association table by myself. Entity Framework can handle it for us by configuring a many to many relationship with the animal class. It requires a table name for the many-many table with a foreign key.

## Set up the controllers, service layer and data access layer

Before even having the service layer, let's use the context directly into the controller and see the database creation. Then, we will change to code every layer but not the unit of work yet. We can use scaffolding to leverage Visual Studio power to get code generation for us. First, right click the controller and select add new controller.

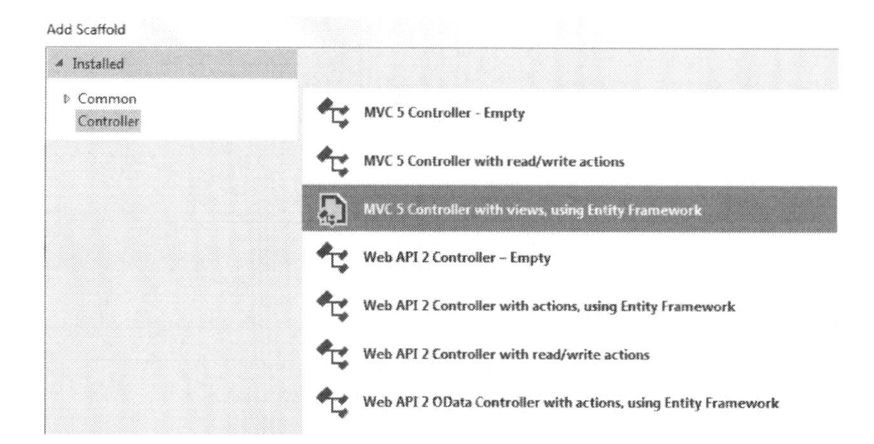


The second step is to select model class; you can select the one of Animal and select the DbContext class. If you do not see your DbContext class (DatabaseContext), close the window and compile your application. The wizard bases its choice on the compiled resource of the project. Once generated, you can execute the code, IIS Express start by default and you just need to go to http://localhost:15635/Animal and the DbContext will start the creation of the database. If you open SQL Server Manager, the unit of work database should have three tables.

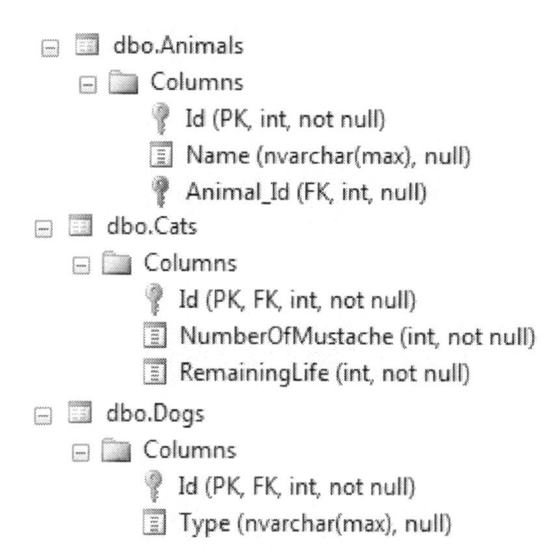


## Transforming to have service layers

At this stage, the architecture of the web application is not enterprise grade. The controller has a strong reference to the database context. The next step is to have everything related to the database inside a service layer which abstracts entity framework. This allows us to test the controller easily without having to care about the database. This is the current controller code at this moment.

```
public class AnimalController : Controller
{
    private DatabaseContext db = new DatabaseContext();

    public ActionResult Index()
    {
        return View(db.Animals.ToList());
    }

    public ActionResult Details(int? id)
    {
        if (id == null)
        {
            return new HttpStatusCodeResult(HttpStatusCode.BadRequest);
        }
        Animal animal = db.Animals.Find(id);
        if (animal == null)
        {
            return HttpNotFound();
        }
        return View(animal);
    }

    public ActionResult Create()
    {
        return View();
    }


    [HttpPost]
    [ValidateAntiForgeryToken]
    public ActionResult Create([Bind(Include = "Id,Name")] Animal animal)
    {
        if (ModelState.IsValid)
        {
            db.Animals.Add(animal);
            db.SaveChanges();
            return RedirectToAction("Index");
        }

        return View(animal);
    }
```

```
public ActionResult Edit(int? id)
{
    if (id == null)
    {
        return new HttpStatusCodeResult(HttpStatusCode.BadRequest);
    }
    Animal animal = db.Animals.Find(id);
    if (animal == null)
    {
        return HttpNotFound();
    }
    return View(animal);
}

[HttpPost]
[ValidateAntiForgeryToken]
public ActionResult Edit([Bind(Include = "Id,Name")] Animal animal)
{
    if (ModelState.IsValid)
    {
        db.Entry(animal).State = EntityState.Modified;
        db.SaveChanges();
        return RedirectToAction("Index");
    }
    return View(animal);
}

public ActionResult Delete(int? id)
{
    if (id == null)
    {
        return new HttpStatusCodeResult(HttpStatusCode.BadRequest);
    }
    Animal animal = db.Animals.Find(id);
    if (animal == null)
    {
        return HttpNotFound();
    }
    return View(animal);
}

[HttpPost, ActionName("Delete")]
[ValidateAntiForgeryToken]
public ActionResult DeleteConfirmed(int id)
{
    Animal animal = db.Animals.Find(id);
    db.Animals.Remove(animal);
    db.SaveChanges();
    return RedirectToAction("Index");
```

```
    }

    protected override void Dispose(bool disposing)
    {
        if (disposing)
        {
            db.Dispose();
        }
        base.Dispose(disposing);
    }
}
```

If you want to rapidly test the database, just add the code in the index.

```
public ActionResult Index()
{
    var animal1 = new Animal { Name = "Boss" };
    var cat1 = new Cat { Name = "Mi" };
    var cat2 = new Cat { Name = "Do" };
    animal1.Enemies = new List<Animal> { cat1,cat2};
    db.Animals.Add(animal1);
    db.Animals.Add(cat1);
    db.Animals.Add(cat2);
    db.SaveChanges();
    return View(db.Animals.AsNoTracking().ToList());
}
```

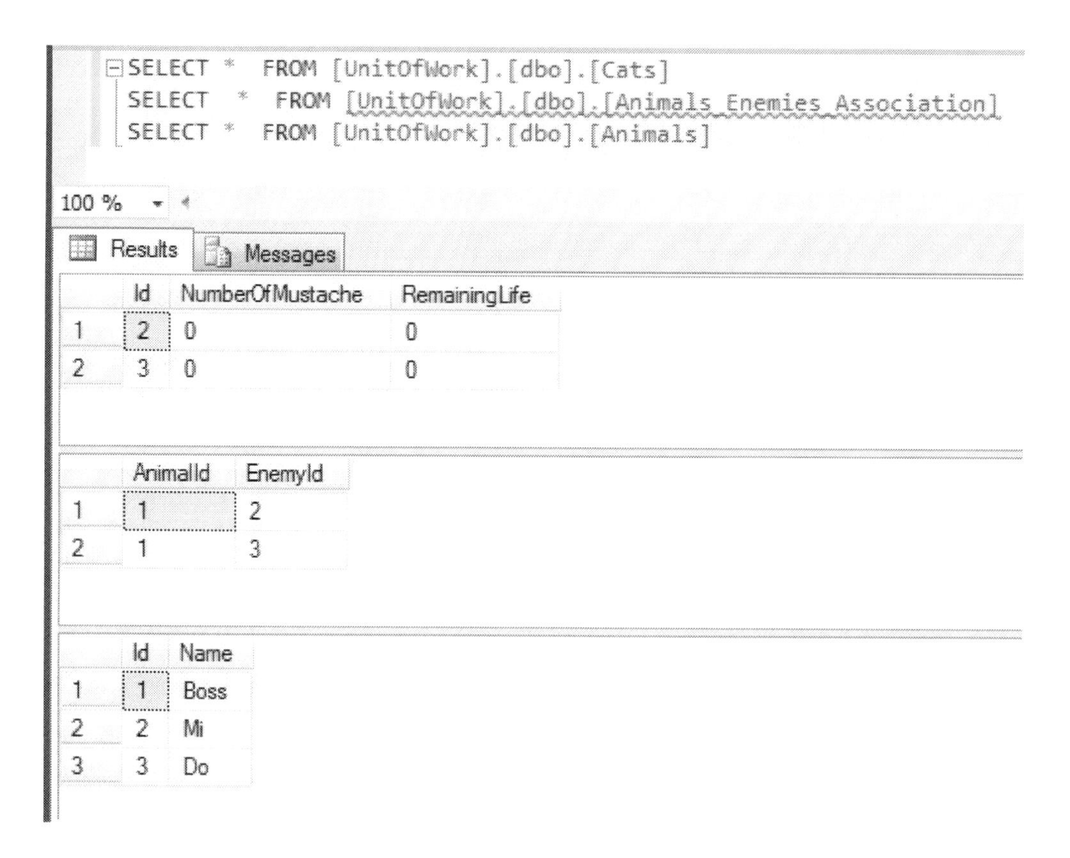


The first step is to create a repository class for animal inside the **DataAccessLayer** folder. Normally, I create a folder called *Repository* to have all repositories.

```
public class AnimalRepository : IAnimalRepository
{
    private DatabaseContext db = new DatabaseContext();

    public Models.Animal Find(int? id)
    {
        return db.Animals.Find(id);
    }

    public void Insert(Models.Animal animal)
    {
        db.Animals.Add(animal);
        db.SaveChanges();
    }

    public void Update(Models.Animal animal)
    {
        db.Entry(animal).State = EntityState.Modified;
```

```
        db.SaveChanges();
    }

    public void Delete(Models.Animal animal)
    {
        db.Animals.Remove(animal);
        db.SaveChanges();
    }

    public void Dispose()
    {
        db.Dispose();
    }

    public IList<Animal> GetAll()
    {
        return db.Animals.AsNoTracking().ToList();
    }
}
```

This class also has an interface with the public method in it. The second step is to create a service layer. Normally, we would create a new project, but to keep everything simple, let's just add a new folder (namespace). Then, we move the *DatabaseContext* class from the controller to the service. The animal service class looks like the following code.

```
public class AnimalService : IAnimalService
{
    private IAnimalRepository animalRepository;

    public AnimalService(IAnimalRepository animalRepository)
    {
        this.animalRepository = animalRepository;
    }

    public Models.Animal Find(int? id)
    {
        return this.animalRepository.Find(id);
    }

    public void Insert(Models.Animal animal)
    {
        this.animalRepository.Insert(animal);
    }

    public void Update(Models.Animal animal)
    {
        this.animalRepository.Update(animal);
    }
```

```
    public void Delete(Models.Animal animal)
    {
        this.animalRepository.Delete(animal);
    }
    public IList<Animal> GetAll()
    {
        return this.animalRepository.GetAll();
    }
}
```

It is all the code from the controller. Later, some improvements should be made. One of these changes is to move the **SaveChanges** because it is not efficient to save every time we add, modify or update an entity. This causes a performance problem when several entities are required to be posted to the database. However, let's focus on the transformation first; later these details will be gone. The role of the service layer is to reassemble every repository. In this situation we have only one repository. In fact, in more complex problems like in enterprise, a service has several repositories and caching classes. The next class that requires changes is the animal controller class. This one now has a constructor that needs an IAnimalService.

```
public class AnimalController : Controller
{
    private IAnimalService _service;

    public AnimalController()
    {
        _service = new AnimalService(new AnimalRepository());
    }

    public AnimalController(IAnimalService animalService)
    {
        _service = animalService;
    }


    public ActionResult Index()
    {
        return View(_service.GetAll());
    }

    public ActionResult Details(int? id)
    {
        if (id == null)
        {
            return new HttpStatusCodeResult(HttpStatusCode.BadRequest);
        }
```

```
    Animal animal = _service.Find(id);
    if (animal == null)
    {
        return HttpNotFound();
    }
    return View(animal);
}

public ActionResult Create()
{
    return View();
}


[HttpPost]
[ValidateAntiForgeryToken]
public ActionResult Create([Bind(Include = "Id,Name")] Animal animal)
{
    if (ModelState.IsValid)
    {
        _service.Insert(animal);
        return RedirectToAction("Index");
    }

    return View(animal);
}

public ActionResult Edit(int? id)
{
    if (id == null)
    {
        return new HttpStatusCodeResult(HttpStatusCode.BadRequest);
    }
    Animal animal = _service.Find(id);
    if (animal == null)
    {
        return HttpNotFound();
    }
    return View(animal);
}

[HttpPost]
[ValidateAntiForgeryToken]
public ActionResult Edit([Bind(Include = "Id,Name")] Animal animal)
{
    if (ModelState.IsValid)
    {
        _service.Update(animal);
        return RedirectToAction("Index");
    }
```

```
            return View(animal);
        }

        public ActionResult Delete(int? id)
        {
            if (id == null)
            {
                return new HttpStatusCodeResult(HttpStatusCode.BadRequest);
            }
            Animal animal = _service.Find(id);
            if (animal == null)
            {
                return HttpNotFound();
            }
            return View(animal);
        }

        [HttpPost, ActionName("Delete")]
        [ValidateAntiForgeryToken]
        public ActionResult DeleteConfirmed(int id)
        {
            Animal animal = _service.Find(id);
            _service.Delete(animal);
            return RedirectToAction("Index");
        }
    }
```

At this stage, the controller is separated from the database by the service and the repository. Still, it is better to not have a strong reference to AnimalService inside the controller. This is why we will extract an interface from AnimalService and we will inject the concrete class by inversion of control. This allows us, when doing a test entry point, to inject a fake AnimalService that will not go to the database. You can use the refactoring tool to extract the interface easily.

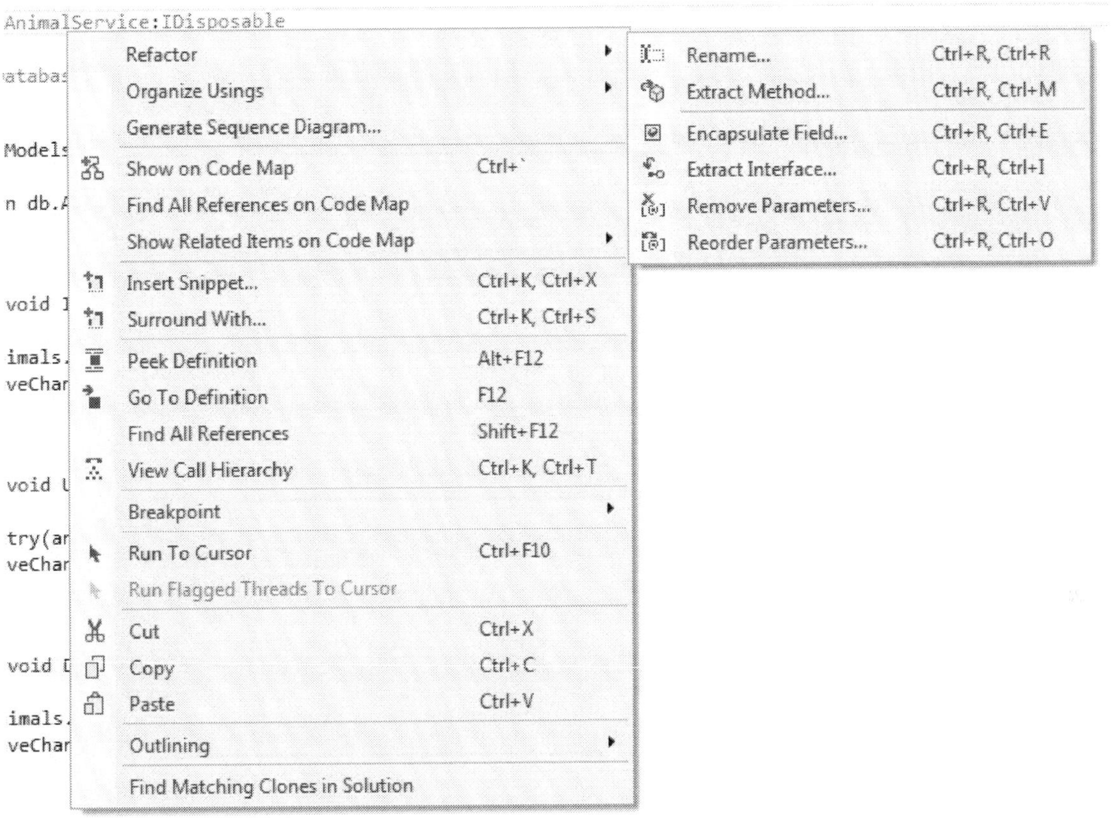

AnimalService:IDisposable

Refactor
Organize Usings
Generate Sequence Diagram...
Show on Code Map Ctrl+`
Find All References on Code Map
Show Related Items on Code Map
Insert Snippet... Ctrl+K, Ctrl+X
Surround With... Ctrl+K, Ctrl+S
Peek Definition Alt+F12
Go To Definition F12
Find All References Shift+F12
View Call Hierarchy Ctrl+K, Ctrl+T
Breakpoint
Run To Cursor Ctrl+F10
Run Flagged Threads To Cursor
Cut Ctrl+X
Copy Ctrl+C
Paste Ctrl+V
Outlining
Find Matching Clones in Solution

Rename... Ctrl+R, Ctrl+R
Extract Method... Ctrl+R, Ctrl+M
Encapsulate Field... Ctrl+R, Ctrl+E
Extract Interface... Ctrl+R, Ctrl+I
Remove Parameters... Ctrl+R, Ctrl+V
Reorder Parameters... Ctrl+R, Ctrl+O

```
public interface IAnimalService
{
    void Delete(Animal animal);
    Animal Find(int? id);
    IList<Animal> GetAll();
    void Insert(Animal animal);
    void Update(Animal animal);
}
```

Inside the controller, we have two constructors. One is to help us for this example which instantiates the service layer, and the other is the real one that takes a single parameter. This is the one that you should have in your enterprise-grade software because it can inject any item of IAnimalService into the controller.

```
public class AnimalController : Controller
{
    private IAnimalService _service;

    public AnimalController(IAnimalService animalService)
    {
```

```
        _service = animalService;
    }
//...
```

Before implementing the unit of work, we will create a new repository to illustrate why the unit of work is required. We will also do a little refactoring by changing the repository to stop automatically calling to SaveChanges. This allows us to insert several entities in a single transaction. This is now the animal service class and interface.

```
public interface IAnimalService
{
    void Delete(Animal animal);
    void Delete(IList<Animal> animals);
    Animal Find(int? id);
    IList<Animal> GetAll();
    void Save(Animal animal);
    void Save(IList<Animal> animal);
}
public class AnimalService : IAnimalService
{
    private IAnimalRepository animalRepository;

    public AnimalService(IAnimalRepository animalRepository)
    {
        this.animalRepository = animalRepository;
    }

    public Models.Animal Find(int? id)
    {
        return this.animalRepository.Find(id);
    }

    public void Delete(IList<Animal> animals)
    {
        foreach (var animal in animals)
        {
            this.animalRepository.Delete(animal);
        }

        this.animalRepository.Save();
    }

    public void Delete(Models.Animal animal)
    {
        this.Delete(new List<Animal> { animal });
    }

    public IList<Animal> GetAll()
```

```
    {
        return this.animalRepository.GetAll();
    }

    public void Save(Animal animal)
    {
        Save(new List<Animal> { animal });
    }

    public void Save(IList<Animal> animals)
    {
        foreach (var animal in animals)
        {
            if (animal.Id == default(int))
            {
                this.animalRepository.Insert(animal);
            }
            else
            {
                this.animalRepository.Update(animal);
            }
        }

        this.animalRepository.Save();
    }
}
```

As you can see, it's better. It also hides the complexity for updates and inserts by having a single method "save." Next, we will create a new repository. We won't code its detail but we will use it inside the AnimalService to simulate a case where we need to interact on several entities.

```
public class HumanRepository : IHumanRepository
{
}

public interface IHumanRepository
{
    void Insert(Models.Human humain);
}
```

We also need to modify the service to have in its constructor the *IHumanRepository*.

```
public class AnimalService : IAnimalService
{
    private IAnimalRepository animalRepository;
    private IHumanRepository humanRepository;
```

```
    public AnimalService(IAnimalRepository animalRepository, IHumanRepository
humanRepository)
    {
        this.animalRepository = animalRepository;
        this.humanRepository = humanRepository;
    }
    //...
}
```

Then we can simulate the need to have something in the same transaction between animal and human repository. This can be in the Save method of the AnimalService. Let's create a new save method in the service which takes an Animal and also a Human. In *IAnimalService* we add.

```
void SaveAll(Animal animal, Human humain);
```

And in the concrete implementation we have :

```
public void SaveAll(Animal animal, Human humain)
{
    this.animalRepository.Insert(animal);
    this.humanRepository.Insert(humain);
}
```

This is where the unit of work is required. The animal repository has its own DbContext and the human repository has its own, too. Since both do not have the same repository, they are in two different transactions. We could wrap both these lines with a **TransactionScope** but since Entity Framework is already a transaction scope and since in more complex scenarios where we would want to use the DbContext further, having to use the same DbContext is something viable.

## Implementing Unit of Work pattern

As we have seen, we need to share the DbContext. This is where the unit of work shines. The first move is to create the unit of work which holds the DbContext.

```
public interface IUnitOfWork
{
    IDbSet<T> Set<T>() where T : class;
    DbEntityEntry<T> Entry<T>(T entity) where T : class;
    void SaveChanges();
}
```

The interface could be richer but this should be the minimal number of methods. The implementation is only having a central point for every database set. In a more domain-driven design application we could restrain entities by having a DbContext that is less general than the one created. "AllDomainContext" contains all entities set. This is perfect to create the whole database or when your application has a limited number of entities (under 50). But if you are using a domain-driven design or with a big application, to have Entity Framework perform well and restrict the domains having several DbContexts is a good solution. With unit of work and its generic T class, you can pass any domain you want to have.

```
public class UnitOfWork<T> : IUnitOfWork where T : DbContext, new()
{
    public UnitOfWork()
    {
        DatabaseContext = new T();
    }

    private T DatabaseContext { get; set; }

    public void SaveChanges()
    {
        DatabaseContext.SaveChanges();
    }

    public System.Data.Entity.IDbSet<T> Set<T>() where T : class
    {
        return DatabaseContext.Set<T>();
    }

    public DbEntityEntry<T> Entry<T>(T entity) where T : class
    {
        return DatabaseContext.Entry<T>(entity);
    }
}
```

This unit of work is very general since it can take T as a set. This means that any entity defined can be used. In our example, with this modified unit of work, the controller needs to be changed, too.

```
public class AnimalController : Controller
{
    private IAnimalService _service;

    public AnimalController()
    {
        var uow = new UnitOfWork<AllDomainContext>();
        _service = new AnimalService(uow, new AnimalRepository(uow)
                                        , new HumanRepository(uow));
    }
```

```
    public AnimalController(IAnimalService animalService)
    {
        _service = animalService;
    }
    //...
}
```

So, the unit of work is instantiated with the domain we want. We still have the “real” constructor that takes only the *IAnimalService* which is the one that should be used in the real application with inversion of control to inject the controller. Since this is an article, to keep it simple, I show you what the **IoC** should do in the background. The animal service is changed, too, to work with the unit of work.

```
public class AnimalService : IAnimalService
{
    private IAnimalRepository animalRepository;
    private IHumanRepository humanRepository;
    private IUnitOfWork unitOfWork;
    public AnimalService(IUnitOfWork unitOfWork, IAnimalRepository
animalRepository, IHumanRepository humanRepository)
    {
        this.unitOfWork = unitOfWork;
        this.animalRepository = animalRepository;
        this.humanRepository = humanRepository;
    }

    public Animal Find(int? id)
    {
        return this.animalRepository.Find(id);
    }

    public void Delete(IList<Animal> animals)
    {
        foreach (var animal in animals)
        {
            this.animalRepository.Delete(animal);
        }

        this.unitOfWork.SaveChanges();
    }

    public void Delete(Models.Animal animal)
    {
        this.Delete(new List<Animal> { animal });
    }

    public IList<Animal> GetAll()
    {
```

```
        return this.animalRepository.GetAll();
    }

    public void Save(Animal animal)
    {
        Save(new List<Animal> { animal });
    }

    public void Save(IList<Animal> animals)
    {
        foreach (var animal in animals)
        {
            if (animal.Id == default(int))
            {
                this.animalRepository.Insert(animal);
            }
            else
            {
                this.animalRepository.Update(animal);
            }
        }

        this.unitOfWork.SaveChanges();
    }

    public void SaveAll(Animal animal, Human humain)
    {
        this.animalRepository.Insert(animal);
        this.humanRepository.Insert(humain);
        this.unitOfWork.SaveChanges();
    }
}
```

The repository now accepts the unit of work. It can work with set defined in the domain without problem.

```
public class AnimalRepository :
WebsiteForUnitOfWork.DataAccessLayer.Repositories.IAnimalRepository
{
    private IUnitOfWork UnitOfWork { get; set; }

    public AnimalRepository(IUnitOfWork unitOfWork)
    {
        this.UnitOfWork = unitOfWork;
    }

    public Models.Animal Find(int? id)
    {
        return UnitOfWork.Set<Animal>().Find(id);
```

```
    }

    public void Insert(Models.Animal animal)
    {
        UnitOfWork.Set<Animal>().Add(animal);
    }

    public void Update(Models.Animal animal)
    {
        UnitOfWork.Entry(animal).State = EntityState.Modified;
    }

    public void Delete(Models.Animal animal)
    {
        UnitOfWork.Set<Animal>().Remove(animal);
    }

    public IList<Animal> GetAll()
    {
        return UnitOfWork.Set<Animal>().AsNoTracking().ToList();
    }
}
```

It is possible to continue to improve the unit of work and Entity Framework by going further in the use of the repository. But, what has been shown here is enterprise graded repository design. It allows you to divide the domain and improve the performance of Entity Framework at the same time. It allows an abstraction between the Asp.Net MVC front and the Entity Framework. It is easily testable because we use an interface which can be mocked easily. Benefits are clear but the price to pay is all the superfluous work required to support this infrastructure. More classes need to be in place. Still, the version presented is light and once the setup is done adding a new entity is only a matter of editing the context in which it belongs and creating in the repository what action is needed.

## Source code

You can find the source code on GitHub : https://github.com/MrDesjardins/WebsiteForUnitOfWork.

# Asp.Net Identity error while seeding with custom field

Release Date: 21-Jan-14
Url: http://patrickdesjardins.com/blog/?post_type=post&p=2596

If you are using the new Asp.Net Identity framework which is working with OWIN, you may fail with an SQL exception. The exception looks like this :

*System.Data.SqlClient.SqlException: Invalid column name 'UserId'*

```
Running Seed method.
System.Data.Entity.Core.EntityCommandExecutionException: An error occurred while executing the command
 definition. See the inner exception for details. ---> System.Data.SqlClient.SqlException: Invalid
column name 'UserId'.
   at System.Data.SqlClient.SqlConnection.OnError(SqlException exception, Boolean breakConnection,
Action`1 wrapCloseInAction)
   at System.Data.SqlClient.SqlInternalConnection.OnError(SqlException exception, Boolean
```

The UserId is a column that is ignored in the configuration of the entity. Why does it try to read from it? Here is how the DbContext looks:

```
public class Configuration : DbMigrationsConfiguration<DatabaseContext>
{
    public Configuration()
    {
    }

    protected override void Seed(DatabaseContext context)
    {
        var userStore = new UserStore<ApplicationUser>();
        var manager = new UserManager<ApplicationUser>(userStore);

        var role = new IdentityUserRole { Role = new
                                  IdentityRole(Model.Roles.ADMINISTRATOR) };
        var user = new ApplicationUser() { UserName = "123123"
                                  , Email = 123123@123.com
                                  , Language = "en-US" };
        user.Roles.Add(role);
        IdentityResult result = manager.Create(user, "123123");

        var role2 = new IdentityUserRole { Role = new
                                  IdentityRole(Model.Roles.NORMAL) };
        var user2 = new ApplicationUser() { UserName = "qweqwe"
                                  , Email = qweqwe@qweqwe.com
                                  , Language = "fr-CA" };
        user.Roles.Add(role2);
        IdentityResult result2 = manager.Create(user2, "qweqwe");

        //...
    }
}
```

The problem resides on the first line of the seeding method. The *UserStore* takes in its first parameter the database context. Since I am not explicitly telling the *UserStore* to take the one passed by parameter, it does not know about the configuration defined in the **DatabaseContext**. To solve the problem just replace the first line with this line:

```
var userStore = new UserStore<ApplicationUser>(context);
```

## The entity type ApplicationUser is not part of the model for the current context.

Release Date: 23-Jan-14
Url: http://patrickdesjardins.com/blog/?post_type=post&p=2604

If you are using Asp.net Identity (OWIN authentication framework) with custom user schema you may stumble into an error that your model is not part of the context.

> *The entity type ApplicationUser is not part of the model for the current context.*

Server Error in '/' Application.

*The entity type ApplicationUser is not part of the model for the current context.*

**Description:** An unhandled exception occurred during the execution of the current web request. Please review the stack trace for more information about the error and where it originated in the code.

**Exception Details:** System.InvalidOperationException: The entity type ApplicationUser is not part of the model for current context.

**Source Error:**

```
Line 62:            if (ModelState.IsValid)
Line 63:            {
Line 64:                var user = await
UserManager.FindAsync(model.UserName, model.Password);
Line 65:                if (user != null)
Line 66:                {
```

**Source File:** c:\Users\Patrick\Documents\GitHub\GymWorkout\WorkoutPlanner\Controllers\AccountController.cs
**Line:** 64

This exception is raised if you go to the login screen and try to log in. It occurs if you have a **DbContext** class that inherits directly to DbContext and not from IdentityDbContext. Your database context must be aware of Identity tables.

```
public class DatabaseContext :IdentityDbContext<ApplicationUser>
```

Having this inheritance solves the problem.

## How to register Model Builder without having to manually add them one by one

Release Date: 31-Jan-14
Url: http://patrickdesjardins.com/blog/?post_type=post&p=2614

When you are using Entity Framework, you must have a class that inherits a **DbContext** class at some point. Multiple options are offered to you to register to Entity Framework (EF) the definition of your entities.

The one we see in this tutorial is based on the overridden method **OnModelCreation** that has a single parameter of type **DbModelBuilder**. This is the entry point for all ways to proceed with registration. Nevertheless, in tutorial the configuration is done directly in the method. The following code shows how it is usually done. For the purpose of being short, only a single primary key is defined for a single entity. The fact is that methods can become very big.

```
public class MyDbContext : DbContext
{
    protected override void OnModelCreating(DbModelBuilder modelBuilder)
    {
        modelBuilder.Entity<YourEntity>().HasKey(d => d.Id);
        base.OnModelCreating(modelBuilder);
    }
}
```

This is why the best practice is to have a single class for every entity configuration. This is done by inheriting every class by **EntityTypeConfiguration**.

```
public class YourEntityConfiguration : EntityTypeConfiguration<YourEntity>
{
    public YourEntityConfiguration()
    {
        this.HasKey(d => d.Id);
```

```
    }
}
```

Once you have your classes defined, the **OnModelCreating** can register them.

```
public class MyDbContext : DbContext
{
    protected override void OnModelCreating(DbModelBuilder modelBuilder)
    {
        modelBuilder.Configurations.Add(new YourEntityConfiguration());
        base.OnModelCreating(modelBuilder);
    }
}
```

The problem is that you have to remember to register the entity and also that this method can become very huge on a big project. Concerning the possibility to forget to register, Entity Framework (EF) will raise an exception saying that it does not know the entity type. It is not a big deal and the message is quite easy to understand. However, having to add this line of code becomes something to do in a big list of things to do. To keep it simpler, the Entity Framework team thought that we could simply specify which assembly every configuration is and to look it up for every class that inherits the **EntityTypeConfiguration**.

```
public class MyDbContext : DbContext
{
    protected override void OnModelCreating(DbModelBuilder modelBuilder)
    {

        modelBuilder.Configurations.AddFromAssembly(Assembly.GetAssembly(GetType()
        )); //Current Assembly
        base.OnModelCreating(modelBuilder);
    }
}
```

The above example shows that configurations are added from an assembly. It takes a single parameter that is the assembly to look up. If you want the current assembly, use *Assembly.GetAssembly(GetType())*.

# Using Migration DbMigration class for Up and Down action

Release Date: 06-Feb-14
Url: http://patrickdesjardins.com/blog/?post_type=post&p=2620

Entity Framework (EF) and Migration tools can be used in several ways. The most effective and complete one is to generate **DbMigration** classes by the Entity Framework Migration Tools. It allows the creation of the table with all attributes like foreign key, size, primary key and so on. It allows rollback in the situation that you have to get an older release. Often, this is possible with a source control but it is harder to have the database be restored in time. Migration tools let you restore the database in the time, which is a big plus. Also, it has the advantage ofcreating a a database quickly, which is very important for automatically testing or to simply create a new database for a developer. Migration also lets you seed data into the database. Instead of having a database empty every time, you can have a database with minimal values.

Before talking about commands that you will use during the development, one command is required to be executed once. It is the one that configures the migration tool.

```
Enable-Migrations
```

You can get help by using: **get-help Enable-Migrations**
You can specify the folder.

First of all, there are commands that you will use often. You can create a solution items folder and create power shell scripts with them. This will simplify the use of them. In both cases, these commands need to be executed in the **Package Manager Console**.

```
param([String]$migrationName)
Write-Host "MigrationName: $migrationName"
Add-Migration -Name $migrationName `
    -ConfigurationType YourDLL.Migration.YourDBContextConfiguration `
    -StartUpProjectName YourStartupDLL `
    -ProjectName YourDLL.Migration `
    -Verbose
```

## Usage:

```
.\AddMigration.ps1 TheMigrationClassToBeGenerated
```

This first script calls the **Add-Migration** command. It takes a configuration type. This file inherits from **DbMigrationsConfiguration** which is generic. The generic type is the **DbContext** class. This DbContext must have all entities so if you have split your context into several files then you must create a specific one for the migration. Your DbMigrationsConfiguration allows you to override a seeding method. This is where you can specify values to be inserted into your tables. It works by giving in parameter the DbContext that lets you insert entity and SaveChanges.

The project name is the parameter that lets you specify the migration project. That should be the same project where you have the configuration type. The StartUpProjectName allows the migration tool to know where to search for the config file. This is needed to get the connection string.

The Power Shell script lets you configure all these settings once and then just lets you specify the file name that contains the generated creation command. The file generated will be prefixed by the data and the time. This allows Entity Framework Migration tool to know the order of the execution of the file.

The second script is to update the database. Let's say that your team has created some script with the Add-Migration. The one that executed the code is up-to-date but not yours. This is why, to update your database, you need to get the code (from your source control) and then execute a command to update.

The update command is **Update-Database**. To make it simpler, like the Add-Migration, a small power script can be used.

```
Update-Database
    -ConfigurationTypeName "YourDLL.Migration.YourDBContextConfiguration" `
    -ProjectName "YourDLL.Migration"  `
    -StartUpProject "YourStartupDLL" `
    -Verbose
```

Parameters are pretty much the same. This time, it will execute the migration file. If you want to update not every file but just a few files you can set the -TargetMigration. It requires after this command the file name to be the last file to be executed. If you have 10 migration files and you want to migrate up to the third file, then you need to target the third file. This can be useful if you need to have a rollback.

This is almost it. You could remove all the files created and use automatic migration. However, you have less control over what is executed. With migration files, you can always edit them to add additional instructions, which is handy in the case of complex situations. This is almost always the case for enterprise applications where a rollback method needs to handle foreign key manipulations.

# Complex Type cannot have reference to entities

Release Date: 18-Mar-14
Url: http://patrickdesjardins.com/blog/?post_type=post&p=2719

If you have a **complex type**, you cannot have within this any reference to other entities. Let's imagine that I have a money class.

```
public class Money
{
    public decimal Value { get; set; }
    public CurrencyType Currency { get; set; }
}
```

As you can see, it has a reference to another class, named *CurrencyType*. This type is abstract and must be set to a Currency class like USD or CND. However, this brings Entity Framework with a ModelValidationException.

*System.Data.Entity.ModelConfiguration.ModelValidationException: One or more validation errors were detected during model generation: DataAccess.Contexts.Implementations.CurrencyType: Name: Each type name in a schema must be unique. Type name 'CurrencyType' is already defined.*

It is not possible to have this configuration. It would be very practical because you can have the Money in any of your classes and the table would have the Money_Value and Money_CurrencyId.

One option is to remove the currency from the *Money* or to have both properties of the Currency class inside the Money class. However, the strong positive that we had with CurrencyType was that this was using Value Object pattern. This means that it was strongly typed in the code and had a reference to a Currency table which had USD and CDN currency.

The question is how to use Entity Framework and still have an association between the amount of the money (value) and the currency without losing the strong association with the table that has all currencies? This leads us to a second option that is to remove the money from the entity that has the money. Instead of having the money directly into the class, you can have all money into a separate table. This removes the use of complex type in the money table. Of course, this causes some overhead by having more tables and more joins to do to get all the information. It also has the problem of having the ID of the Money inside your Entity.

A possible solution that I have used is to lose the strong Foreign Key but still have the data go directly into the entity that uses the money. This way, fewer tables, more speed, and in the code we use the value object pattern. Here is the money class and the value object class for currency:

```
public class Money
{
    public decimal Value { get; set; }
    public int CurrencyTypeId
    {
        get { return this.Currency.Id; }
        set { this.Currency = CurrencyType.GetCurrencyFromId(value); }
    }
    ///
    /// This is ignored by EntityFramework
    ///
    public CurrencyType Currency { get; set; }
}

public abstract class CurrencyType : ValueObject
{

    public static readonly CurrencyType Canada = new CanadianCurrency();
    public static readonly CurrencyType UnitedStatesOfAmerica = new USACurrency();

    public static CurrencyType GetCurrencyFromId(int value)
    {
        Type type = typeof(CurrencyType);

        var fields = type.GetFields(BindingFlags.Public | BindingFlags.Static);
        foreach (var field in fields)
        {
            var fieldValue = field.GetValue(null) as CurrencyType;
            if (fieldValue != null)
            {
                if (fieldValue.Id == value)
                {
                    return fieldValue;
                }
            }
        }
        throw new KeyNotFoundException(string.Concat(value
                                , " cannot be found in any static fields."));
    }
}
```

As you can see, the money class does have the value and the CurrencyType property. This property is ignored by Entity Framework so Money can be as **Complex Type**. However, we have an integer field that can be used but should not since we have a strongly typed currency property. Here is how to make it work with Entity configuration.

```
public class MoneyConfiguration : ComplexTypeConfiguration
{
    public MoneyConfiguration()
```

```
    {
        this.Ignore(d => d.Currency);
    }
}
```

How to use this money class? The best way is to check the unit tests.

```
[TestMethod]
public void
GivenAnInteger_WhenIntegerIsAKeyOfACurrency_ThenReturnConcreteCurrency()
{
    // Arrange
    var idOfCanada = CurrencyType.Canada.Id;
    var expected = CurrencyType.Canada;

    // Act
    var found = CurrencyType.GetCurrencyFromId(idOfCanada);

    //Assert
    Assert.IsInstanceOfType(found,typeof(CanadianCurrency));
    Assert.AreEqual(expected.Id,found.Id);
}
```

This is required because when we load from Entity Framework we will only get the integer. But, in the business logic the code will use the property. This is why the property of *CurrencyTypeId* is tightly bound with Currency with the reflection code. If the ID is not legit (does not exist), an exception is thrown. This should never occur but we should still test the case.

```
[TestMethod]
public void
GivenAnInteger_WhenIntegerIsNotAnExistingKeyOfACurrency_ThenThrowException()
{
    // Arrange
    const int idNonExisting = -1;

    // Act & Assert
    TestExtensions.Thrown(() => CurrencyType.GetCurrencyFromId(idNonExisting));
}
```

<ValueObjectsUnitTest> (2 tests)
ValueObjectsUnitTest.Currencies (2 tests)
CurrenciesTest (2 tests)
GivenAnInteger_WhenIntegerIsAKeyOfACurrency_ThenReturnConcreteCurrency
GivenAnInteger_WhenIntegerIsNotAnExistingKeyOfACurrency_ThenThrowException

To conclude, this might not be the best solution since it would be cleaner not to have this integer in the class. It would also be better not to have this integer without a foreign key to the CurrencyType table. However, since the value will be filled up and handled by Entity Framework only, we still control the integrity with the code. It would be possible for us to add manually the foreign key too.

# How to use Entity Framework with a list of Value Objects

Release Date: 25-Mar-14
Url: http://patrickdesjardins.com/blog/?post_type=post&p=3397

A value object can be anything that would be in an Enum in C#. However, we have this one in the database since it is an entity. The difference is that inside the code you have the ID and description. This way, we have a fast access in the code without needing to go in the database and we have a strong database that has all foreign keys to the value object class. Even if Entity Framework supports Enum, it is not strongly typed inside the database. The database does not have a foreign key so it would be possible to set a value that would not be in C#.

Because of how Entity Framework works, we cannot simply have an entity with a list of value objects. This would cause Entity Framework to set the entity ID into the value object table. The desired effect is to have only one entry per value object. For example, I have a Contest entity that has a list of possible Stock Markets. I want the value object, Stock Market, to have in its table all possible stock exchange markets and not have duplicates for different contests.

To fix this problem, we need to create an association table that will act as an association table in the database.

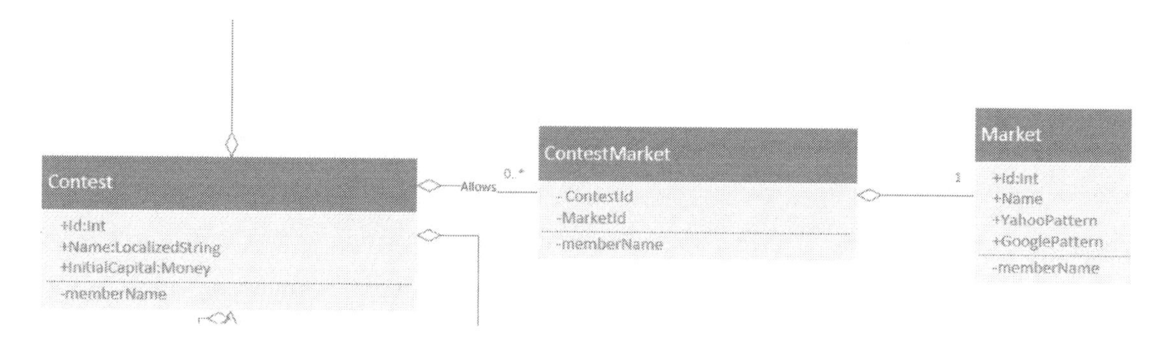

Concerning Entity Framework, we need to specify the new entity in the configuration. We need to specify that its primary key is the combination of both primary keys (Contest and Market). It would also be able to add additional properties for the association like having a date. This association can be set by setting a key with an anonymous object.

```
public class ContestMarketConfiguration : AssociationConfiguration
{
    public ContestMarketConfiguration()
        : base(Constants.SchemaNames.Contest)
    {
        this.HasKey(c => new { MarketId = c.MarketId, ContestId = c.ContestId });
    }
}
```

It is not required to specify the name of the property (MarketId, ContestId) but it is required to have these properties directly inside the Entity. The following code **does not** work:

```
public class ContestMarketConfiguration : AssociationConfiguration
{
    public ContestMarketConfiguration()
        : base(Constants.SchemaNames.Contest)
    {
        this.HasKey(c => new { MarketId = c.Market.Id
                             , ContestId = c.Contest.Id });
    }
}
```

This is unfortunate because you have to play with the Model to add an additional property just for the association. The entity looks like this:

```
public class ContestMarket
{
    public Contest Contest { get; set; }
    public int ContestId { get; set; }
    public MarketType Market { get; set; }
    public int MarketId { get; set; }
}
```

The Contest entity has a **Collection** of *ContestMarket* and the *MarketType* does not have anything. This way, it can be used anywhere even without the Contest context.

# Why it is wrong to use the Asp.Net MVC MetaDataType Attribute

Release Date: 03-Apr-14
Url: http://patrickdesjardins.com/blog/?post_type=post&p=3414

First of all, lets talk about **MetaDataType** attribute and why it exists. This one is from the **System.ComponentModel.DataAnnotations.MetadataTypeAttribute** namespace. Its role is to add attributes to a class without having to modify it. You can add this attribute that takes a single parameter to a class that will have all the attributes.

Some rules restrain the use of **MetaDataType**. It cannot be applied to a property and can only be applied to a single class for each class type. This attribute cannot be inherited, so you cannot customize it. On the other side, this attribute can be applied to **partial class** which is the main purpose of this attribute. This attribute will be respected by ASP.NET MVC but will not be read by Entity Framework. This is something interesting if you want to add additional validations or display attributes that do not affect the database. However, it is a good wakeup call for anybody who uses this strategy for validation attributes to know why it should be validated only during the input of the value and not during the save.

Second, from the description we can come to the conclusion that it was implemented for the scenario of Entity Framework with the **Database First Approach**. The model classes are automatically generated from the **EDMX file** and even if they are in C# and you can edit them, you should not. The reason is that if you change your database you will have to generate the model again which will override your changes. This is why Entity Framework creates those generated classes as partial class. This allows you to create your own class with the same name and define additional properties, fields and methods. But, what about existing properties that you would want to add attributes to? This is where **MetaDataType** comes into play.

```
//Class from Entity Framework Database First
public partial class YourModelClass
{
    public string YourProperty{get;set;}
}

//Your Partial Class
[MetadataType(typeof(YourModelClassMetaData))]
public partial class YourModelClass
{
}
```

```
//The class that add your attributes
public class YourModelClassMetaData
{
    [Required]
    public object YourProperty{get;set;};
}
```

To illustrate the use of MetaDataType, let's see an example with Entity Framework. As you can see, the first class of the code snippet is the generated class. This one has all your properties that represent every column of your table. This class should not be edited by your since the file can be overridden by an automatic tool. This is why the second class comes into play. It uses the **partial** keyword to give you a leverage. You can add new items without touching the generated file. The only constraint is to have the partial keyword and the same class name. This way, .Net can match the classes and merge them into a single class. In this example, we add the MetaDataType attribute that gives the capability to a class to delegate the attribute association. This is what we want — to add an attribute to existing properties. Having only partial class is not enough because you can add but not attribute because these must be set over an existing property.

The last class in the code snippet is the one referenced by the MetadataType attribute of the second. It tells .Net Framework to go into this third class, do reflection to get a property-property association and move the attribute from the referenced class into the class that the MetadataType attribute has set. This is why the property type does not matter, only the name.

In another scenario, where you do not want to add attributes to a class that comes from Entity Framework, you could place directly into your model class the MetadataType attribute and unclutter your model from any attribute by having them all in another class.

At the end, what is wrong with MetadataType? It does not seem to hurt anything. Well, this is where I have something that bothers me. How come the model classes are directly used in the view? This means that you are using ViewBag, ViewData or something else to pass additional information to the view. This means that your design is less testable since it relies on a static object mechanism. It is also not required and someone could omit it without breaking anything. It also means that you are splitting your model class into three files — one generated, one of yours and one with attributes. This generates a lot of noise just to bypass a view model approach or to not use Entity Framework Code First (that can be used even if you are working with the database first).

I believe this approach is viable for a small application that you know will not be over 15 entities with not a lot of business logic. It is a tool in the middle of a lot of others.

Nevertheless, this is far from being an approach that should be opted to be "the one" that must be used absolutely. This approach ends often by having UIHint, mixed with Required, mixed with Display attribute. Some are back end, some are front end, and everything is mixed up in a huge class that seems not that huge because it is divided in three.

## Failed to initialize the PowerShell host

Release Date: 24-Apr-14
Url: http://patrickdesjardins.com/blog/?post_type=post&p=3452

During the migration of Entity Framework to 6.1.0 I received an error about PowerShell host that failed to initialize.

*Adding 'EntityFramework 6.1.0' to BusinessLogicUnitTest. Successfully added 'EntityFramework 6.1.0' to BusinessLogicUnitTest. Executing script file 'C:\Code\BourseVirtuelle\packages\EntityFramework.6.1.0\tools\install.ps1'.*

Failed to initialize the PowerShell host. If your PowerShell execution policy setting is set to AllSigned, open the Package Manager Console to initialize the host first. The problem was the system has its **executions policy too restrictive**. One way to fix the problem is to open a PowerShell console as administrator and to set the execution policy to unrestricted.

```
Set-ExecutionPolicy Unrestricted
```

```
Administrator: Windows PowerShell
Windows PowerShell
Copyright (C) 2013 Microsoft Corporation. All rights reserved.

PS C:\Windows\system32> Set-ExecutionPolicy Unrestricted
PS C:\Windows\system32>
```

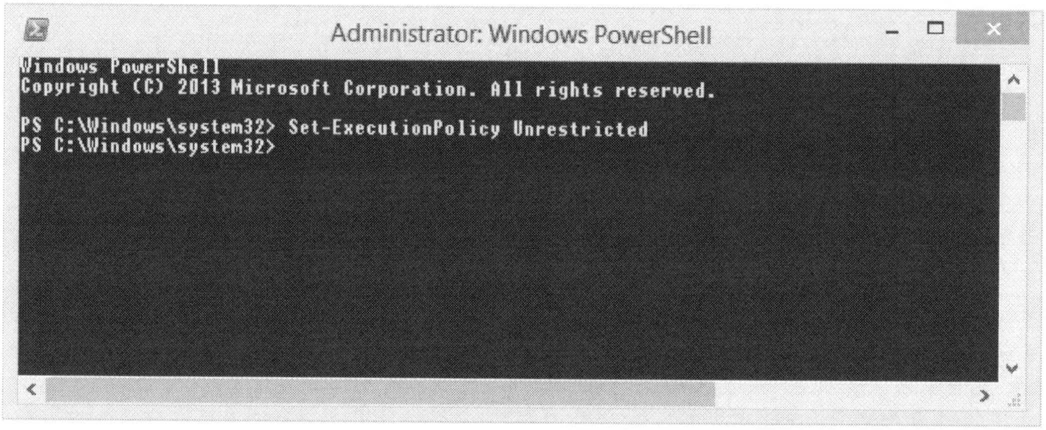

From there, open again Visual Studio 2013 and open the **Package Manager Console**. This was also required before using NuGet to update Entity Framework. Opening the Package Manager Console seem to execute a Power Shell script named **Profile.ps1** located in your Program Files folder.

```
C:\Program Files (x86)\Microsoft Visual Studio
12.0\Common7\IDE\Extensions\b331wcwx.fbh\Modules\NuGet\Profile.ps1
```

# Entity Framework Finds an Entity by its Primary Key

Release Date: 03-May-14
Url: http://patrickdesjardins.com/blog/?post_type=post&p=3514

Entity Framework allows you to search entity by many criteria, like you would do with SQL query. However, Entity Framework has a special method that is specialized to **search by primary key**. This method is named **Find**. The Find method takes a single parameter that is the primary key. If more than one parameter is specified, then Entity Framework will use all these parameters for the primary key. This is the case if you have multiple columns as the primary key (composite key).

```
private static void FindUser()
{
    using (var context = new YourContext())
    {
        var person = context.Persons.Find(1);
        Console.WriteLine(person.Name); //Output SeededPerson
    }
}
```

If nothing is found, the method returns null. It is important to always verify if the find method returned a value or not. If this validation is omitted, your code could crash like the following code:

```
private static void FindUser()
{
    using (var context = new YourContext())
    {
        var person = context.Persons.Find(2);
        Console.WriteLine(person.Name); //Crash because person is null
    }
}
```

This is the result of this code, a Find that returns null and throws a **NullReferenceException**:

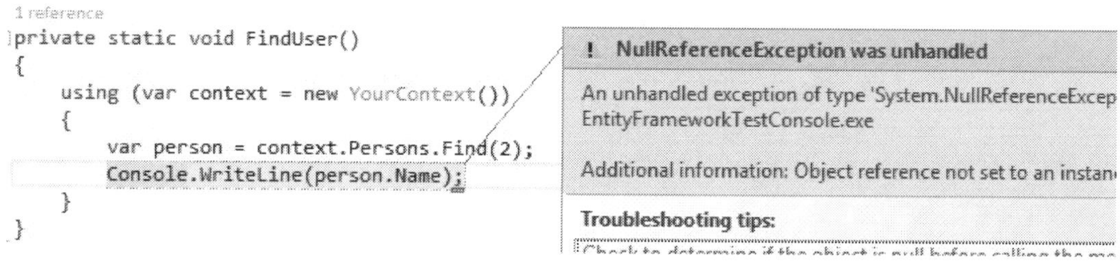

```
1 reference
private static void FindUser()
{
    using (var context = new YourContext())
    {
        var person = context.Persons.Find(2);
        Console.WriteLine(person.Name);
    }
}
```

! NullReferenceException was unhandled

An unhandled exception of type 'System.NullReferenceExcep
EntityFrameworkTestConsole.exe

Additional information: Object reference not set to an instan

Troubleshooting tips:

The Find method looks the same as the **SingleOrDefault** method with condition on the column that represents the primary key. The SingleOrDefault generates this SQL statement:

```
SELECT TOP (2)
    [Extent1].[Id] AS [Id],
    [Extent1].[Name] AS [Name],
    [Extent1].[BirthDate] AS [BirthDate],
    [Extent1].[Person_Id] AS [Person_Id],
    [Extent1].[Residence_Id] AS [Residence_Id],
    [Extent1].[House_Id] AS [House_Id]
    FROM [dbo].[People] AS [Extent1]
    WHERE 1 = [Extent1].[Id]
```

This is not the case of the Find method that does not generate anything in the SQL Profiler. So, it has something different, other than being limited to search only by primary key.

The first difference is that the Find method looks in DbContext memory to see if it is already present. If it finds the entity then it returns it. No round trip to the database. The Find method looks for an entity that has already been added to the DbContext and also those that have been marked to be added. If it is not found, it executes the same query as the SingleOrDefault. If you are curious about the TOP (2), just remember that, like Single, it expects to have only a single entity returned. By having TOP 2, if it has two or more entities for the primary key, then it would raise an exception.

Another difference is that Find calls DetectChanges. Here is the code source of Entity Framework for the Find method.

```
public TEntity Find(params object[] keyValues)
{
  this.InternalContext.ObjectContext.AsyncMonitor.EnsureNotEntered();
  this.InternalContext.DetectChanges(false);
  WrappedEntityKey key = new WrappedEntityKey
                    (this.EntitySet, this.EntitySetName, keyValues, "keyValues");
  object obj = this.FindInStateManager(key) ?? this.FindInStore(key, "keyValues");
  if (obj != null && !(obj is TEntity))
```

```
  throw Error.DbSet_WrongEntityTypeFound((object) obj.GetType().Name, (object)
typeof (TEntity).Name);
  else
  return (TEntity) obj;
}
```

Line 4 calls the DbContext DetectChanges. So, by default, performance can be reduced. It would be a good idea to set the **AutoDetectChangesEnabled** to false. We will discuss later detect changes.

If you call Find twice, only one round trip to the database is done. But if you are doing a call twice with SingleOrDefault, two round trips are executed.

```
using (var context = new YourContext())
{
    var person = context.Persons.SingleOrDefault(d => d.Id == 1);
    Console.WriteLine(person.Name);
    var person2 = context.Persons.SingleOrDefault(d => d.Id == 1);
    Console.WriteLine(person2.Name);
}
```

The result is:

| EventClass | TextData |
|---|---|
| SQL:BatchCompleted | select serverproperty('EngineEdition') |
| SQL:BatchCompleted | SELECT TOP (2) [Extent1].[Id] AS [... |
| SQL:BatchCompleted | SELECT TOP (2) [Extent1].[Id] AS [... |

This is completely different with Find.

```
private static void DoubleFindDatabase()
{
    using (var context = new YourContext())
    {
        Console.WriteLine(context.Persons.Local.Count); //0
        var person = context.Persons.Find(1);
        Console.WriteLine(person.Name);
        Console.WriteLine(context.Persons.Local.Count); //1
        var person2 = context.Persons.Find(1);
        Console.WriteLine(person2.Name);
        Console.WriteLine(context.Persons.Local.Count); //1
    }
}
```

If we have added a person into the context but not saved anything in the database, the Find method will return this entity.

```
private static void FindUserNotInDatabaseButInContext()
{
    using (var context = new YourContext())
    {
        Console.WriteLine(context.Persons.Local.Count); //0
        var newPerson = new Person {Id=500, Name = "New Person"
                                  , BirthDate = new DateTime(2000, 1, 2)};
        context.Persons.Add(newPerson);
        Console.WriteLine(context.Persons.Local.Count); //1
        var person = context.Persons.Find(500);
        Console.WriteLine(person.Name);
        Console.WriteLine(context.Persons.Local.Count); //1
    }
}
```

This is not the case with **SingleOrDefault**. It returns NULL.

```
using (var context = new YourContext())
{
    Console.WriteLine(context.Persons.Local.Count); //0
    var newPerson = new Person {Id=500, Name = "New Person"
                              , BirthDate = new DateTime(2000, 1, 2)};
    context.Persons.Add(newPerson);
    Console.WriteLine(context.Persons.Local.Count); //1
    var person = context.Persons.SingleOrDefault(d=>d.Id==500);
    //Console.WriteLine(person.Name);//Commented because would crash. Person= NULL
    Console.WriteLine(context.Persons.Local.Count); //1
}
```

The reason is the **SingleOrDefault**, contrary to **Find**, does not go to the Local memory of the DbContext.

# Entity Framework Complex Type and its Tracking

Release Date: 04-May-14
Url: http://patrickdesjardins.com/blog/?post_type=post&p=3534

Entity Framework has something called **complex type**. They are classes that do not have a unique identifier. They are used as a subset of an entity. For example, you can have an Address class that you want to have inside another class but do not want to have to have a table for the Address. This is useful for concepts that can be shared across entities without having to refer to them as an entity themselves. Another example could be Audit. An Audit table can be a solution, but you may want to have a ModifiedDate and ModifiedUser for some of your entities. The solution would be to copy and paste those two properties on all your entities or to have a class that has those two properties and to use this class inside entities that want to have audit. Let's see a coding example.

```
public class House
{
    public int Id { get; set; }
    public double Price { get; set; }
    public Address Address { get; set; }
}

public class Address
{
    public string Street { get; set; }
    public int Number { get; set; }
    public string City { get; set; }
}
```

A *house* has an *Address*. Later on, if we add *Business* entity, this could also refer to the *Address* entity without having to copy and paste all *Address* properties.

# Linq to Entity to get the number of days between two dates

Release Date: 08-May-14
Url: http://patrickdesjardins.com/blog/?post_type=post&p=3468

If you want to get the number of day between two dates, you can get those dates back to C# and calculate the difference between them. However, it is possible to tell SQL Server to do it for you by Linq To Entity.

It has changed since **Entity Framework (EF) 6**. You have to use DbFunctions class now to execute complex operations to SQL Server. The operation that interests us is named **DiffDays**. It takes two parameters. The first one is the smallest date, the second one is the biggest date. If you invert these parameters, the count will be negative.

Here is an example of its use:

```
var allActiveContest = GetAllActiveContestForUser(userId)
              .Select(d=>new ContestWithSmallStatistics(){
                            Id=d.Id,
                            Name=d.Name,
                            NumberOfDaysRemainingBeforeEndDate =
             DbFunctions.DiffDays(d.RegistrationRules.StartingTime
                              ,d.RegistrationRules.EndingTime).Value,
                            NumberOfUsersRegistered = d.Contester.Count
          });
```

The main advantage is that you can have from the database exactly what you want instead of having a class that would have two dates. You could also use it for having some logic that will not return everything. For example, we could return only Active Contest for a contest that has more than 30 days.

## CreateIdentityAsync value cannot be null when logging with User created with Migration Tool

Release Date: 15-May-14
Url: http://patrickdesjardins.com/blog/?post_type=post&p=3473

If you create a user from your Asp.Net MVC (**Identity**) and log in with this one, it should work. However, if you create your users by code, for example with Entity Framework Migration seeding method, you may have for results an error page. The error is not very clear. It can say that the value cannot be null and that the parameter name is value. This does not give a lot of information about where the error is. The stack trace shows some information about security claims and the problem is triggered by the call to the UserManager **CreateIdentityAsync** method.

# Server Error in '/' Application.

*Value cannot be null.*
*Parameter name: value*

**Description:** An unhandled exception occurred during the execution of the current web request. Please review the stack trace for more information about the where it originated in the code.

**Exception Details:** System.ArgumentNullException: Value cannot be null.
Parameter name: value

**Source Error:**

```
Line 44:        public async Task<ClaimsIdentity> CreateIdentityAsync(ApplicationUser user, str
Line 45:        {
Line 46:            return await userManager.CreateIdentityAsync(user, applicationCookie);
Line 47:        }
Line 48:        public ClaimsIdentity CreateIdentity(ApplicationUser user, string applicationCo
```

**Source File:** c:\Users\Patrick\Documents\TFS\BourseVirtuelle\Code\BourseVirtuelle\DataAccess\UserManager\Implementations\UserManager.cs **Line:** 46

**Stack Trace:**

```
[ArgumentNullException: Value cannot be null.
Parameter name: value]
   System.Security.Claims.Claim..ctor(String type, String value, String valueType, String issuer
   System.Security.Claims.Claim..ctor(String type, String value, String valueType, String issuer
   System.Security.Claims.Claim..ctor(String type, String value) +59
   Microsoft.AspNet.Identity.<CreateAsync>d__0.MoveNext() +1641
   System.Runtime.ExceptionServices.ExceptionDispatchInfo.Throw() +48
   System.Runtime.CompilerServices.TaskAwaiter.ThrowForNonSuccess(Task task) +235
```

In fact, the problem is that the Security Stamp was not set. This was found after seeing a difference in **AspNetUsers** table.

| Id | Email | Grav... | Display... | FirstNa... | LastName | LastLog... | Creation... | Validat... | Emai... | Passwo... | SecurityStamp |
|---|---|---|---|---|---|---|---|---|---|---|---|
| 9e4-cc01ea52bbfe | system@syste... | NULL | System | System | System | NULL | 2014-04-2... | 2014-04... | False | AJKDBa... | NULL |
| 379b6b8d-5136... | super@super.c... | NULL | super | NULL | NULL | NULL | 2014-04-2... | 2014-04... | False | AET8M... | b448c7e1-4ab1... |
| 49ecda70-bf64-... | 123@123.com | NULL | pdesjardi... | Patrick | Desjardins | NULL | 2014-04-2... | 2014-04... | False | AO2X+z... | b448c7e1-4ab1... |
| 58cff640-98b1-... | asd@asd.com | NULL | jdoe | Jim | Doe | NULL | 2014-04-2... | 2014-04... | False | AJKooh... | NULL |
| 9a7a7fa5-5a9f-... | qwe@qwe.com | NULL | msavaria | Melodie | Savaria | NULL | 2014-04-2... | 2014-04... | False | AKjF7ps... | NULL |
| f5d9dfff-3f2a-4... | test@test.com | NULL | Test | Test | Test | NULL | 2014-04-2... | 2014-04... | False | ADDUS... | NULL |
| NULL | NULL | NULL | NULL | NULL | NULL | NULL | NULL | NULL | NULL | NULL | NULL |

As you can see, the column was not set for the user created by the Entity Framework Migration Seed method. To solve this issue, the seed method was changed to generate a **Security Stamp**. The security stamp can be generated with a random GUID.

```
var adminUser = new ApplicationUser { Id = Guid.NewGuid().ToString()
```

```
    , FirstName = "Patrick"
    , LastName = "Desjardins"
    , DisplayName = "pdesjardins"
    , Email = EMAIL_ADMIN
    , CreationDateTime = runningContext.GetCurrentTime()
    , UserName = userValueGenerator.GenerateUserName(EMAIL_ADMIN)
    , PasswordHash = ApplicationUser.HashPassword("123123")
    , ValidationDateTime = runningContext.GetCurrentTime()
    , SecurityStamp = Guid.NewGuid().ToString()
};
```

With the Security Stamp set, it is possible to log in without having CreateIdentityAsync raising any exception.

## Entity Framework Database Setup for Code First

Release Date: 22-May-14
Url: http://patrickdesjardins.com/blog/?post_type=post&p=3496

This article is part of a series of Entity Framework articles. This first article is how to generate the database from mode classes. First, let's define model classes that will be used across all articles.

```
public class Person
{
    public int Id { get; set; }
    public int Name { get; set; }
    public DateTime BirthDate { get; set; }

    public ICollection<Person> Friends { get; set; }

    public House Residence { set; get; }
}

public class House
{
    public int Id { get; set; }
    public double Price { get; set; }

    public Address Address { get; set; }

    public ICollection<Person> Resident { get; set; }
    public Person Owner { get; set; }
}

public class Address
```

```
{
    public string Street { get; set; }
    public int Number { get; set; }
    public string City { get; set; }
}
```

But first we will comment on the Address class and all references to it. The reason is that we do not want for the moment to configure anything. Then we need to add Entity Framework to your project.

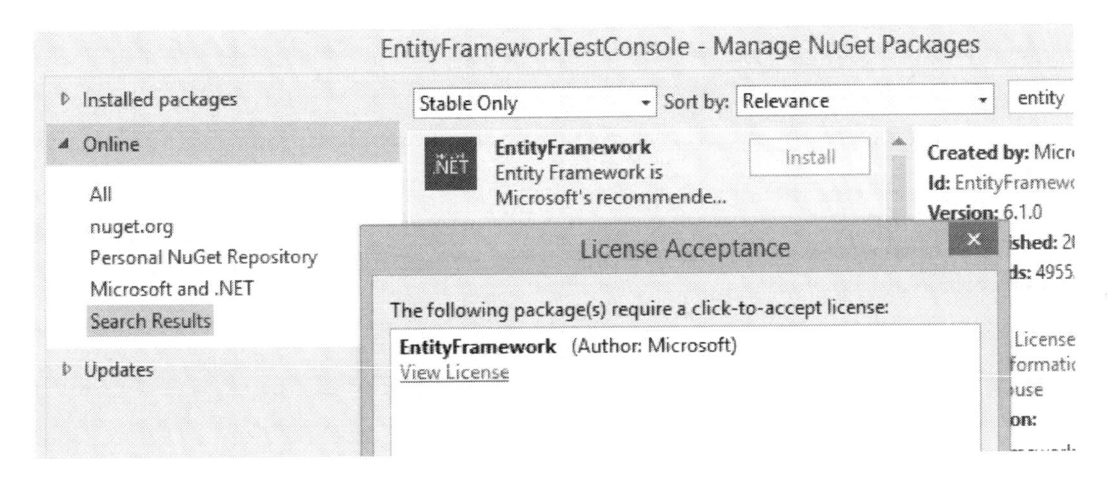


The last step is to tell Entity Framework to initialize the database. This will create the database and all tables defined by the DbContext.

```
public static void BuildDatabase()
{
    using (var context = new YourContext())
    {
        context.Database.Initialize(true);
    }
}
```

We could also add an Entity to the database to generate the database automatically. This would produce the same result.

```
public static void BuildByAddingEntity()
{
    using (var context = new YourContext())
    {
        var stud = new Person() { Name = "Person1"
                                , BirthDate = new DateTime(1990, 01, 01) };
        context.Persons.Add(stud);
        context.SaveChanges();
```

```
    }
}
```

The result is not very interesting because it creates something without the help of any connection string. This means that the database name is generated with the context name and the namespace. For example, the code executed to generate a database would be "EntityFrameworkTestConsole.DataAccessLayer.YourContext." To fix this issue, we need to define a connection string and then set it in the YourContext. It also has used the default SQL Server defined for your machine. In general, it is SQL Express. This is very restrictive.

EntityFrameworkTestConsole.DataAccessLayer.YourContext
Database Diagrams
Tables
System Tables
FileTables
dbo._MigrationHistory
dbo.Houses
dbo.People

If you set up a connection string with a name (for example you could use "DefaultConnection") this one will be used if set in the context. The **app.config** is where the connection string can be defined.

```
<configSections>
  <!-- For more information on Entity Framework configuration, visit
http://go.microsoft.com/fwlink/?LinkID=237468 -->
  <section name="entityFramework"
          type="System.Data.Entity.Internal.ConfigFile.EntityFrameworkSection,
EntityFramework, Version=6.0.0.0, Culture=neutral,
PublicKeyToken=b77a5c561934e089"
          requirePermission="false" />
</configSections>
<connectionStrings>
  <add name="DefaultConnection"
       connectionString="Data Source=(LocalDb)\v11.0;Initial
Catalog=EntityFrameworkTestConsole;Integrated Security=True"
       providerName="System.Data.SqlClient" />
</connectionStrings>
```

This generates the database with the name specified in the **Catalog** from the connection string. You could also specify directly the connection string into the base() but this will be a show stopper if you are building an application that must change the server and database depending on the environment (dev, test, prod).

EntityFrameworkTestConsole
Database Diagrams
Tables
System Tables
FileTables
dbo._MigrationHistory
dbo.Houses
dbo.People

Entity Framework takes care of everything for you. Tables are created from your entity defined in your context. It also takes care of all primary keys and foreign keys for you.

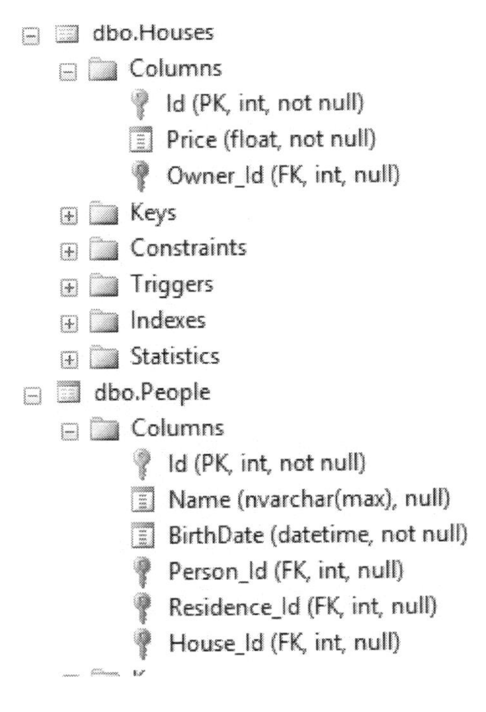


So far, we have seen that Entity Framework can generate the database from minimalist code. Only a context needs to be defined. Of course, setting a connection string and associating the connection string name with the context gives you more control of which server and database to connect Entity Framework.

You can find this code at GitHub (https://github.com/MrDesjardins/EntityFrameworkTestConsole).

# Entity Framework Database Initialization

Release Date: 27-May-14
Url: http://patrickdesjardins.com/blog/?post_type=post&p=3505

Initializing a database with Entity Framework is essential. It creates the database, tables and all constraints. In a previous article, we saw that it is possible to generate the database when the context specifies to the database to initialize itself or when adding an entity to the database. However, when the database exists and we have changed model classes, how can we control how the database schema is altering? This is the goal of this article. We will see how we can control Entity Framework to create and especially how to update database schema.

We have already seen the **default initializer**. It is named **CreateDatabaseIfNotExists**. This is only interesting when you start a brand new application. The reason is that a small change like adding a new property to a class will throw an exception. This is because Entity Framework realizes that the model from the code is not still synchronized with the table schema. This results in an **InvalidOperationException** that looks like this:

*Additional information: The model backing the 'YourContext' context has changed since the database was created. Consider using Code First Migrations to update the database.*

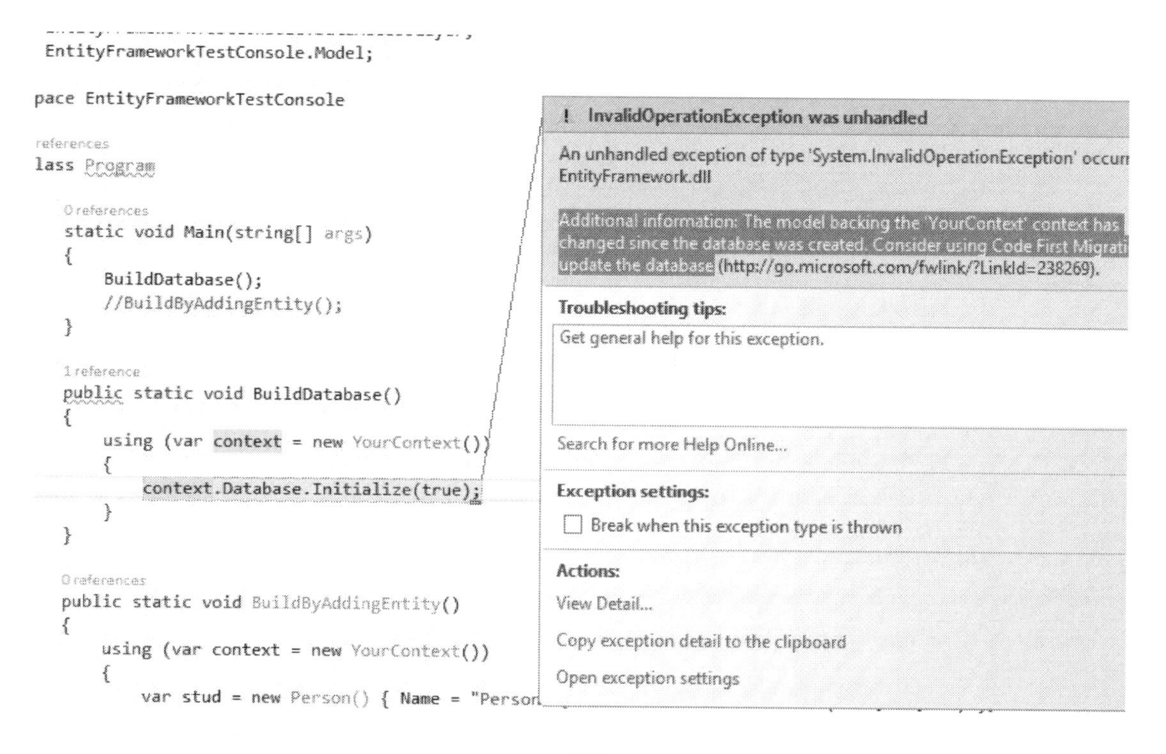

If you want to use that type of initializer, you have to manually delete the whole database for every modification of your context. For your information, the default intializer could also be explicitly specified in the contructor of your DbContext.

```
public YourContext(): base("DefaultConnection")
{
    Database.SetInitializer<YourContext>(new
            CreateDatabaseIfNotExists<YourContext>()); //Default one
}
```

Instead of having to manually delete the database every time, you can use the second initializer that will drop the database for you if any change has been detected. This second initializer that drops the database for you is named **DropCreateDatabaseIfModelChanges**.

```
public YourContext(): base("DefaultConnection")
{
    Database.SetInitializer<YourContext>(new
            DropCreateDatabaseIfModelChanges<YourContext>()); //Drop database if
        changes detected
}
```

It is important to note that this initializer will not delete the database if you do not change the model. If you run your application multiple times, it could start to have a lot of data that you may not want. In the scenario where you would prefer to erase every piece of data from your database even if you do not change the model, then you have to use a third initializer. **DropCreateDatabaseAlways** drops the database every time the application starts.

```
public YourContext(): base("DefaultConnection")
{
    Database.SetInitializer<YourContext>(new
            DropCreateDatabaseAlways<YourContext>()); //Drop database every times
}
```

The problem with all these initializers is that all of them at some point let you down with a default value. You have to have an SQL script to fill up tables with initial data. This is where the most useful initializer exists. It is the custom initializer. You can create your own initializer and inherit from one of the three we just discussed. For example, you can drop all the databases every time the schema is changed, which will create all tables but also in this custom initializer tell Entity Framework to insert default demo values. You can also create one that does not inherit any of the three but inherits from **IDatabaseInitializer**. The advantage of inheriting from an existing initializer is that you can use the leverage of basic functionality and only override the Seed method to push data into the website.

```
public YourContext(): base("DefaultConnection")
{
    Database.SetInitializer<YourContext>(new CustomInitializer<YourContext>());
//Custom if model changed and seed values
}
//...
public class CustomInitializer<T> : DropCreateDatabaseIfModelChanges<YourContext>
{
    protected override void Seed(YourContext context)
    {
        base.Seed(context);
    }
}
```

The *CustomInitializer* method overrides the **Seed** method. This is where you can use the context passed by parameter to insert data into your database. You do not have to call SaveChanges to save anything because the class that calls the seed method calls the **SaveChanges** right after calling the seeding method.

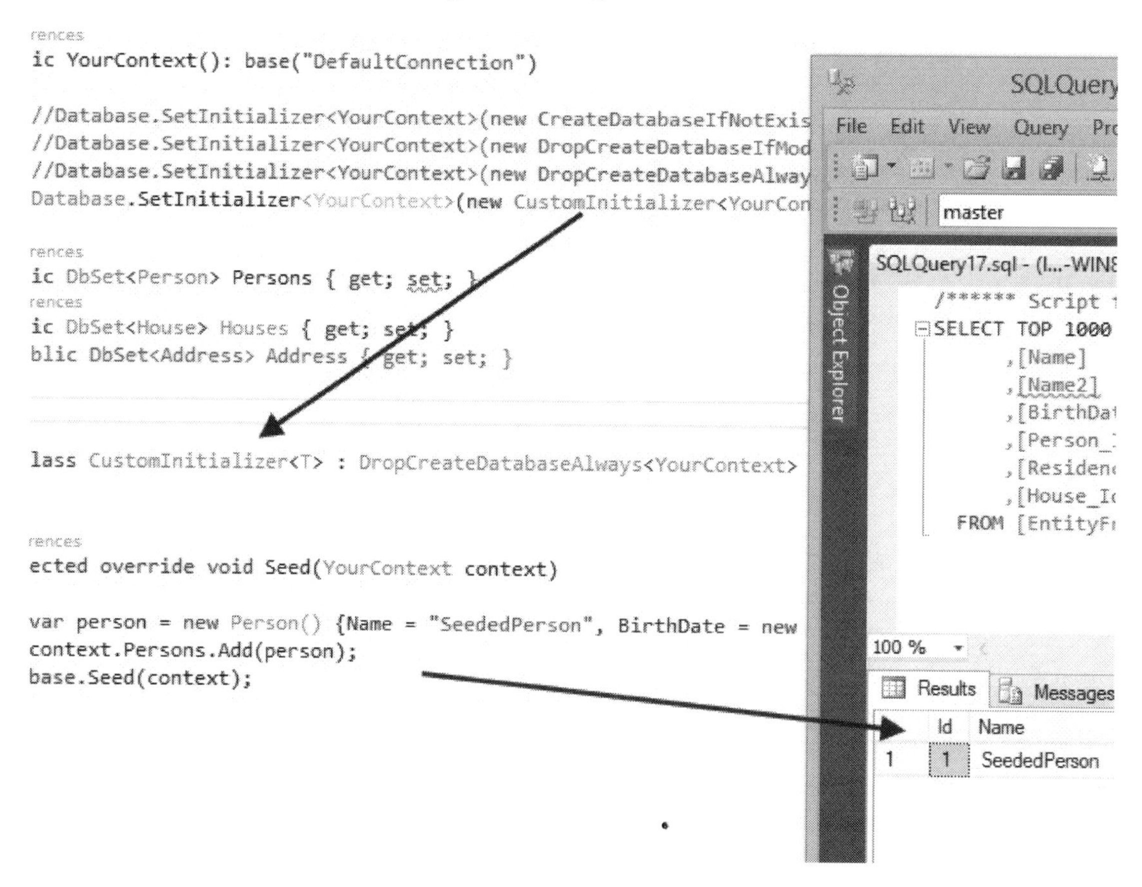

If the database already exists, you may stumble into an error. The exception "Cannot drop database because it is currently in use" can raise. This problem occurs when an active connection remains connected to the database that is in the process of being deleting. A trick is to override the **InitializeDatabase** method and alter the database. This tells the database to close all connections and if a transaction is open to roll back this one.

```
public class CustomInitializer<T> : DropCreateDatabaseAlways<YourContext>
{
    public override void InitializeDatabase(YourContext context)
    {
        context.Database.ExecuteSqlCommand(TransactionalBehavior
                    .DoNotEnsureTransaction
                    , string.Format("ALTER DATABASE {0} SET SINGLE_USER WITH
ROLLBACK IMMEDIATE"
                    , context.Database.Connection.Database));

        base.InitializeDatabase(context);
    }

    protected override void Seed(YourContext context)
    {
        var person = new Person() { Name = "SeededPerson"
                                , BirthDate = new DateTime(1900, 1, 1) };
        context.Persons.Add(person);
        base.Seed(context);
    }
}
```

The last configuration is to remove all initialization. This will not check if the database has changed, or check if something is not synchronized between tables and model classes. This is perfect if you have an existing database that is not handled by Entity Framework for the creation and insertion of initial values.

```
public YourContext(): base("DefaultConnection")
{
    Database.SetInitializer<YourContext>(null); //No initialization
}
```

Before concluding, I have to say that any of the initializers should have been set in the static constructor of your context. The static constructor is called before any constructors and is executed once. This is what we want. The reason is that in some of your applications, you may initialize more than once the context. You do not want to execute all the processes to check if the database is ready to be changed or not.

```
static YourContext()
{
```

```
    //Database.SetInitializer<YourContext>(new
CreateDatabaseIfNotExists<YourContext>()); //Default one
    //Database.SetInitializer<YourContext>(new
DropCreateDatabaseIfModelChanges<YourContext>()); //Drop database if changes
detected
    //Database.SetInitializer<YourContext>(new
DropCreateDatabaseAlways<YourContext>()); //Drop database every times
    //Database.SetInitializer<YourContext>(new CustomInitializer<YourContext>());
//Custom if model changed and seed values
    Database.SetInitializer<YourContext>(null); //Nothing is done
}
```

We have seen how to use Entity Framework to initialize a database but also how to seed it with testing values. We have seen many different way to initialize the database, tables and model classes with Entity Framework. So far, we have not discussed the Entity Framework Migration Tool to initialize the database. This tool allows a manual call with Entity to the database to perform initialization. It has the advantage of having full control of when and what is done but has the disadvantage of having more to do. Information about the Migration tool will be discussed later. You can find all code discussed in this article at GitHub (https://github.com/MrDesjardins/EntityFrameworkTestConsole).

# Entity Framework DbContext Local

Release Date: 03-Jun-14
Url: http://patrickdesjardins.com/blog/?post_type=post&p=3522

Entity Framework uses the **DbContext** as a proxy to connect to the database. The DbContext keeps information that came from the database but also information set from your C# code. It is the *middleman* between your entity in your code and your entity in your database. To be more accurate, it is the **Local** of the **DbSet** that contains the DbContext where the information remains for the lifetime of the DbContext.

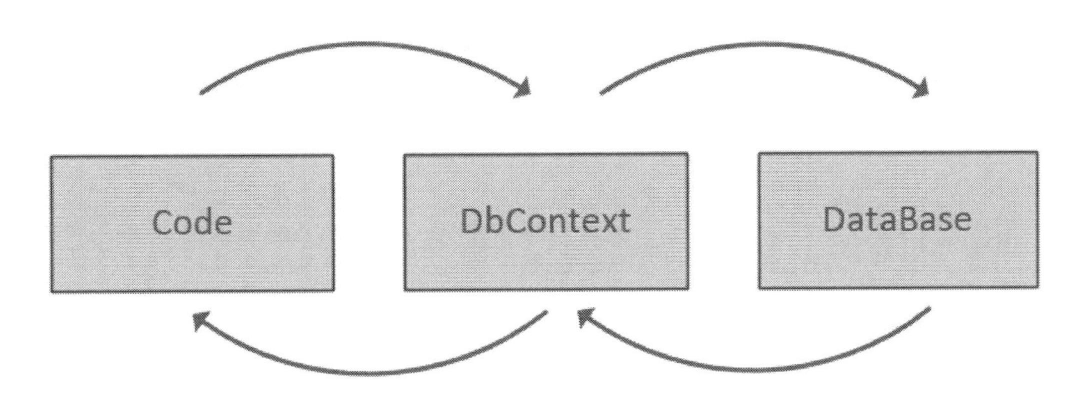


The DbContext has for every set a local storage. This is a temporary place where information resides before going into the database. It is possible to access this container to get information already queried.

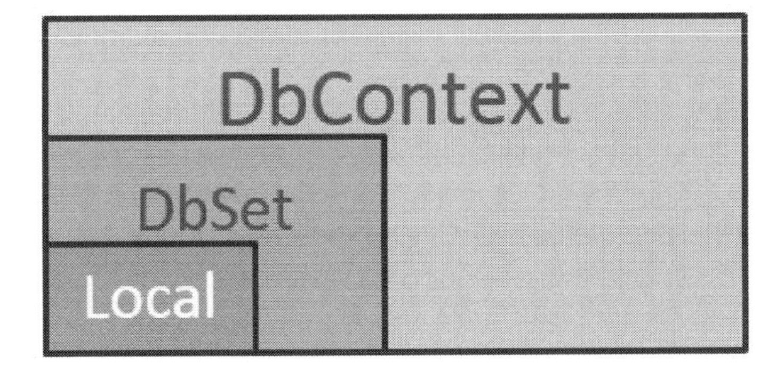


The **Finds** method uses the Local to get for the primary key the entity before querying the database. Methods like **Single** and **Where** do not. However, it is possible to explicitly do a query against the Local. This can be proved easily by doing a simple test. This test can be as easy as making two calls to the database with **SingleOrDefault**. We can see in the profiler two calls made to the database. Conversely, querying the local with **SingleOrDefault** means no query is done to the database.

```
private static void QueryLocal()
{
    using (var context = new YourContext())
    {
        Console.WriteLine(context.Persons.Local.Count); //0
        var newPerson = new Person { Id = 500, Name = "New Person"
```

```
                , BirthDate = new DateTime(2000, 1, 2) };
        context.Persons.Add(newPerson);
        Console.WriteLine(context.Persons.Local.Count); //1
        var person = context.Persons
                .SingleOrDefault(d => d.Id == 1); //Query the database
        Console.WriteLine(context.Persons.Local.Count); //2
        var person2 = context.Persons
                .SingleOrDefault(d => d.Id == 1); //Query the database again
        Console.WriteLine(context.Persons.Local.Count); //2
        var person3 = context.Persons.Local
                .SingleOrDefault(d => d.Id == 1); //Does not query the database
        Console.WriteLine(context.Persons.Local.Count); //2
    }

}
```

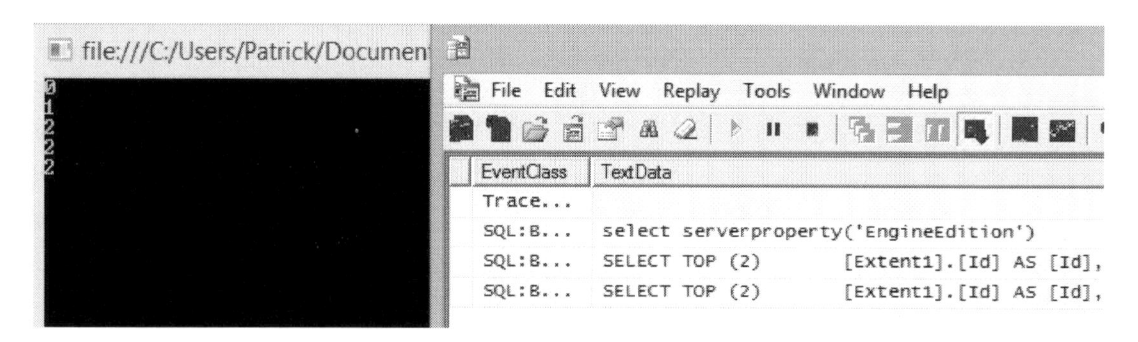


Querying with a **Where** clause loads information into the Local storage but does not load everything from the database, just the data filtered by the Where. If you want to load all entities into your local you can use **explicit loading**.

```
private static void ExplicitLoadIntoLocal()
{
    using (var context = new YourContext())
    {
        Console.WriteLine(context.Persons.Local.Count); //0
        context.Persons.Load(); //Explicit loading
        Console.WriteLine(context.Persons.Local.Count); //1
    }
}
```

The explicit loading does a single query that loads everything from the database. The SQL profiler shows the Select statement below.

```
SELECT
    [Extent1].[Id] AS [Id],
    [Extent1].[Name] AS [Name],
```

```
    [Extent1].[BirthDate] AS [BirthDate],
    [Extent1].[Person_Id] AS [Person_Id],
    [Extent1].[Residence_Id] AS [Residence_Id],
    [Extent1].[House_Id] AS [House_Id]
    FROM [dbo].[People] AS [Extent1]
```

In a future article, we will see that it is possible with explicit loading (.Load) to not load everything from the database. The goal here is to show that the **DbSet.Local** is filled up. It is also important to notice that if you call Load twice, it will load everything from the database. If you remember one conclusion from this article it should be that you have to be aware of which operations always go to the database and which ones are optimized by using the **Local** cache.

```
private static void ExplicitLoadIntoLocal()
{
    using (var context = new YourContext())
    {
        Console.WriteLine(context.Persons.Local.Count); //0
        context.Persons.Load();
        Console.WriteLine(context.Persons.Local.Count); //1
        context.Persons.Load(); //Call the database one more time
    }
}
```

If you are interested in executing the code in this post, you can get the source code from GitHub (https://github.com/MrDesjardins/EntityFrameworkTestConsole).

## Entity Framework Entry Property to Access Tracking Information for Scalar Properties

Release Date: 05-Jun-14
Url: http://patrickdesjardins.com/blog/?post_type=post&p=3528

Entity Framework has a **change tracker API** exposed by the **Entry** property of the **DbContext**. The Entry method or the **Entries** method can be used to find or to change information that is tracked by Entity Framework. It is possible to know the current value but also the original value. It is also possible to track the state of every entity, to read it and to modify it. This article covers the use of Entry for scalar properties. Scalar properties are properties that have a primitive type like integer, string, datetime, double, etc. It does not include any of your classes. In a subsequent post, we will cover how to track an entity inside an entity, and also collection of an entity.

The entry method has two methods that let you drill down inside an entity to change a collection of other entities from an entity or to have access to other references of entities. From there, we could use the explicit loading method, Load, to load a specific portion of information without loading the whole table (as seen in a previous article with DbSet).

This is a simple example to add a new entity with Entry. The code displays the *Person* in the **Local** memory. The new entry is only set in the Local when its state is changed to Added.

```
private static void EntryToAddNewEntity()
{
    using (var context = new YourContext())
    {
        Console.WriteLine(context.Persons.Local.Count); //0
        var newPerson = new Person {Name = "New Person"
                                   , BirthDate = new DateTime(1980, 1, 2) };
        var entryPerson = context.Entry(newPerson);
        Console.WriteLine(context.Persons.Local.Count); //0
        entryPerson.State = EntityState.Added;
        Console.WriteLine(context.Persons.Local.Count); //1
        context.SaveChanges();
    }
}
```

Modifying an existing entity with Entry is also possible without loading this one from the database and without having to update every field.

```
private static void EntryToModifyExistingEntityWithoutLoadingFromDatabase()
{
    using (var context = new YourContext())
    {
        Console.WriteLine(context.Persons.Local.Count); //0
        var existingPerson = new Person { Id=1, Name = "Updated Name"};
        context.Persons.Attach(existingPerson);
        var entryPerson = context.Entry(existingPerson);
        Console.WriteLine(context.Persons.Local.Count); //1
        entryPerson.Property(d => d.Name).IsModified = true;
        Console.WriteLine(context.Persons.Local.Count); //1
        context.SaveChanges();
    }
}
```

It produces an SQL statement with only a single SET.

```
exec sp_executesql
N'UPDATE [dbo].[People]
  SET [Name] = @0
```

```
  WHERE ([Id] = @1)
',N'@0 nvarchar(max) ,@1 int',@0=N'Updated Name',@1=1
```

The advantage of loading from the database is that we do not have to specify which property has been changed.

```
private static void EntryToModifyExistingEntityByLoadingFromDatabase()
{
    using (var context = new YourContext())
    {
        Console.WriteLine(context.Persons.Local.Count); //0
        var existingPerson = context.Persons.Find(1);
        Console.WriteLine(context.Persons.Local.Count); //1
        existingPerson.Name = "Updated from database";
        Console.WriteLine(context.Persons.Local.Count); //1
        context.SaveChanges();
    }
}
```

By modifying the property, Entity Framework has inside the tracking the original value and the current value. It knows that the only property changed is the name property. When you are developing a Client-Server application, you may want to modify only properties that are changed by the Html form. For example, if you have a web form that has all field and the user modifies one value, you would want to have an update executed with only the field that has changed to be in the update sql statement. Entity Framework has a method in the **Entry** property named *CurrentValues*. *CurrentValues* lets you set the value to something you want. Setting a value changes the state of the entry. If this one differs from the OriginalValues, then it is updated to the repository. To simplify the process, the CurrentValues properties has a SetValues method. It takes from an object all scalar properties and maps them into the entry. Scalar properties are a property that is not another entity or a collection.

```
private static void EntryToModifyByPropertyChanged()
{
    var objectFromUser = new Person {Id = 1, Name="Test"
                                , BirthDate = new DateTime(1801, 12, 25)};
    using (var context = new YourContext())
    {
        Console.WriteLine(context.Persons.Local.Count); //0
        var existingPerson = context.Persons.Find(1);
        Console.WriteLine(context.Persons.Local.Count); //1
        context.Entry(existingPerson).CurrentValues.SetValues(objectFromUser);
        Console.WriteLine(context.Persons.Local.Count); //1
        context.SaveChanges();
    }
}
```

This code updates Name and BirthDate only if the entity with the ID has not already got the name and birthday in the database. If the name is the same, then only the birthday changes. If you execute this method twice, nothing will be updated.

It is also possible to update without doing any select statement from the database by setting to Modified the state of the object that came from the client side.

```
private static void EntryToModifyByPropertyChangedWithoutUsingFind()
{
    var objectFromUser = new Person { Id = 1, Name = "Tester #2"
                                , BirthDate = new DateTime(1941, 12, 25) };
    using (var context = new YourContext())
    {
        Console.WriteLine(context.Persons.Local.Count); //0
        context.Entry(objectFromUser).State = EntityState.Modified;
        Console.WriteLine(context.Persons.Local.Count); //1
        context.SaveChanges();
    }
}
```

So far we have seen how to access the tracking information for all scalar properties with the **Entry** method. Three other scenarios exist that have not been covered. First is Complex Object, the second is an entity that references another (optional or required) property,and the third is an entity that has a collection of entities. All code in this article is accessible through
GitHub (https://github.com/MrDesjardins/EntityFrameworkTestConsole).

# Entity Framework Default Collection Value

Release Date: 17-Jun-14
Url: http://patrickdesjardins.com/blog/?post_type=post&p=3560

If you have a class that has collections, the default value of these collections is NULL when your Entity is loaded by Entity Framework. If you are using Lazy Loading, then these properties are virtual. It is not recommended to initialize the collection in the constructor if these are virtual. Not because it is Entity Framework but because initializing a property that is virtual is never a good practice in .Net. The reason is beyond the scope of this article but just keep in mind that even if it is initialized by the constructor, the class that inherits your class may still use the property before it is initialized, which could cause an exception.

Still, if you are using Entity Framework without Lazy Loading, your properties should not be virtual, and by default these collections must be initialized; otherwise, a NULL value is returned.

# Entity Framework Eager Loading and Lazy Loading Produce Same Queries

Release Date: 19-Jun-14
Url: http://patrickdesjardins.com/blog/?post_type=post&p=3562

If you are using Entity Framework with **Lazy Loading** or **Eager Loading** you may realize that both work the same way. With Lazy Loading, you have to access the property and Entity Framework loads the property on-demand. On the other side, with Eager Loading, we need to specify the property to load before accessing it. Lazy Loading has the disadvantage that you must have a virtual property and it has some overhead code that is executed to remember if it must load from the database or from the context, while Eager Loading lets you handle everything so you can optimize your database calls. In a scenario where you have a one to one relationship, for example a Person that has a House,

```
var person = new Person {Id = 1, Name = "SeededPerson"
            , BirthDate = new DateTime(1900, 1, 1)
            , Friends = new Collection<Person> {person2, person3}};
person.Residence = new House {Id = 1, Address = new Address
                    {City = "Montreal", Number = 123, Street = "Owl"}
                    , Price = 350000};
context.Persons.Add(person);
```

you can load the *Residence* by using **Eager Loading** this way:

```
private static void LazyLoadingAndEagerLoadingSameResult()
{
    using (var context = new YourContext())
    {
        Console.WriteLine("No Lazy Loading, Eager Loading");
        var person = context.Persons.Find(1);
        context.Entry(person).Reference(d=>d.Residence).Load(); //Eager Loading
        Console.WriteLine("City is " + person.Residence.Address.City);
    }
}
```

If we kick in the Microsoft **SQL Profiler**, we see two queries. One loads the *Person* and one loads the *Residence* object.

```
SELECT
    [Limit1].[Id] AS [Id],
    [Limit1].[Name] AS [Name],
    [Limit1].[BirthDate] AS [BirthDate],
```

```
    [Limit1].[Residence_Id] AS [Residence_Id],
    [Limit1].[House_Id] AS [House_Id]
    FROM ( SELECT TOP (2)
        [Extent1].[Id] AS [Id],
        [Extent1].[Name] AS [Name],
        [Extent1].[BirthDate] AS [BirthDate],
        [Extent1].[Residence_Id] AS [Residence_Id],
        [Extent1].[House_Id] AS [House_Id]
        FROM [dbo].[People] AS [Extent1]
        WHERE [Extent1].[Id] = @p0
    )  AS [Limit1]

SELECT
    [Extent2].[Id] AS [Id],
    [Extent2].[Price] AS [Price],
    [Extent2].[Address_Street] AS [Address_Street],
    [Extent2].[Address_Number] AS [Address_Number],
    [Extent2].[Address_City] AS [Address_City],
    [Extent2].[Owner_Id] AS [Owner_Id]
    FROM  [dbo].[People] AS [Extent1]
    INNER JOIN [dbo].[Houses] AS [Extent2] ON [Extent1].[Residence_Id] =
[Extent2].[Id]
    WHERE ([Extent1].[Residence_Id] IS NOT NULL) AND ([Extent1].[Id] =
@EntityKeyValue1)
```

The Lazy Loading version is similar but without the Reference/Load line.

```
using (var context = new YourContext())
{
    context.Configuration.LazyLoadingEnabled = true;
    Console.WriteLine("Lazy Loading, No Eager Loading");
    var person = context.Persons.Find(1);
    Console.WriteLine("City is " + person.Residence.Address.City);
}
```

Also, it requires you to change the Person class to have the Residence be virtual.

```
public class Person
{
    public int Id { get; set; }
    public string Name { get; set; }
    public DateTime BirthDate { get; set; }
    public ICollection<Person> Friends { get; set; }
    public virtual House Residence { set; get; }
}
```

If you forget to set the virtual, you will not receive an error message about the virtual but about a **NullReferenceException**. Unfortunately, the exception does not speak for itself!

You have to remember to change the property to virtual.

You can find the source code of this article on GitHub (https://github.com/MrDesjardins/EntityFrameworkTestConsole).

## Entity Framework and DetectChanges

Release Date: 24-Jun-14
Url: http://patrickdesjardins.com/blog/?post_type=post&p=3565

**DetectChanges** can be set to false inside the configuration of the **DbContext**.

```
public class YourContext : DbContext
{
    public YourContext()
        : base("DefaultConnection")
    {
        this.Configuration.AutoDetectChangesEnabled = false;
    }
}
```

or can be turned off for the context life cycle:

```
using (var context = new YourContext())
{
    context.Configuration.AutoDetectChangesEnabled = false;
}
```

This will increase the overall performance of Entity Framework because it will not execute the verification of changes of the entities inside the **DbContext** and the database. Disabling the auto detection of changes comes with the cost that if you do not call it manually you will not have a good result. If **AutoDetectChangesEnabled** is kept to true, or set to true again, then you can be sure that a verification is done when:

- DbSet.Add
- DbSet.Find
- DbSet.Remove
- DbSet.Local
- DbSet.Attach
- DbContext.SaveChanges
- DbContext.GetValidationErrors

- DbContext.Entry
- Any Linq query on DbSet

If you are doing a few queries or you add several new entities you may want to detect change only after all commands instead of letting Entity Framework detect change on every command.

To tell Entity Framework to detect changes, you must use the **DbContext** and call the **ChangeTracker** property that has the **DetectChanges** method. The following example will not update the user.

```
private static void DetectChangesExample()
{
    using (var context = new YourContext())
    {
        context.Configuration.AutoDetectChangesEnabled = false;
        var personToModify = context.Persons.Find(1);
        personToModify.BirthDate = new DateTime(3050, 12, 12);
        context.SaveChanges();
    }
}
```

This is because the DbContext does not know about the change of the Person ID 1. If we change the above code by adding the **DetectChanges** then the database is noticed of the change.

```
private static void DetectChangesExample()
{
    using (var context = new YourContext())
    {
        context.Configuration.AutoDetectChangesEnabled = false;
        var personToModify = context.Persons.Find(1);
        personToModify.BirthDate = new DateTime(3050, 12, 12);
        context.ChangeTracker.DetectChanges();
        context.SaveChanges();
    }
}
```

It is also possible to get from the **Entry** collection the state of the entity. If we execute both examples by adding a simple check of the state, the one that has auto detect changes set to false will return an unmodified state while the other one will have a modified state.

```
private static void DetectChanges()
{
    using (var context = new YourContext())
    {
        context.Configuration.AutoDetectChangesEnabled = false;
        var personToModify = context.Persons.Find(1);
        personToModify.BirthDate = new DateTime(3050,12,12);
        Console.WriteLine(context.Entry(personToModify).State);
        //context.ChangeTracker.DetectChanges(); //Remove this line and it w
        context.SaveChanges();
    }
}
```

```
file:///C:/Users/Patrick/Documents/GitH
Unchanged
```

With DetectChanges:

```
1 reference
private static void DetectChanges()
{
    using (var context = new YourContext())
    {
        context.Configuration.AutoDetectChangesEnabled = false;
        var personToModify = context.Persons.Find(1);
        personToModify.BirthDate = new DateTime(3051,12,12);
        Console.WriteLine(context.Entry(personToModify).State);
        context.ChangeTracker.DetectChanges(); //Remove this line
        Console.WriteLine(context.Entry(personToModify).State);
        context.SaveChanges();
    }
}
```

```
file:///C:/Users
Unchanged
Modified
```

Something interesting about **Complex Type** is that the whole class has a single state. If you change one property of the whole class that is marked as complex type, the whole complex type is marked as modified. The reason is that Entity Framework does not create a proxy object for complex type.

This said, you must use **DetectChanges** before saving; otherwise your changes will never reach the database. You can find the code in this post on GitHub (https://github.com/MrDesjardins/EntityFrameworkTestConsole).

# Entity Framework Create Entity

Release Date: 15-Jul-14
Url: http://patrickdesjardins.com/blog/?post_type=post&p=3583

Creating a new instance and having Entity Framework handling this one in its context requires some manipulations. You have two different paths to accomplish this goal. The first one is to create the entity and add it to the DbSet. The second one is to create the instance from the DbSet directly instead of instantiated, with a **new** keyword. Here is a code that adds two entities, one that is not tracked by Entity Framework, and that is because it has been created with the **Create** method.

```
using (var context = new YourContext())
{
    // Create a new instance with Add
    var person = new Person {Name = "New person with New Keyword"
                             ,BirthDate = DateTime.Now};
    Console.WriteLine("Person non-proxy state: " + context.Entry(person).State);
    context.Persons.Add(person);// Now EF added the object but not tracking

    // Create a new instance with Entity Framework (proxy)
    var person2 = context.Persons.Create();
    Console.WriteLine("Person proxy state: " + context.Entry(person2).State);
    person2.Name = "New Person from EF";
    person2.BirthDate = DateTime.Now;
    context.Persons.Add(person2); // Still need to add but EF was tracking changes
    var x1 = context.Persons.Local.Count();
    Console.WriteLine("The count is at " + x1);

    // Detect Changes
    context.ChangeTracker.DetectChanges();
    Console.WriteLine("Person non-proxy state: " + context.Entry(person).State);
    Console.WriteLine("Person proxy state: " + context.Entry(person2).State);
    var x2 = context.Persons.Local.Count();
    Console.WriteLine("The count is at " + x2);

    context.SaveChanges();
}
```

The result is the same for those two creations because we do not use anything from the Entity Framework Proxy. Choosing from one or the other method to create is more a preference than a guidance. You have to choose which one you prefer and keep your whole system using the same method. Otherwise, it will be confusing to know if we need or not to bind the entity to Entity Framework proxies.

```
Person non-proxy state: Detached
Person proxy state: Detached
The count is at 2
Person non-proxy state: Added
Person proxy state: Added
The count is at 2
```

You can get the source code on GitHub (https://github.com/MrDesjardins/EntityFrameworkTestConsole).

## Entity Framework Disconnected Graph and the root

Release Date: 23-Jul-14
Url: http://patrickdesjardins.com/blog/?post_type=post&p=3590

Entity Framework works with entities that can be attached or not. Attached entities are tracked by Entity Framework. This way, Entity Framework can detect if a change has been made or if something has been deleted. Having an entity not loaded from Entity that exists inside the database is called a disconnected entity. When persisting an object into Entity Framework, we are working with a graph. This means that an entity has another reference to entities which can also have other entities. The entity that we are performing an operation on is the root of the graph. Depending on the situation, the root can change. For example, you can have E1 referencing E2 which references E3. If you are using E2 to do some operation, the root is E2. It is important to understand what is the root because an operation executed on the root can have side effects on the rest of the graph.

A simple example is the following one. You have an entity that has a list of another type of entities. If you instantiate this entity and add to its list some entities and only do a Context.Add to the root, all entities from the added entity will also be added.

```
using (var context = new YourContext())
{
    var newHouse = new House {Address = new Address
                {City="TestCity",Number = 123,Street="Street Name here"}};
    newHouse.Owner = new Person {Name = "Automatically added from the property"
                              , BirthDate = DateTime.Now};
    newHouse.Resident = new Collection<Person>(new []
              {new Person{BirthDate = DateTime.Now
                         ,Name = "Automatically added from the collection"}
              });
    context.Houses.Add(newHouse);
    context.SaveChanges();
}
```

In this example, all *Person* entities do not exist in the database. The *House* entity does not exist. Rather than adding the *House* entity and all *Persons*, we just need to add the root element the *House*. This is what the code is doing. This execution produces three entries into the database: one for the *House*, one for the *Owner* (a *Person*) and a last one for the *Resisdent* (a *Person*).

Results | Messages

| | Id | Price | Address_Street | Address_Number | Address_City | Owner_Id |
|---|---|---|---|---|---|---|
| 1 | 1 | 0 | Street Name here | 123 | TestCity | 1 |

| | Id | Name | BirthDate | Residence_Id | House_Id |
|---|---|---|---|---|---|
| 1 | 1 | Automatically added from the property | 2014-06-08 20:37:32.550 | NULL | NULL |
| 2 | 2 | Automatically added from the collection | 2014-06-08 20:37:32.567 | NULL | 1 |

It is important to notice that Entity Framework is bright enough to not mark children as "Added" if this is already tracked by its context. For example, you load from the database a Person entity and add it to the collection. This will not be added but will be attached. You can find this example on GitHub
(https://github.com/MrDesjardins/EntityFrameworkTestConsole).

## Entity Framework ChangeTracker

Release Date: 29-Jul-14
Url: http://patrickdesjardins.com/blog/?post_type=post&p=3703

Entities have a single state during their life cycle that can change among these four defined states: **Added, Deleted, Unchanged, Modified**. If the entity already exists in the database the state is **unchanged**. If you apply a modification the state changes to **modified**. Otherwise, if the entity does not exist and is brand new, the state is **added**. It is also the case if you specify to Entity Framework to delete an entity, it is set to **undeleted**. States can be changed by using Entity Framework Context methods like Add, Attach, Remove but also by setting the entity state by using the Entity Framework Entry method to get information about the entity state.

## How to work with Value Object In C#

Release Date: 19-Aug-14
Url: http://patrickdesjardins.com/blog/?post_type=post&p=3641

Implementing value objects in your project is something that every software has to do. It may sound like a simple task but from my experience I can tell you that it is less easy than it looks. In fact, it is easy but a developer does not really understand the differences between an enum, an entity or a value object.

Before going any deeper, let's define what is a value object. A value object is a class that has information that does not have a unique identifier for every usage but a unique identifier for the instance itself. A value object is reused across your application many times, which removes a lot of complexities that you would have by having a unique identity for each of these instances. For example, you have a *Person* class that has a relationship by a property to a *Status* class. This is the perfect example for a value object. You create a class for each status like one for *Married* and one for *Single*. You could have a *Married* entry for each person but that would result in a lot of duplicates. You could have used a C# enum or a C# constant but this would result in a **weak integrity** between your classes and also in your persistence storage. The integrity is weak in the code because you would pass between methods string or enum which could be casted from integer. The string could be anything and would require a lot of validations. In the database, you save in a column a string or an integer (for the enum). In both cases, you do not have any validation from the persistence storage, only from custom code. This is where a value object can shine. You can have a strong integrity in code but also in the database. You can also have a big performance saving by having the same object reused across the application. For example, if you have 1 million *Persons* that are *Single*, 1 million will be linked to the same object. You do not have the redundancy of having 1 million *Single* entities.

Before going any deeper, let's examine a second example that is from **Eric Evans** in his book **Domain Driven Design**. Imagine a box of markers with different colors. Each marker has a value object that defines the color. Each color does not have a different ID for each marker, nor does it have a different ID for each line drawn. You would have simply the class *Marker* having a reference to the value object that defines the color. You also have for each *Line* class a reference to the value object color to know the color of the line. In both cases, it would be too big in resources to save a new entity for each *Marker* and *Line*.

Another example could be with a simple state that changes between *Active*, *Inactive*, *NotSet*. Those three states can use a value object to define the state of any entity that requires a defined state. Or another example could be that you have several currencies that you want to handle in your program. Every amount is set to a currency. The list is well defined and does not change dynamically so you can create a class by currency. This is crucial to have your value object not dynamic. It is the cost of this pattern. You cannot have something dynamic because you need to have the value object defined in code, in a class.

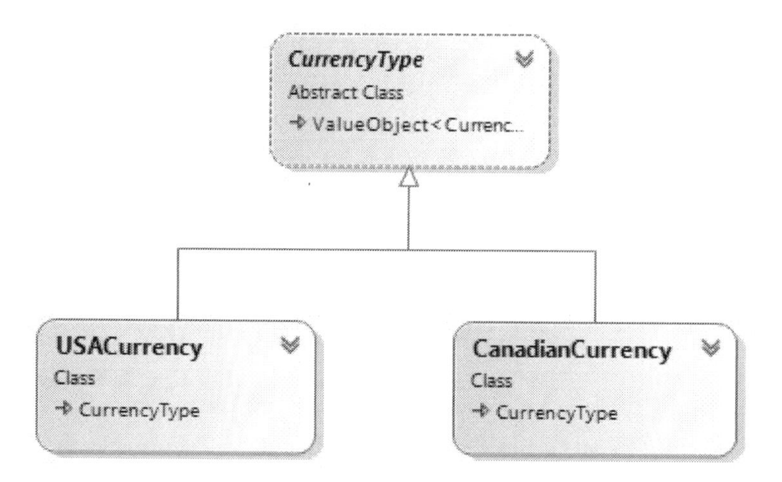


The image above shows that we have a value object named *CurrencyType*. This means that if you have a class that has a *CurrencyType* property it will use it. The image also displays two values for the value object: USA and Canadian.

```
public void Money
{
    public CurrencyType Currency { get; set; }
    public decimal Amount { get; set; }
}
```

This usage is very strong because you can only assign a *CurrencyType* to the currency property of the class. It would be weak to have used a string for the currency like the code below.

```
public void Money
{
    public string CurrencyType { get; set; }
    public decimal Amount { get; set; }
}
```

The problem would have been the same for an integer property. The *Money* class could have used an enum but at the time of saving everything, the table would have the decimal value for the amount and an integer for the currency type. The problem is now at the database level where the integer could have been altered and when loaded back in the software would cause instability. However, the value object pattern cannot be unstabilized because of the database integrity that supports the class type integrity. Since every value object is reflected by a table entry, those entries are referenced by a foreign key to the one that uses the value object. For example, if you have an *Item* that has a price of type *Money*, you could set the *CurrencyType* to USD. In the database, the table *Item* would have a column *price* and a column *currency type*. The currency type would have a foreign key to the table currency type. Every value of the value object is a class. For example, if you have a Canadian currency and an American currency you need two classes.

```
public class CanadianCurrency:CurrencyType
{
  public CanadianCurrency()
  {
    base.Id = 1;
    base.Name = "$CDN";
    base.Culture = new CultureInfo("fr-CA");
  }
}

public class USACurrency:CurrencyType
{
  public USACurrency()
  {
    base.Id = 2;
    base.Name = "$USD";
    base.Culture = new CultureInfo("en-US");
  }
}
```

You can have anything you want in the value object. The minimum is to have an identifier that will be the primary key in the database. In the example above, it is an integer but could be a string. The important thing is to have all your implementation inherit the same class. In this case, it is *CurrencyType*.

```
public abstract class CurrencyType : ValueObject<CurrencyType>
{
  public static readonly CurrencyType Canada = new CanadianCurrency();
  public static readonly CurrencyType UnitedStatesOfAmerica = new USACurrency();
}
```

The two static properties of the value object class act as a factory and are not required. It is just easy to select values because, instead of instantiating the entity yourself, you use the factory, which offers all possibles choices with Microsoft IntelliSense.

```
//Instead of :
item.CurrencyType = new CanadianCurrency();
//Use :
item.CurrencyType = CurrencyType.Canada;
```

You do not have to inherit to ValueObject like in the example above, but if you do, it will give you some additional possibilities like having automatic parsing from primary value (integer in our example but could have been string) to the value object. Imagine a scenario where you let the user choose from a combobox the value object. The value is returned as the unique identifier. In the case of the money currency, the value 2 could be returned to the controller and you have from this value to get the value object back into the model object. This can be done by a method that maps the ID to the value object.

```
public abstract class ValueObject : IEntity
{
    public int Id { get; set; }
    public string Name { get; set; }

    public override bool Equals(object obj)
    {
        if (ReferenceEquals(null, obj))
        {
            return false;
        }
        if (ReferenceEquals(this, obj))
        {
            return true;
        }
        if (obj.GetType() != this.GetType())
        {
            return false;
        }
        return Equals((ValueObject)obj);
    }
    protected bool Equals(ValueObject other)
    {
        return Id == other.Id;
    }

    public override int GetHashCode()
    {
        return Id;
    }

    public static bool operator ==(ValueObject left, ValueObject right)
    {
        return Equals(left, right);
    }

    public static bool operator !=(ValueObject left, ValueObject right)
    {
        return !Equals(left, right);
    }
}
```

```
public abstract class ValueObject<TValueObject>
                            : ValueObject where TValueObject : IEntity
{
    public static TValueObject GetFromId(int value)
    {
        Type type = typeof(TValueObject);

        var fields = type.GetFields(BindingFlags.Public | BindingFlags.Static);
        foreach (var field in fields)
        {
            var fieldValue = (TValueObject)field.GetValue(null);

            if (fieldValue.Id == value)
            {
                return fieldValue;
            }

        }
        throw new KeyNotFoundException(string.Concat(value
                                , "cannot be found in any static fields."));
    }
}
```

It may look like a lot of code but it is not. The first class that is not generic only overrides some operator to simplify the comparison between value objects of the same type. The generic version has the possibility to get from the the IDdd the value object. It uses reflection to get for each implementation the value object type if one has the ID passed by parameter. If you do not inherit your values classes from the **ValueObject** class, you must still inherit them from a common class to associate all values into a specific value object type. My suggestion is to use the value object class because it gives you more action that can be used across all value object types.

```
item.CurrencyType = CurrencyType.GetFromId(viewModel.CurrencyIdFromWebForm);
```

This pattern works very well with Entity Framework.

```
public class CurrencyTypeConfiguration : ValueObjectConfiguration<CurrencyType>
{
    public CurrencyTypeConfiguration()
    {
    }
}
```

The configuration is very similar to every one of your value objects. The trick is all in the inherited class, **ValueObjectConfiguration,** that takes the type in its generic parameter.

```
public abstract class ValueObjectConfiguration<T>
                            : EntityTypeConfiguration<T> where T : ValueObject
```

```
{
    protected ValueObjectConfiguration()
    {
        Map(a => a.MapInheritedProperties());
        HasKey(p => p.Id);
        ToTable(typeof(T).Name, Constants.SchemaNames.ValueObject);
    }
}
```

The configuration sets the inheritance to **MapInheritedProperties**. This creates a single table with all classes. This means that all values of your value object are in a single table named by the name of the generic class name. In our example, the table created by Entity Framework is named *CurrencyType* and has two entries, one with ID 1 and one with ID 2. This solution is easy to use because you must only inherit this value object configuration class by setting the type of the class of the value object, and Entity Framework handles the creation of each entry in the table under the name of the value object.

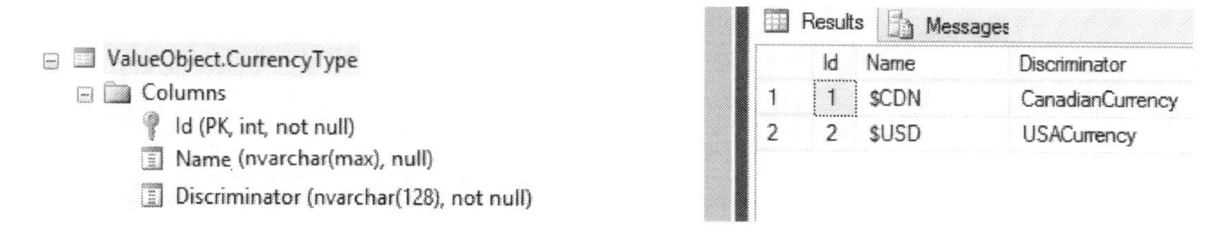


As you can see in the code and also in the screenshot of the table above this text, a primary key is created. This ensures that you have a unique value object identifier but also that if you use the value object in another entity this one is strongly referenced.

One more thing. This is very efficient in terms of performance. If you have your *Item*, you do not need to load from the database the currency information. First, you can have the *ID* directly from the entity that uses the value object. This is because the foreign key is already in the table that uses the value object. You only need to load if you have created a lot of data that is not stored in the class but since it is a value object all this information is already in the class. Second, you can load the whole value object from the method we have defined in the **ValueObject** class. A trick is to never include/load the value object but to use the method to get back the whole object.

```
public class Item
{
    public int CurrencyTypeId
    {
        get { return this.Currency.Id; }
        set { this.Currency = CurrencyType.GetFromId(value); }
    }
```

```
    /// <summary>
    /// This is ignored by EntityFramework
    /// </summary>
    public CurrencyType Currency { get; set; }
}
```

The code above shows one way to do it. You can tell Entity Framework to ignore property and use the *CurrentyTypeId*. This way, it loads and it saves only the unique identifier and allows you to use the value object property in your business logic. As you can see, the setter of the currency type sets the value object value from the **GetFromId**. The getter also does not link to an integer but to the currency value object. This guarantees us to use the simplest way to save value to entity (by having the foreign key in the class) and to have integrity in the value because it passes through the **GetFromId** method that throws an exception if the value is not valid.

The last example is good in the scenario where you have an **Entity Framework Complex Object. Complex Object** cannot have a navigability association. But, if you have a normal entity, then the best way is to have the foreign key in the database. If we also want to have the performance, this means that we do not want to load the value object with an Include (to avoid join). To be able to have performance and integrity the best way is to have the entity use a scalar property that holds the foreign key. Continue to read the next section to see the real solution for all cases because the current solution does not solve the problem of a nullable value object.

## Full Working Version of Value Object

We have discussed a few ways to implement value object. Let's wrap up everything in a small console application for a working demo. This final version works for every situation. This means that it works with required attribute, works by setting the property to null and having a scalar property to the value object, and it also works without having to use an Include statement to reduce the amount of join. Finally, it can use Entity Framework when saving to avoid adding the value object but just referring to it.

First of all, let's define our context. The context defines the connection string and removes everything in the configuration about lazy loading, detection and proxy. It also sets up two entities. The first one is *Parent* and the second one is *Child*. A *Child* will have a reference to a *Parent*. The *Child* is referencing a *Parent* which simulates the **value object.**

```
public class MyContext : DbContext
{
    public MyContext()
        : base("MyContextConnectionString")
    {
```

```
        base.Configuration.LazyLoadingEnabled = false;
        base.Configuration.AutoDetectChangesEnabled = false;
        base.Configuration.ProxyCreationEnabled = false;
    }

    protected override void OnModelCreating(DbModelBuilder modelBuilder)
    {
        base.OnModelCreating(modelBuilder);
        modelBuilder.Entity<Parent>();
        modelBuilder.Entity<Child>();
    }
}
```

The *Parent*, simulating the value object, has a unique identifier, *ID*, and a name. It also has the "Create" method which is, in fact, the method that we would use to get the value object. It is the method that we have previously named **GetFromId**. This time, we make it very simple for the purpose of the example.

```
public class Parent
{
    public int Id { get; set; }
    public string NameParent { get; set; }

    public static Parent Create(int id)
    {
        return new Parent { Id = id };
    }
}
```

The *Child* class, the one that has the value object, the *Parent* in this example, is more complex. First of all, we do not use auto-property. This time, we are using properties and fields, one for the class and one for the scalar that represents the foreign key. We do want to not have to include (create a SQL Join) every time. *TheOnlyParent* property returns the field directly. That means that if the field is Null we will have Null as a value. This is what we want for Entity Framework,to only save back the ID and not to verify if it has a match with the property. The *Child* class also has the scalar property that returns the field but has something special in the setter to create the object from the method of the value object that can create the value object by its ID.

```
public class Child
{
    private Parent theOnlyParent;
    private int theOnlyParentId;
    public int Id { get; set; }
    public string NameChild { get; set; }
    [Required]
```

```
    public Parent TheOnlyParent
    {
        get
        {
            return theOnlyParent;
        }
        set
        {
            theOnlyParent = value;
            if (value != null)
                TheOnlyParentId = value.Id;
        }
    }

    public int TheOnlyParentId
    {
        get { return theOnlyParentId; }
        set
        {
            theOnlyParentId = value;
            theOnlyParent = Parent.Create(value);
        }
    }
  }
```

To be very bulletproof with Entity and this scenario of having a reference to an existing object, let's add a **Required** attribute into the property field. This means that Entity will verify if this property is set. That also means that setting to Null will raise a validation exception. This is why every value object (or any entity that links an existing entity) must be set to unchanged.

```
static void Main(string[] args)
{
    Console.WriteLine("Start create database");
    Database.SetInitializer(new DropCreateDatabaseAlways<MyContext>());
    Console.WriteLine("Start adding Parent");
    var p1 = new Parent { NameParent = "Test Parent Name#1" };
    int parentCreatedId;
    Console.WriteLine("Context");
    using (var context = new MyContext())
    {
        context.Set<Parent>().Add(p1);
        context.SaveChanges();
        parentCreatedId = p1.Id;
    }
    Console.WriteLine("Start adding a child from a different context");
    var c1 = new Child { NameChild = "Child #1" };
    c1.TheOnlyParentId = parentCreatedId;
```

```
    c1.TheOnlyParent = new Parent { Id = parentCreatedId };

    Console.WriteLine("Context");
    using (var context = new MyContext())
    {
        Console.WriteLine("*Change State Child");
        context.Entry(c1).State = EntityState.Added;
        Console.WriteLine("*Change State Child->Parent Navigability Property");
        context.Entry(c1.TheOnlyParent).State
                = EntityState.Unchanged; // We do not want to create but reuse
        Console.WriteLine("*Save Changes");
        context.SaveChanges();
    }
    Console.WriteLine("End");
    Console.ReadLine();
}
```

This code runs without a problem. The property can be set to a value object OR can be null and in both cases the association is created in the database. This code has a strong integrity by having the foreign key created but also is aiming for performance with the possibility to load the entity (for example Child) without having to include the associate entity (the Parent).

Here is a last example, a value object for an *OrderType*, a *TransactionType and OrderStatus*. The *Order* class has a property for the *OrderStatus* that can be null. The *TransactionType* is mandatory and is an example of a default value that is calculated dynamically. The *OrderStatus* is another required value object. This example shows three cases of value object.

```
public class Order
{
    /// <summary>
    /// This allow to return NULL from the navigability method.
    /// This is required to be sure when saving with Entity Framework
    /// that we only save the OrderTypeId. Not setting this to null
    /// cause EF to have a role problem.
    /// </summary>
    private bool noOrderType = false;
    public int OrderTypeId
    {
        get
        {

            if (!PriceStop.IsNull && !PriceLimit.IsNull)
                return OrderType.StopLimit.Id;
            if (!PriceStop.IsNull && PriceLimit.IsNull)
                return OrderType.Limit.Id;
            return OrderType.Market.Id;
```

```
    }
    set { this.OrderType = OrderType.GetFromId(value); }
}

public OrderType OrderType
{
    get
    {
        if (noOrderType)
            return null;
        if (!PriceStop.IsNull && !PriceLimit.IsNull)
            return OrderType.StopLimit;
        if (!PriceStop.IsNull && PriceLimit.IsNull)
            return OrderType.Limit;
        return OrderType.Market;
    }
    set
    {
        if (value == null)
        {
            noOrderType = true;
        }
    }
}

// ---------------------------------------------------
private int transactionTypeId;
private TransactionType transactionType;

public int TransactionTypeId
{
    get { return transactionTypeId; }
    set
    {
        this.transactionTypeId = value;
        this.transactionType = TransactionType.GetFromId(value);
    }
}

[Required]
public TransactionType TransactionType
{
    get { return transactionType; }
    set
    {
        if (value != null)
        {
            this.transactionTypeId = value.Id;
        }
        this.transactionType = value;
```

```
        }
    }

    // ---------------------------------------------------------
    private int orderStatusId;
    private OrderStatusType orderStatus;

    public int OrderStatusId
    {
        get { return orderStatusId; }
        set
        {
            orderStatusId = value;
            orderStatus = OrderStatusType.GetFromId(value);
        }
    }

    [Required]
    public OrderStatusType OrderStatus
    {
        get { return orderStatus; }
        set
        {
            if (value != null)
            {
                this.orderStatusId = value.Id;
            }
            orderStatus = value;
        }
    }
}
```

Finally, value object is a simple pattern that should not be a nightmare to implement in your project. If well designed, it can be very easy to use. Entity Framework works very well with value object and performance is as fast as any other solution.

## Entity Framework Using Foreign Key Property Instead of Property

Release Date: 01-Oct-14
Url: http://patrickdesjardins.com/blog/?post_type=post&p=3697

Entity Framework allows two types of association. The first one requires less change in your classes because it uses the normal way to have an association in an oriented object. This is called **independent association**. For example, if you have a *Car* class that has an *Owner* then you just need to have in your *Car* class a property of *Owner* type. With Entity Framework, you will need to do something when saving the entity if you do not want to have a new instance of the *Owner*. This can be done by attaching or by setting the property with Entity Framework to EntityState.Unchanged. However, it is simpler if you add in your classes not only the property of the type but also an additional property with the foreign key. For example, your *Car* class could have the property of *Owner* but also *OwnerID*.

```
public class Car
{
    public int Id { get; set; }
    public string Type { get; set; }
    public Person Owner { get; set; }
    public int OwnerId { get; set; }
}

public class Person
{
    public int Id { get; set; }
    public string Name { get; set; }
    public DateTime BirthDate { get; set; }
}
```

Creating a new **Car** and associating the car to a *Person* (**Owner**) can be done without having to do any hard code. The code below adds a **Person** and then creates a new **Car** with an association to the person that owns the car.

```
private static void AddByIdInsteadOfProperty()
{
    using (var context = new YourContext())
    {
        var person = new Person { Name = "Automatically added from the property"
                                , BirthDate = DateTime.Now };
        context.Set<Person>().Add(person);
        context.SaveChanges();
        Console.WriteLine("Person id = " + person.Id);
        var car = new Car {OwnerId = person.Id, Type = "Honda"};
        context.Set<Car>().Add(car);
        context.SaveChanges();
        Console.WriteLine("Car id = " + car.Id);
    }
}
```

Without this property you would have to set the *Owner* property to a new **Person** with this at the ID of the existing person previously created. But this will try to add the person and will crash because Entity Framework will try to insert an entity with an existing ID. To fix this, we need to set the property state to attached and everything would commit without

a problem. The reason that it is simpler to use the property ID defined is that Entity Framework tracks only scalar property. Scalar property is a property with primitive value. You can find the code on GitHub:
https://github.com/MrDesjardins/EntityFrameworkTestConsole.

# Entity Framework Copies All Scalar Properties From An Existing Entity

Release Date: 07-Oct-14
Url: http://patrickdesjardins.com/blog/?post_type=post&p=3705

Entity Framework gives the possibility to create a new instance with properties of an existing entity with a single line instruction. The function that verifies every property and compares them with the one in the context is inside the **Entry** function under the name **SetValues**.

Let's set up the code to try an update on an existing entity. First, let's create the entity in its own context. This way we insert the entity in the database and kill the context.

```
//Create a person
using (var context = new YourContext())
{
  var person = new Person { Name = "WorkingWithEntry", BirthDate = DateTime.Now };
  context.Set<Person>().Add(person);
  context.SaveChanges();
}
```

The second step is to load from the database the person into a variable that will be used in another context. This simulates the scenario of a disconnected entity. It is loaded with values but the next context will not know about it.

```
using (var context = new YourContext())
{
    personLoaded = context.Set<Person>()
                          .Single(sd => sd.Name == "WorkingWithEntry");
}
```

Finally, we do a single change or multiple changes to the disconnected entity and call the **SetValues**. But before calling this method, we must change at least one property. In the example below, we change the name.

```
personLoaded.Name = "Modified Name";
using (var context = new YourContext())
{
    context.Configuration.AutoDetectChangesEnabled = false;
```

```
    context.Configuration.ProxyCreationEnabled = false;
    var copy = new Person();
    context.Entry(copy).State
        = EntityState.Added;//The context must know the entity to do the copy to.
    context.Entry(copy).CurrentValues
       .SetValues(personLoaded); //The context must knows the entity to copy from.
    copy.Name = "This is a copy AKA clone";
    context.SaveChanges();
}
```

After changing the name, we create a new instance of *Person* and add this new instance to the context by using the **Entry** method and set the state to **Added**. We could also use the **Add** method which does the same thing. The next step is to use the **SetValues** with the entity that contains all changes. Entity Framework will match all properties' names and assign values if required. Of course, it is possible to change properties after calling this method to have something unique.

It is not required to use that method if you are modifying an existing entity. Changing the state to **Modified** does the job. Here is the complete code with the **Modified** used with an existing entity.

```
private static void WorkingWithEntryAndAllScalarProperties()
{
    Person personLoaded;

    //Create a person
    using (var context = new YourContext())
    {
        var person = new Person { Name = "WorkingWithEntry"
                                , BirthDate = DateTime.Now };
        context.Set<Person>().Add(person);
        context.SaveChanges();
    }

    //Load the person (new context)
    using (var context = new YourContext())
    {
        personLoaded = context.Set<Person>()
                              .Single(sd => sd.Name == "WorkingWithEntry");
    }

    personLoaded.Name = "Modified Name";

    //Save the person (modified its properties, new context)
    using (var context = new YourContext())
    {
        context.Configuration.AutoDetectChangesEnabled = false;
```

```
        context.Configuration.ProxyCreationEnabled = false;

        context.Entry(personLoaded).State = EntityState.Modified;
        context.SaveChanges();

        var copy = new Person();
        context.Entry(copy).State
        = EntityState.Added;//The context must know the entity to do the copy to.
        context.Entry(copy).CurrentValues
            .SetValues(personLoaded); //The context must also know the entity to
        copy from.
        copy.Name = "This is a copy AKA clone";
        context.SaveChanges();
    }
}
```

The SQL generated by this code for the **SaveChanges**() after the **EntityState.Modified** is a huge one with all properties updated, even those that have not changed.

```
exec sp_executesql N'UPDATE [dbo].[People]
SET [Name] = @0, [BirthDate] = @1
WHERE ([Id] = @2)
',N'@0 nvarchar(max) ,@1 datetime2(7),@2 int',@0=N'Modified Name',@1='2014-07-31
12:00:05.9600000',@2=12
```

If you want to update only specific fields in the table you have to set the property to modified instead of the whole entity, like the code below.

```
private static void UpdatingASpecificFieldOfATable()
{
    Person person;

    //Create a person
    using (var context = new YourContext())
    {
        person = new Person { Name = "Update only a single property"
                            , BirthDate = DateTime.Now };
        context.Set<Person>().Add(person);
        context.SaveChanges();
    }

    //Update a single field
    using (var context = new YourContext())
    {
        context.Configuration.AutoDetectChangesEnabled = false;
        context.Configuration.ProxyCreationEnabled = false;
        context.Entry(person).State
            = EntityState.Unchanged; //In the context without any modification
```

```
        person.BirthDate = new DateTime(1984, 08, 01);
        person.Name = "This will not be saved in the database";
        context.Entry(person).Property(d => d.BirthDate).IsModified = true;
        //context.Entry(person).Property(d => d.Name).IsModified = false;
        context.SaveChanges();
    }
}
```

It is important to see that I have commented in the line that set the name IsModified to False. We do not need to specify properties that are not modified if we have AutoDetectChangesEnabled to false. In the case that it is set to true, you need to set it manually to false because Entity Framework detects a change when setting the properties. The goal here is to modify the Name and the BirthDate property but only allow the update of the BirthDate. Here is a screenshot of the database.

| Id | Name | BirthDate | House_Id | Residence_Id |
|---|---|---|---|---|
| 15 | Update only a single property | 1984-08-01 00:00:00.000 | NULL | NULL |

We are finished with the subject of **SetValues** with the **Entry** and **Modified** property. However, it is interesting to see that you can have a lot of control over what you want to be modified or not with Entity Framework. You can see the code of this article on GitHub (https://github.com/MrDesjardins/EntityFrameworkTestConsole).

# Entity Framework Does Not Allow Nullable Complex Type

Release Date: 12-Nov-14
Url: http://patrickdesjardins.com/blog/?post_type=post&p=3803

Once in a while, I forget that a weakness of Entity Framework makes me change the design of my database. Entity Framework (well, for the first six versions at least) cannot save an entity that has a **complex type** to null.

Let's assume that you have a class named *Order*, and this one has a *Price* property. The *Price* property is of type *Money* which is a complex type. You cannot set your Price property to null without having Entity Framework crash during the commit phase.

*DbUpdateException: Null value for non-nullable member. Member: 'PriceLimit'.*

Once you realize that Entity Framework will not help you in this path, you have to change your design. There are multiple ways to handle this kind of scenario but one that I prefer and I really think is quite easy is to have an additional property inside the complex class that specifies whether the complex class is null or not. Of course, this would be cleaner not to have that property, but at least it is a viable solution if you own the complex type. It also has the advantage of being cohesive and not altering all of your classes that use that complex type. In the complex class we change the value to be nullable now.

```
private decimal? value;

public decimal? Value
{
     get { return value; }
     set { this.value = value; }
}
```

This is the first change that will let the database save a null value not to the complex type but to the value of this one. The next step is to create a new property that will specify if the complex type is null or not.

```
public bool IsNull
{
    get { return !this.Value.HasValue; }
    set {
        if (value)
        {
            this.Value = null;
        }
        else
        {
            this.Value = default(decimal);
        }
    }
}
```

As you can see, the **IsNull** property does not contain a value but is calculated on the fly. We also will not store this value in the database. This means that we need to ignore this property for Entity Framework.

```
public MoneyConfiguration()
{
    this.Ignore(d => d.IsNull);   // Required because Entity Framework cannot
                              have two properties that load the same property(value)
}
```

The reason is twofold. First, we do not need to save this value because we can calculate it on the fly. Second, Entity Framework does not allow us to read this type of property. Indeed, Entity Framework can save both values (the value and the IsNull flag) but when this tries to load the data from the database, it will not be able to resolve the value correctly, primarily because both properties depend on each other. When setting the **Value**, the **IsNull** does not change, so it is fine. However, when Entity Framework sets **IsNull** to false the default value is set. Since we cannot tell Entity Framework to avoid loading a single property and we cannot specify the order of the properties to be loaded, it is better to avoid having to save the value.

# 7. GIT

This chapter groups every post written during 2013 and 2014 about Git. Like all chapters in this book, every article is a snapshot of a real scenario that has a high probability of happening if you are using these technologies. You will notice that every article that has been chosen to be included in this book contains the release date to identify when it was written. A permanent link is also provided that allows you to go in and read updates and comments. Feel free to go on the website to add your own comment if you wish.

## GitHub Command Line Basic

Release Date: 02-Dec-14
Url: http://patrickdesjardins.com/blog/?post_type=post&p=3840

The first thing is to create a repository. You can create one free at **GitHub**. After created the repository on GitHub get the URL of the repository and copy and paste to the console with the **clone** command.

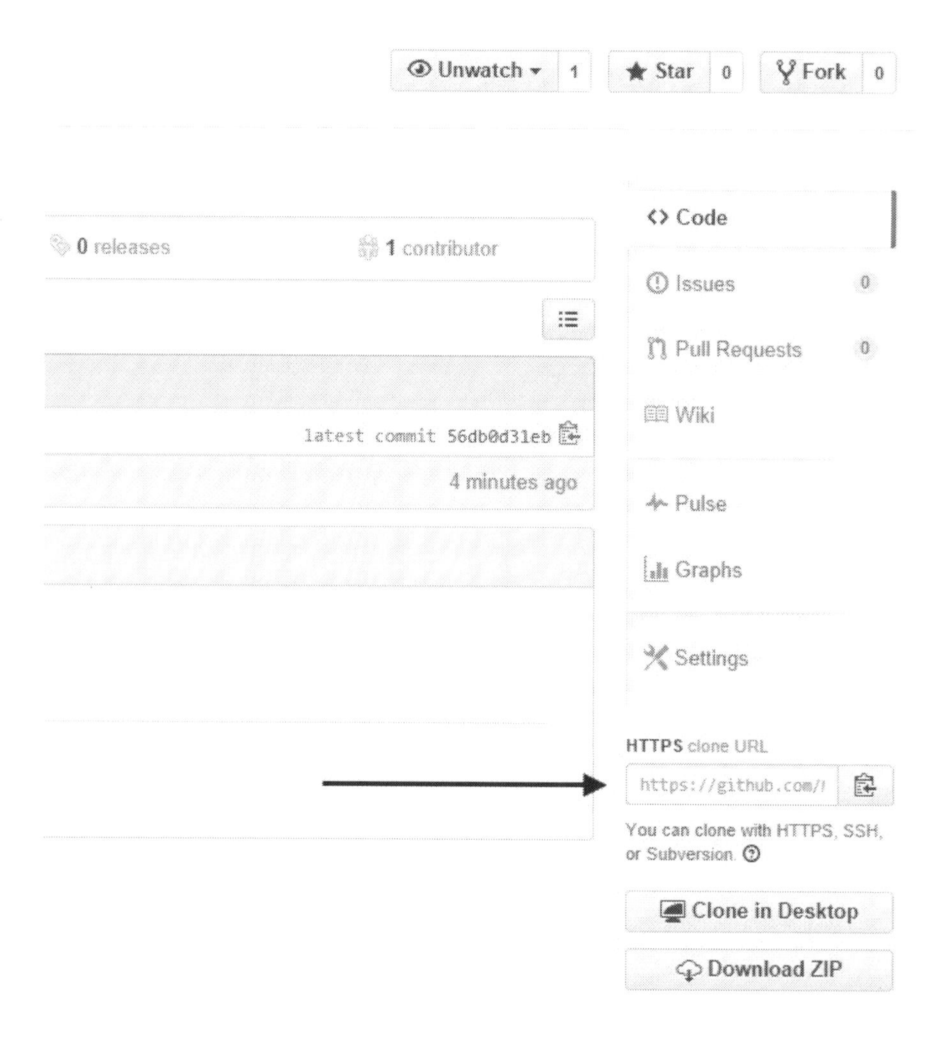


Download the repository to your computer with the **clone** command.

```
git clone https://github.com/MrDesjardins/TestingGit.git
```

```
C:\Users\Patrick\Documents\GitHub> git clone https://github.com/MrDesjardi
Cloning into 'TestingGit'...
remote: Counting objects: 3, done.
remote: Total 3 (delta 0), reused 0 (delta 0)
Unpacking objects: 100% (3/3), done.
Checking connectivity... done
C:\Users\Patrick\Documents\GitHub>
```

Open notepad and modify an existing file. You can do it manually by specifying the file

```
git add README.md
```

You can use the **add** command with the the **-u** for all modified files but not for adding a new file. In both cases, if you check the status you will see that the file is modified.

```
git status
git commit -m "Message here"
git status
```

Checking the status will not say that the file is modified but that your branch is ahead of **origin/master** by one commit. Doing another change on the same file will set back the status to modified. You need to commit again before sending everything to the server. If you do not want to have the latest change, before commiting you can roll back the file with the checkout command.

```
git checkout readme.md
```

Before having your code available to everybody, it is possible to see all branches.

```
git branch -r git branch -a
```

To send the code to the server, we need to push. We need to specify the remote Git push origin master. This was the easy step. Now let's do a branch that we will later merge back into this master branch.

```
git checkout -b "Branch1"
//or
git branch Branch1
git checkout Branch1
```

If we are checking the branches, we will see one local branch and not a remote one.

```
git branch -a
//create file test1.txt
git add text1.txt
git commit -m "Added test1.txt from branch1"
git checkout -b Branch2
//create file test1.txt
git add text1.txt
git commit -m "Added test1.txt from branch2"
```

From there we can do several things like a pull request, pulling directly or pushing to another branch. Let's first start with a pull request. To do so, you need to go on GitHub.

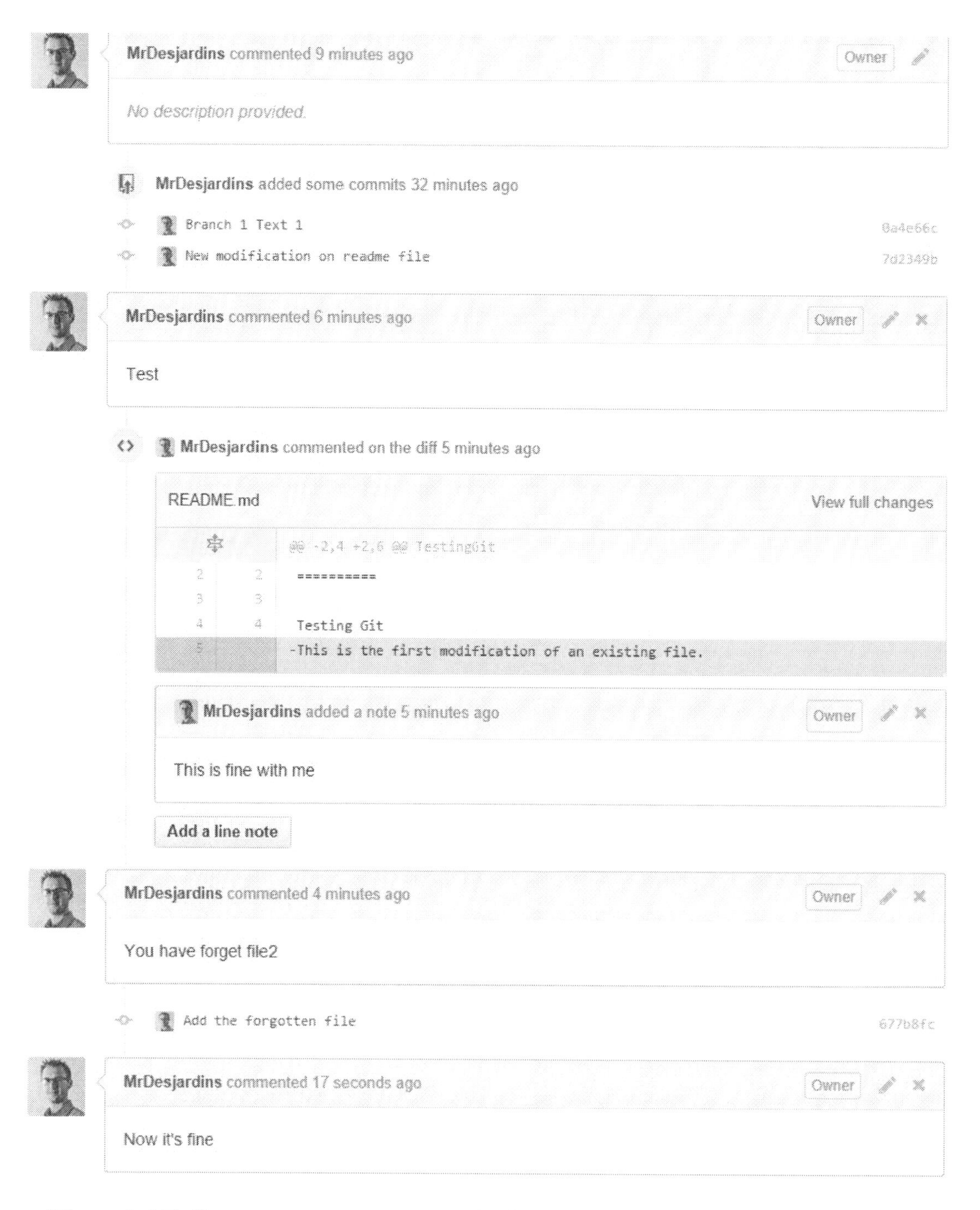


The web UI allows you to comment on the branch, but also inside every file. At the end, we can close the pull request. You can close the pull request if you are not satisfied or you can accept and merge from the website or the console. The console allows you to get the code and test it before pushing it back to the server. If you do not have the branch on your computer then you need to fetch it and check it out. Finally, merge the master to the branch to check the pull request with the whole main branch.

```
git fetch origin
git checkout -b branch1 origin/branch1
git merge master
```

Once everything is done (merging, making sure that it builds, unit test works, etc), then it is time to merge everything in the master,or if you already have the branch in your computer, you can get the code with the fetch command and then check the modification with the Git log. Finally, you can merge.

```
git fetch origin origin/branch1
git log origin/branch1
git merge origin/branch1
```

To accept the pull request, checkout the master and merge the branch into it. Finally, push everything to the server.

```
git checkout master
git merge --no-ff branch1
git commit -m "Merging Blah Blah"
git push origin master
```

As in this example, conflict can occur.

```
C:\Users\Patrick\Documents\GitHub\TestingGit [master]> git merge --no-ff branch1
Auto-merging test1.txt
CONFLICT (add/add): Merge conflict in test1.txt
Auto-merging README.md
CONFLICT (content): Merge conflict in README.md
Automatic merge failed; fix conflicts and then commit the result.
```

You can also see the conflict with the **git status** command.

```
Automatic merge failed; fix conflicts and then commit the result.
C:\Users\Patrick\Documents\GitHub\TestingGit [master +2 ~0 -0 !| ]> git status
# On branch master
# Your branch is ahead of 'origin/master' by 1 commit.
#   (use "git push" to publish your local commits)
#
# You have unmerged paths.
#   (fix conflicts and run "git commit")
#
# Changes to be committed:
#
#       new file:   forget.txt
#
# Unmerged paths:
#   (use "git add <file>..." to mark resolution)
#
#
#
#
C:\Users\Patrick\Documents\GitHub\TestingGit [master +2 ~0 -0 !| ]>
```

Before resolving the conflict, you need to be sure that you have configured the merging tool. Here is the configuration for WinMerge. This configuration must be set in your .gitconfig from your user folder. You can access it by using : **%USERPROFILE%/.gitconfig**

```
[merge]
    tool = winmerge
[mergetool "winmerge"]
    cmd = "'C:/Program Files (x86)/WinMerge/WinMergeU.exe'" -e "$MERGED"
    keepBackup = false
    trustExitCode = false
    tool = winmerge
[difftool "winmerge"]
    cmd = "'C:/Program Files (x86)/WinMerge/WinMergeU.exe'" -e "$LOCAL" "$REMOTE"
-dl "Local" -dr
```

If you prefer **kdiff3** tool, which is a 3-way commit tool, use this command

```
[merge]
    tool = kdiff3
[mergetool "kdiff3"]
    path = C:\\Program Files (x86)\\KDiff3\\kdiff3.exe
    keepBackup = false
    trustExitCode = false
```

From there you can use **git mergetool** and Git will go through all files that need to resolve a conflict.

```
git mergetool
```

Once all conflicts are resolved, merge done, commit done and push to the server done, then the pull request is automatically closed for you. We still have branch2 to merge. Let's do it without a pull request. But before that, let's move into branch2 and delete the readme file. Then let's try to undo this delete.

```
git checkout branch2
del readme.md
git checkout -- readme.md
```

Same thing with a new file.

```
git add readme.md2
git reset readme.md2
```

Last thing with a modified date.

```
//modify file
git checkout -- readme.md
```

So you have to remember two different commands to undo something to a file. One is checkout and one is reset. Concerning undoing, if you have commit, you can also undo this command. In fact, committing only puts the file in the stage area. To undo a commit use the **git reset** command.

```
git reset --soft HEAD~1
```

## How to Rebase your Working Branch Without Commiting your Working Files

Release Date: 04-Dec-14
Url: http://patrickdesjardins.com/blog/?post_type=post&p=3859

Let's start by building the scenario where you have two files that you want to share to everybody and one that is a configuration file that should not be shared. In some point in the development you want to get the latest version of the master branch into your feature branch. This requires you to do a merge or to rebase. **Merging** is interesting but will cause all files in your feature branch to be modified, which will be hard later for the pull request. The reason is that you want to pull request only your modification and not the files that have been merged. This is where **rebase** can be interesting. The problem is that if you try to rebase you will get a message saying that you need to commit or stash or change first. This is comprehensive since when you rebase you are moving the HEAD of your feature branch in front of the master one. It needs to have a "node" to move. To do this, you have to go into your feature branch, add all files you want to commit, and commit.

```
git checkout Feature1
git add File1
git add File2
git rebase master
```

The last line will fail. The reason is that you still have the configuration file not commited, and you do not want to do so. This is where the **stash** command shines. The git stash command allows you to put the remaining files somewhere that has changed into a **stash** which will allow you, later, to get it back (after the rebase). To execute the stash, you have to execute the stash command in the branch you want the files not staged to be stashed.

```
git checkout Feature1
git stash
git rebase master
git stash pop
```

You should be all set with the latest version of the master branch and also your files back (the configuration file in our example).

# Git Adding a File to a Previous Commit

Release Date: 06-Dec-14
Url: http://patrickdesjardins.com/blog/?post_type=post&p=3868

Imagine that you are doing a commit and you forgot to bring a file or multiple files. You can do a second commit but this would have the consequence of having two commits for something that in fact would have been in one. Git allows you to alter a past commit with the **amend** parameter. For example, here is a small commit of one file.

```
git add main.cs
git commit -m "This is my first commit"
```

This is how to add a second file to this first commit.

```
git add util.cs
git commit --amend --no-edit
```

The **--no-edit** parameter specifies that we do not want to modify the message. If you are doing a Git log, you will see a single commit.

# Create a New Git Branch with Uncommited Code

Release Date: 08-Dec-14
Url: http://patrickdesjardins.com/blog/?post_type=post&p=3863

If you started doing some code modification but you realize that you should have done these modifications in a branch instead of directly into the branch where you did the modification, you can move all files into a new branch. The command is checkout with the parameter **-b** which creates the branch if it does not exist.

```
git checkout -b NewBranch
git add .
```

The Git **add .** simply adds all uncommited files into the staged area. Other possibilities exist like using **git stash** to move uncommited code into a temporary place and unstash into another branch.

```
git stashgit checkout NewBranch
git stash apply
```

# Git Combining Commit Not Pushed Yet

Release Date: 14-Dec-14
Url: http://patrickdesjardins.com/blog/?post_type=post&p=3874

You are working on your computer, did several commits and you are ready to push. However, you may not want to push all the commits but only one that combines all your commits. Multiple cases exist where you want all the code but not some of the comments related to commits. Another case could be that the commit was not significant and you want to get rid of it. This is often the case of a commit without a message. The changes are required, but an empty commit is not. To combine commits you need to use the rebase method inside your own branch. This is done by using the **rebase interactive** command.

```
git rebase -i              #All since the last commit
git rebase -i HEAD~5       #Last 5 commits
```

I wrote two commands that are doing almost the same thing. The first one does not specify the commit to take. By default, it will take all commits not pushed. The second command takes the last five commits. This will redirect you to the interactive rebase screen. From that screen, it is possible to squash, edit or pick a command. You will also notice that the screen displays all commits from the oldest to the newest commit. You will see one line per commit. This allows you to edit every line by choosing if you want to keep the commit with **pick**, to get the code but not the message with **squash,** or to edit the commit with **edit**.

Let's take the scenario that we want to combine everything in one commit. In that case, you **pick** the first commit and **squash** all the other ones. You save and Git will open your default editor to allow you to edit the final message. Save and you are all set. At any time, if a conflict occurs you can abort. You just need to do the abort method of the git rebase command.

```
git rebase --abort
```

# How To Use Git From Visual Studio Online

Release Date: 16-Dec-14
Url: http://patrickdesjardins.com/blog/?post_type=post&p=3730

If you have a Git repository in Visual Studio Online and want to use a third party to manage your source code, like SourceTree, you need to configure something in Visual Studio. First, open your Visual Studio Online portal and go into your profile to set up an alternative authentication. The profile is in the top right corner of Visual Studio. Click your name and then click **My Profile**.

Second, click the **Crendentials** tab. This will allow you to have an alternative login name and a password to use for applications like SourceTree (or any other system).

USER PROFILE 

Patrick Desjardins

GENERAL LOCALE **CREDENTIALS** CONNECTIONS

**ALTERNATE AUTHENTICATION CREDENTIALS**

Some applications that work outside the browser (including Team Explorer Everywhere command line client and the git-tf utility) require basic authentication credentials. Other applications do not properly handle using an e-mail address for the user name during authentication.

To work with these applications, you need to enable alternate credentials, set a password, and optionally set a secondary user name not in the form of an e-mail address. Please note that alternate credentials cannot be used to sign in to the service from a web browser or outside of these applications. Learn more

User name (primary)

User name (secondary) patrickdesjardins Edit

Password •••••••••••• Change

Confirm password •••••••••••• Change

Disable alternate credentials

Save changes Cancel

When this is done, the third step is to copy the Git Http path, which is the one you see in your browser when you click in the project you want to code, and then code. The syntax should look like the example below.

```
https://YOURRepositoryNAME.visualstudio.com/DefaultCollection/_git/Project
```

You need that http url to paste it into your software and be able to clone the repository. From there, you can use Git to do any other command you wish.

# 8. IIS

This chapter groups every post written during 2013 and 2014 about IIS. Like all chapters in this book, every article is a snapshot of a real scenario that has a high probability of happening if you are using these technologies. You will notice that every article that has been chosen to be included in this book contains the release date to identify when it was written. A permanent link is also provided that allows you to go in and read updates and comments. Feel free to go on the website to add your own comment if you wish.

## Installing IIS on Windows 7 Home Edition and running your Asp.Net MVC application

Release Date: 21-Aug-13
Url: http://patrickdesjardins.com/blog/?post_type=post&p=2226

If you go to the administrator panel, you may not see IIS anywhere. To make sure, go to Control Panel\All Control Panel Items\Administrative Tools\

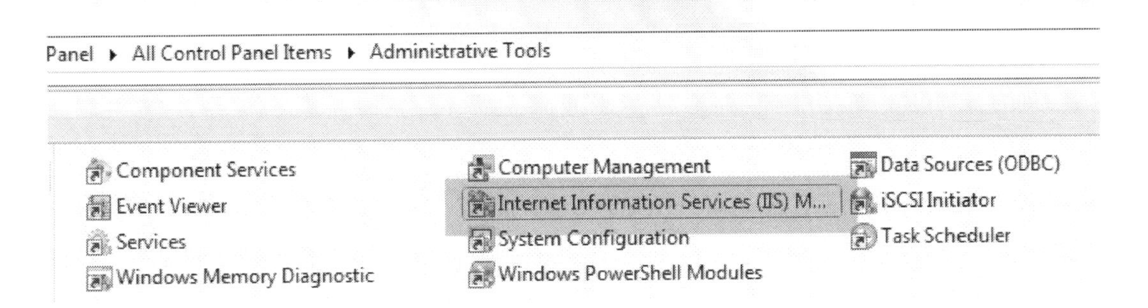


If you have IIS, you will see an icon with the text **Internet Information Services (IIS) Manager**. If not, you will have to install it, which is already part of Windows 7, it is just not enabled. To install it, go to Control Panel\All Control Panel Items\ and select Programs and Features. In the left side bar, you will see a link called **Turn Windows features on or off**. Select this and a new window opens.

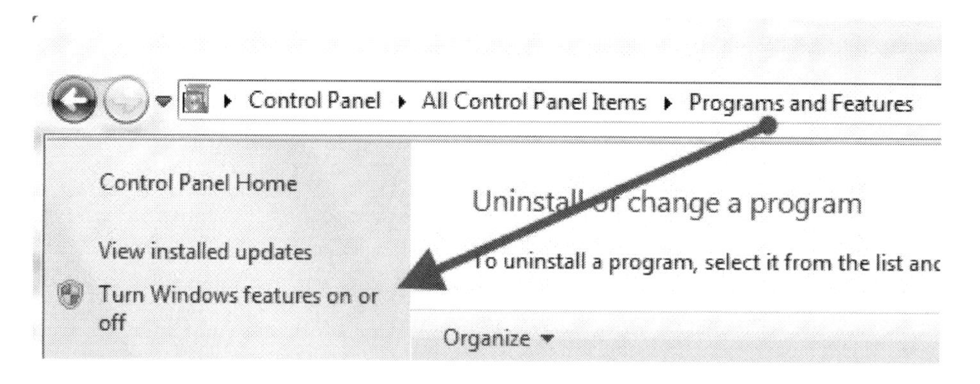


You have to select IIS and go into a subfolder to select what you see in the following image.

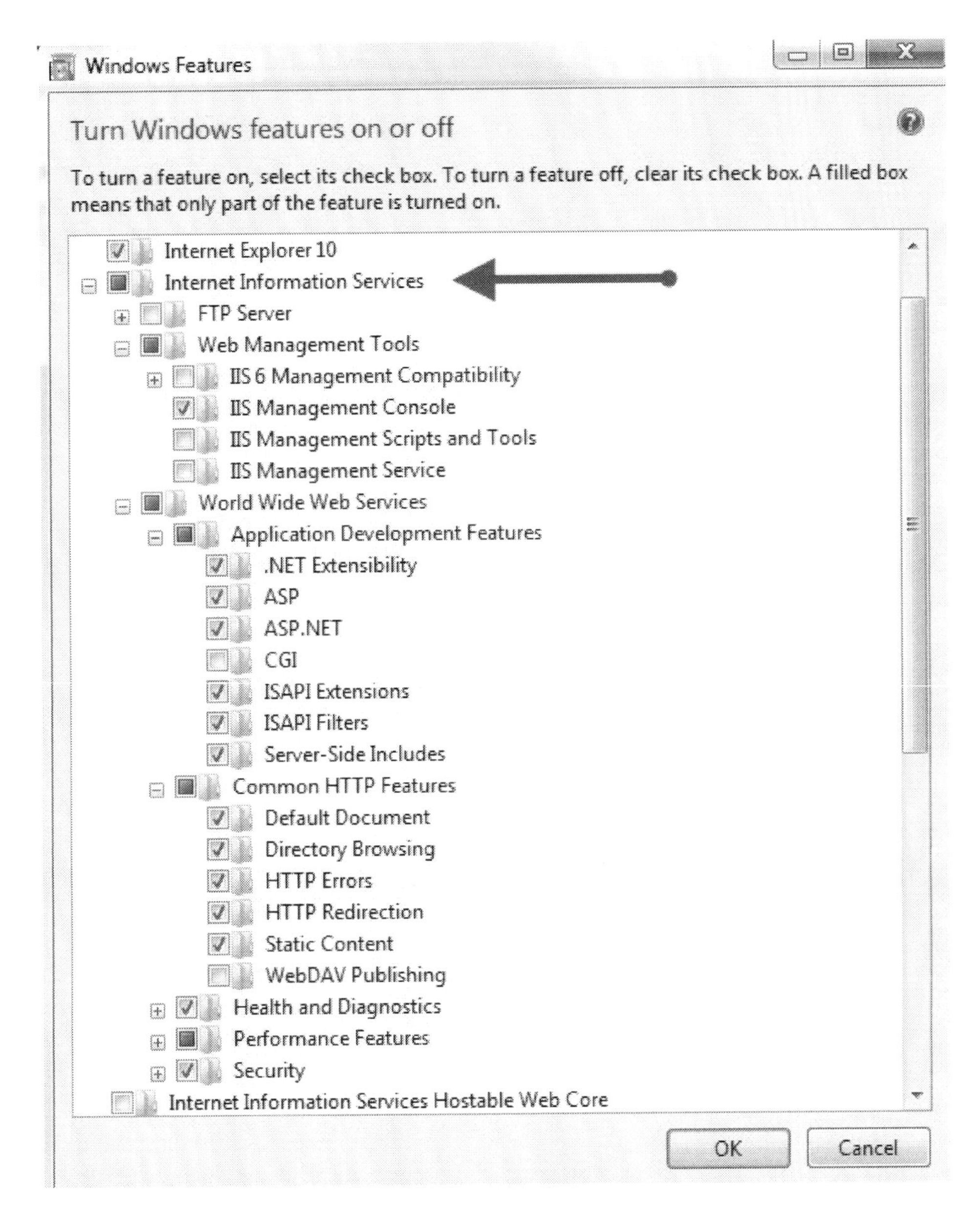


This will take several minutes depending on your machine. When everything is done, the control panel will now have IIS in the administrative tools.

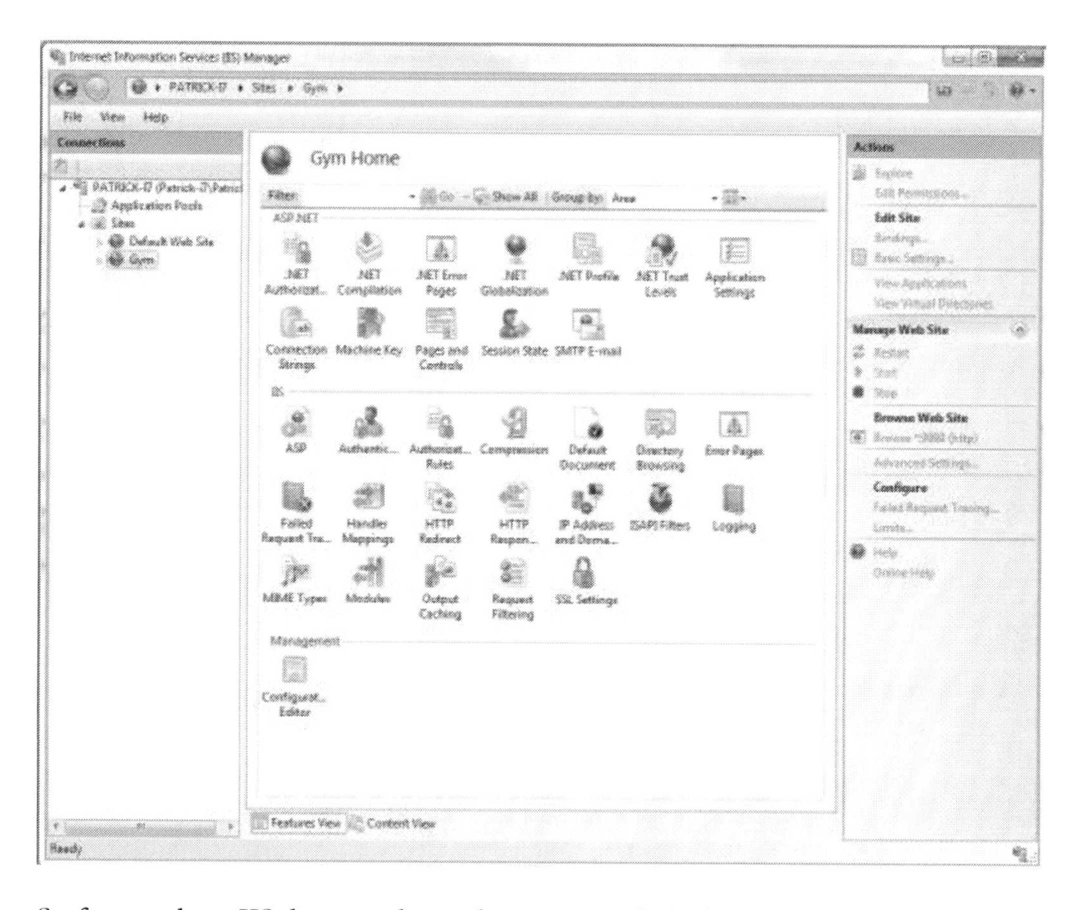


So far, you have IIS, but you do not have your website linked to it. If you are a developer, the best way to make it work is to link IIS to the path where your code resides. I prefer not having my code in My Documents because it will cause some security problems with default configuration. In fact, the user on which IIS will run the application pool won't have access to your file inside your My Documents. Nevertheless, we can run IIS with an application pool that uses your credentials. First, open IIS and create a new website to which you will select the root of your web application (where the solution is). Be sure to have the website running on a good framework. I have found that it selects framework 2.0 by default which should be the latest framework (4.0) if you run an MVC website. If you are using code inside your My Documents, you also need to set your application pool to your account.

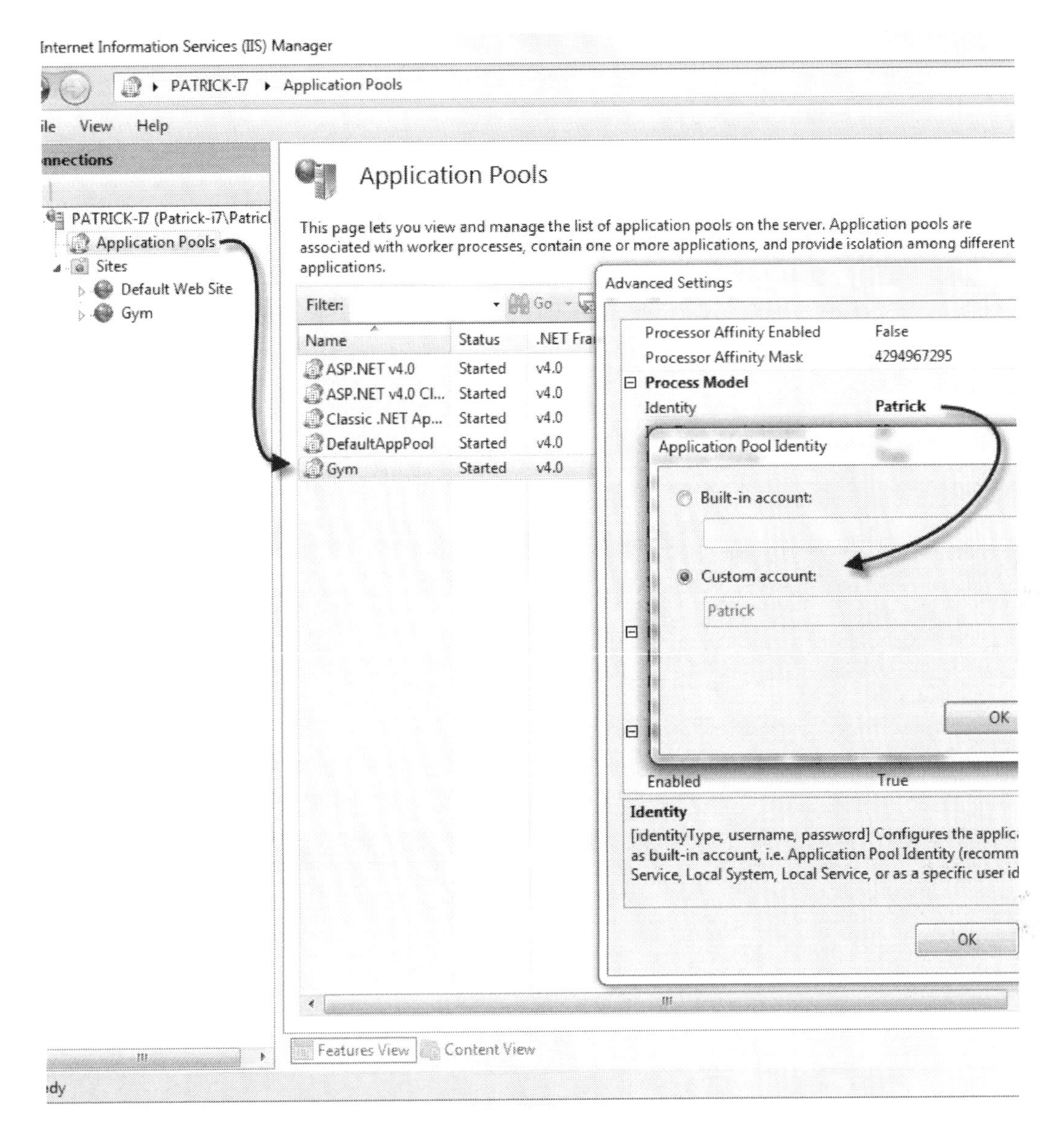


Now, if you try to run your website, you should be able to see it. If you get this message:

*IIS – this configuration section cannot be used at this path*

It means that you have not selected every option in the image above when installing IIS. The good news is that it is not too late. You need to go back into the **Windows Features and select the Application Development Features**. If you get the error message:

*HTTP Error 500.19 – Internal Server Error – The requested page cannot be accessed because the related configuration data for the page is invalid.*

This means that IIS does not have access to the folder. This means that you need to change the Identity of the application pool as instructed before.

Another point of failure may be that IIS is not running with all the new installed configuration. You will know this if you get the message

*Handler "ExtensionlessUrlHandler-Integrated-4.0" has a bad module "ManagedPipelineHandler" in its module list*

To have IIS use all new modules, open a Console as an administrator and execute the following line: c:\Windows\Microsoft.NET\Framework\v4.0.30319\aspnet_regiis.exe –i

```
Administrator: C:\Windows\System32\cmd.exe
Microsoft Windows [Version 6.1.7601]
Copyright (c) 2009 Microsoft Corporation.  All rights reserved.

C:\Windows\system32>c:\Windows\Microsoft.NET\Framework\v4.0.30319\aspnet_regiis.exe -i
Microsoft (R) ASP.NET RegIIS version 4.0.30319.17929
Administration utility to install and uninstall ASP.NET on the local machine.
Copyright (C) Microsoft Corporation.  All rights reserved.
Start installing ASP.NET (4.0.30319.17929).
........
Finished installing ASP.NET (4.0.30319.17929).

C:\Windows\system32>
```

The last problem may be that you see your website but without JavaScript and CSS loading. You can notice this not only because your website won't display correctly but also because JavaScript and CSS errors will be marked in every browser tool.

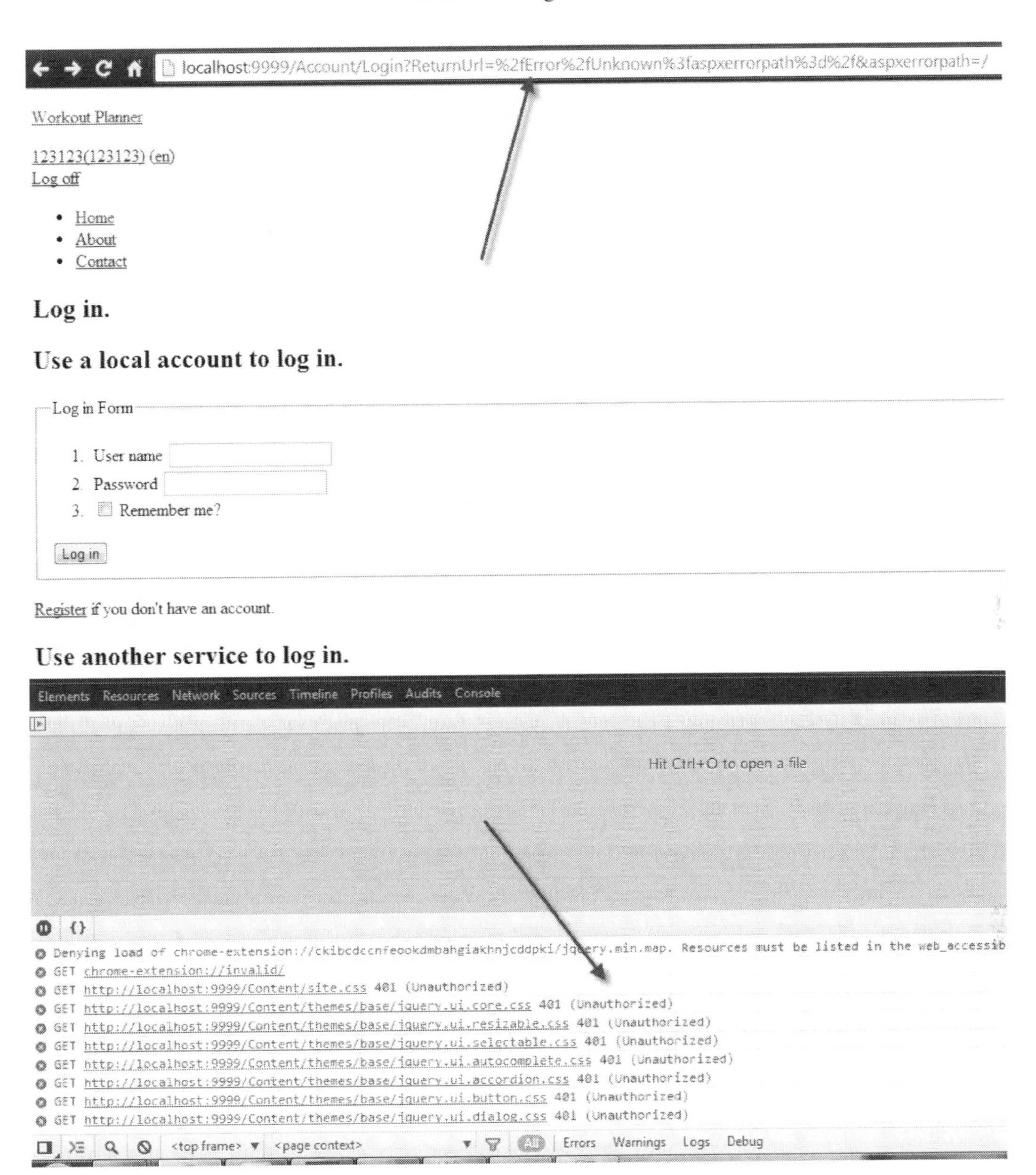


To fix this, two things must be set. First, you have to have the **Static Content** installed. This has to be checked when installing IIS. If not, you can go into Control Panel\All Control Panel Items\ and select Programs and Features. In the left side bar, you will see a link called **Turn Windows features on or off** and under **Common Http functions** of IIS you will see the option.

Second, you need to execute not only the application pool under your credential but also set the authentication of the website under yours. To do it, select Basic Settings > Connect as… > Specific user.

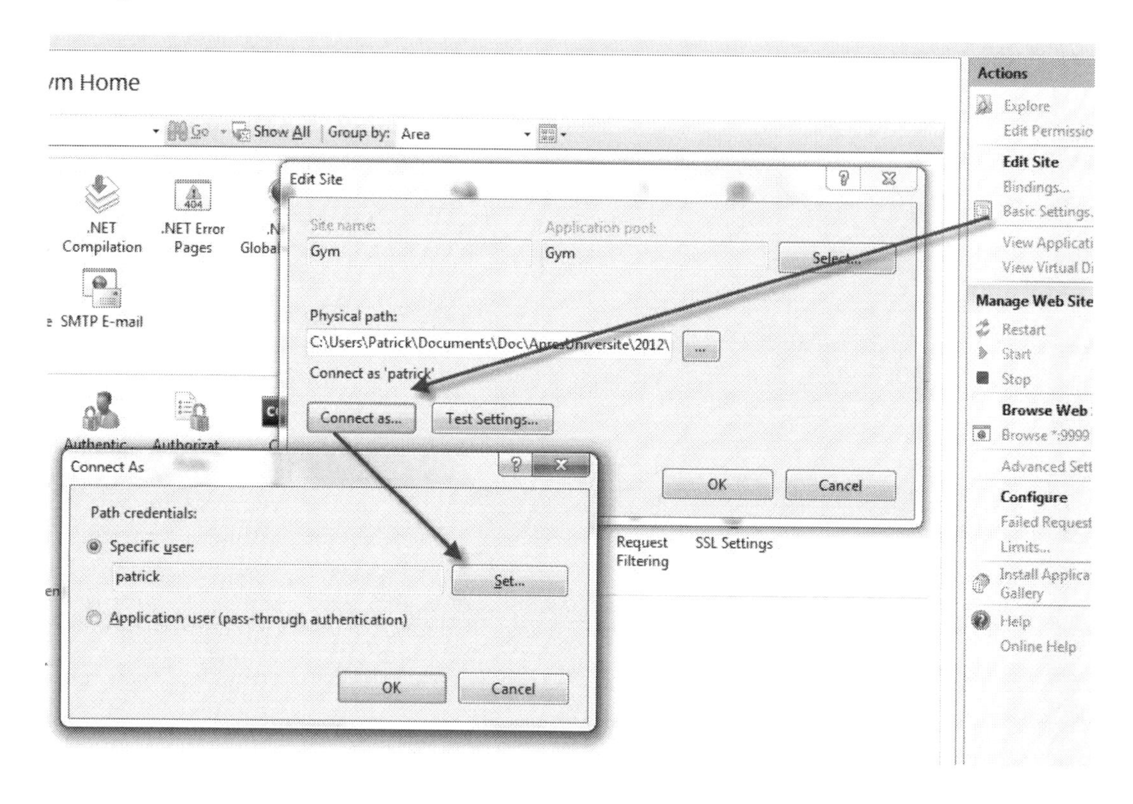


From here, your website should work from any location (even your My Documents folder).

## IIS 8.0 Application Initialization for fast startup every time

Release Date: 14-Feb-14
Url: http://patrickdesjardins.com/blog/?post_type=post&p=2635

Since IIS 8, application pool has an advanced option that allows it to never sleep instead of being active on demand, which boots up the application pool only when someone calls the website. This is problematic for performance because the first person to hit the website has a booting time that can be several seconds if not minutes. Even with the configuration that indicates to not recycle the application pool, there is the problem of the first startup. Also, having the application pool never reset is not a good practice. In fact, it is a good practice to reset the application pool on a schedule when your website is not in an active time window. For example, if you do not have a lot of visits at 2 am, you can specify to recycle at 2 am.

Still, before IIS 8.0, this was possible but the first person to hit the website paid the price. Before going any further, you need to have installed the Application Initialization module. It is free and available by Web Platform. A link is available if you select inside IIS the root node of your server.

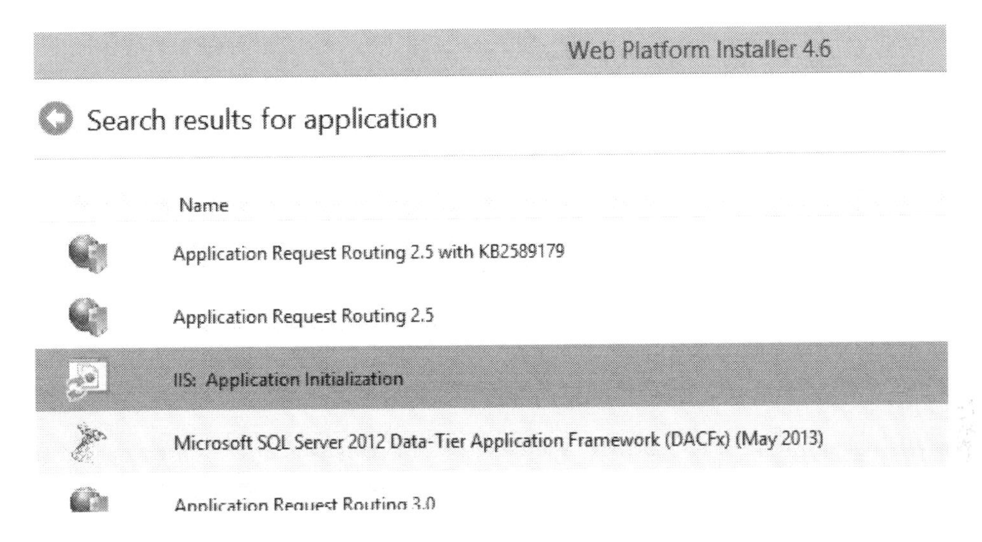


With IIS 7.5 and after, it is possible to select the **Start Mode**. The Start mode can be **On Demand** or **Always Running**. **On demand** starts the application pool from an HTTP request. **Always running** uses the Windows Process Activation Service (WAS) to start the application pool. This was available with IIS 7.5 but IIS 8.0 does have this configuration within IIS without having to modify any applicationhost.config file. It is more convenient.

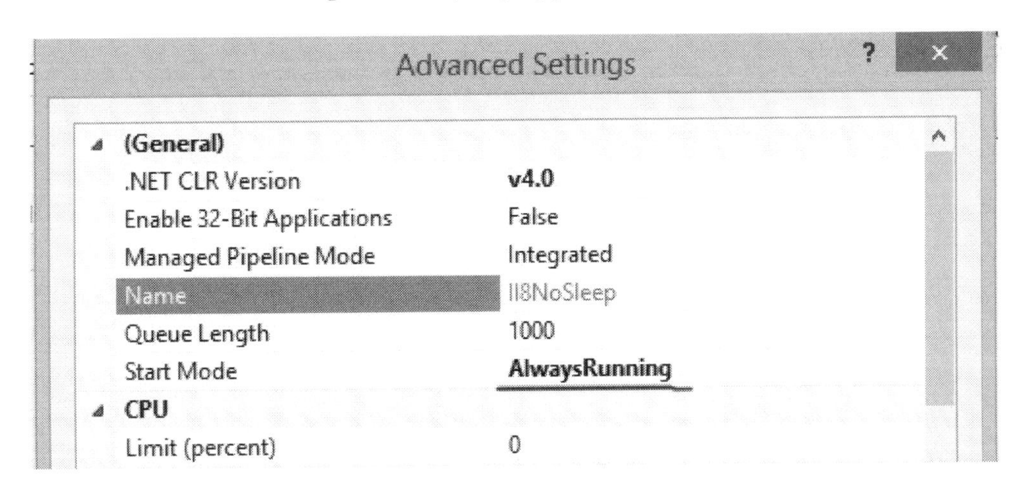


To enable it to be preloaded, a modification to the machine configuration is required. IIS 8 does not have any screen that allows you to enable it. The file is located here:

C:\Windows\System32\inetsrv\config\applicationHost.config

```
<sites>
    <site name="Default Web Site" id="1">
        <application path="/">
            <virtualDirectory path="/"
                              physicalPath="%SystemDrive%\inetpub\wwwroot" />
        </application>
        <application path="/TestToDelete" applicationPool="II8NoSleep"
                                          preloadEnabled="true">
            <virtualDirectory path="/" physicalPath="C:\inetpub\wwwroot" />
        </application>
        <bindings>
            <binding protocol="http" bindingInformation="*:80:" />
        </bindings>
    </site>
   ...
```

Line 6 of the previous XML is the one you want. In fact, you need to search for your site which is under the site's XML element. Then you see the application path that needs to be modified. The **preloadedEnabled=true** is the attribute to add. This file needs to be edited with administration privileges.

At this point, any time the application pool is recycled, it will boot it to be available. But, since it sends a fake request to your website to boot up, wouldn't it be great if you could choose which page that WAS uses? Yes, and it can be configurable. This is a must if you have a page that loads data into the cache, or to manually wake up other resources. To customize the page to be called by IIS, you need to open the web.config of your website and add an XML element.

```
<applicationInitialization
    remapManagedRequestsTo="Startup.htm"
    skipManagedModules="true" >
  <add initializationPage="/default.aspx" />
</applicationInitialization>
```

The XML has a **remapManagedRequestsTo** which is the page to be displayed when the loading is executed. Instead of having a blank screen with a long loading progress bar, this allows a static message to be displayed to the visitor. The **initializationPage** is the page to be called by the WAS.

# How to use Chrome browser with an IIS web application and Windows Authentication (AD)

Release Date: 11-Mar-14
Url: http://patrickdesjardins.com/blog/?post_type=post&p=3389

Having an intranet that is using single sign-on with Active Directory (AD) is something that we see daily in the industry. Most of the time, Microsoft Internet Explorer is used and everything seems to be transparent. However, in some cases, like when using Google Chrome, you can get an annoying popup that asks for credentials. The problem is that even if the user enters his credentials the popup keeps popping.

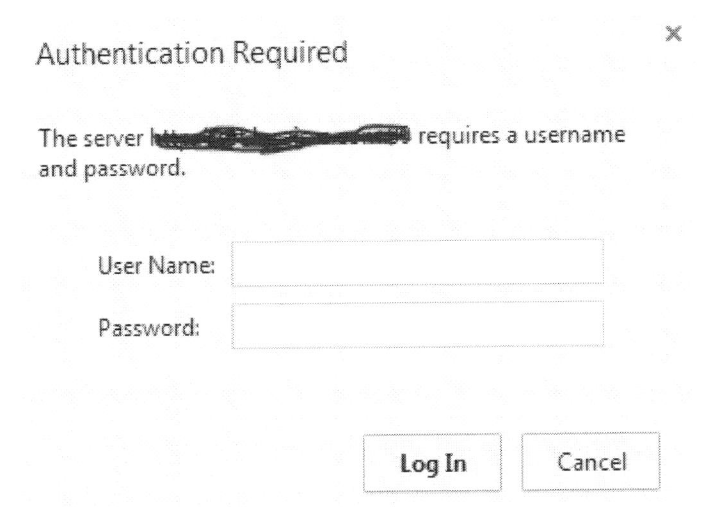


First of all, why does it work with Microsoft Internet Explorer but not with Chrome? This is interesting because both of them share the same internet configuration. This is not the same for Mozilla Firefox that has its own configuration. Nevertheless, Chrome uses the **Internet Options** in the Control Panel\All Control Panel Items. If the configuration is fine for Internet Explorer, then it should be fine for Chrome too. This eliminates the problem of having your intranet website not in the trusted list of intranet websites.

Second, it is not a problem of code. Your code should be all fine if it worked with Internet Explorer. In fact, if you have a credential problem it is more likely that something is not validated correctly. This gives us a final place to search for this problem — the server. **IIS** has for each of your websites an **authentication** configuration, located at the root of the website. This is where you should have already set the authentication to **Windows Authentication.**

# IIS No Sleep (idle) and AutoStart with Values

Release Date: 24-Jun-14
Url: http://patrickdesjardins.com/blog/?post_type=post&p=3548

It is important to have not only a good code but to have it in a hosting environment that will make it look good. One negative point that we hear with IIS is that when the application pool sleeps, the user that does a query has a penalty of time on its first query. This can lead to several seconds of waiting. It is interesting to note that for at least five years we can have IIS auto start. It is also interesting to note that we can also make IIS not become idle.

## Changing IIS Idle Time

The first step to improve IIS performance is to remove the timeout. This can be done by opening IIS, opening the **Application Pool** you want to change the setting in, and opening the Advanced Setting Window. The window has a Process Model section where you will find **Idle Time-out (minutes)** setting. You can set this property to 0. By default, the Application Pool also recycles every few minutes. You can set it to 0 to have it not recycle. This will cause a higher availability of IIS during the day where most clients are. If your application has a low period, let's say that you are building for an internal website for a company, you can set an absolute time to recycle. This can be set in the same screen as before, the **Advanced Setting** of the **Application Pool**, by changing the **Specific Times**. For example, we can set it to recycle the pool at 1 am every day.

Advanced Settings

| | |
|---|---|
| **(General)** | |
| **CPU** | |
| **Process Model** | |
| Generate Process Model Event Log Entry | |
| Identity | **ApplicationPoolIdentity** |
| Idle Time-out (minutes) | **0** |
| Idle Time-out Action | Terminate |
| Load User Profile | True |
| Maximum Worker Processes | 1 |
| Ping Enabled | True |
| Ping Maximum Response Time (seconds) | 90 |
| Ping Period (seconds) | 30 |
| Shutdown Time Limit (seconds) | 90 |
| Startup Time Limit (seconds) | 90 |
| **Process Orphaning** | |
| **Rapid-Fail Protection** | |
| **Recycling** | |
| Disable Overlapped Recycle | False |
| Disable Recycling for Configuration Changes | False |
| Generate Recycle Event Log Entry | |
| Private Memory Limit (KB) | 0 |
| Regular Time Interval (minutes) | **0** |
| Request Limit | 0 |
| Specific Times | **TimeSpan[] Array** |
| Virtual Memory Limit (KB) | 0 |

## Auto Start

The auto start functionality is something that allows you to perform an action when IIS starts your application pool. For example, you could load in your caching system information from your database. You can also have some code that verifies the availability of an external webservice, etc. This requires some manual editing of files on the server where your IIS resides. The file that needs to be edited is named **applicationHost.config** and it is located in the system folder: c:\windows\system32\inetsrv\config\.

The first section that you need to edit is the one that has your application pool name. You must ensure that you have **autoStart = true** and the **startmode** to **alwaysrunning**.

```
<add name="YourAppPoolName"
     autoStart="true"
     startMode="AlwaysRunning"
```

```
    managedRuntimeVersion="v4.0">
    <processModel
          identityType="SpecificUser"
          userName="DefaultAppUserName"
          idleTimeout="00:00:00" />
</add>
```

In the same file, the second section to find is the application path. You can find this section by searching your application name. You must have **serviceAutoStartEnabled=true** and set a **serviceAutoStartProvider** to a unique name that we will define soon.

```
<application path="/YourApplicationPath"
             applicationPool="YourAppPoolName"
             serviceAutoStartEnabled="true"
             serviceAutoStartProvider="YourProvider" >
             <virtualDirectory path="/"

physicalPath="C:\inetpub\wwwroot\YourApplicationPath" />
 </application>
```

The provider name we just set needs to be defined. This can be done by adding a new section (if it is not yet there) in the applicationHost.config file (the same file where we are currently modifying the XML) under the section **serviceAutoStartProviders**.

```
<serviceAutoStartProviders>
     <add name="YourProvider"
               type="YourProvider, Full.NameSpace.To.YourProvider,
version=1.0.0.0, Culture=neutral" />
</serviceAutoStartProviders>
```

IIS will get the DLL from your application bin folder and start running your custom code for your application when the application pool boots.

The last part is to code the custom code of your provider. This can be done by implementing a specific interface. This interface has a PreLoad method that is executed by IIS. The interface that you must implement is named **IProcessHostPreloadClient**.

```
public class YourProvider : IProcessHostPreloadClient
{
    public void Preload(string[] parameters)
    {

    }
}
```

Do not forget that this feature is available only for **IIS 7.5 and above**. Also, do not forget that you may have to write some additional code if you want to use your repository with your IoC container. If you are using the Http Cache that Asp.Net provides, you need to have the namespace added to your project that has the custom provider.

# Developing with IIS Express to Full IIS

Release Date: 28-Oct-14
Url: http://patrickdesjardins.com/blog/?post_type=post&p=3758

Developing with IIS Express has its limitations. The more you are developing the more you may have several websites, web api, WCF and other systems that must run together. You can increase your compilation process by only compiling and publishing the system that has changed. Visual Studio is bright enough to not recompile every library but it also has its pitfalls with IIS Express that suddenly has some of its references not synchronize. The result is obvious. First of all, the "startup" project will work but some of the others will not. For example, if you have a web project and a web api with the web as a startup project, you may have the web working when the web api will result in many types of possible errors.

A solution is to use IIS instead of IIS Express. This way, with every compilation only the libraries that have changed are compiled but once it is compiled, all your systems will stay in a working stage (indeed it must have been in a working stage). To switch is pretty easy. Open IIS and create one website for your web project and so on. Define different ports for all your websites and that's it. Not so fast! You can have an error 500:

*This configuration section cannot be used at this path. This happens when the section is locked at a parent level. Locking is either by default.*

**HTTP Error 500.19 - Internal Server Error**

**The requested page cannot be accessed because the related configuration data for the page is invalid.**

**Detailed Error Information:**

| | | | |
|---|---|---|---|
| **Module** | IIS Web Core | **Requested URL** | http://localhost:80/ |
| **Notification** | BeginRequest | **Physical Path** | C:\Users\Patrick\Documents\TFS\BourseVirtuelle uelle |
| **Handler** | Not yet determined | **Logon Method** | Not yet determined |
| **Error Code** | 0x80070021 | **Logon User** | Not yet determined |
| **Config Error** | This configuration section cannot be used at this path. This happens when the section is locked at a parent level. Locking is either by default (overrideModeDefault ="Deny"), or set explicitly by a location tag with overrideMode="Deny" or the legacy allowOverride="false". | | |

This error occurs if you have not added some IIS features. To add those features, open the Windows Features by typing **Turn Windows features on or off** in the start menu. This opens a window with some Windows features. Select **Internet Information Services**, **World Wide Web Services** and all of the others.

- Internet Information Services
  - FTP Server
  - Web Management Tools
  - World Wide Web Services
    - Application Development Features
    - Common HTTP Features
    - Health and Diagnostics
    - Performance Features
    - Security

From there, be sure that your web application in IIS points to the web project and to the web api project. Not the DLL folder, but the folder where the project is located. You just need to compile and you are up and running. If you need to debug with breakpoint, you need to go in Visual Studio and go to Debug > Attach To Process. Click **Show Process from all users** and select the **w3wp.exe** process. Click attach and you are ready to debug.

# 9. JAVASCRIPT

This chapter groups every post written during 2013 and 2014 about JavaScript. Like all chapters in this book, every article is a snapshot of a real scenario that has a high probability of happening if you are using these technologies. You will notice that every article that has been chosen to be included in this book contains the release date to identify when it was written. A permanent link is also provided that allows you to go in and read updates and comments. Feel free to go on the website to add your own comment if you wish.

## How with JQuery to disable click until animation is done

Release Date: 21-Jan-13
Url: http://patrickdesjardins.com/blog/?post_type=post&p=1687

You may want to animate something before doing an action and remove the possibility that the user will click again. This is often a desired behavior because it might break the current animation, or simply do nothing, which will give the user a false impression of a bug.
The solution is to disable the button (or link) during the animation.

```
function clickFunction(obj) {
    //If animated than we wait the animation to be over
    if ($(':animated').length) {
        return false;
    }

    obj.animate({
        //Animation here that is executed one but if clicked before
        //this one is over won't be reached
    }, 4000);
}
```

The above code works with JQuery framework and checks if the animated queue contains any element. If yes, the function called by the click returns false and does not do anything. In fact, you could here write something to the screen if you want to inform the user that something is occurring and that he should wait.

## Jquery selector Parent vs Closest to search element through upper levels of hierarchical structure

Release Date: 23-Jan-13
Url: http://patrickdesjardins.com/blog/?post_type=post&p=1690

With JQuery you can use **Parent**, **Parents** and **Closest** to search elements at a higher level of the one selected. What are the differences?

## JQuery Parent selector

Parent() will search one level up only. For example, here is the HTML code of a situation where you can see two levels deep of div and a paragraph.

```
<div class="parent1">
   <div class="parent2">
      <p>Hello Again</p>
   </div>
  </div>
```

If we use the Parent selector on the paragraph it will select parent2 division.

```
$("p").parent().css("background", "yellow");
```

You can see this example in action here: http://jsfiddle.net/C5Shz/
Even by specifying the class of the second level, nothing will be selected.

```
$("p").parent('parent1').css("background", "yellow");
```

You can see the result: http://jsfiddle.net/L953U/
The reason is that parent goes only one level up.

## JQuery Parents selector

Parents will return an array of elements. It returns all elements from root to the selected element.

```
$("p").parents('div').css("background", "yellow");
```

This returns two divisions, the parent1 and the parent2. The reason is that the parent1 is the root parent and parent2 is the parent between the selected one (p) and the searched element.

You can see the example in action here: http://jsfiddle.net/u7SaF/

## JQuery Closest selector

Closest() looks up the tree like .parent() but stops when the search element is found. It returns a single element or nothing if nothing is found.

```
$("p").closest("div").css("background", "blue");
```

This will color in blue the closest division from the p.
Here is the example in action. http://jsfiddle.net/ZNQ5Q/

If we summarize everything in bullet points:

**Parent:**
- Begins with the current element and goes only one level up
- The returned jQuery object contains zero or one element

**Parents:**
- Begins with the parent element
- Travels up the DOM tree but returns elements in reverse
- The returned jQuery object contains zero, one, or multiple elements

**Closest:**
- Begins with the current element
- Travels up the DOM tree until it finds a match for the supplied selector
- The returned jQuery object contains zero or one element

Finally, I often see code with multiple parents() called. For example, $("p").parent().parent()..css("background", "blue"). Instead, you can use *eq* with *parents*.

```
<div>
    <div>
        <div>
            <p>Hello Again</p>
        </div>
    </div>
</div>

$("p").parents().eq(2).css("background", "blue");
```

This will get all parents and since the order is from the parent selection the list will return the level up. Do not forget that the index you provide starts with 0 which is the immediate parent element. In the example above, only the first div will have a background blue while the two inner divisions will remain white. Here is an example : http://jsfiddle.net/U4msb/1/

# How to shake (or vibrate) an HTML element

Release Date: 05-Apr-13
Url: http://patrickdesjardins.com/blog/?post_type=post&p=1970

When your user makes an error, it might be interesting to select the control and to make it shake a few seconds just to get the user's attention. It is not something you should do for every validation but sometime you may come across a situation where the user might be more confused about which controls or elements he needs to take care of. Therefore, a way to point it out is to shake the element on the screen and highlight the correct one.

The code in this post is not in the form of a JQuery plugin but it should be. It is more intended to be educational. The first part of the code shows you that you need to call the method "Vibrate" that takes the element to shake as a parameter.

```
var vibrateIndex = 0;
var selector;
//Animate the selector with the animation function
function Vibrate(item) {
    selector = $(item);
    var interval = 10;
    var duration = 500;
    vibrateIndex = setInterval(Vibe, interval);
    setTimeout(StopVibration, duration);
}
```

The second part is doing the animation of shaking the control. In fact, we are randomly moving the left and top position of the control and setting this one relative. This is important. Otherwise, the control will not move. It also sets the border to red.

```
//Animation
function Vibe() {
    var shake = 3;
    $(selector).stop(true, false)
        .css({
            position: 'relative',
            left: Math.round(Math.random() * shake) + 'px',
            top: Math.round(Math.random() * shake) + 'px',
            borderColor: 'red'
        });

};
```

The last part is executed when the animation is over. This is called by the **setTimout** method previously set with a duration.

```
//Remove all CSS applied to the selector
function StopVibration() {
    clearInterval(vibrateIndex);
    $(selector).stop(true, false)
                .css({
                    position: 'static',
                    left: '0px',
                    top: '0px',
                    borderColor: ''
                });
};
```

This could be improved by having everything inside a JQuery plugin, which would be cleaner. The problem with the code above is that we used a global variable to remember to control that is incorporated into the animation and the interval reference is also global.

You can see a working example at http://jsfiddle.net/kEVd3/.

## Plugin

Here is the JQuery Plugin version: http://jsfiddle.net/kEVd3/3/

```
(function ($) {
    $.fn.vibrate = function (options) {
        options = $.extend({}, $.fn.vibrate.defaultOptions, options);
        var control = $(this);
        var vibrateIndex = 0;
        var selector;

        vibrateIndex = setInterval(vibe, options.interval);
        setTimeout(stopVibration, options.duration);
        function vibe() {
            var shake = 3;
            $(control).stop(true, false)
                .css({
                    position: 'relative',
                    left: Math.round(Math.random() * shake) + 'px',
                    top: Math.round(Math.random() * shake) + 'px',
                    borderColor: 'red'
                });

        };

        function stopVibration() {
            clearInterval(vibrateIndex);
            $(control).stop(true, false)
                        .css({
```

```
                                position: 'static',
                                left: '0px',
                                top: '0px',
                                borderColor: ''
                            });
        };
        return this;
    }

    $.fn.vibrate.defaultOptions = {
        interval: 10
       , duration: 500
    }
})(jQuery);
```

Here is an example of how to use it:

```
$('#btnShake').click(function () {
    $('input[type=text]').vibrate();
});
```

You can also specify an option like the duration:

```
$('input[type=text]').vibrate({ duration: 3000 });
```

I'll do a post concerning how to create a JQuery plugin soon to explain in detail how and why the plugin has been created this way.

# JQPlot with Internet Explorer 7 and 8: Do not forget excanvas.js

Release Date: 23-May-13
Url: http://patrickdesjardins.com/blog/?post_type=post&p=2073

JQPlot (http://www.jqplot.com/) is a JavaScript library that makes it easy to have a graphic on your website. By default, it uses all the power of Html5.

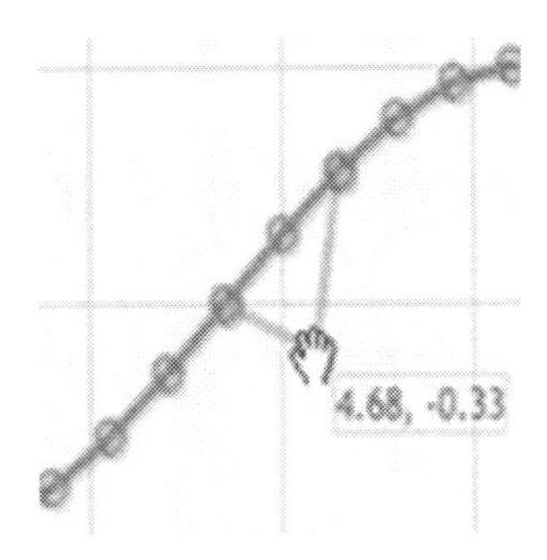


If you want to use JQPlot with Internet Explorer 8, add this line before adding the JQPlot's JavaScript files.

```
<!--[if IE]><script language="javascript" type="text/javascript"
src="@Url.Content("~/Scripts/libs/plot/excanvas.js")"></script><![endif]-->
```

The JavaScript library can be found on https://code.google.com/p/explorercanvas. This will let the library use the excanvas.js instead of the Html5 one.

# Jquery Get Html Text Without Children Elements

Release Date: 03-Oct-13
Url: http://patrickdesjardins.com/blog/?post_type=post&p=2324

Sometimes, you have an hmtl list inside another HTML list, or in fact any HTML element inside html, and you want to have the text but not other HTML tags. How can you do this?

You cannot use .html() because it will return the inner HTML tag. You cannot use .text() because it will return the text of the HTML element with the text inside an inner HTML element. For example:

```
<ul>
    <li id="step1">
        This is Step 1
        <ul>
            <li>This is inside Step 1</li>
        </ul>
    </li>
    <li id="step2">
        This is Step 2
    </li>
</ul>
```

If we use "step1.html()". The output is:

```
This is Step 1
<ul>
    <li>This is inside Step 1</li>
</ul>
```

If we use "step1.text()". The output is:

```
This is Step 1
 This is inside Step 1
```

But if you want to get only "This is Step 1" you will have to use several Jquery calls.

```
$("#step1").clone()
           .children()
           .remove()
           .end()
          .text();
```

The **clone** instruction makes a copy of the ul structure. It contains the whole structure with an inner list. The **children** get everything under step 1. This is the **ul** right under the step1 ID. The remove takes out all children. In our case, it removes only the **ul** under the step1 ID. The **end** method tells Jquery to select back the initial selector which is the cloned element and get its text. Since we have removed every child, the **text** method will return only the text of the element.

## How to create a JQuery plugin that accepts public function

Release Date: 18-Oct-13
Url: http://patrickdesjardins.com/blog/?post_type=post&p=2338

If you have a web project that uses JQuery framework and you have a lot of functions that have cohesive meaning in a single JavaScript file, maybe you should think about creating a plugin. The choice to create a JQuery plugin lets you act on an Html element by using JQuery. You extend JQuery. I will not write here how to create a plugin but how to add to your plugin some public functions. This is something important that may have turned you off of converting all your functions into a JQuery plugin. But in this article I will show you how to extend JQuery for a simple plugin and allow it to use plugin public function. Those public functions will be called commands.

```
(function ($) {
    //define the commands that can be used
    var commands = {
        publicMethod1Name: innerPluginMethod1,
        publicMethod2Name: innerPluginMethod2
```

```
    };

    $.fn.yourPlugin = function () {
        if (typeof arguments[0] === 'string') {
            var property = arguments[1];
            //Erase command name which is index 0.
            var args = Array.prototype.slice.call(arguments);
            args.splice(0, 1);
            //Execute command with the rest of argument (1...n)
            commands[arguments[0]].apply(this, args);
        }
        else {
            initialize.apply(this, arguments);
        }
        return this;
    };

    function initialize(options) {

    }

    function innerPluginMethod1(param1) {

    }

    function innerPluginMethod2() {

    }
})(jQuery);
```

The code above can be used this way:

```
$('#htmlElement').yourPlugin({ option1: value1, option2: value2 });
$('#htmlElement').yourPlugin("innerPluginMethod1", "parameter1");
```

As you can see, the plugin can be called in two different ways. The first line initializes the JQuery plugin and the second line calls a public function. The weak point is that you have to pass the name of the function (command) by a string. The strong point is that commands have access to all the plugin variables. They can access your option initialized by the first line in the example above or can set values which will be available to all other commands.

The code is pretty simple, as you can see. The first line verifies that we pass a string as the first parameter. This is the case when we call the command by string. Otherwise, we pass an object which is the options of the plugin or we pass nothing. If it is a string, we take the string and get the function. This is why we have a dictionary of command names to function. Before calling the function, we remove the first parameter because it's the name of the function; we do it by calling **slice**. The next call is **apply,** which takes the context of the "this" into the function. This gives the the command all references of the JQuery plugin. If the first parameter was not a string, it can be nothing or an object (for plugin option). We simply call the method initialized that let you set up the option and execute the main goal of your plugin. We also call **apply** to give all arguments.

# An Introduction Of How To Load Asynchronously JavaScript Files

Release Date: 10-Oct-14
Url: http://patrickdesjardins.com/blog/?post_type=post&p=3713

JavaScript files are loaded synchronously from the top to the bottom of the script tag in your HTML page. This has the advantage of handling references correctly. You can use, from a file that is loaded later, functions from a file that was loaded earlier. For example, if you set the script tag to load JQuery as the first script to load, every subsequent JavaScript file will be able to use JQuery. However, the problem is that you are losing performance because every file is in a queue to be downloaded. Several options exist, like bundling all JavaScript into a single file, or activating in your web server SPDY protocol. But, it still does not fix another problem, which is to divide the JavaScript file to work by module. This way, you could have reusable modules that could be loaded depending on the need instead of having a huge bundle. This technique is called AMD. AMD for Asynchronous Module Definition. It is a mechanism for defining modules and their dependencies, and can load asynchronously all of them.

Open source projects exist that do AMD for JavaScript. One of them is **amdjs** and a second one is **RequireJS.** Both work with the same principle of defining a module ID which associates one or multiple JavaScript files to a unique identifier.

In this article, I will concentrate on RequireJS, which is in my opinion very well documented and easier to understand. To get started, you need to remove from your project all your JavaScript references. You only need to have the RequireJS and to define its bootstrapper function. In the example below, you have your bootstrapper method called main.js that must be defined in the **data-main** attribute of a script tag that defines the source to **require.js.**

```
<script data-main="scripts/main.js" src="scripts/require.js"></script>
```

The example above could have been written without the .js for the main attribute. This is because **RequireJS** knows that we are handling a JavaScript file and will handle extensions by itself if the reference does not start with an http protocol (http or https) or does not start with a slash (/). Advanced configurations are possible for paths like defining a specific path alias for folders, or to define the base path. You can find more information directly on the RequireJS Api Web Page.

Once paths are defined you can now decide which JavaScript file to load for the page you want. The example below is from RequireJs. It loads JQuery, a JavaScript for canvas and something that uses a predefined subpath called *app* that uses a module named *sub*.

```
requirejs(['jquery', 'canvas', 'app/sub'],
function ($, canvas, sub) {
    // Every module are loaded here
});
```

Inside your JavaScript files, you can define dependencies. This is where all the modularity kicks in. This example also comes from RequireJS Api Web Page. It is the code that is set at the top of the shirt.js file which depends on the cart.js and inventory.js file. The define functions takes as its first parameter an array of modules that depends on the file. The second parameter is a function that takes the same amount of the dependent module. This allows us to have a reference to the dependent module. You can see that in the Dependency Injection pattern.

```
define(["./cart", "./inventory"], function (cart, inventory) {
    //return an object to define the "my/shirt" module.
    return {
        color: "blue",
        size: "large",
        addToCart: function () {
            inventory.decrement(this);
            cart.add(this);
        }
    }
}
);
```

Let's dive into a short demo. Create a simple Html file that calls the bootstrap of Require.js.

```
<!DOCTYPE html>
<html>
<head>
    <script data-main="scripts/main"
            src="scripts/require.js"></script>
</head>
<body>
</body>
</html>
```

This example implies that we set the require.js file, that you can download from the official website, to be installed into a scripts directory. In that directory we will set the main.js file and a folder that will contain another JavaScript file. This will let you demo JavaScript files in different folders.

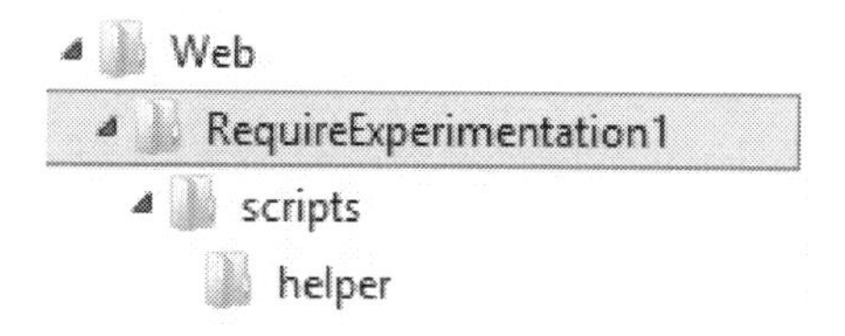


The main JavaScript will require the use of the other JavaScript in the other folder.

```
console.log("Main: Before Require");
require(["helper/util"], function (util) {
    console.log("Main: After Util loaded");
});
console.log("Main: After Require");
```

And the *util* will be a plain JavaScript that just shows the output in the console.

```
console.log("Util: Util file is loaded");
```

The end result is what we expect —the two logs of main.js are executed before the one in util.js. The last log is the one defined in the function inside the require which is triggered only when the util.js is finally loaded.

```
Main: Before Require
Main: After Require
Util: Util file is loaded
Main: After Util loaded
```

So far we have seen the possibility of the modularity but not the asynchronous feature. To show this in action, let's create some more JavaScript files and modify the main.js to load more than only a single file.

```
console.log("Main: Before Require");
require(["helper/util", "helper/util2", "helper/util3"], function (util) {
    console.log("Main: After all Util loaded");
});
console.log("Main: After Require");
```

The output is about the same but now we have three JavaScript files loaded in parallel.

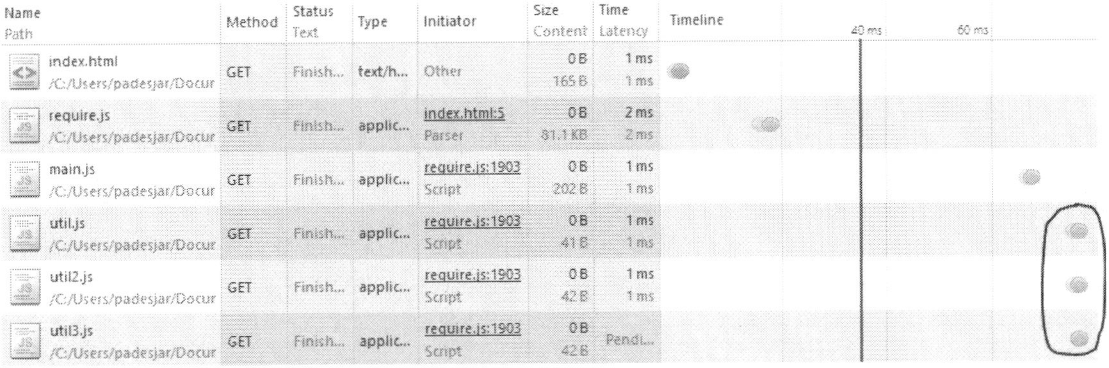

| Name<br>Path | Method | Status<br>Text | Type | Initiator | Size<br>Content | Time<br>Latency | Timeline (40 ms, 60 ms) |
|---|---|---|---|---|---|---|---|
| index.html<br>/C:/Users/padesjar/Docur | GET | Finish... | text/h... | Other | 0 B<br>165 B | 1 ms<br>1 ms | |
| require.js<br>/C:/Users/padesjar/Docur | GET | Finish... | applic... | index.html:5<br>Parser | 0 B<br>81.1 KB | 2 ms<br>2 ms | |
| main.js<br>/C:/Users/padesjar/Docur | GET | Finish... | applic... | require.js:1903<br>Script | 0 B<br>202 B | 1 ms<br>1 ms | |
| util.js<br>/C:/Users/padesjar/Docur | GET | Finish... | applic... | require.js:1903<br>Script | 0 B<br>41 B | 1 ms<br>1 ms | |
| util2.js<br>/C:/Users/padesjar/Docur | GET | Finish... | applic... | require.js:1903<br>Script | 0 B<br>42 B | 1 ms<br>1 ms | |
| util3.js<br>/C:/Users/padesjar/Docur | GET | Finish... | applic... | require.js:1903<br>Script | 0 B<br>42 B | Pendi... | |

Let's do a comparison of these JavaScript files loaded without Require.js to see how it would have looked.

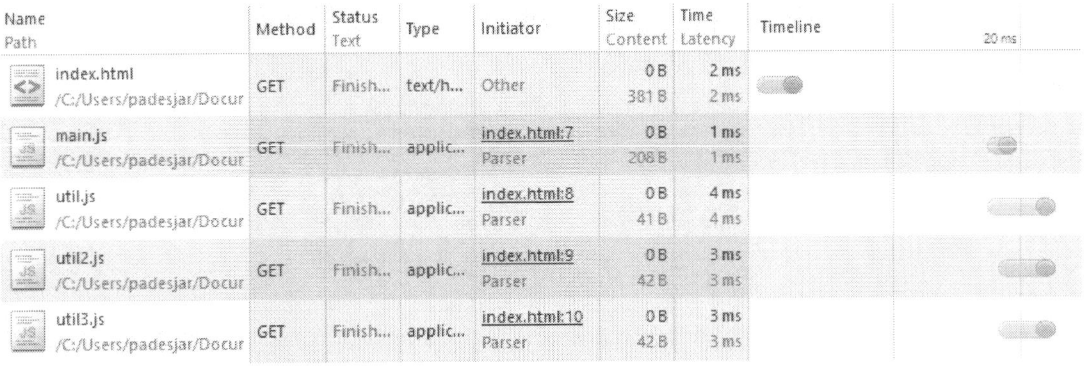

| Name<br>Path | Method | Status<br>Text | Type | Initiator | Size<br>Content | Time<br>Latency | Timeline (20 ms) |
|---|---|---|---|---|---|---|---|
| index.html<br>/C:/Users/padesjar/Docur | GET | Finish... | text/h... | Other | 0 B<br>381 B | 2 ms<br>2 ms | |
| main.js<br>/C:/Users/padesjar/Docur | GET | Finish... | applic... | index.html:7<br>Parser | 0 B<br>208 B | 1 ms<br>1 ms | |
| util.js<br>/C:/Users/padesjar/Docur | GET | Finish... | applic... | index.html:8<br>Parser | 0 B<br>41 B | 4 ms<br>4 ms | |
| util2.js<br>/C:/Users/padesjar/Docur | GET | Finish... | applic... | index.html:9<br>Parser | 0 B<br>42 B | 3 ms<br>3 ms | |
| util3.js<br>/C:/Users/padesjar/Docur | GET | Finish... | applic... | index.html:10<br>Parser | 0 B<br>42 B | 3 ms<br>3 ms | |

It is not really different because these files are small but they are not loaded at the same time. However, we see that using Require.js has a performance penalty for small JavaScript files. The time is almost double when using Require.js in this very small test. It is worth it to check it out with a bigger library. It is also important to keep in mind that it is not only about performance but about modules.

# How To Debug With Visual Studio And TypeScript

Release Date: 14-Oct-14
Url: http://patrickdesjardins.com/blog/?post_type=post&p=3742

If you have Visual Studio 2013 Service Pack 3 it is easy to debug TypeScript within Visual Studio, directly from TypeScript source code. First of all, go in the Solution Explorer and right click the solution you are executing. Second, go in the project property under the TypeScript Build tab. Check in the **Debugging Panel** > **Generate source maps**.

Output

TypeScript Build

- [x] Keep comments in JavaScript output
- [ ] Combine JavaScript output into file:
- [ ] Redirect JavaScript output to directory:
- [ ] Generate declaration files

Debugging

- [x] Generate source maps
- [ ] Specify root directory of source maps:
- [ ] Specify root directory of TypeScript files:

That'sit. You just need to set a breakpoint and you are in business.

## QUnit - A JavaScript Unit Test Framework

Release Date: 17-Oct-14
Url: http://patrickdesjardins.com/blog/?post_type=post&p=3734

QUnit is a unit testing framework developed by JQuery Team. It is available at http://qunitjs.com/ but can be found also if you go to the JQuery website and click the last button of the header toolbar. The framework has assertion methods that you are used to using with Java or C# but also a webpage that has all your tests' status displayed in a clean way. This is interesting to have the big picture of your test suites' health.

To start testing, you need to create an Html page that refers to the .css and the .js file of the QUnit Framework. The last required action that you must do before coding your test is to define in the HTML two placeholders. One must have the ID qunit and the other one qunit-fixture. The first one contains all your unit tests and unit test results. The second one is used to insert Html that your test can test against it.

```
<div id="qunit"></div><div id="qunit-fixture"></div>
```

Here is the result of a failing test.

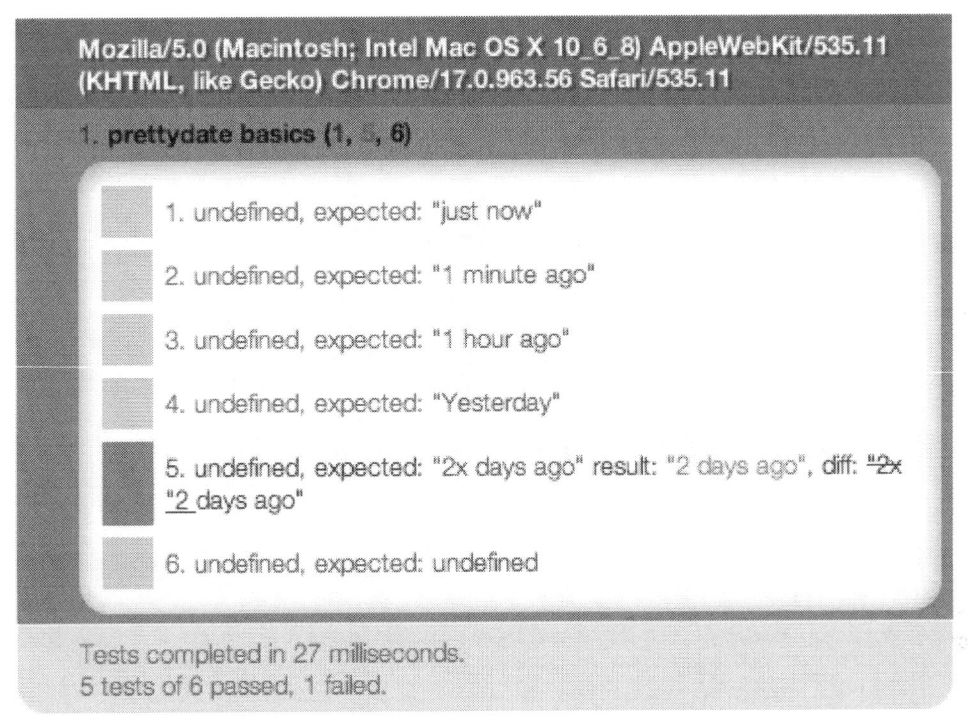


In a nutshell, Qunit provides a method to organize your test, to compare values, to test your assertion expectation, and to test exceptions.

To organize your test into categories, you must call the **module** method. At its simplest expression, only a name can be defined. Otherwise, you can specify some lifecycle methods, one method before each test of your category and one method after each test of your category.

```
QUnit.module('Category of test'); // Create a group of test
```

QUnit specifies each test within the method **test**. The first parameter is the name of your test, the second is a function that contains your test.

```
QUnit.test('This is test 1', function()
{
        //Test goes here
});
```

The function can use several methods of assertion and expectation. The first one is the **equal** method. This is the same as any equal method of any other unit testing framework. You do not have to provide a third parameter for the message, this is optional. It is also possible to use the notEqual method to compare something that should not be equal to a specific value. These methods use the double equal and if you need something more robust, like you would with the triple equal, then you must use the strictEqual.

```
QUnit.equal('x','x'); // Assert a value
QUnit.equal('x','y', 'X and Y are not equal and it must be'); // Assert a value
QUnit.notEqual('x','z', 'X and Z are equal and must not'); // Assert a value
QUnit.strictEqual( 1, 1, "1 and 1 have the same value and type");
QUnit.notStrictEqual( 1, "1", "1 and '1' are not the same");
```

As you see, we are using the QUnit on every assertion call. In fact, you can use a shorter version by using the parameter of the testing function.

```
QUnit.test('This is test 1', function(q){
        q.equal(...);
});
```

Another primitive assertion is to test against a boolean. This can be done with the **ok** method.

```
QUnit.ok(true, 'This is true');//If true it passes
```

If you know that something must throw an exception in a specific case, than you can call the expected method that throws inside the **throws** method. You can specify an expected error object to match the thrown exception also.

```
QUnit.throws(()=>{});// Test if something has been thrown with  throw "error"...
```

Another way to test is to see how many assertions have been called. This is useful in cases of looping and callback functions. The **expect** method must be used before any assertion inside the **test** method.

```
QUnit.expect(3); // Expect to have 3 asserts, good for call back method testing
```

QUnit is a small framework that allows you to test your JavaScript. It is compatible with TypeScript and you can find the definition file at GitHub.

# TypeScript Hashmap Equivalence in JavaScript

Release Date: 21-Oct-14
Url: http://patrickdesjardins.com/blog/?post_type=post&p=3748

TypeScript is transformed into JavaScript and sometimes you start some of your code in TypeScript and finish in JavaScript. This is a scenario that you can see when developing some code in TypeScript and at some point it is integrated into some existing JavaScript code.
TypeScript allows you to have a hash map in which you define the type for your key and for the value that it will hold. Let's take the example of a hash map that has a string key and a string value.

```
var arr = { [path:string]:string; }; //Hashmap that has for key a string and for
value a string
```

If you need to use this variable in JavaScript and be sure that it will continue to work when coming back into some JavaScript generated by TypeScript, you have to keep in mind that this is in fact a double array. If you want to define some values for this variable, you must define for each key a property that contains an array of values. For example, imagine two keys with two values each like the example below.

```
var arr = { 'k1': ['p1', 'p2'], 'k2': ['2p1', '2p2'] }
```

This is a working example that can be read back in TypeScript. It is also possible with JavaScript to get back all information by looping through all the keys and values even if the k1 and k2 of the previous example are properties.

```
for (var key in arr) {
    var allValues = arr[key];
    for (var keyValue in allValues) {
        console.log('Key ' + key + ' has value : ' + allValues[keyValue]);
    }
}
```

# How To Delay Some of your Web Resources

Release Date: 23-Oct-14
Url: http://patrickdesjardins.com/blog/?post_type=post&p=3754

If you are working with JavaScript and Asynchronous Module Definition (AMD) you know that you have the possibility to have a module that depends on others. At some point, you may want to test what would happen if one of your scripts takes a lot of time to load. For example, if you have a JavaScript module named "A" that depends on "B" and "C" and only when "A" is loaded can execute a task, you may want to test if the task required is really triggered when both dependencies are loaded.

To test that, you can use **Fiddler**. Fiddler lets you see all Http traffic but it can also let you play with responses. To do this, open the **AutoResponse** tab.

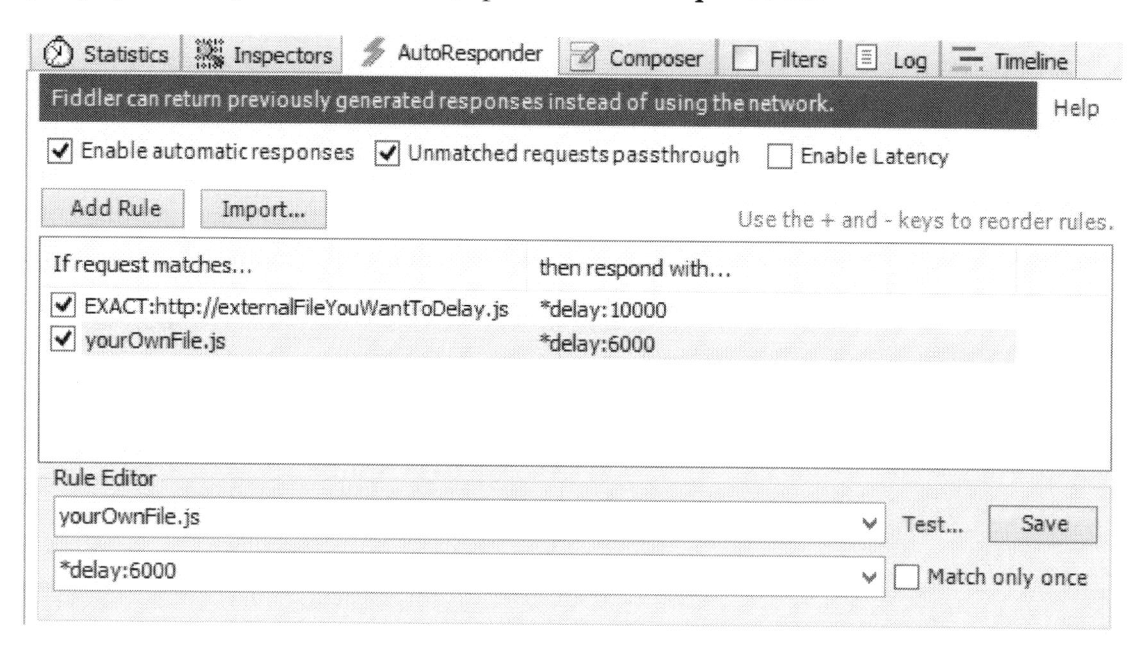


You need to set up for the URL you want a response action. You can use an exact math, a file name, or use any Regex you want. The example above shows you both. When the url comparison is true by one of your matches then the response is launched. For us, adding a delay is done by adding the following command ***delay:####**followed by the number of milliseconds to have the delay.

```
*delay:5000
```

During your test, the code that must be executed after both dependencies load will be delayed if you have set up a delay for one or many of the dependencies.

# JavaScript The Good Things to Know

Release Date: 31-Oct-14
Url: http://patrickdesjardins.com/blog/?post_type=post&p=3764

## Null and array

The type **null** or the type **array** are in fact of type object. You can verify this by using **typeof**.

```
console.log(typeof(null));
console.log(typeof([1,2,3]);
```

## Variables Name

Variables names can have an illegal character if used with quotation marks when defined. For example, you can use **numeric** and **alphanumeric character** with **underscore** but you cannot use directly a dash. The variable name this-is-illegal is not legal but if you define your object with the property name "this-is-illegal" it works.

```
var yourObject = {
    "this-is-illegal": "but it works because of the quote",
    this_is_legal: "and does not require quote"
};
```

Even if the illegal character can be bypassed by the first approach, using quotes, it is not recommended to write your code this way., retreving the value required to use the array notation instead of the dot notation.

```
var v1 = yourObject["this-is-illegal"];
//instead of
var v1 = yourObject.this_is_legal;
```

## arguments variable

Every function can access the **arguments** keyword. This variable is not an official JavaScript array (lack of Array method) but can access every element with the square bracket.

```
function add(a, b) {
    return a + b;
    // or
    return arguments[0] + arguments[1];
}
```

But this goes far beyond that. You can define your function to not have any arguments and use it with multiple arguments. The **arguments** variable will hold all arguments passed to the function and not only those officially specified.

```
function add() {
    var index;
    var sum = 0;
```

```
    for (index = 0; index < arguments.length; index += 1) {
        sum += arguments[index];
    }
    return sum;
}

var result = add(1, 2, 3, 4, 5); // 15
```

## Default Initialization

If you are not sure if a variable has already been initialized you can use the **||** **operator** to check and assign.

```
var variableWithValueForSure = anotherVariable.variable1 || "defaultValue";
```

What it does is checks if the first expression returns **undefined**. If it is undefined, then this returns **false**. Since it returns **false**, the next expression is evaluated, which sets the value. If it is not **undefined**, it returns, not **true,** but the value directly. This is why often in JavaScript we see the same variable doing this trick to itself to be sure that it is defined. The next example ensures that the variable *me* is defined and not undefined.

```
var me = me || {};
```

## Object and Dynamic Variables

It is possible to add variables at any time with JavaScript. You just need to set a value to have the variable defined inside your object. This is also true for functions.

```
var obj = {
    variable1: 1
};
obj.newVariable = 2; //newVariable is added to the object obj
```

## References is used, not copy

Every time you set an existing object to another variable it passes its reference. This is true for function parameters but also for variables inside a function.

```
var x1 = x2; //x1 and x2 are the same now
x2.v1 = 'value1';
//x1.v1 is also at 'value1'
```

## Prototype

Prototype is the concept in JavaScript that allows you to share information through different objects of the same type. When calling a function or variable on an object, if this does not find the function or variable it checks to see if it can find it in its prototype. If it does not find it, it goes to the prototype of the prototype and so on until it reaches object.prototype. If nothing is found, it returns **undefined**.

## hasOwnProperty

If you want to loop your object property (variables and functions) than you will stumble into prototype properties which you may not want to see. If you want to see only methods that you have defined for the object and not those from the prototype you must use the function **hasOwnProperty('propertyToCheck').**

```
var propertyName ;
for (propertyName in yourObject)
{
    if (yourObject.hasOwnProperty(propertyName]))
    {
        //Do what you want with the property that is inside YourObject
        //and not inside the its prototype
    }
}
```

We used the "for in" statement to loop through all properties. This gives us properties in a nonspecific order. If you want to have properties in the order defined in the code, you must use a for with an integer that loops every property in an array.

## Delete keyword

Using delete can remove a property. For example, if you define a property named *prop1* and you execute delete on it, this will return undefined except if the prototype has a *prop1* method, because of the nature of the prototype.

## Adding Method to Prototype

You can add methods to an object with the prototype. You just need to use the prototype keyword after the type you want to enhance. The example below adds a trim method to any string.

```
String.prototype['trim'] = function ()
{
    return this.replace(/^\s+|\s+$/g, '');
};
```

This code adds the trim method to all String types.

## Variables Declaration

In JavaScript it is better to define variables in the beginning of the function instead of the best practice that suggests to declare the variable nearest its use. The reason is that JavaScript scope works differently than other languages. JavaScript variables defined in a scope can access other variables outside its scope.

```
var Program = function () {
    var var1 = 1;
    var Program2 = function () {
        var1 = var1 + 1; // This can access var1 function which is not the case in
other scoped language.
    }
    Program2(); // Call f2 function
    //The value of var 1 is 2;
}
```

For example, this does not work in C#:

```
class Program
{
    private int a;

    private class Program2
    {
        public Program2()
        {
            a = a + 1; // Do not compile
        }
    }
}
```

## Apply Keyword

You can call any function by following this function with the method **apply**. This takes two parameters. The first one is the value you want to set to **this** for the method you call. The value can be set to null if you do not want to pass a value to the **this** of the function. The second parameter is an array. This array is converted into the function parameter.

```
function add(a, b) {
    return a + b;
}

//Can be called this way:
var result1 = add(1, 2); //3
//or
var result2 = add.apply(null, [1, 2]); //3
```

## Exceptions

You can throw exceptions and catch them. The exception throws an object you want. You can use anything.

```
throw { name: 'Error Name', message: 'message you want' };
```

A thrown statement is read by catch block. If you want to catch multiple exceptions, then you must do an if statement on a property you want, for example the name.

```
try {
    throw { name: 'StackOverFlow', message: 'message you want' };
}
catch (e) {
    if (e.name === 'StackOverFlow') {
        console.log('***' + e.name + ': ' + e.message + '***');
    }
    console.log(e.name + ': ' + e.message);
}
```

## Chaining Calls

It is always good to return the this keyword if your method returns nothing. This allows you to do chaining calls.

```
var Human = function () {
    this.name = 'Not Defined';
    this.gender = 'm';
};

Human.prototype.setName = function (name) {
    this.name = name;
    return this;
};

Human.prototype.setGender = function (gender) {
    this.gender = gender;
    return this;
};
```

This allows us to chain because every function returns the **this** reference.

```
var patrick = new Humain()
                .setName('patrick')
                .setGender('male');
```

## JavaScript Encapsulation with Closure

JavaScript provides **encapsulation** with something named **closure**. Since everything in JavaScript uses functions, this one does, too. The principle of closure is to encapsulate every variable and method into a cohesive function. This allows us to scope what is private to the object from what is public. It is very similar to object oriented class. Private methods and variables are not returned by the closure while public methods and variables are. Let's start with an example to demystify the concept of closure.

```
var referenceToTheObject = (function ()
{
    var privateVariable = 0;
    return
    {
        publicMethod1: function () {       }
        ,publicMethod2: function () {       }
    };
}()
);
```

This is interesting because, in fact, we are invoking an anonymous function (see the line before the last one). This function returns an object with two public functions. As you must know now, these functions can call any methods and variables in their outer scope. This means that both public methods can call each other but also the private variable. The private variable is not reachable outside the anonymous function because it is not returned by the anonymous function.

# 10. NO SQL, SQL, UNITY

This chapter groups every post written during 2013 and 2014 about No Sql, Sql, Unity. Like all chapters in this book, every article is a snapshot of a real scenario that has a high probability of happening if you are using these technologies. You will notice that every article that has been chosen to be included in this book contains the release date to identify when it was written. A permanent link is also provided that allows you to go in and read updates and comments. Feel free to go on the website to add your own comment if you wish.

## Installing MongoDB on a Windows Machine

Release Date: 20-Nov-14
Url: http://patrickdesjardins.com/blog/?post_type=post&p=3818

The first step is to install **MongoDB** on your machine. You can go on the official website, and in the top menu you will see Download. Click the Download link (http://www.mongodb.org/downloads) and then select the Windows version. You can download the 64 bit or 32 bit. In this tutorial of MongoDB we will use the **MongoDB 64 bit for Windows**. The file is about 132 megs and is a setup.

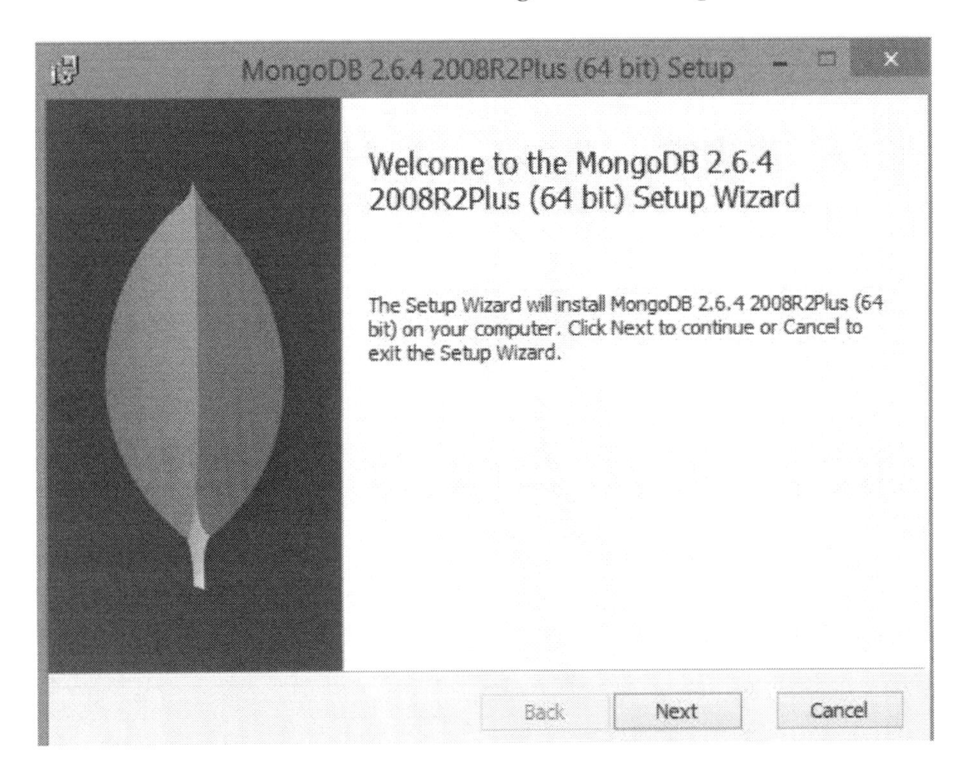

The installation is pretty straightforward. You can select the typical installation to have a basic setup. During the installation, you will have to accept elevating the permission.

From here, it is time to open a Command Prompt with administration rights. Let's go in the folder we just installed, MongoDB. Since we have installed the typical package with the 64 bit version, the installation should be in **program files**.

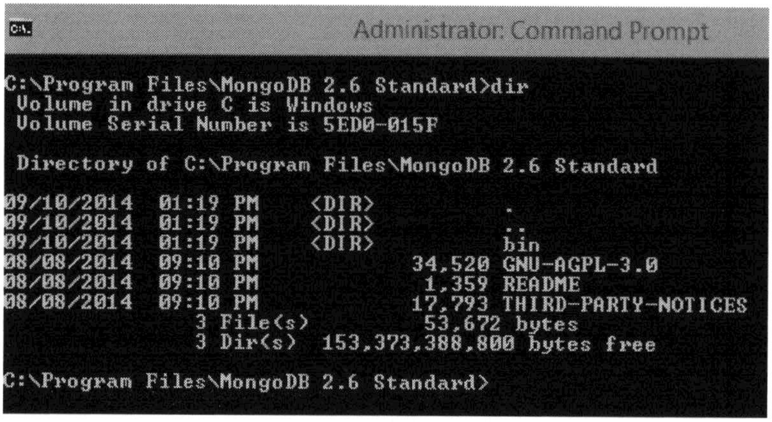

```
Administrator: Command Prompt

C:\Program Files\MongoDB 2.6 Standard>dir
 Volume in drive C is Windows
 Volume Serial Number is 5ED0-015F

 Directory of C:\Program Files\MongoDB 2.6 Standard

09/10/2014  01:19 PM    <DIR>          .
09/10/2014  01:19 PM    <DIR>          ..
09/10/2014  01:19 PM    <DIR>          bin
08/08/2014  09:10 PM            34,520 GNU-AGPL-3.0
08/08/2014  09:10 PM             1,359 README
08/08/2014  09:10 PM            17,793 THIRD-PARTY-NOTICES
               3 File(s)         53,672 bytes
               3 Dir(s)  153,373,388,800 bytes free

C:\Program Files\MongoDB 2.6 Standard>
```

You can after that configure MongoDB. The next steps are taken directly from MongoDB documentation. You must create a directory to save the content. This can be anywhere so let's do a data folder at the root of the installation path. The md command lets you create a directory. The code below is what you can write to create the default path that MongoDB uses.

```
cd "C:\Program Files\MongoDB 2.6 Standard"
md \data\db
```

Then, you can start MongoDB.

```
cd bin
mongo.exe
```

The first time I started MongoDB I got a warning followed by an error saying that it was not possible to connect.

*C:\Program Files\MongoDB 2.6 Standard\bin>mongo.exe MongoDB shell version: 2.6.4 connecting to: test 2014-09-10T13:34:40.878-0700 warning: Failed to connect to 127.0.0.1:27017, reason: errno:10061 No connection could be made because the target machine actively* *refused it. 2014-09-10T13:34:40.882-0700 Error: couldn't connect to server 127.0.0.1:27017 (127.0.0.1), connection attempt failed at src/mongo/shell/mongo.js:146 exception: connect failed*

Than I realized that I was launching **mongo.exe** instead of **mongod.exe**. Once the administration console launches the mongod.exe you can start a new console (no need to have administration privileges on this one) and start mongo.exe. Here is what you should see.

```
Administrator: Command Prompt

C:\Program Files\MongoDB 2.6 Standard>dir
 Volume in drive C is Windows
 Volume Serial Number is 5ED0-015F

 Directory of C:\Program Files\MongoDB 2.6 Standard

09/10/2014  01:19 PM    <DIR>          .
09/10/2014  01:19 PM    <DIR>          ..
09/10/2014  01:19 PM    <DIR>          bin
08/08/2014  09:10 PM            34,520 GNU-AGPL-3.0
08/08/2014  09:10 PM             1,359 README
08/08/2014  09:10 PM            17,793 THIRD-PARTY-NOTICES
               3 File(s)         53,672 bytes
               3 Dir(s)  153,373,388,800 bytes free

C:\Program Files\MongoDB 2.6 Standard>
```

Do not forget to specify the **–dbpath** when starting the **mongod.exe** because otherwise it will store everything on your **c:** drive.

## Basic Commands

Here are a few commands that may be useful during the development. **dbs shows** the database you have

```
show dbs
```

You can create a new database or switch the database by using the **use** command.

```
use mydb
```

Information is added into the collection. You can add data into a collection with the command **db.insert()**. Here is an example of three insertions into a collection named *testdata* of the dotnet database.

```
use dotnet
db.testdata.insert({id:1})
db.testdata.insert({id:2})
db.testdata.insert({id:3,name:"three"})
```

It is possible to see if the collection of the active database really exists with **show collections** command.

```
show collections
```

The last command that is really useful is to see the content of a collection. You can use the **find()** command.

```
db.testdata.find()
```

Keep in mind that if you see nothing it might be because you typed the collection name with the wrong case sensitivity. MongoDB is case sensitive. Here is a screenshot of the output of all commands that we just discussed.

```
Command Prompt - mongo
2014-09-10T13:53:41.327-0700 ReferenceError: dbs is not defined
> show dbs
admin  (empty)
local  0.078GB
> use dotnet
switched to db dotnet
> db
dotnet
> show dbs
admin  (empty)
local  0.078GB
> db
dotnet
> db.testData.insert({id:1})
WriteResult({ "nInserted" : 1 })
> db.testData.insert({id:2})
WriteResult({ "nInserted" : 1 })
> db.testData.insert({id:3, name="three"})
2014-09-10T14:00:39.703-0700 SyntaxError: Unexpected token =
> db.testData.insert({id:3, name:"three"})
WriteResult({ "nInserted" : 1 })
> db
dotnet
> dotnet
2014-09-10T14:00:53.039-0700 ReferenceError: dotnet is not defined
> show collections
system.indexes
testData
> db.testdata.find()
> db.testData.find()
{ "_id" : ObjectId("5410bbebd3215d068ab42678"), "id" : 1 }
{ "_id" : ObjectId("5410bbefd3215d068ab42679"), "id" : 2 }
{ "_id" : ObjectId("5410bbfbd3215d068ab4267a"), "id" : 3, "name" : "three" }
```

# MongoDB —— Good to Know

Release Date: 27-Nov-14

Url: http://patrickdesjardins.com/blog/?post_type=post&p=3833

Recently I have been working with MongoDB. Here are some highlights that might help you to make the decision to use that No-SQL database.

In MongoDB, write operations are atomic at the **document level**. If you design your data to use reference (which is possible) forget about atomic transactions. Also, if you design by referencing other documents, it will not be possible to get the information with a single query.

It is possible to query MongoDB with operators such as comparing with $gt, $gte, $lt, $lte, $in, $nin, $ne. Logical operationx exist with $or, $and, $not, $not. Other types of operator exist and can be used for querying the database or to project. Here are some examples.

```
db.users.insert({name:"patrick", age:30})
db.users.insert({name:"mélodie", age:26})
db.users.insert({name:"vincent", age:30})
db.users.insert({name:"julie", age:28})
db.users.find({age:{$lt:30}}) // Return 2 elements
```

When your document gets over **16 megs**, Mongo divides it into parts. GridFS is then required to reassemble every part of the document. In MongoDB you can allow the system to generate the unique identifier by not setting any _id. But, you can also take the liberty to assign the _id when inserting your document. It is better to store a one to many reference into the "one side". This way, you do not have a huge array in the "many side." You can also reference something that does not exist yet. For example, if A references B, you can insert A with a reference to B and then insert B.

It is possible to set an index, like in SQL, to improve performance. This can be done with the **ensureIndex** method. This method is available on the database.

```
db.users.ensureIndex({name:1})
```

It is possible to store in a string information such as a hiearchical path and then query against that string property with a regex to find. It is possible to write with the MongoDb command **insert**, **update**, **findAndModify** and **remove**.

The update command can be executed against a collection. This has three parameters. The first one is the query. You can specify the unique identifier of the data you want to update or to any other criteria. This can be useful for an embedded resource to query multiple documents that have the same embedded information. The second parameter is what we are updating. We can update the whole document or a part of it. It is also possible to push ($push) information into an existing array or to increment/decrement the value of a field. The following example comes from the MongoDB website and it updates a book by its ID only if the book is available on the shelf. It updates by decreasing the number of available copies and pushes a new entry about who checked out the book. This is all done atomically.

```
db.books.update(
   { _id: 123, available: { $gt: 0 } },
   {
       $inc: { available: -1 },
       $push: { checkout: { by: "abc", date: new Date() } }
   }
)
```

Doing operations like **update**, **insert**, and **delete** returns some information into a **WriteResult** object. Some properties, like the number of found elements by the query, or the number of inserted or modified documents, are returned. The number of inserted can be above 0 when updating if in the third parameter of the update you specify the option of inserting if not found.

When defining an index on an array, MongoDB creates index entries for each element. This means that if you have a document with an index on an array of three elements in the backend the information will be set in three index collections. For example, if you have a car document with an array of colors and you set an index on the color array, the document will be indexed three times and also stored one time as the car itself. This has an impact in the inserting time (like in SQL).

If you are working with money and want to be exact, you need to multiply your number to have an integer. For example, storing 9.99 with a precision of 2 decimals would require you to store 999 in MongoDB. But then you have to divide by 100 to get back the real value. Depending on the precision you want, you multiply and divide by the power of 10 desired.

The primary key is defined with MongoDB ObjectId. This ObjectId is generated by using the Unix TimeStamp, the machine identifier, the process ID and a random value. The result looks like a GUID. You can generate one by calling **ObjectId().**

```
> ObjectId()
ObjectId("5411c0ceb4c966ae79a65372")
> ObjectId()
ObjectId("5411c0d9b4c966ae79a65373")
> ObjectId()
ObjectId("5411c0d9b4c966ae79a65374")
> ObjectId()
ObjectId("5411c0dab4c966ae79a65375")
```

# The difference between SQL Delete statement and SQL Truncate statement

Release Date: 04-Jul-13
Url: http://patrickdesjardins.com/blog/?post_type=post&p=2136

Sometimes, tasks that we do often seem easy but when we stop to go deeper we realize that we do actions by reflex and that we have forgotten the meaning of the detail underneath the action.

One action that we have to do quite often is to remove data from tables. This can be done with the keyword delete or truncate. Here are two examples.

```
--Delete
DELETE FROM Table123
```

```
--Truncate
TRUNCATE TABLE Table123
```

But behind those two statements, what's really happening? First of all, the delete statement is row oriented. This means that it deletes one row after another. This means that it has to lock the row, delete it, log it, etc, then unlock it. This whole process consumes resources and time.

On the other side, truncate statement does not log anything, it does not go row by row. All these advantages come with the disadvantage of not being able to delete specific rows or be able to restore what you have deleted.

```
--This will work
DELETE FROM Table123 WHERE startDate <= 2013-06-14

--This won't work
TRUNCATE TABLE Table123 WHERE startDate <= 2013-06-14 -- Error!
```

Truncate also does not have any trigger. **OnDelete** or **OnUpdate** does not trigger, which could have caused undesired behavior. However, another advantage that truncate does have is that it will reset the seed for identity.

To conclude, using delete is the way to go if you are inside an application and you need to remove an entity of your model. The business defined behind the trigger will be executed while you will be able to specify which entry to delete. On the other side, truncate is a must to use if you need to reset a table or move several rows to a temporary table, truncate and reinsert rows.

# Truncate a table without removing all constraints

Release Date: 01-May-14
Url: http://patrickdesjardins.com/blog/?post_type=post&p=3460

**Truncating** a table has the advantage of removing all data without logging or locking every row. This is a huge advantage over the **Delete** statement. This means that a truncated table cannot be restored, neither can you have a where clause in the SQL statement. Truncate also has the ability to reset the seed to its initial value. **On delete** triggers are also not fired and all foreign keys constraints must be removed or disabled. Instead of removing all constraints, it is possible to tell SQL Server to not check any foreign key.

```
SET FOREIGN_KEY_CHECKS = 0;
TRUNCATE TABLE [Schema].[Table];
SET FOREIGN_KEY_CHECKS = 1;
```

This will result in removing data from the table in the fastest way possible. If you want more details you can check the article I previously wrote about Truncate vs Delete.

## Working with BigInteger with C# .Net and SQL Server

Release Date: 29-Jul-14
Url: http://patrickdesjardins.com/blog/?post_type=post&p=3597

If you must pass to a Store Procedure or just for a simple query a variable of type **BigInt** beware, you could be surprised by the result. **BigInt** in SqlServer has nothing to do with the **BigInteger** class of .Net. **BigInt** in SQL existed a long time before **BigInteger** from .Net (4.0). If you are using **BigInteger** you will get a **System.InvalidCastException**.

*An exception of type 'System.InvalidCastException' occurred in System.Data.dll but was not handled in user code*

*Additional information: Failed to convert parameter value from a BigInteger to a Int64.*

To pass a value to SQL Server of type **BigInt**, you must use a **long** in .Net.
For example, here is how to pass a **long** to SqlServer using SqlParameter.

```
long myBigNumber = 1;
var myParameter = new SqlParameter("@myParameterName", myBigNumber)
                        { SqlDbType = SqlDbType.BigInt };
```

You have to use a long for the value, but you specify the type to be of **SqlDbType.BigInt**. As you can see, we do not need to specify the **DbType** but only the **SqlDbType**. We are using a long because a **long** and **Int64** are the same type.

## Unity Lifetime management

Release Date: 07-Jan-13
Url: http://patrickdesjardins.com/blog/?post_type=post&p=1598

When you use Unity to get an instance of a class, Unity passes through the lifetime manager. The lifetime manager's responsibility is to indicate to unity how to instance the class into an object. This may already have an instanced object for the class requested and thus give the existing one instead of creating a new instance.

## TransientLifetimeManager

**TransientLifetimeManager** is the default lifetime manager used by Unity if none is specified. This is the simplest form of lifetime manager. It creates a new instance every time unity needs an instance of the class.

```
var container = new UnityContainer();
container
    .RegisterType(typeof(IMyClass), typeof(MyClass), "namedMyClass")
    .RegisterType(typeof(IMyClass), typeof(MyClass), "named2MyClass",
                                             new TransientLifetimeManager());
```

In the above example, you can see two registrations with unity of IMyClass interface with the concrete implementation of MyClass. Both of them are using the **TransientLifetimeManager**. The first one is implicit because it uses the default lifetime manager, while the second is explicit by having a third parameter which specifies to use **TransientLifetimeManager** lifetime manager.

## Singleton

The singleton is a pattern (or anti-pattern) that specifies that only one instance will live in memory. With Unity, the singleton lifetime manager is called **ContainerControlledLifetimeManager**. The **ContainerControlledLifetimeManager** will instance on the first call the class into an object and all subsequent calls will simply give a pointer (reference) to the same object.

```
var container = new UnityContainer();
container
    .RegisterType(typeof(IMyClass), typeof(MyClass), "SingletonMyClass"
                                    , new ContainerControlledLifetimeManager());
```

Of course, it is only possible to use the explicit registration for singleton since the implicit would create a **TransientLifetimeManager**. A small note before we pass to the next lifetime manager. If you are using a web application, be aware that the object will be shared among all your users.

## Others lifetime managers

Unity does have multiple other lifetime managers like **PerThreadLifetimeManager** or **PerResolveLifetimeManager**. Neither of them will be discussed here. The first one can be useful with a system where you are using parallel operations and the second one in some custom cases where the lifetime manager needs to be recreated every time.

In a web application, the default lifetime manager, **TransientLifetimeManager**, is the one to use. It will create an instance per web request. Of course, **ContainerControlledLifetimeManager** is also used in the case of instancing the data access layer, the caching system, the logging system, etc. Those are used across the system without containing *user* objects.

## Registering with Microsoft Unity an interface to a concrete class with multiple constructors

Release Date: 13-Mar-14
Url: http://patrickdesjardins.com/blog/?post_type=post&p=2712

If you are using inversion of control, you may come across the scenario where you want to register your interface to a concrete class that has **multiple constructors**. Registering with Microsoft Unity an interface to a concrete class with multiple constructors is something that requires specifying to Unity which of the constructors to use.

```
container.RegisterType<IMainDbContext, MainDbContext>();
```

The code above can work if *MainDbContext* has only one constructor. Even if this requires several parameters, it does not matter. Unity will try to solve every parameter. However, in the case that *MainDbContext* has several constructors, Unity does not know which one to evaluate. Well, that is not totally true. In fact, Microsoft Unity tries the one with the most parameters. This can be problematic if you have more than one constructor with the same number of parameters.

To select which constructors, you have to use the **InjectionConstructor** class. This class allows you to specify parameter type. You can use the ResolvedParameter that is generic. You can specify for every parameter the type you want.

```
container
        .RegisterType<IMainDbContext, MainDbContext>(
        new InjectionConstructor(
            new ResolvedParameter<IRunningContext>()
        )
        );
```

As you can see, this indicates to Microsoft Unity to resolve the *IRunningContext* from its container and inject the object into the single parameter constructor of MainDbContext. In that case, we take the single constructor of *MainDbContext* that has its parameter of *IRunningContext*.

# 11. VISUAL STUDIO

This chapter groups every post written during 2013 and 2014 about Visual Studio. Like all chapters in this book, every article is a snapshot of a real scenario that has a high probability of happening if you are using these technologies. You will notice that every article that has been chosen to be included in this book contains the release date to identify when it was written. A permanent link is also provided that allows you to go in and read updates and comments. Feel free to go on the website to add your own comment if you wish.

## Visual Studio 2012 Automatic Checkout Not Working with TFS

Release Date: 14-Aug-13
Url: http://patrickdesjardins.com/blog/?post_type=post&p=2206

This is annoying and can come from a lot of places. How come sometimes you cannot automatically check out a file when editing inside Visual Studio? First of all, the most obvious thing to do is to be sure that Visual Studio has the option to automatically check out a file when it is edited. This can be verified by going to Tools>Options>Source Control>Environment, and be sure that Visual Studio does have in the Editing setting the option **Check out automatically** selected.

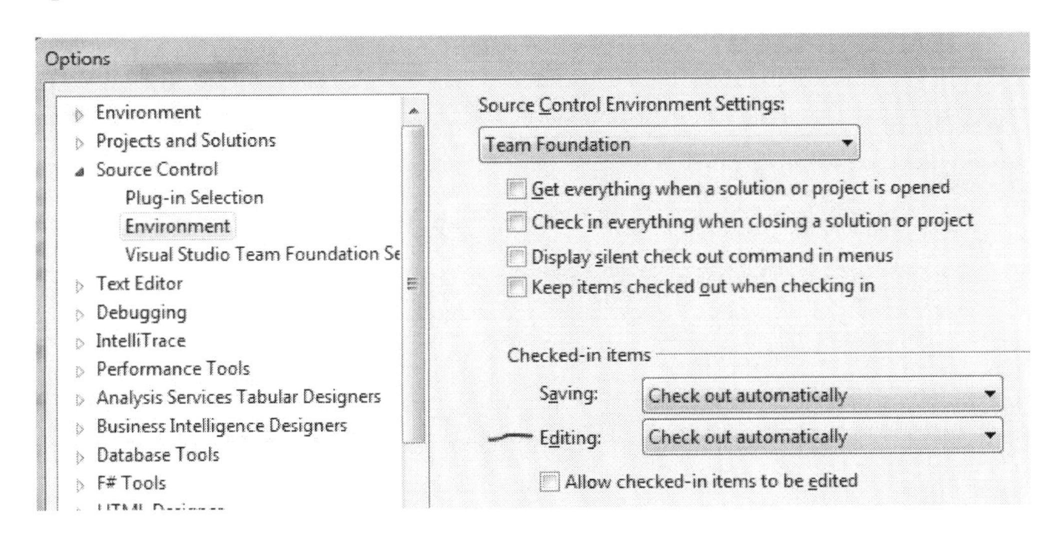


Second, your Windows account is linked with TFS and your password might be expired or changed since the last time it was verified by Visual Studio. To be sure, just select Team>Connect to Team Foundation Server.

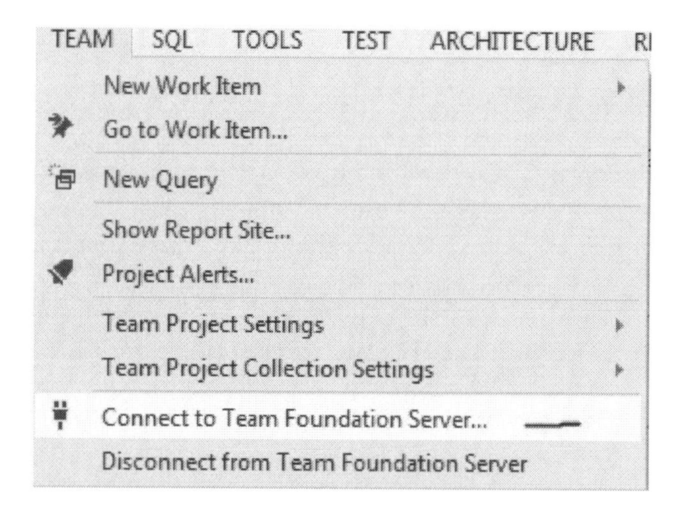


This will open a panel and you'll be able to click "Connect." The problem is that it might do nothing if you are already connected.

The last step is to verify that the solution might be offline. This is often the case if you are branching with TFS. If you open the solution in your new branch, the solution may not be "online." To be sure to be "online," you need to go to File>Source Control>Go Online. From here, if you were not connected, you will see in the output window some movement of activities.

## How to unit test a method that is not from an interface orvirtual with Visual Studio 2012

Release Date: 03-Sep-13
Url: http://patrickdesjardins.com/blog/?post_type=post&p=2277

Microsoft has the ability to fake methods but has the disadvantage that it needs to be from an interface or be virtual. This is the case of most testing frameworks. Nevertheless, Microsoft has the principle of shim which allows you to replace the method behavior with yours for the time of a test. You can get additional information on MSDN. This blog article explains briefly how to use shim. For the purpose of this article, let's say that we have a library with a single class which contains a single method, *MyClass,* with the method *MyMethod.* We will call that method from another method that we want to test. So, we want to mock the *MyMethod* from the *ToTest* method.

```
namespace ShimpProjectClassesToShim
{
    public class MyClass
```

```
    {
        public string MyMethod(string variable)
        {
            return "From MyClass = " + variable;
        }
    }
    public class MyClass2
    {
        public string ToTest()
        {
            var m = new MyClass();
            return m.MyMethod("InsideMyClass2");
        }
    }
}
```

This *MyMethod* method is not virtual, which removes the possibility of using a conventional mocking framework. It does not come from an interface, either, so we cannot mock or stub. However, we can shim. To continue with our example, we need a second project, the one for the test. This one will have a reference to the library previously created. Once done, right click the reference and click **Add Fake Assembly**.

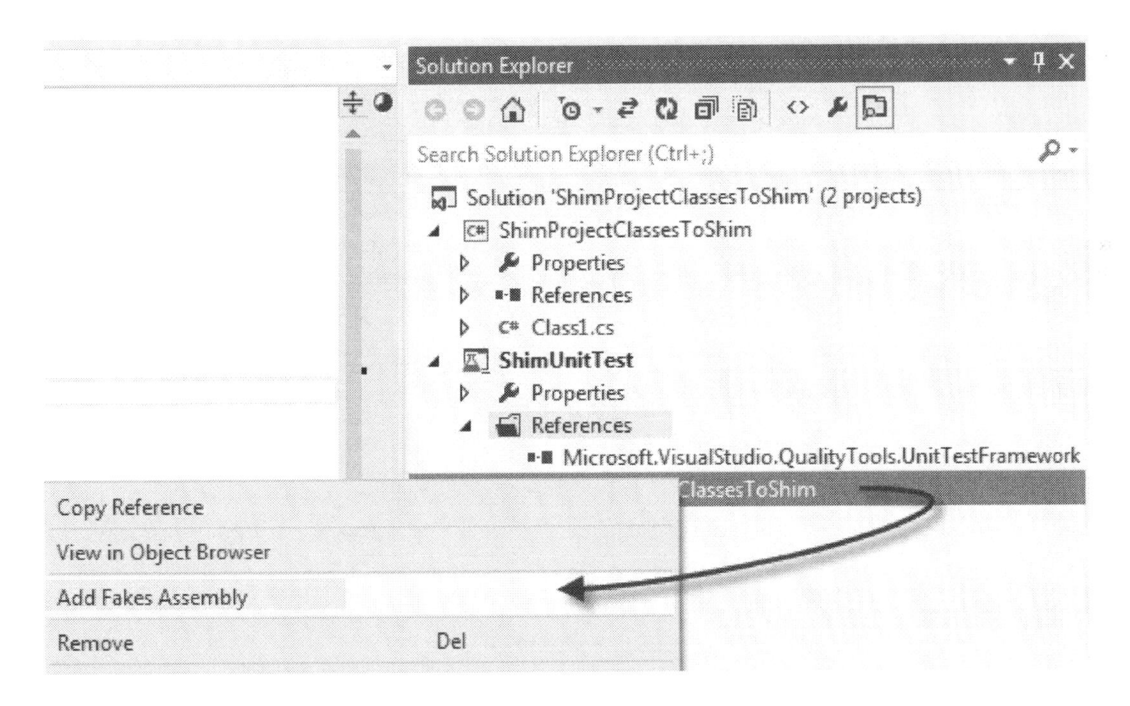


Do not worry, you have already added the reference from the unit project to the library project. Maybe a better naming of the action should have been **Transform to Fake**

**Assembly**. When done, you will see a Fakes folder created with the fake reference. Indeed, this requires having the project with the class already compiled.

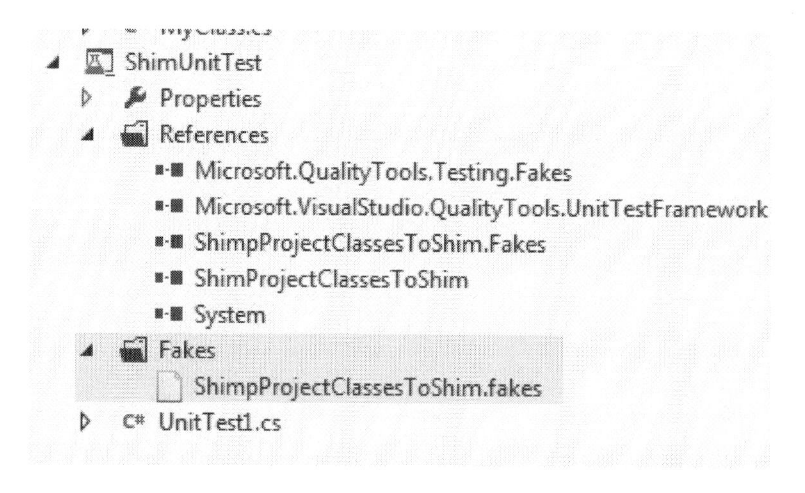


If you are curious about what this file contains, here is one for the example we are setting up.

```
<Fakes xmlns="http://schemas.microsoft.com/fakes/2011/">
  <Assembly Name="ShimpProjectClassesToShim"/>
</Fakes>
```

So the test will consist of shimming *MyClass* that is used by *MyClass2*. This is a common scenario where you want to test a method that uses another class that you do not want to test. In our case, we want to test *MyClass2* and not *MyClass*, so we shim *MyClass* to have a known return value. The test must be inside the scope of a **ShimContext** to be able to set the shim to the fake return values.

```
[TestClass]
public class UnitTest1
{
    [TestMethod]
    public void TestMethod1()
    {
        //Shim
        using (ShimsContext.Create())
        {
            //Arrange
            ShimMyClass.AllInstances.MyMethodString =
                                            (theClass, s) => "FAKE " + s;
            var classToUnitTest = new MyClass2();

            //Act
```

```
            string result = classToUnitTest.ToTest();

            //Assert
            Assert.AreEqual("FAKE InsideMyClass2", result);
        }
    }
}
```

The **arrange** section sets for all instances of the method the desired return value. As you can see, we use *ShimMyClass* class to set all instances. In your case, if your class is called *XYZ*, you will have to use *ShimXYZ*. This convention is by design. The class has been created for you with the prefix **Shim**. From there, you will be able to set the return value for all methods. The rest of the unit test is as usual. The only difference is when the method shim is called, the shim code is executed.

## Visual Studio 2013 Peak Definition

Release Date: 16-Sep-13
Url: http://patrickdesjardins.com/blog/?post_type=post&p=2301

Visual Studio 2013 brings many new improvements and one of these is the peak definition feature. This feature is available by the default shortcut **alt+F12** when the cursor of your mouse is on a method.

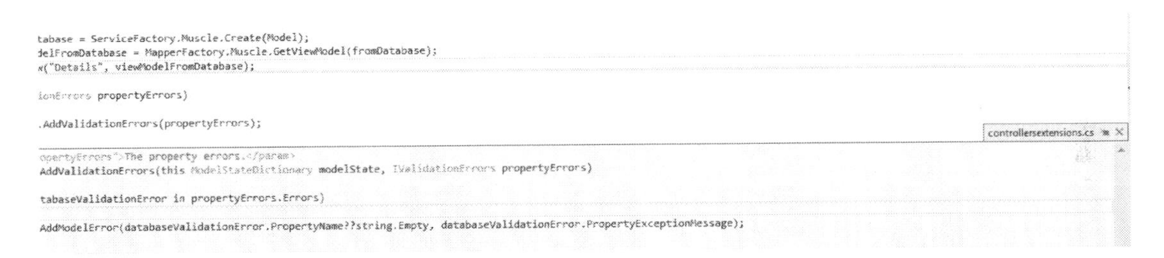


The goal of the **peak definition** is to display the content of the method inside the file, where the method is called. A picture is worth a thousand words, so here is an example. I have clicked the *AddValidationErrors* and I have pressed **alt+F12**. What happens is that a block with the title "controllersextension.cs" appears. It displays the code that would have been called. You can close this window any time by clicking the "X" or by pressing escape.

The goal of this feature is to limit the number of files open for just watching what's happening. It's very fast, and allows you to have a peek at what's happening. The only limit this new tool has is that it doesn't work well when the method is from an interface. In that case, you see the interface definition.

```
[HttpGet]
[Authorize(Roles = Roles.ADMINISTRATOR)]
public ActionResult Edit(int id)
{
    var x = ServiceFactory.Muscle.Get(new Muscle{Id=id});
```

```
    TModel New();
    TModel Get(TModel model);
    TModel Create(TModel model);
    int Update(TModel model);
    int Update(TModel model, params Expression<Func<TModel, object>>[] properties);
    int Delete(TModel model);
}
```

# Visual Studio 2013 Scrollbar Customization With Bar Mode and Map Mode

Release Date: 20-Sep-13
Url: http://patrickdesjardins.com/blog/?post_type=post&p=2305

Visual Studio 2013 lets you have two types of scroll bar. The first one is the same as in Visual Studio 2012, which contains additional information like where errors are located marked with a red rectangle, and allows you to mark every keyword searched with a yellow mark. It also contains a dark brown color for breakpoint and a blue line for the current line. The last thing it can display is what has changed.

Now, you can switch to have a visual representation of the code. This new scroll bar visualization is called the map mode. To activate the map mode, right click on any scroll bar and select the options entry in the context menu.

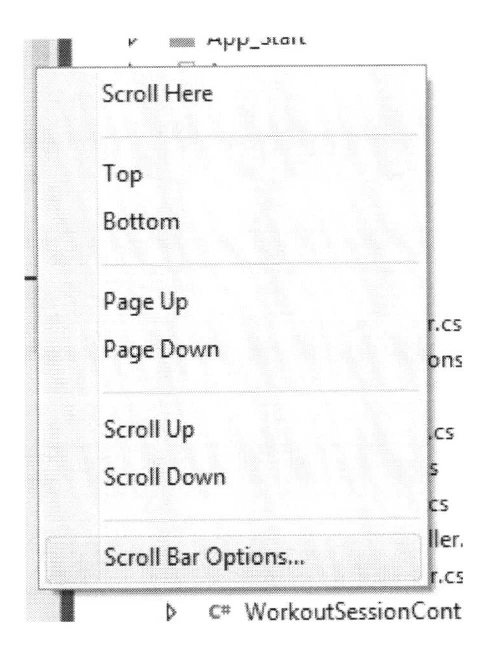


This will bring the options menu for the scroll bar. At the right of the dialog window, a behavior frame contains the two available options.

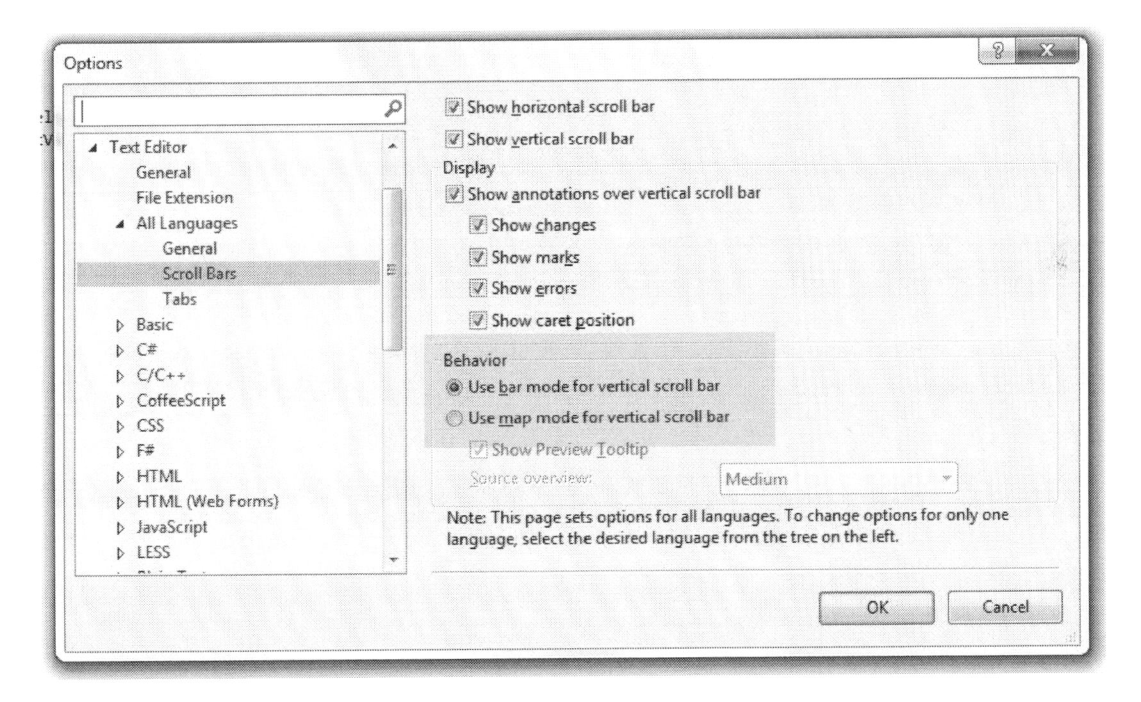


Not only can you see the code but you can also, if you put your mouse over the scroll bar, see what the code is.

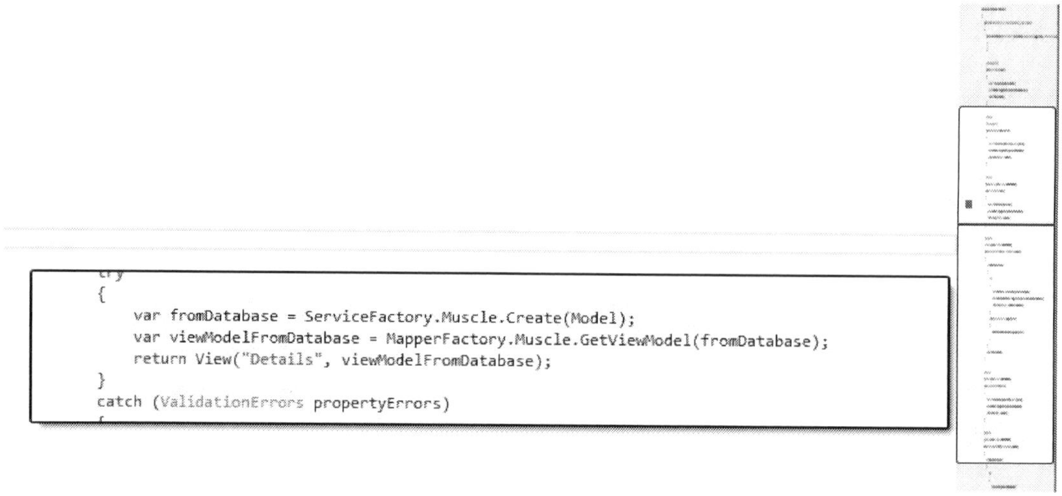

```
{
    var fromDatabase = ServiceFactory.Muscle.Create(Model);
    var viewModelFromDatabase = MapperFactory.Muscle.GetViewModel(fromDatabase);
    return View("Details", viewModelFromDatabase);
}
catch (ValidationErrors propertyErrors)
```

The main goal of this new feature is to allow you to move less when developing. It allows the developer to not move back and forth inside a page. With the combination of the **peak definition** feature, the focus remains more and more on the task and not moving around files and lines.

# Microsoft .Net 4.5.1 Binding Redirect

Release Date: 24-Sep-13
Url: http://patrickdesjardins.com/blog/?post_type=post&p=2313

With the new version of Microsoft .Net, the 4.5.1, you will be able to use an assembly that has been compiled with another framework version dependency. For example, a project that uses a library that itself uses a library that we might use in the project but with another version won't work normally. But, with the new feature called binding redirect, an entry inside the web.config (or app.config) is added to tell the .Net virtual machine to use a specific library for the version of the dependency. Here is an example of the web.config:

```
<dependentAssembly>
        <assemblyIdentity name="assemblyWithDependencyProblem"
publicKeyToken="32ab4ba45e0a69a1" culture="en-us" />
        <bindingRedirect oldVersion="1.0.0.0" newVersion="2.0.0.0" />
</dependentAssembly>
```

```
Project A --> Library A --> Dependency 1 (version1)
  |---------> Dependency 2 (version2)
```

The example above would have an entry in the web.config (or app.config) that tells the dependency to use version 1 if used by Library A and use version 2 when directly used by the project. It might not be an impressive feature because it is not visual but it is very useful. Often, a library from the .Net framework could be problematic but this is a thing of the past.

## Visual Studio 2013 Displaying Return Value Of Method

Release Date: 26-Sep-13
Url: http://patrickdesjardins.com/blog/?post_type=post&p=2315

Visual Studio 2013 has an awesome feature for those who like debugging. One limitation before Visual Studio 2013 was that we couldn't see the return value of a method, or the return value of the method that called another method. Now, with Visual Studio 2013, it's possible to see the return value with the Debugging windows "Auto." It's also possible to see the returning value by using the **$ReturnValue** keyword in the immediate windows.
Here is an example.

```
class Program
{
    static void Main(string[] args)
    {
        var x = Method1();
        Console.WriteLine(x);
        Console.ReadLine();
    }

    private static string Method1()
    {
        return "Method1 call " + Method2();
    }

    private static string Method2()
    {
        return "From Method2" + Method3();
    }

    private static string Method3()
    {
        return "From Method3";
    }
}
```

If we set a breakpoint to the *Method1* and we hit next, we will be at the ending curly bracket. Normally, we won't see the value of *"Method1 call " + Method2();*

Now, we can see it.

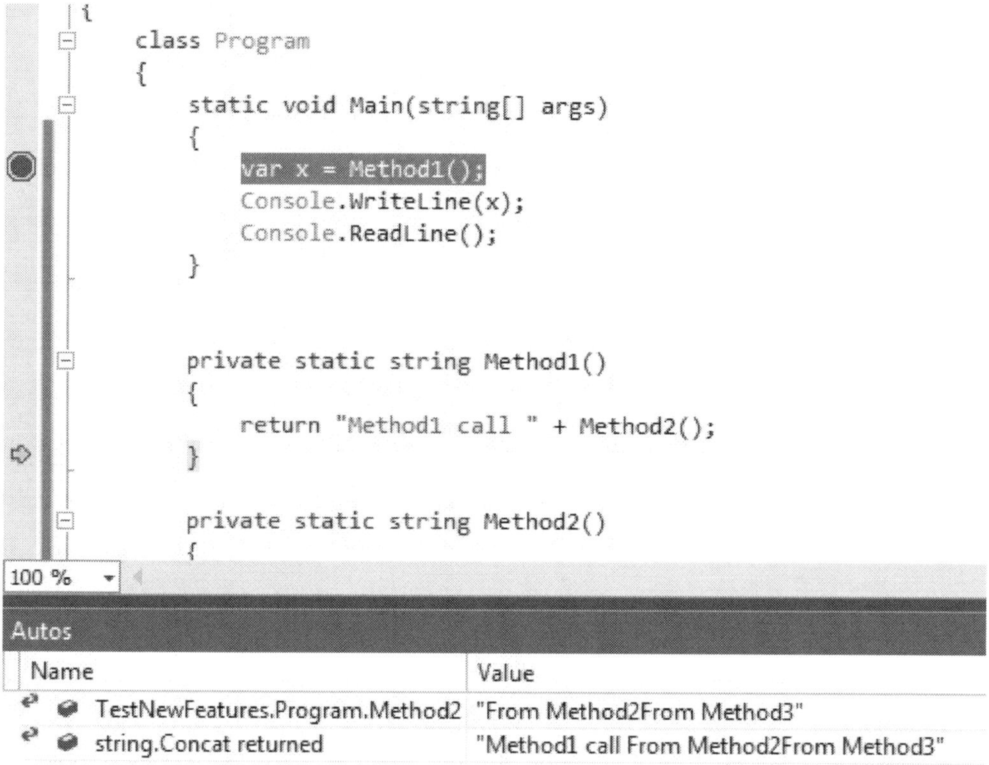

```
{
    class Program
    {
        static void Main(string[] args)
        {
            var x = Method1();
            Console.WriteLine(x);
            Console.ReadLine();
        }


        private static string Method1()
        {
            return "Method1 call " + Method2();
        }

        private static string Method2()
        {
```

100 %

Autos

| Name | Value |
|---|---|
| TestNewFeatures.Program.Method2 | "From Method2From Method3" |
| string.Concat returned | "Method1 call From Method2From Method3" |

As you can see in the image above, we see in the left bottom corner the **Auto Windows Panel**. The first line is the value inside *Method2* and the second line is the return value of *Method1*.

## Visual Studio 2013 remove Development Server AKA Cassini

Release Date: 01-Oct-13
Url: http://patrickdesjardins.com/blog/?post_type=post&p=2320

I have been developing with Visual Studio since the 2003 version and most of the time directly executing the code with the default server which is the one that Visual Studio triggers when you press F5 (Build and Execute). More and more, I had to use IIS because that bigger website (enterprise application) requires a lot of IIS features, which is more convenient than **IIS Express** or **Cassini** (the Development Server integrated with Visual Studio).

Since Visual Studio 2013, Cassini is gone. The default choice is IIS Express. You can change it to IIS or any external host.

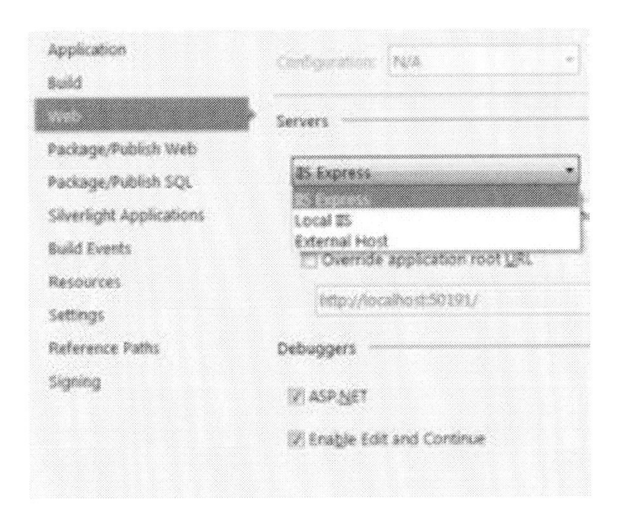


This is a feature that I will miss because for a small project it was easy to execute with just Visual Studio. IIS Express is fine but the lack of visual help to configure makes it good for people who are familiar with IIS settings. Cassini had removed this learning curve. Nevertheless, it makes developers learn more about IIS and possibly create better applications because developers will understand the whole picture.

# Unit Test and References with CodeLens

Release Date: 31-Oct-13
Url: http://patrickdesjardins.com/blog/?post_type=post&p=2355

**CodeLens** is a new feature that enhances your code by adding additional information over your methods. CodeLens adds information concerning references, unit testing and TFS. We will not talk about TFS in this article but concentrate on the two first features that are available even if you do not use TFS. CodeLens is available only with Visual Studio 2013 Ultimate.

The first information CodeLens adds over your method's signature is the number of references that the method has. References are all code entries that your code contains in the method where the information is added. If you are using **ReSharper**, you may find it similar to the **Find Usage** feature but with the advantage of being dynamically available for all your methods directly in Visual Studio. Visual Studio adds this information directly above the method, which allows it to very rapidly figure out if the method is used and where the method is called. To see it in action, open Visual Studio 2013 Ultimate Edition and select any of your existing projects. The reference count will be written in small gray letters above each class and each method.

```
3 references
public class WorkoutService : BaseS
{
    1 reference
    public WorkoutService(IReposit
    {
    }
```

To be able to get additional information concerning references, pressing **ALT+2** or clicking on the numbers of a reference opens a contextual window with all call occurrences. You can from there select a reference to be transported directly to the file and the line that calls the method.

```
Services\Implementations\WorkoutService.cs (2)
    47 : SetWorkoutSessionExerciseOrder(model);
    66 : SetWorkoutSessionExerciseOrder(model);
Show on Code Map | Collapse All

2 references
private static void SetWorkoutSessionExerciseOrder(Workout model)
{
    foreach (var workoutSession in model.Sessions)
    {
        int index = 1;
        foreach (var workoutSessionExercise in workoutSession.WorkoutSessionExercises)
        {
            workoutSessionExercise.Order = index++;
        }
    }
}
```

It is also possible from the same menu to generate the **Code Map** of the method. This is an interesting way to see all references' links.

```
54 : var x = ServiceFactory.Exercise.New();
WorkoutPlanner\Controllers\MuscleController.cs (1)
47 : var x = ServiceFactory.Muscle.New();
WorkoutPlanner\Controllers\WorkoutSessionController.cs (1)
49 : var newModel = ServiceFactory.Workout.New();
WorkoutPlanner\Controllers\WorkoutSessionExerciseController.cs (1)
57 : var x = ServiceFactory.WorkoutSessionExercise.New();

10 references
public Workout New()
{
    return new Workout();
}

29 references | 2/3 passing
public Workout Get(Workout model)
{
    var modelToBound = Repository.Workout.Get(model.Id);
    return modelToBound;
}
```

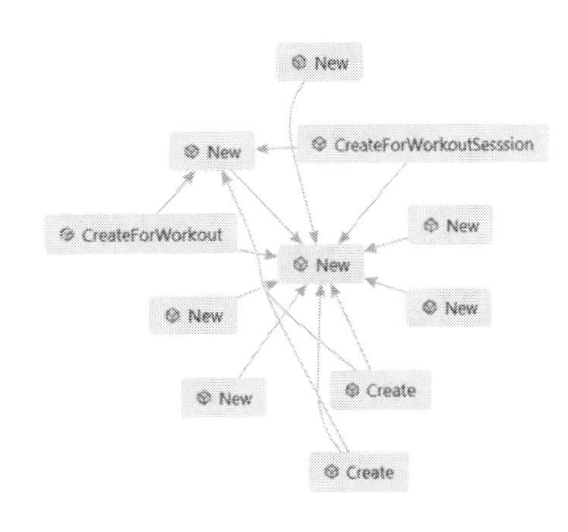


If you do not want to move to the usage of your method because you just want to have a look but not move from where you are, you can. To see the code that uses it, you can see a small snapshot of two lines before and two lines after the call by moving the focus to a reference without clicking.

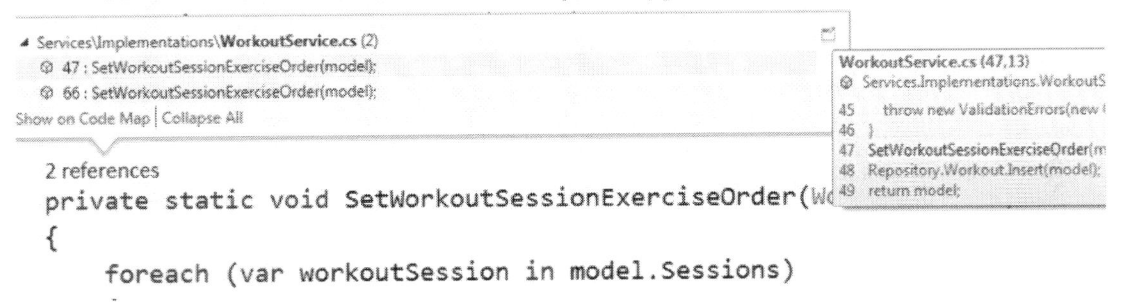


The second information that is added by **CodeLens** is the number of unit tests that are successful for the method compared to the number of total unit tests. This is one of the greatest features to improve your code quality because in a single look, you can see if a method is tested or not. You can also visualize which tests are in error or have passed. With a single click you can move from your method to your test. Another piece of information that is provided is the amount of time the test took. This is a new metric used by executing unit testing and it allows you to improve your code by having near each code the time that it takes to execute it.

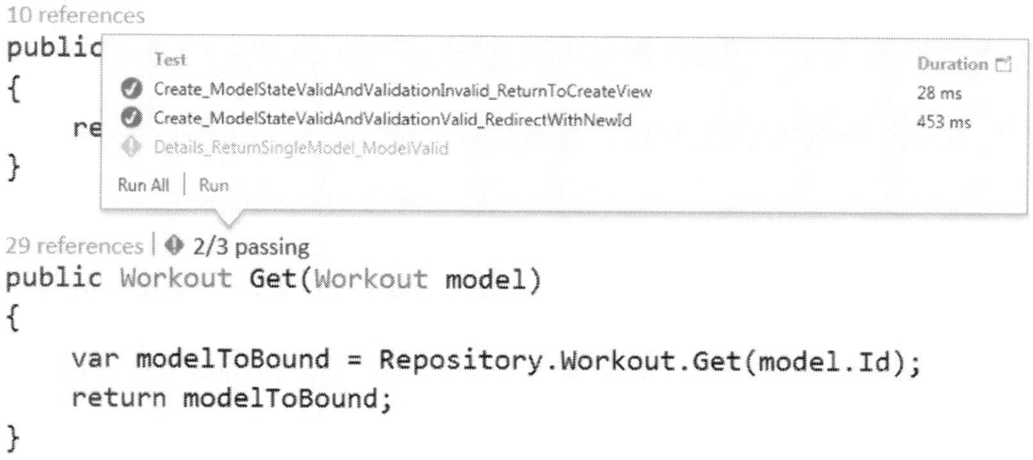

```
10 references
public
{
    re
}
```

Test | Duration
--- | ---
Create_ModelStateValidAndValidationInvalid_ReturnToCreateView | 28 ms
Create_ModelStateValidAndValidationValid_RedirectWithNewId | 453 ms
Details_ReturnSingleModel_ModelValid |

Run All | Run

```
29 references | 2/3 passing
public Workout Get(Workout model)
{
    var modelToBound = Repository.Workout.Get(model.Id);
    return modelToBound;
}
```

As you can see, Visual Studio 2013 improves the integration of good software development by having near your hands different information. Reference is a key information to have and unit testing helps you and your team to work toward the objective of better code quality.

# NuGet package, how to not commit all libraries to your source control

Release Date: 26-Dec-13
Url: http://patrickdesjardins.com/blog/?post_type=post&p=2395

I am publishing more and more code to GitHub (https://github.com/MrDesjardins) when I am posting blog posts to have something for the reader to test. The problem is that if I want to have something that works, I need to have all references published into the source control. This can start to be huge if I have several packages. NuGet gives three advantages to not have these libraries in the source control.

- Source control includes every version of every file within the repository, and binary files that are updated frequently can lead to significant repository bloat and more time required to clone the repository.
- With the packages included in the repository, team members may add references directly to package contents on disk rather than referencing packages through NuGet.
- It becomes harder to clean your solution of any unused package folders, as you need to ensure you don't delete any package folders still in use.

But, how can we send a project into a repository and have NuGet know that it needs to download every reference on the first build? This can be done by changing the solution to use **NuGet Package Restore**. To enable this feature, right click the solution in the Solution Explorer and select **Enable Restore NuGet Package Restore.**

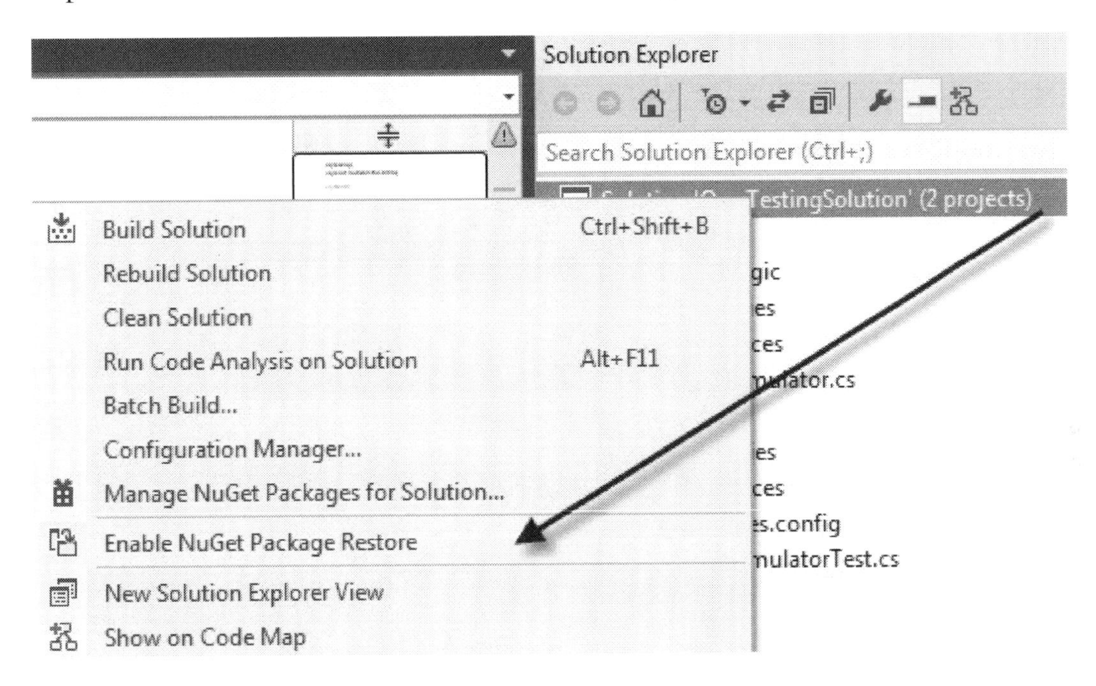


This will create a folder named **.nuget** with three files.

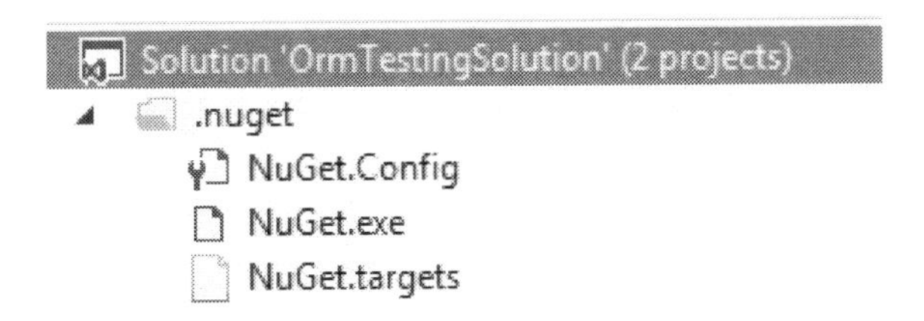


This will install all referenced packages before a project is built, thereby ensuring that all dependencies are available to a project without requiring them to be stored in source control. Also, you must ignore the **.nuget** repository and its content.

## Two NuGet Restore Approaches

When NuGet Restore is enabled, you have two different options. The first one allows Visual Studio to download automatically the reference. This is the default approach and the recommended one. The second approach is the console one that is more manual.

## Automatic Approach

The automatic approach is the default one since NuGet 2.7. When the code is compiled, Visual Studio raises an event that NuGet is hooked to. This allows NuGet in a pre-event to execute itself. NuGet reads the packages.config file and downloads every package not present. This means that the first time you get the code the build is slower. The speed is not reduced because of the compilation but because NuGet downloads every package. The second time you compile, the speed will be back because of only having the source code to compile. Of course, Visual Studio needs to have the option to download NuGet package. This can be found in the Tools>Options menu of Visual Studio.

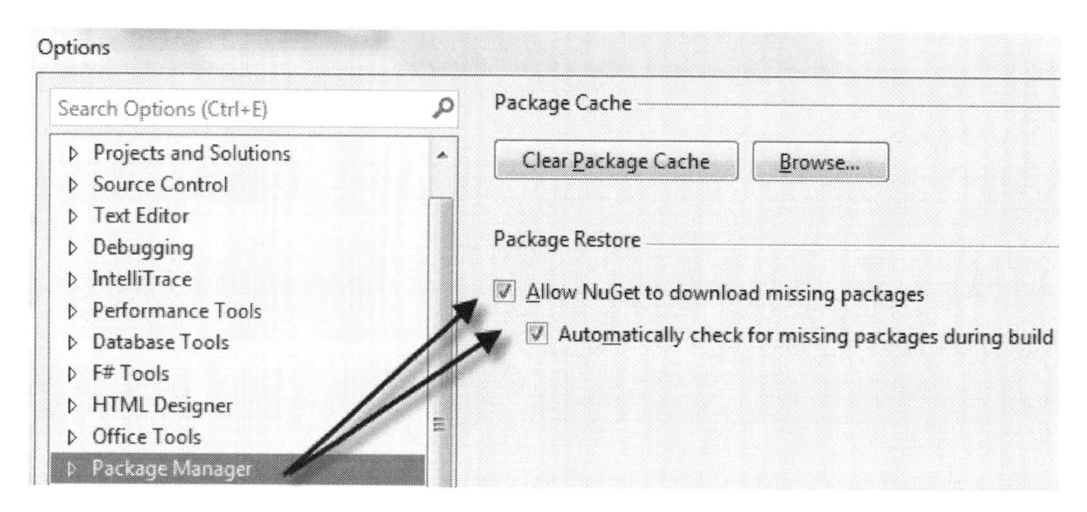


## Manual Approach

As we have mentioned, NuGet added three files. One is an executable called NuGet.exe that can be called manually to download a package from the packages.config. Here is an example of the command you can write to get every file.

```
nuget.exe restore YourSolutionFile.sln
```

# Tutorial about how to create your first NuGet package

Release Date: 07-Jan-14
Url: http://patrickdesjardins.com/blog/?post_type=post&p=2533

This is a tutorial about how to create your first NuGet package.

## Part 1 : Setting up the basic information of NuGet

The first step is to get Nuget.exe. This is required to create the NuGet package but also to create the first draft of the metadata of the package. It is open source and can be found at CodePlex.

The second step is to create the metadata package. This is where you specify the name of the application, the version of the NuGet and other information. Another very important section of the metadata is the dependencies list. It allows you to specify other package names and versions that need to be installed before installing your package. To get a brand new metadata file, open a Windows console and type:

```
nuget spec
```

This will create a new file like the following one.

```
<?xml version="1.0"?>
<package >
  <metadata>
    <id>Package</id>
    <version>1.0.0</version>
    <authors>Patrick</authors>
    <owners>Patrick</owners>
    <licenseUrl>http://LICENSE_URL_HERE_OR_DELETE_THIS_LINE</licenseUrl>
    <projectUrl>http://PROJECT_URL_HERE_OR_DELETE_THIS_LINE</projectUrl>
    <iconUrl>http://ICON_URL_HERE_OR_DELETE_THIS_LINE</iconUrl>
    <requireLicenseAcceptance>false</requireLicenseAcceptance>
    <description>Package description</description>
    <releaseNotes>Summary of changes made in this release of the
package.</releaseNotes>
    <copyright>Copyright 2013</copyright>
    <tags>Tag1 Tag2</tags>
    <dependencies>
      <dependency id="SampleDependency" version="1.0" />
    </dependencies>
  </metadata>
</package>
```

For my example, it was to transform the open source project (https://github.com/MrDesjardins/DragAndDropWebList) that I published a few weeks ago. What I want to transform is the part that is an MVC template. Here is my transformed file.

```
<?xml version="1.0"?>
<package >
  <metadata>
    <id>DragAndDropMultiSelectorList</id>
    <version>1.0.0</version>
    <authors>Patrick</authors>
    <owners>Patrick</owners>
    <projectUrl>https://github.com/MrDesjardins/DragAndDropMultiSelectorList
    </projectUrl>
<iconUrl>https://raw.github.com/MrDesjardins/DragAndDropMultiSelectorList/master/i
conNuget.png</iconUrl>
    <requireLicenseAcceptance>false</requireLicenseAcceptance>
    <description>This nuget package installs the Javascript, the CSS and the
Templates to allow to
    have UIHint to have special control to drag and drop items from an available
    list of item to a selected list.</description>
    <releaseNotes>First version</releaseNotes>
    <copyright>Copyright 2013</copyright>
    <tags>drag-and-drop </tags>
    <dependencies>
      <dependency id="jQuery" version="2.0.3" />
      <dependency id="jQuery.UI.Combined" version="1.10.3" />
    </dependencies>
  </metadata>
</package>
```

You can also use this open source project, the NuGet Explorer (http://nuget.codeplex.com/), that allows you to edit every metadata property. It also allows you to publish directly to NuGet once you have an account and an API key.

## Part 2 : The content of the NuGet package

The next part is the content of the NuGet package. Create a folder with the name *content*. Everything in this folder will be moved to the solution. This means if you have inside the folder **content** a folder *Content* and inside this one you have *Images* and you set a file *forward.png*, when the NuGet package is installed, the image will be set at this position. For my example, here is the file structure:

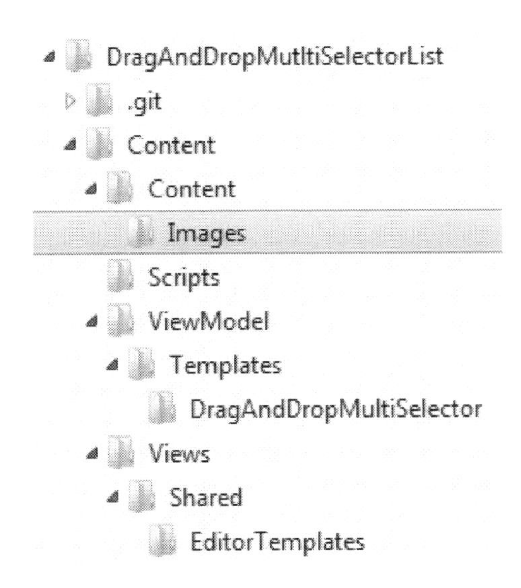


The second step of this part is to have some pre-processing. NuGet allows you to change part of every file dynamically. This can be done if you rename your file by adding .pp at the end. For example, I want to use the user namespace for three files. I changed these three file extensions and open them to add the namespace tag.

Documents library
DragAndDropMultiSelector

Name

ISelectorAvailableItemViewModel.cs.pp
MultiSelectorWithSingleValueExtended.cs.pp
MultiSelectorWithSingleValueExtendedItem.cs.pp

```
namespace $rootnamespace$.ViewModel.Templates.DragAndDropMultiSelector
{
    public interface ISelectorAvailableItemViewModel
                                <TUniqueIdentifierType, TExtendedValueType>
    {
      TUniqueIdentifierType ID { get; set; }
      string Description { get; set; }
      TExtendedValueType ExtendedProperty { get; set; }
    }
}
```

As you can see, the first line contains **$rootnamespace$** which will dynamically change the namespace to the user namespace. The last step of this part is to add a

**web.config.transform** file to add configuration in the web.config if required. In my scenario, nothing was required so I have not added it.

## Part 3 : Publish the NuGet package

When everything is set up, it's time to create the NuGet package. This can be done by using the nuget.exe previously downloaded. You need to execute the .nuspec created by the first step.

```
nuget pack
C:\Users\Patrick\Documents\GitHub\DragAndDropMutltiSelectorList\DragAndDropMutltiS
electorList.nuspec
```

This will create a file called *DragAndDropMutltiSelectorList.1.0.0.nupkg* (of course it will be your NuGet name and version).

This can be published to NuGet's website or your own NuGet repository. To do a fast test, open Visual Studio and add a local folder that has your new NuGet package. This way, you will be able to install any local NuGet package inside this folder. To do this, go to **Manage NuGet Packages For Solution** that is located under Tools>Library Package Manager. Then, click Settings at the bottom of the screen. This will pop up the option window for NuGet. Here, you can add your folder.

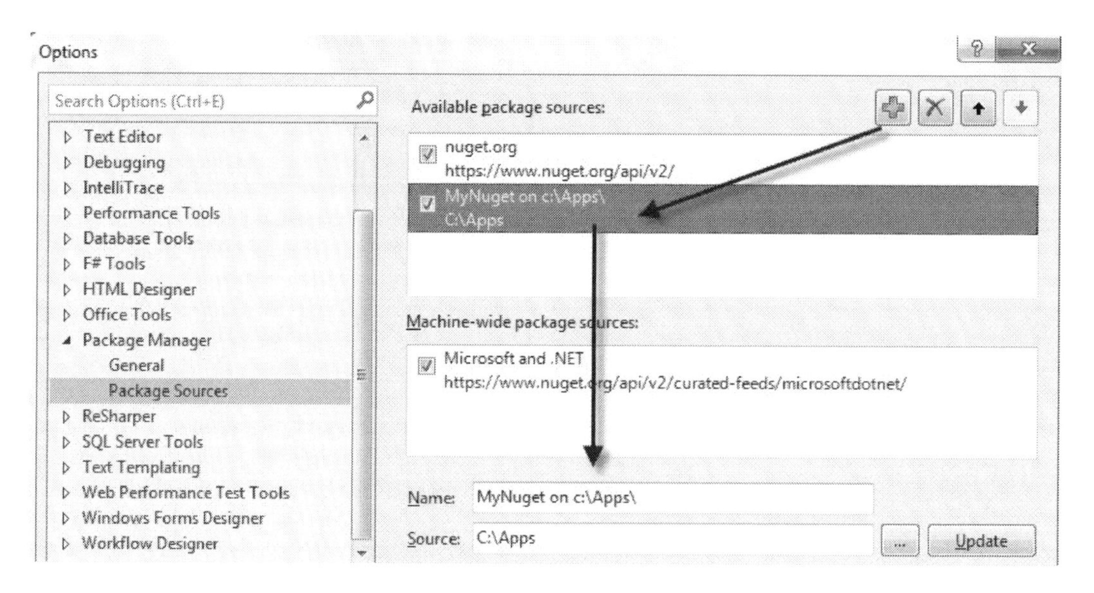


If you double click your package, it will be installed. This allows you to test your package before publishing it on the web. But, once it is tested, you can publish it on Nuget.org. This step is very fast. You need to create an account, then you upload the .nukg and that is it. You can find the package that I just created at this url now: https://www.nuget.org/packages/DragAndDropMultiSelectorList/

# Code coverage with Visual Studio 2013

Release Date: 17-Jan-14
Url: http://patrickdesjardins.com/blog/?post_type=post&p=2572

Microsoft Visual Studio has the ability to tell you what is covered by your unit test. Not all editions have this feature, but Premium and Ultimate do.

First of all, where is the code coverage tool in Visual Studio? It's in the **Test** menu under **Analyze Code Coverage**.

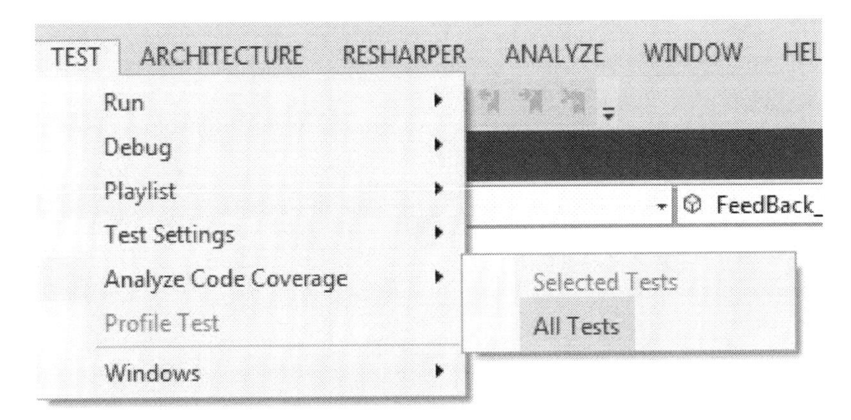


Once done, the Code Coverage Result panel opens. You can open this panel by going to Test>Windows>Code Coverage Result if you want to open it later. This panel indicates the number of code blocks and the percentage covered by all code. As you can see, even the unit test project is in the statistics (red arrow). What is important is the blue arrow, the project tested. As you can see in the image below, everything is unit tested (100%).

Code Coverage Results

Patrick_PATRICK-I7 2013-12-15 20_53_35.co

| Hierarchy | Not Covered (Blocks) | Not Covered (% Blocks) | Covered (Blocks) | Covered (% Blocks) |
|---|---|---|---|---|
| Patrick_PATRICK-I7 2013-12-15 20_53_35.coverage | 0 | 0,00 % | 69 | 100,00 % |
| unittestmessaginglibrary.dll | 0 | 0,00 % | 40 | 100,00 % |
| messaginglibrary.dll | 0 | 0,00 % | 29 | 100,00 % |
| {} MessagingLibrary | 0 | 0,00 % | 29 | 100,00 % |
| FeedBack | 0 | 0,00 % | 29 | 100,00 % |
| FeedBack(string, string, MessagingLibrary.FeedBackType) | 0 | 0,00 % | 3 | 100,00 % |
| FeedBack(string, string) | 0 | 0,00 % | 3 | 100,00 % |
| FeedBack(string, MessagingLibrary.FeedBackType) | 0 | 0,00 % | 3 | 100,00 % |
| FeedBack(string) | 0 | 0,00 % | 3 | 100,00 % |
| FeedBack() | 0 | 0,00 % | 5 | 100,00 % |
| AddMessage(string, string, MessagingLibrary.FeedBackType) | 0 | 0,00 % | 4 | 100,00 % |
| AddMessage(string, string) | 0 | 0,00 % | 3 | 100,00 % |
| AddMessage(string, MessagingLibrary.FeedBackType) | 0 | 0,00 % | 3 | 100,00 % |
| AddMessage(string) | 0 | 0,00 % | 2 | 100,00 % |

Another feature is to display directly into the code which line has been hit and which one has not been hit during testing. Visual Studio and the code coverage tool can highlight directly into the code the background in green for all codes that have been reached by unit tests and in red if no test has executed the line. To enable this feature, click on the **Code Coverage Result,** the icon with multiple blocks.

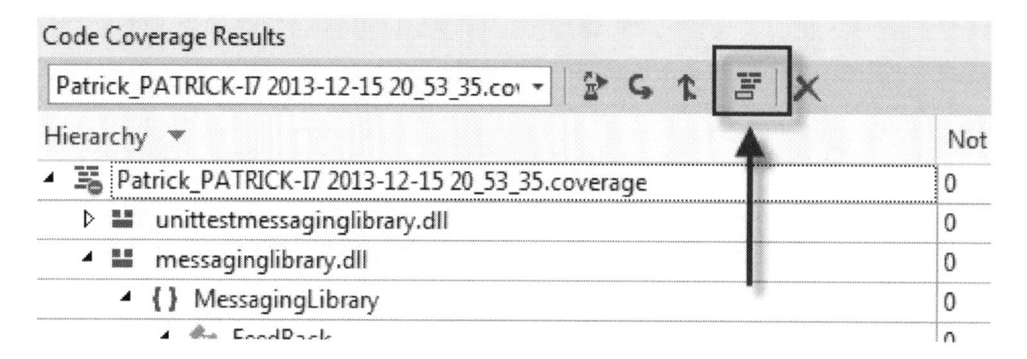


Once clicked, you will see the code changing.

```
namespace MessagingLibrary
{
    14 references
    public class FeedBack:IFeedBack
    {
        5 references | 1/1 passing
        public FeedBack()
        {
            this.Code = string.Empty;
            this.Message = string.Empty;
            this.Type = FeedBackType.Unknown;
        }
         1 reference | 1/1 passing
         public FeedBack(string code, string mess
        {
            this.AddMessage(code,message,type);
        }
```

I have entitled this post with Visual Studio 2013 but, in fact, this has been available since 2008 without much change. It is not well known but very interesting if you are using unit testing.

# How to generate web.config in every compilation for every build configuration

Release Date: 04-Feb-14
Url: http://patrickdesjardins.com/blog/?post_type=post&p=2616

This article explains how to generate a web.config or an app.config to every build configuration when compiling. This can be useful if you want to apply transformations for every build without having to compile multiple times. Normally, you have to specify the target build to apply the configuration to the web.config. This is the default Visual Studio process. You build one time for Debug and you have to build one more time for Release. The problem is it requires compiling multiple times for the same code. If you are working in a DEV then TEST then PROD, you have to compile three times, which could insert a bug if a code changes or is not compiled in the same environment.

This is why it is better to have all configuration files generated when everything is compiled before any testing. The challenge is that the transformation file is a good system. You do not have to copy and paste the whole configuration files to change only a few settings. To be able to use the transformation within a single compilation, we have to modify the web project file in notepad. This is the xml code that needs to be pasted into the .csproj at the end of the file within the project xml element.

```
<Target Name="BeforeBuild">
  <!-- Variable that contains the path of where the configuration file will be
located -->
  <ItemGroup>
    <TransformedWebConfigsDir Include="$(OutDir)..\_TransformedWebConfigs" />
  </ItemGroup>
    <!-- MSBuild transform the web.config into the destination folder-->
  <!-- Remove the temporary folder where transformation are located. This is used
only after this process as run once -->
    <RemoveDir Directories="@(TransformedWebConfigsDir)" />
  <!-- Create the transformation directory only if not existing. -->
    <MakeDir Directories="@(TransformedWebConfigsDir)"
Condition="!Exists('@(TransformedWebConfigsDir)')" />
  <!-- Transform for debug -->
    <TransformXml Source="Web.config" Transform="Web.Debug.config"
Destination="@(TransformedWebConfigsDir)\Web.Debug.config" StackTrace="true" />
  <!-- Transform for release -->
    <TransformXml Source="Web.config" Transform="Web.Release.Dev.config"
Destination="@(TransformedWebConfigsDir)\Web.Release.Dev.config" StackTrace="true"
/>
  </Target>
  <Target Name="BeforeClean">
    <RemoveDir Directories="@(TransformedWebConfigsDir)" />
   </Target>
```

The XML creates a target before the build that specifies an output directory, which in my case is named *_TransformedWebConfigs*, in the project directory. It cleans everything and then it creates the directory and applies the transformation for **Debug** and **Release Dev**. If you have a Test and Production then you have to have additional lines that specify the Transformation name (build name in Visual Studio) and the destination of the file. As you can see, the XML has an ItemGroup that lets you reuse the path everywhere in your **MsBuild** command.

## Power Shell refuses to execute script inside Visual Studio

Release Date: 01-Apr-14
Url: http://patrickdesjardins.com/blog/?post_type=post&p=3410

If you are running Visual Studio 2013 and execute inside the **Package Manager Console** a Power Shell script, you may stumble into a failure, a message concerning PSSecurityException that cannot load the script because of something disabled. Even if a few minutes ago you were able to run the command, this can appear.

*Script.ps1 cannot be loaded because the execution of scripts is disabled on this system. Please see "get-help about_signing" for more details.*

The trick is to execute the following line:

```
Set-ExecutionPolicy RemoteSigned
```

This will raise a question that you have to write "y" to accept.

*Execution Policy ChangeThe execution policy helps protect you from scripts that you do not trust. Changing the execution policy might expose you to the security risks described in the about_Execution_Policies help topic. Do you want to change the execution policy?[Y] Yes [N] No [S] Suspend [?] Help (default is "Y"):y*

# How to add an Area with Visual Studio for an Asp.Net MVC project

Release Date: 29-Apr-14
Url: http://patrickdesjardins.com/blog/?post_type=post&p=3447

Adding an area can be done manually by adding a folder inside your website project under the **Areas** folder. From there you can add a folder for your controller. However, a better way exists that creates for you the area with all folders required. It also adds the **_ViewStart.cshtml** for you. If you right click the Areas folder you will not find anything related to **Add Area**.

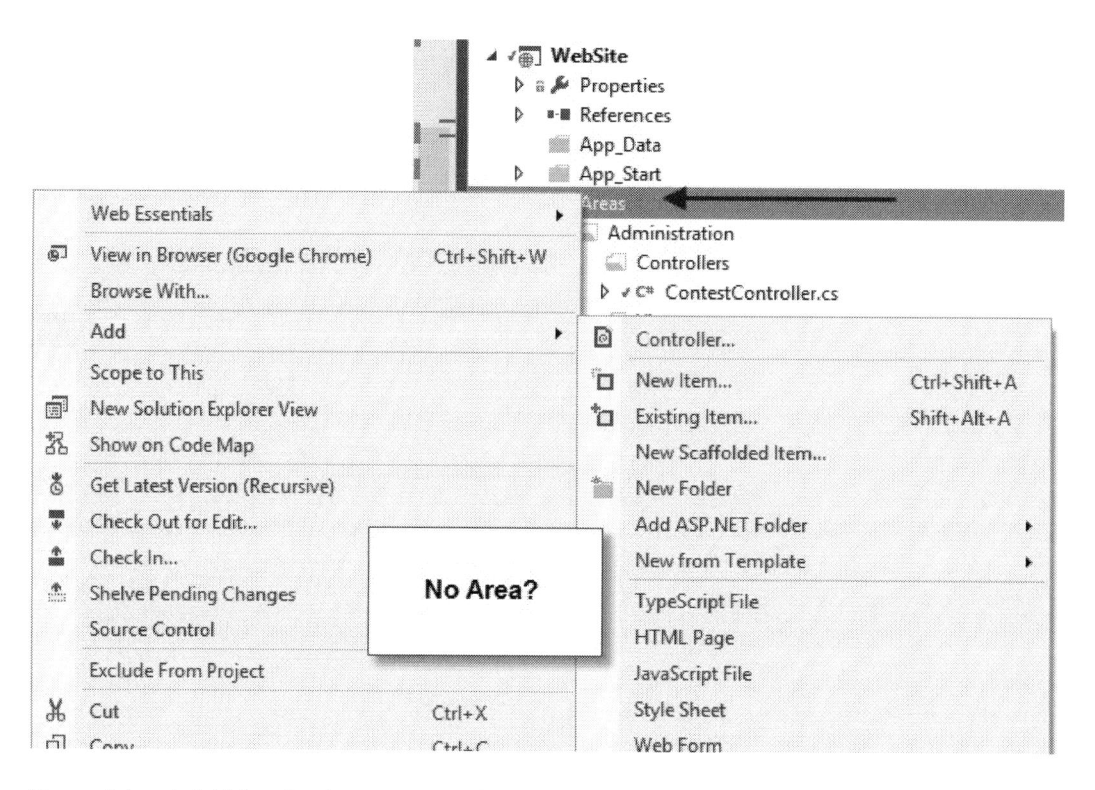


Everything is hidden in the contextual menu of the website project.

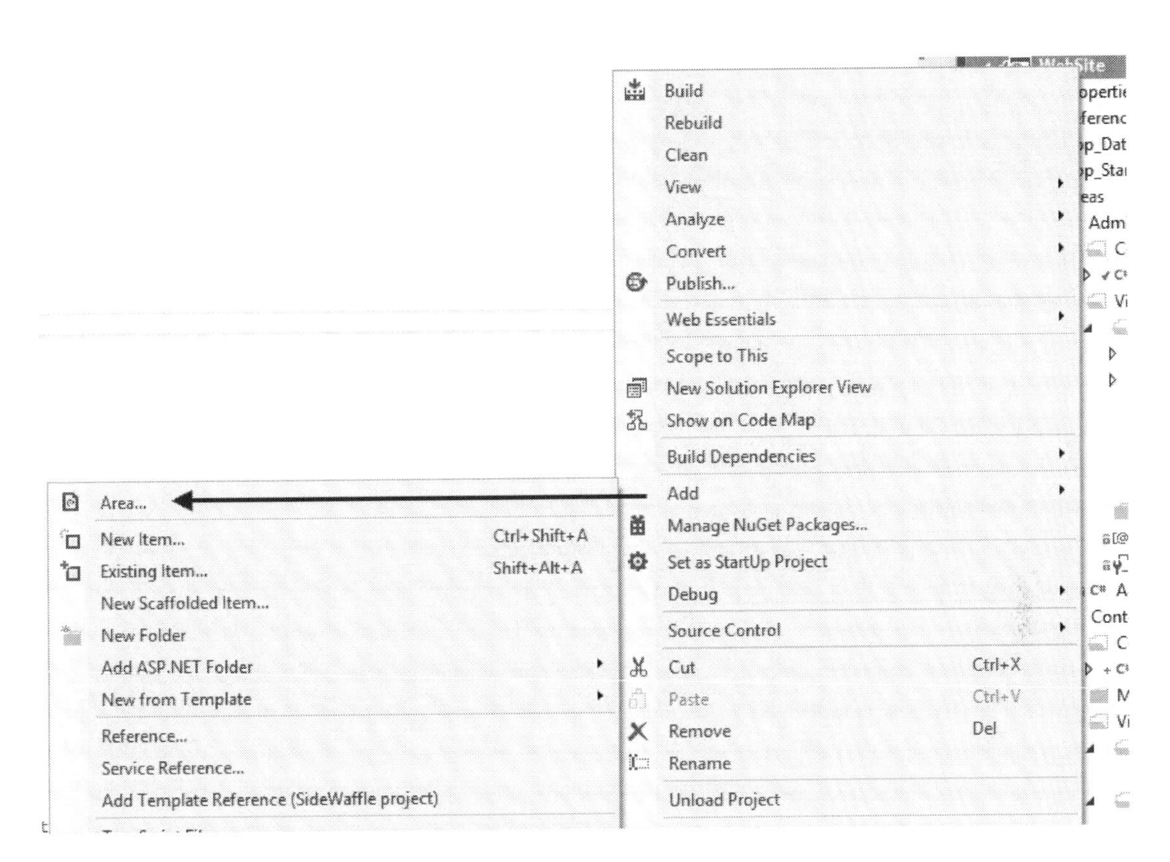


This will add for you your area. If no Area folder exists, it will add it for you. It will also take care to register the area with the map route.

# Modifying TFS Bug states for a specific collection

Release Date: 17-Sep-14
Url: http://patrickdesjardins.com/blog/?post_type=post&p=3553

If you want to modify the workflow state in TFS for a specific collection, you must use a command line tool named **witadmin**. This tool is located in the **bin** folder of Visual Studio.

```
%programfiles(x86)%\Microsoft Visual Studio 12.0\Common7\IDE
```

Here is an example for a collection named *TEST*. The first command named **listwith** gives you the list of wit types.

```
witadmin listwitd /collection:http://yourtfsserver:8080/tfs/yourpath /p:TEST
```

```
C:\Program Files (x86)\Microsoft Visual Studio 11.0\Common7\IDE>witadmin listwitd
Task
Bug
Impediment
Product Backlog Item
Shared Steps
Sprint
Test Case
```

This is interesting because if you want to modify the state for the Bug then you have the confirmation with **witadmin** and **listwitd** that you will have all types that we can edit, like the Bug.

If you want to modify the state, you need to export the definition into an XML file. You can apply your modification and then import it into TFS. It is a good practice to keep a version that was not altered before modifying the wit. In case the importation goes wrong, you will be able to get it back to its previous state.

```
//Get the definition for BUG
witadmin exportwitd /collection:http://yourtfsserver:8080/tfs/yourpath /p:TEST
                /n:BUG /f:"C:\Code\FileName.xml"

//After your changes, you import back
witadmin importwitd /collection:http://yourtfsserver:8080/tfs/yourpath /p:TEST
                /f:"C:\Code\FileName.xml"
```

The file that you get from TFS allows you to specify states and transitions between them. In the example above, we specify the type of TFS item we want to edit with the switch **/n**. The list of possible values comes from **listwitd**. It is interesting to note that if you have already used a state it will continue to exist in TFS until it goes back to a state defined.

```
<WORKFLOW>
  <STATES>
    <STATE value="Done">
      <FIELDS>
        <FIELD refname="Microsoft.VSTS.Scheduling.Effort">
          <READONLY />
        </FIELD>
      </FIELDS>
    </STATE>
    <STATE value="New (1/4)" />
    <STATE value="Resolved (2/4)" />
    <STATE value="Deployed (3/4)" />
    <STATE value="Closed (4/4)" />
  </STATES>
  <TRANSITIONS>
    <TRANSITION from="" to="New (1/4)">
      <REASONS>
```

```
        <DEFAULTREASON value="Nouveau bug" />
      </REASONS>
      <FIELDS>
        <FIELD refname="Microsoft.VSTS.Common.BacklogPriority">
          <DEFAULT from="value" value="1000" />
        </FIELD>
      </FIELDS>
    </TRANSITION>
    <TRANSITION from="New (1/4)" to="Resolved (2/4)">
      <REASONS>
        <DEFAULTREASON value="Solve" />
      </REASONS>
    </TRANSITION>
    <TRANSITION from="Resolved (2/4)" to="Deployed (3/4)">
      <REASONS>
        <DEFAULTREASON value="Need to be tested" />
      </REASONS>
    </TRANSITION>
    <TRANSITION from="Deployed (3/4)" to="Closed (4/4)">
      <REASONS>
        <DEFAULTREASON value="Fixed" />
      </REASONS>
    </TRANSITION>
    <TRANSITION from="Deployed (3/4)" to="New (1/4)">
      <REASONS>
        <DEFAULTREASON value="Bug still present" />
      </REASONS>
    </TRANSITION>
    <TRANSITION from="New (1/4)" to="Closed (4/4)">
      <REASONS>
        <DEFAULTREASON value="Not a real bug" />
      </REASONS>
    </TRANSITION>
  </TRANSITIONS>
</WORKFLOW>
```

After importing your modification into TFS your change will be reflected right after the command line..

## VisualStudio.com Build Problem With System.Object is defined in an assembly that is not referenced

Release Date: 26-Sep-14
Url: http://patrickdesjardins.com/blog/?post_type=post&p=3774

Visual Studio 2013 builds correctly your Asp.Net MVC under .Net Framework 4.5.2 but when you commit to Visual Studio TFS online the Build Server gives you an error about

System.Object. The error can be something about **System.Object that is not defined in an assembly**. Here is the full exception.

*Entities\Trading\Portefolio.cs (41): The type 'System.Object' is defined in an assembly that is not referenced. You must add a reference to assembly 'System.Runtime, Version=4.0.0.0, Culture=neutral, PublicKeyToken=b03f5f7f11d50a3a'.*

This is because on your computer Visual Studio knows to get them by going into a system folder. For example, the folder *C:\Program Files (x86)\Reference Assemblies\Microsoft\Framework\.NETFramework\v4.5\Facades* has a lot of assemblies that Visual Studio knows are on your computer .

To fix this problem you need to open your **Web.Config** file and add under System.Web a compilation section.

```
<system.web>
  <compilation debug="true" targetFramework="4.5.2">
    <assemblies>
      <add assembly="System.Runtime, Version=4.0.0.0, Culture=neutral,
PublicKeyToken=b03f5f7f11d50a3a" />
    </assemblies>
  </compilation>
  <httpRuntime targetFramework="4.5.2"/>
</system.web>
```

An important notion is that the **httpRuntime target framework** must be the same as the one defined in the compilation. The last thing that might be required is to force msbuild to use the target framework you want. To do so, open Visual Studio Online or edit within Visual Studio the **Build Definition** to use the framework 4.5.2 (or the one defined in your web.config). You have to set the framework to the same as the web.config. If you already have an argument after **/p** you just need to append the target framework version with the framework version desired.

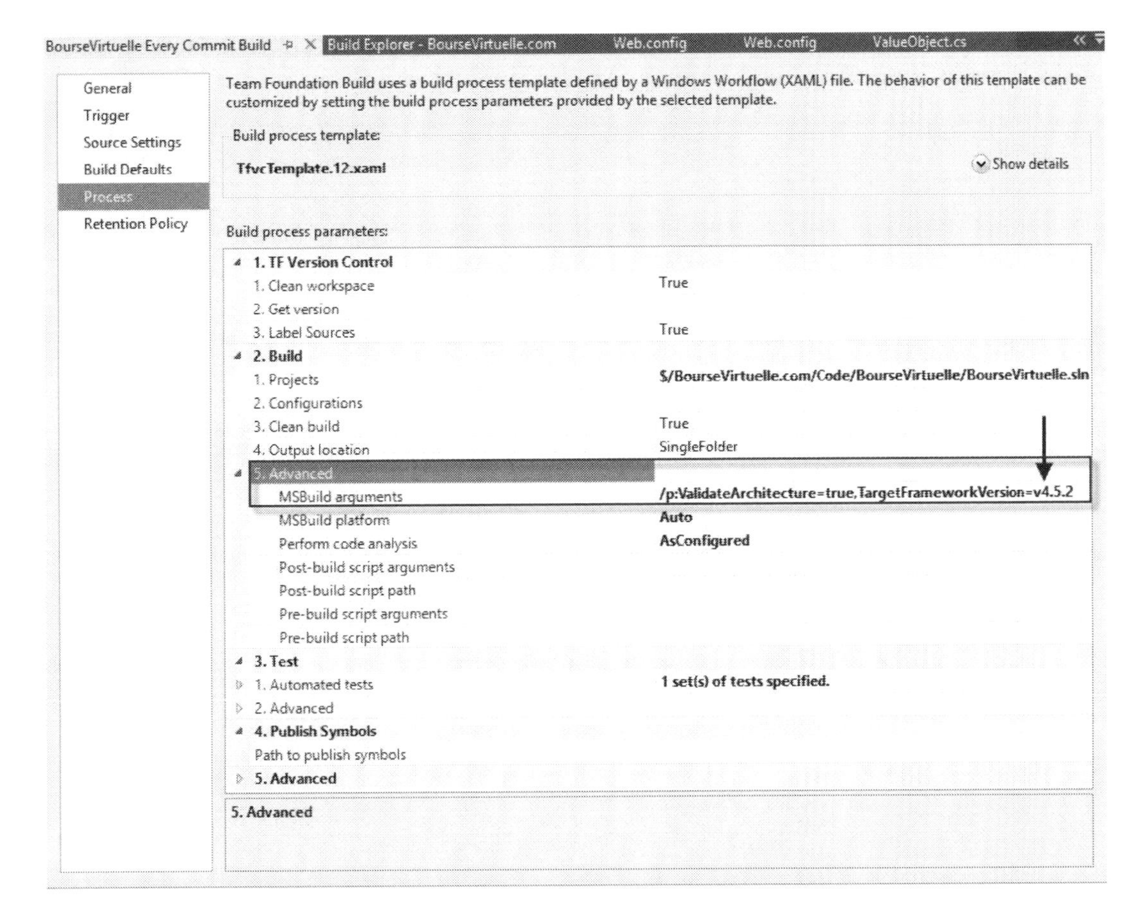


Finally, if you still have problems building with Visual Studio, at the time I am writing this article the Visual Studio Online team has confirmed to me that they do not support the latest framework of .Net. This should be solved in a few months.

## Visual Studio Extension to Attach to IIS with a Single Key

Release Date: 06-Nov-14
Url: http://patrickdesjardins.com/blog/?post_type=post&p=3788

Developing web applications requires at some point using IIS. Visual Studio lets you debug easily with IIS Express by pressing F5. This starts Visual Studio Express and automatically attaches Visual Studio's debugger to the IIS Express process. However, if you are using IIS, nothing is automatic. You have to go into the **Debug** menu, select **Attach to Process** and then in the list select **w3wp.exe**. This is something that you may have to do more than a dozen times per day.

Today, I found something interesting in the Visual Studio Extension Gallery. It is an extension that lets you do that with a single click.

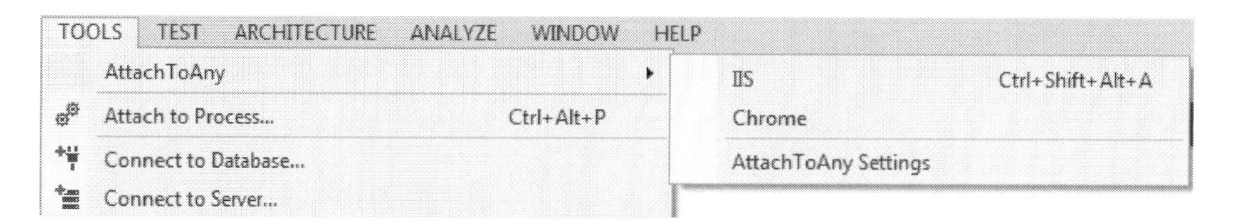


Since this extension is adding the action to the menu, it is possible to assign a shortcut to the action "Attach to process". IIS is assigned to *attach to any 001*.

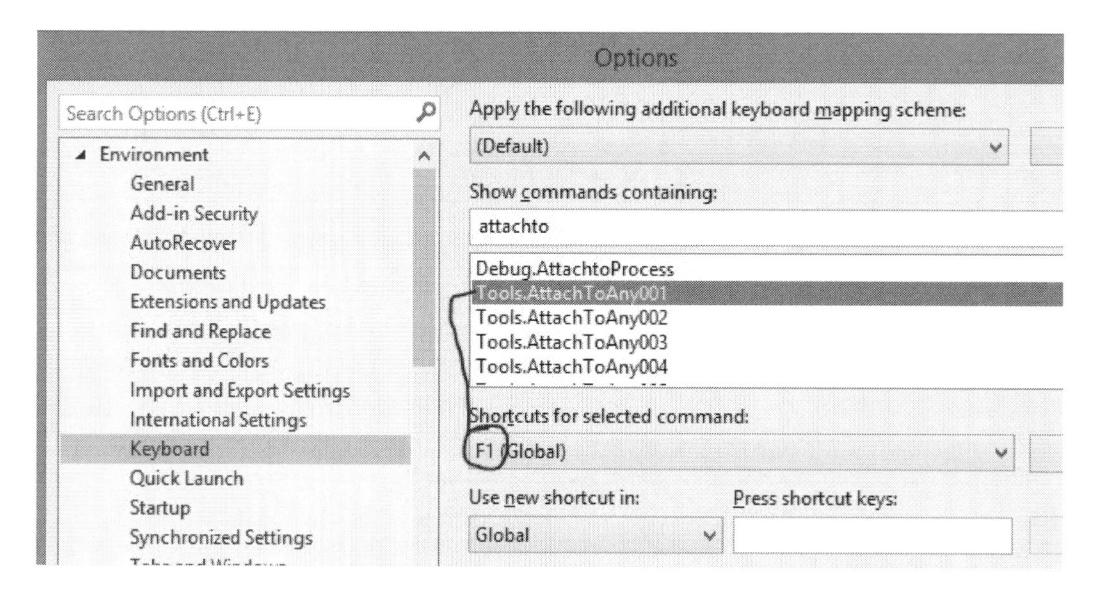


I have assigned mine to the F1 key. Every time I want to debug, I just need to hit F1 and I am ready to go.

# Visual Studio Build Notification

Release Date: 17-Nov-14
Url: http://patrickdesjardins.com/blog/?post_type=post&p=3780

Visual Studio comes with multiple interesting tools. One of the tools is the **Build Notification** application. This tool can be located in the Common7\IDE folder. Here is an example with Visual Studio 2013:

*C:\Program Files (x86)\Microsoft Visual Studio*

*12.0\Common7\IDE\BuildNotificationApp.exe*

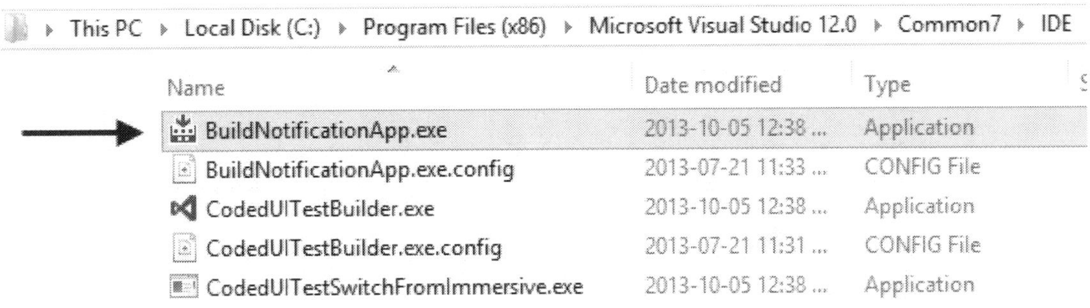

This PC ▸ Local Disk (C:) ▸ Program Files (x86) ▸ Microsoft Visual Studio 12.0 ▸ Common7 ▸ IDE

| Name | Date modified | Type |
|---|---|---|
| BuildNotificationApp.exe | 2013-10-05 12:38 ... | Application |
| BuildNotificationApp.exe.config | 2013-07-21 11:33 ... | CONFIG File |
| CodedUITestBuilder.exe | 2013-10-05 12:38 ... | Application |
| CodedUITestBuilder.exe.config | 2013-07-21 11:31 ... | CONFIG File |
| CodedUITestSwitchFromImmersive.exe | 2013-10-05 12:38 ... | Application |

Once open, you have to configure the tool to let it know what build to check. Here is an example that has been automatically filled since I am already using Visual Studio and TFS for a project.

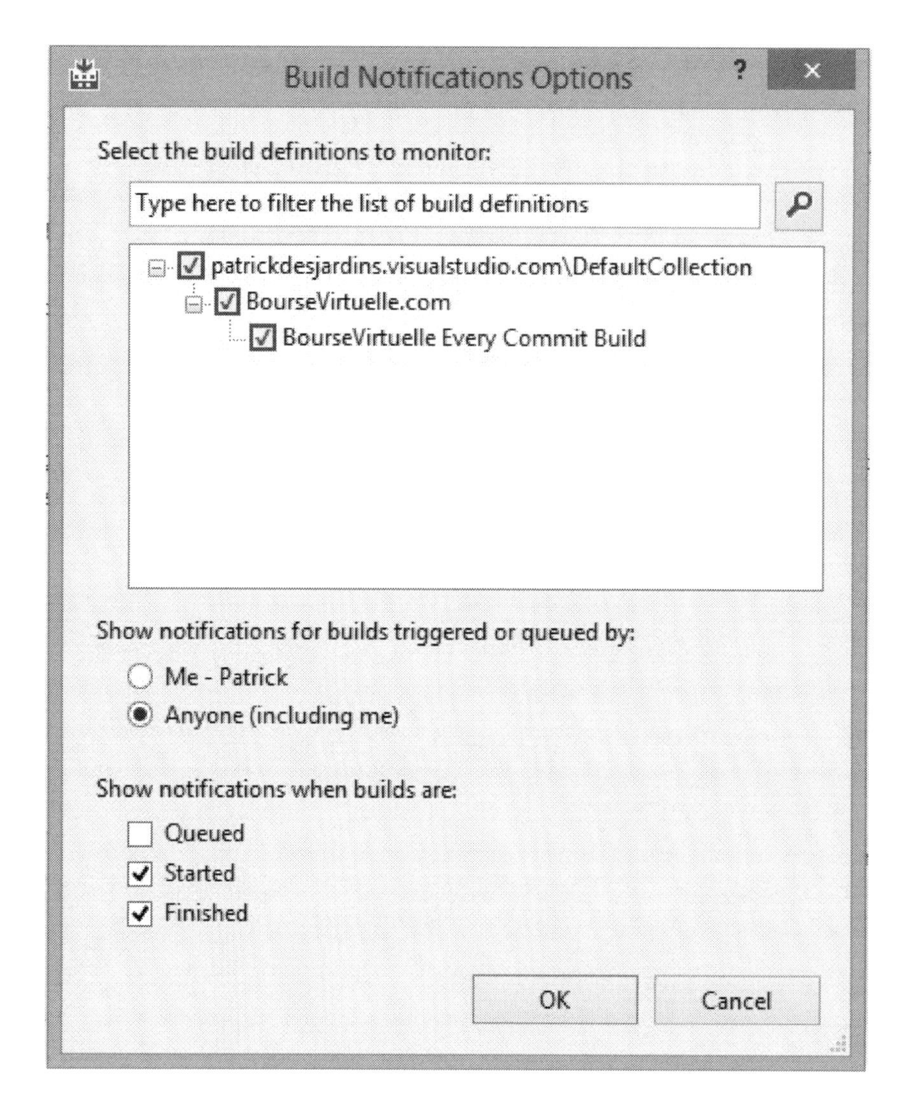


When the configuration is set, the system tray shows an icon with the status of the last build. For example, here is the icon when the build fails:

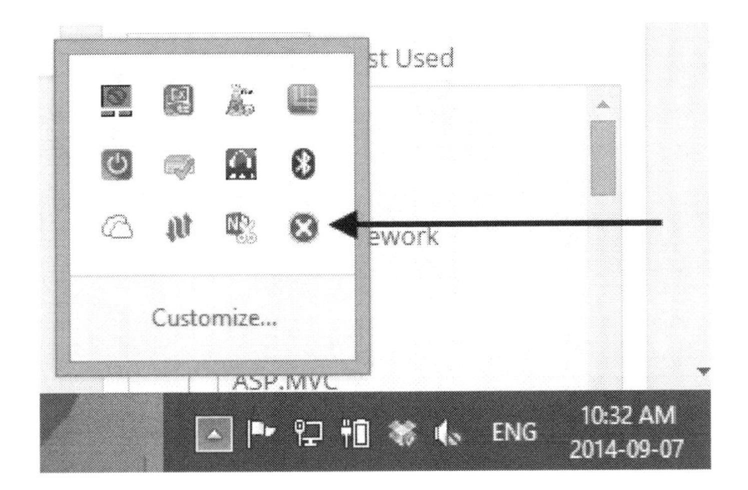


This tool is quite handy if you have a team that is using TFS and you are using the build server. This way, you can know exactly when the build fails and be ready to react.

# 12. WEB SERVICES

This chapter groups every post written during 2013 and 2014 about Web Services. Like all chapters in this book, every article is a snapshot of a real scenario that has a high probability of happening if you are using these technologies. You will notice that every article that has been chosen to be included in this book contains the release date to identify when it was written. A permanent link is also provided that allows you to go in and read updates and comments. Feel free to go on the website to add your own comment if you wish.

## Where is ScvUtil.exe located?

Release Date: 13-Mar-13
Url: http://patrickdesjardins.com/blog/?post_type=post&p=1930

To use the **ScvUtil.exe** you can use the Visual Studio's command prompt and type **svcutil.exe**. If you want to use it from a command prompt, you can go to the following path (in Microsoft Windows 7 operating system):

*C:\Program Files\Microsoft SDKs\Windows\v6.0A\Bin*

The easiest way is to use the Visual Studio Command's prompt since it is already in the correct folder. To use this Visual Studio's console, go to the **Start Menu** and go to the Visual Studio folder under the **Tools** subdirectory.

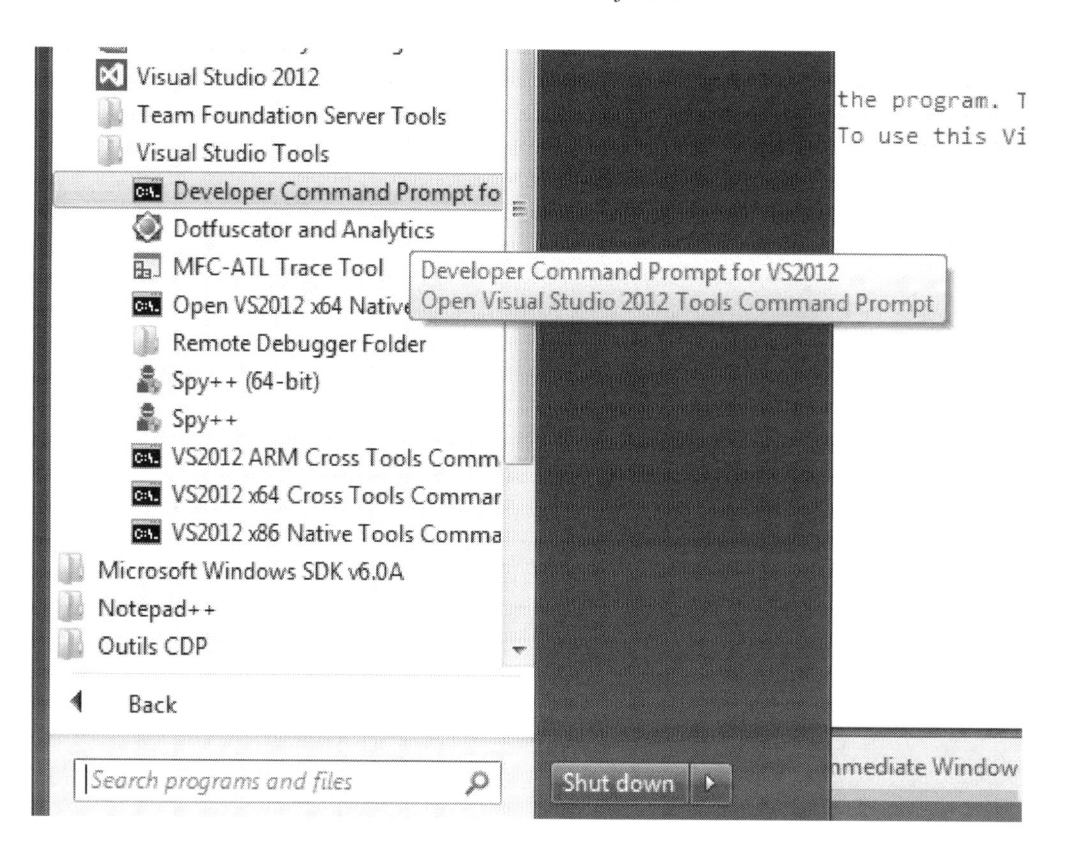


## What is ScvUtil.exe?

Release Date: 15-Mar-13
Url: http://patrickdesjardins.com/blog/?post_type=post&p=1935

If you want to consume web services inside your .Net application, a tool exists to help you create the .Net code to interact with web services. This tool is a console application called **ScvUtil.exe**. This blog post contains information concerning the location of this tool. This application generates two files. The first file is a .cs file that contains the code of the proxy and the code of the DTO classes (complex class used by the service). The second file is a .config file that contains the information about how to connect to the web services. To generate those files, you can simply call the ScvUtil application with the path of the webservice (the WSDL path). This is the URL:

```
svcutil.exe http://localhost:1234/MyService.svc?wsdl
```

The problem is that doing it with only a single parameter will output those files to your

C:\windows\system32\ which is not clean and can cause a security problem. However, it is possible to indicate where to output those two files by adding two parameters to the svcutil.exe tools.

```
svcutil.exe http://localhost:1234/MyService.svc?wsdl /out:"c:\myPath\proxy.cs"
/config:"c:\myPath\config.config"
```

Explicit destinations give you the leverage to output the CS file and the configuration file where you want.

## What is WcfTestClient and where is it?

Release Date: 23-Mar-13
Url: http://patrickdesjardins.com/blog/?post_type=post&p=1938

When you are consuming a web service, either if you are creating it and you want to debug it, or just do a quick use of a service, Visual Studio comes with an external tool that can help you invoke methods of service. This tool is called **WcfTestClient** and can be executed from the Developer Console.

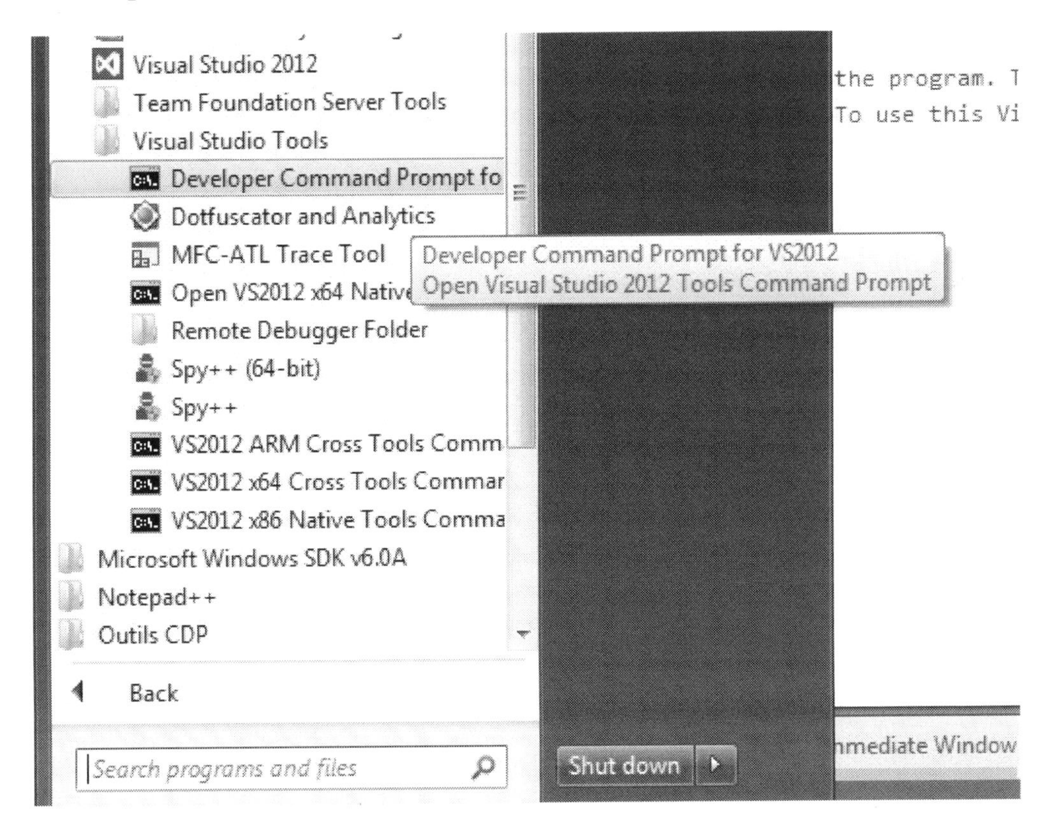

Inside the console you do not need to insert any parameter (but you could set the url of the service).

From here, inside the menu you can add services with a complete url to the webservice. Once it is added, you will get all methods that can be invoked.

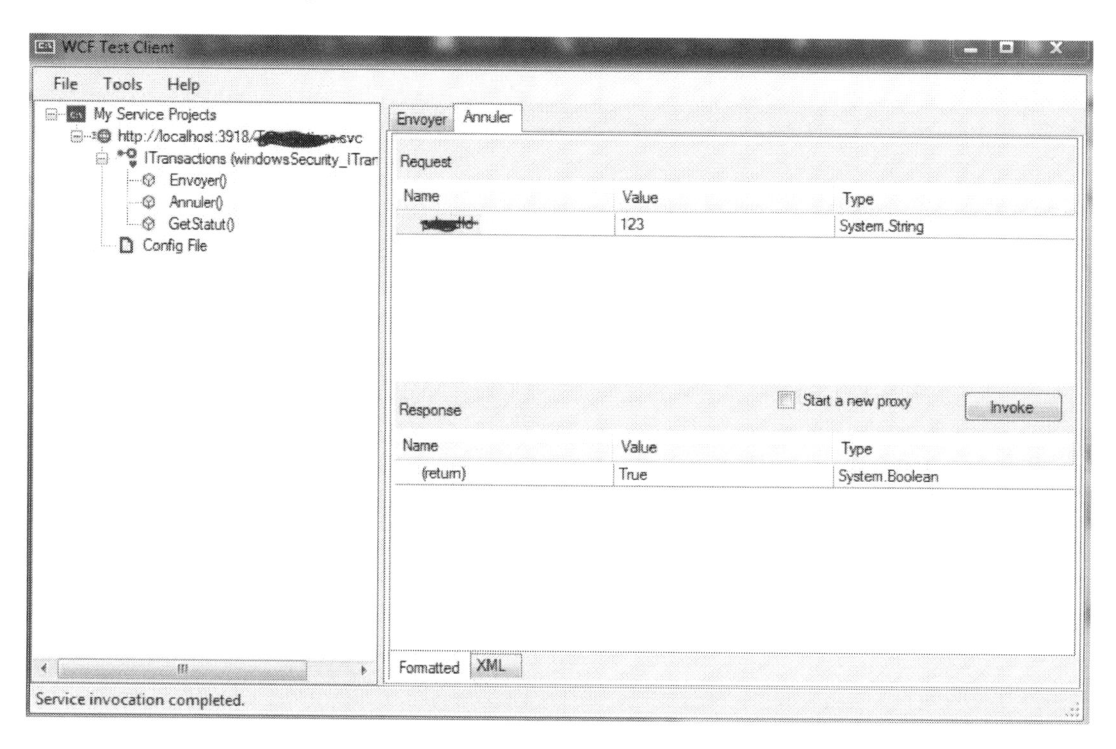


That is about it. From here you can invoke methods by setting parameters (if those are not complex object) and see results.

# How to log every call of your WCF service's methods

Release Date: 09-Apr-13
Url: http://patrickdesjardins.com/blog/?post_type=post&p=1994

If you want to log information like which method has been called with which parameters on every method of your WCF service, you should not set the log every time on each method. Two approaches are possible to create something clean.

The first option is to create an **attribute** and when this is present it will log. The second is to automatically log every call. I will show you the second approach since it seems more logical than to log every method. If you are curious about how to do it with an attribute, I will post the code to apply security with WCF with attribute, which will show you how to do it. This article shows you how to log every call of WCF's methods. It uses **Microsoft Unity** as IOC. The first step is to modify your service definition. This can be done by editing the **.scv** (not the .svc.cs).

```
<%@ ServiceHost Language="C#"
Debug="true"
Service="MyNameSpace.MyServices.MyService"
CodeBehind="MyService.svc.cs"
Factory="MyNameSpace.MyServices.Common.MyServiceHostFactory " %>
```

The important modification is the **Factory** attribute. This one is required to be able to use Unity. This acts as the global.asax.cs. By this, I mean it is called when the service is initialized and not at every call. Behind this factory, your own class is instanced and you are able to return your own **ServiceHost** class. This is a door to initialize Unity (IoC), AutoMapper and many other utilities classes that need to be instanced once.

```
public class MyServiceHostFactory : ServiceHostFactory
{
    protected override ServiceHost CreateServiceHost(Type serviceType
                                                    , Uri[] baseAddresses)
    {
        var serviceHost = new MyServiceHost(serviceType, baseAddresses);
        //ConfigureUnity(serviceHost.Container);
        //ConfigureAutoMapper();
        return serviceHost;
    }
}
```

The **MyServiceHostFactory** creates a **MyServiceHost** and configures the inversion of control container. It also initializes the Automapper configuration. The MyServiceHost inherits from ServiceHost, which lets you add the implementation of the IoC container and handle behaviors. To be able to log every service's method, a new behavior needs to be defined.

```
public class MyServiceHost : ServiceHost
{
    public UnityContainer Container { get; set; }

    public MyServiceHost()
    {
        Container = new UnityContainer();
```

```
    }

    public MyServiceHost(Type serviceType, params Uri[] baseAddresses)
                                    : base(serviceType, baseAddresses)
    {
        Container = new UnityContainer();
    }

    protected override void OnOpening()
    {
        base.OnOpening();

        if (this.Description.Behaviors.Find<MyServiceBehavior>() == null)
        {
            this.Description.Behaviors.Add(new MyServiceBehavior(Container));
        }
    }
}
```

The *MyServiceHost* initializes the container and adds a single behavior which handles the logging feature.

```
public class MyServiceBehavior : IServiceBehavior
{
    public UnityInstanceProvider InstanceProvider { get; set; }

    public MyServiceBehavior()
    {
        InstanceProvider = new UnityInstanceProvider();
    }

    public MyServiceBehavior(UnityContainer unity)
    {
        InstanceProvider = new UnityInstanceProvider { Container = unity };
    }

    public void AddBindingParameters(ServiceDescription serviceDescription,
                    ServiceHostBase serviceHostBase,
                    Collection<ServiceEndpoint> endpoints,
                    BindingParameterCollection bindingParameters)
    {
    }

    public void ApplyDispatchBehavior(ServiceDescription serviceDescription
                                    , ServiceHostBase serviceHostBase)
    {
        InstanceProvider.ServiceType = serviceDescription.ServiceType;
        foreach (ChannelDispatcherBase cdb in serviceHostBase.ChannelDispatchers)
        {
```

```
            var cd = cdb as ChannelDispatcher;
            if (cd != null)
            {
                foreach (EndpointDispatcher ed in cd.Endpoints)
                {
                    ed.DispatchRuntime.InstanceProvider = InstanceProvider;
                }
            }
        }

        var log = InstanceProvider.Container.Resolve<ILog>();
        IOperationBehavior behavior = new LoggingOperationBehavior(log);
        foreach (ServiceEndpoint endpoint in serviceDescription.Endpoints)
        {
            foreach (OperationDescription operation in
                                            endpoint.Contract.Operations)
            {
                if (!operation.Behaviors.Any(d => d is LoggingOperationBehavior))
                {
                    operation.Behaviors.Add(behavior);
                }
            }
        }
    }

    public void Validate(ServiceDescription serviceDescription
                                  , ServiceHostBase serviceHostBase)
    {
    }
}
```

This is where we attach, for all endpoints and all operations (methods), the behavior to be executed. This is where we add the logging behavior. The first foreach is required for Unity to be the provider while the second foreach is there to add the logging behavior.

```
public class UnityInstanceProvider : IInstanceProvider
{
    public IUnityContainer Container { set; get; }
    public Type ServiceType { set; get; }


    public UnityInstanceProvider()
        : this(null)
    {
    }

    public UnityInstanceProvider(Type type)
    {
        ServiceType = type;
```

```
            Container = new UnityContainer();
        }

        public object GetInstance(InstanceContext instanceContext, Message message)
        {
            return Container.Resolve(ServiceType);
        }

        public object GetInstance(System.ServiceModel.InstanceContext instanceContext)
        {
            return GetInstance(instanceContext, null);
        }

        public void ReleaseInstance(InstanceContext instanceContext, object instance)
        {

            var myInstance = instance as IDisposable;

            if (myInstance != null)
            {
                myInstance.Dispose();
            }
        }
    }

    public class LoggingOperationBehavior : IOperationBehavior
    {
        private readonly ILog _myLog;

        public LoggingOperationBehavior(ILog myLog)
        {
            _myLog = myLog;
        }

        public void ApplyDispatchBehavior(OperationDescription operationDescription
                                            , DispatchOperation dispatchOperation)
        {
            dispatchOperation.Invoker = new LoggingOperationInvoker(_myLog
                                    , dispatchOperation.Invoker, dispatchOperation);
        }

        public void Validate(OperationDescription operationDescription)
        {
        }

        public void ApplyClientBehavior(OperationDescription operationDescription
                                                , ClientOperation clientOperation)
        {
        }
```

```
    public void AddBindingParameters(OperationDescription operationDescription
                                , BindingParameterCollection bindingParameters)
    {
    }
}
```

At this point, we need to invoke the log. We need to specify an invoker that will be executed. This is why we need to create a logging invoker which takes the log that comes from Unity.

```
public class LoggingOperationInvoker : IOperationInvoker
{
    private readonly IOperationInvoker _baseInvoker;
    private readonly string _operationName;
    private readonly string _controllerName;
    private readonly ILog _myLog;

    public LoggingOperationInvoker(ILog myLog, IOperationInvoker baseInvoker
                                                , DispatchOperation operation)
    {
        _myLog = myLog;
        _baseInvoker = baseInvoker;
        _operationName = operation.Name;
        _controllerName = operation.Parent.Type == null ? "[None]" :
operation.Parent.Type.FullName;
    }

    public object Invoke(object instance, object[] inputs, out object[] outputs)
    {
        _myLog.Log("Method " + _operationName + " of class "
                                    + _controllerName + " called");
        try
        {
            return _baseInvoker.Invoke(instance, inputs, out outputs);
        }
        catch (Exception ex)
        {
            _myLog.Log(ex);
            throw;
        }
    }

    public object[] AllocateInputs() { return _baseInvoker.AllocateInputs(); }

    public IAsyncResult InvokeBegin(object instance, object[] inputs
                                    , AsyncCallback callback, object state)
    {
        _myLog.Log("Method " + _operationName + " of class "
                                            + _controllerName + " called");
```

```
        return _baseInvoker.InvokeBegin(instance, inputs, callback, state);
    }

    public object InvokeEnd(object instance, out object[] outputs
                                                        , IAsyncResult result)
    { return _baseInvoker.InvokeEnd(instance, out outputs, result); }

    public bool IsSynchronous { get { return _baseInvoker.IsSynchronous; } }
}
```

This is where the log is really written. It uses the interface to log which came from Unity and which from the Factory. The log is written when the method is invoked.

# How to use Unity with Web API

Release Date: 29-Apr-13
Url: http://patrickdesjardins.com/blog/?post_type=post&p=2026

Web API's controllers are instantiated by Asp.Net MVC framework, and by default the parameterless constructor is called. If you want to instantiate your class with your IoC, like Microsoft Unity, you will have to customize the instantiation of those Web API Controllers. The customized instanciator is called a **Dependency Resolver** and can be configured in the **Global.asax**.

```
public class WebApiApplication : System.Web.HttpApplication
{
    protected void Application_Start()
    {
        AreaRegistration.RegisterAllAreas();

        WebApiConfig.Register(GlobalConfiguration.Configuration);
        FilterConfig.RegisterGlobalFilters(GlobalFilters.Filters);
        RouteConfig.RegisterRoutes(RouteTable.Routes);
        BundleConfig.RegisterBundles(BundleTable.Bundles);

        UnityConfiguration.Initialize();
        MapperConfiguration.Initialize(UnityConfiguration.Container
                                        .Resolve<IMapperFactory>());
        UnityConfiguration.Container.Resolve<IDatabaseContext>()
                                        .InitializeDatabase();
        GlobalConfiguration.Configuration.DependencyResolver
                    = new IoCContainer(UnityConfiguration.Container);
    }
}
```

The first thing to do is to modify the **Application_Start** of your WebApi project. You need to execute the configuration of all your interfaces with Unity. In the example above, this is done by calling *UnityConfiguration.Initialize()* which Resolves every interface to a concrete class. The second thing to do is to set to the **GlobalConfiguration** a **DependencyResolver** to an IocContainer that we will create to use Unity container.

```
internal class ScopeContainer : IDependencyScope
{
    protected readonly IUnityContainer _container;

    public ScopeContainer(IUnityContainer container)
    {
        if (container == null)
        {
            throw new ArgumentNullException("container");
        }
        this._container = container;
    }

    public object GetService(Type serviceType)
    {

        if (!_container.IsRegistered(serviceType))
        {
            if (serviceType.IsAbstract || serviceType.IsInterface)
            {
                return null;
            }
        }
        return _container.Resolve(serviceType);
    }

    public IEnumerable<object> GetServices(Type serviceType)
    {
        return _container.IsRegistered(serviceType) ?
             _container.ResolveAll(serviceType) : new List<object>();
    }

    public void Dispose()
    {
        _container.Dispose();
    }
}

internal class IoCContainer : ScopeContainer, IDependencyResolver
{
    public IoCContainer(IUnityContainer container) : base(container)
    {
    }
```

```
    public IDependencyScope BeginScope()
    {
        var child = _container.CreateChildContainer();
        return new ScopeContainer(child);
    }
}
```

The *GetService* is made in a way that it does not require you to register every controller with **Unity** but only registered types will go through Unity. From here, every Web API controller will be instanced by passing by the *ScopeContainer*, which will check every parameter's type and resolve the type with Unity. The Web API will create a new instance of Unity and dispose of it at every http request.

# How to secure your Web API Controller globally without having to use the Authorize attribute

Release Date: 05-May-13
Url: http://patrickdesjardins.com/blog/?post_type=post&p=2039

If you are using **Web API** of .Net 4.5 framework and you want to have the same behavior of Asp.Net MVC which lets you have global authorization set to every http request, then you need to configure your website differently. In Asp.Net you would add a new filter to the **FilterConfig** file.

```
public static void RegisterGlobalFilters(GlobalFilterCollection filters)
{
    filters.Add(new HandleErrorAttribute());
    filters.Add(new AuthorizeAttribute());
}
```

But this does not work with the API controller. You have to set the AuthorizeAttribute to the WebApiConfig file.

```
public static void Register(HttpConfiguration config)
{
  config.Routes.MapHttpRoute(
    name: "DefaultApi",
    routeTemplate: "api/{controller}/{id}",
    defaults: new { id = RouteParameter.Optional }
  );

  config.Filters.Add(new AuthorizeAttribute());
}
```

From here, every method of all your controllers requires authorization. If you want to remove this required authorization for a specific web method, you need to add the attribute **[AllowAnonymous]**.

## How to use Microsoft Data Service OData with Unity

Release Date: 03-Jun-13
Url: http://patrickdesjardins.com/blog/?post_type=post&p=2083

If you want to use Unity with a **Microsoft Data Service (OData)**, you need to set up your IoC container once, and the perfect time to do it is in the startup. **OData**'s service does not have global.asax, neither does it have a **ServiceHostFactory** where you could set up your container. With Microsoft Data Service you want to set up your **Unity** container with the method **CreateDataSource,** which is available since you must inherit from **DataService**.

```
public class MyDataService : DataService<MyContext>
{
    public UnityContainer Container { get; set; }

    public static void InitializeService(DataServiceConfiguration config)
    {
        config.SetEntitySetAccessRule("*", EntitySetRights.AllRead);
        config.DataServiceBehavior.MaxProtocolVersion =
                                              DataServiceProtocolVersion.V3;
        config.UseVerboseErrors = true;
    }

    protected override ODataDbContext CreateDataSource()
    {
        Container = new UnityContainer();
        Bootstrapper.Initialise(Container);
        return new MyDataSourceContext(Container.Resolve<IMyInterface>());
    }
}
```

As you can see, you just need to define your **UnityContainer** as a property to your class (or you could use an attribute) and then initialize it inside the **CreateDataSource** method. Not only can you initialize your container here, but you can override the one defined in DataService to use yours (MyDataSourceContext) which uses unity for its parameters.

So, if you have a context for test and for your Data Service, then you could simply put any of the two in the class signature: *public class MyDataService : DataService*, and define the real context to use later in the override method. The main advantage is that you can inject with Unity (or any IoC container you use) classes to your context.

# Using Service Trace Viewer Tool to debug WCF service

Release Date: 10-Jun-13
Url: http://patrickdesjardins.com/blog/?post_type=post&p=2085

Microsoft provides a free tool to test your WCF service. This tool lets you see a lot of things that you can define at whichever level you want to see. The first step to configure the tool is to go inside your service project and open the configuration file. You should add into the **Configuration** tag the code below:

```
<system.diagnostics>
    <trace autoflush="true" />
    <sources>
            <source name="System.ServiceModel"
                    switchValue="Information, ActivityTracing"
                    propagateActivity="true">
            <listeners>
               <add name="sdt"
                    type="System.Diagnostics.XmlWriterTraceListener"
                    initializeData= "yourFileName.log" />
            </listeners>
         </source>
    </sources>
  </system.diagnostics>
```

Your file can contain any extension. The tool by default searches for a few files but you can at the end select All and see every extension.

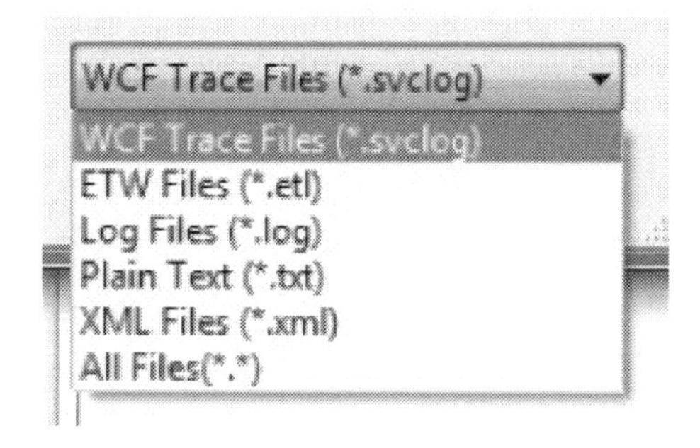


You can also specify to log only errors instead of information. ActivityTracing will trace every activity, which can be heavy on the log file. To use this tool, open a developer's console and type: **SvcTracerViewer**.

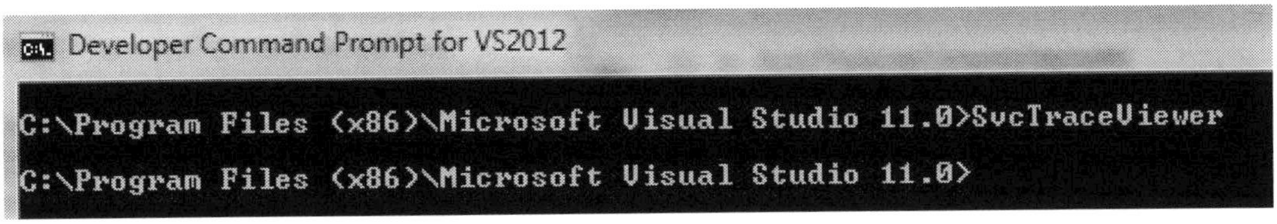

```
Developer Command Prompt for VS2012

C:\Program Files (x86)\Microsoft Visual Studio 11.0>SvcTraceViewer

C:\Program Files (x86)\Microsoft Visual Studio 11.0>
```

A Windows application will start and will let you select your tracing file and apply several filters.

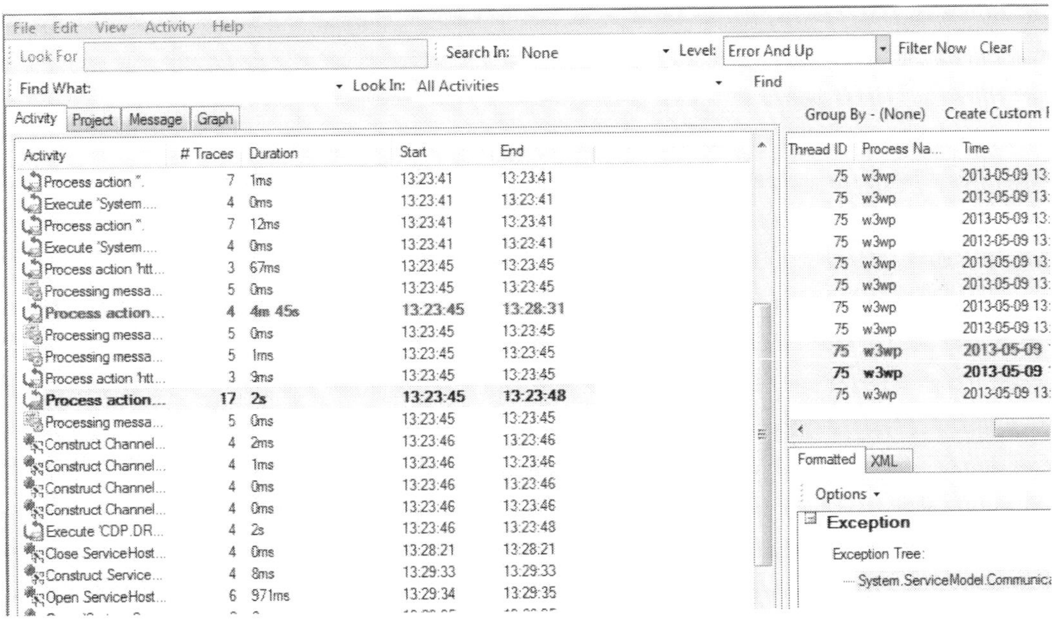

From here you should be able to see what is wrong with your WCF without having to attach any process to a remote WCF service.

## How to add active directory (AD) security to WCF services with attribute

Release Date: 27-Jun-13
Url: http://patrickdesjardins.com/blog/?post_type=post&p=2125

If you are using WCF web services with active directory (AD) you may want to have a more atomic authorization process than setting the security by IIS. You may want to allow a specific method for some groups when others may only have access to other groups. The first step is to create a custom attribute. This example shows you how to add a single role but you could modify this code to allow multiple roles.

```
public class SecureOperationAttribute : Attribute, IOperationBehavior
{
    public string Role { get; set; }
    public void AddBindingParameters(OperationDescription operationDescription
                                , BindingParameterCollection bindingParameters) { }
    public void ApplyClientBehavior(OperationDescription operationDescription
                                        , ClientOperation clientOperation) { }
    public void Validate(OperationDescription operationDescription) { }
    public void ApplyDispatchBehavior(OperationDescription operationDescription
                                        , DispatchOperation dispatchOperation)
    {
        dispatchOperation.Invoker = new SecureOperationInvoker(Role
                                                    , dispatchOperation);
    }
}
```

Once the attribute is set you need to create the **invoker**.

```
public class SecureOperationInvoker : IOperationInvoker
{
    private readonly IOperationInvoker _baseInvoker;
    private readonly string _operationName;
    private readonly string _role;

    public SecureOperationInvoker(string role, DispatchOperation operation)
    {
        _role = role;
        _baseInvoker = operation.Invoker;
        _operationName = operation.Name;
    }

    public object Invoke(object instance, object[] inputs, out object[] outputs)
    {
        if (!UserIsInRole(_role))
        {
            throw new FaultException(string.Format("Authentication fail. The
operation '{0}' requires the role '{1}'.", _operationName, _role), new
FaultCode("Authentication"));
        }
        return _baseInvoker.Invoke(instance, inputs, out outputs);
    }

    public object[] AllocateInputs()
    {
        return _baseInvoker.AllocateInputs();
    }

    public IAsyncResult InvokeBegin(object instance, object[] inputs
                                , AsyncCallback callback, object state)
```

```
    {
        return _baseInvoker.InvokeBegin(instance, inputs, callback, state);
    }

    public object InvokeEnd(object instance, out object[] outputs
                                                    , IAsyncResult result)
    {
        return _baseInvoker.InvokeEnd(instance, out outputs, result);
    }

    public bool IsSynchronous
    {
        get
        {
            return _baseInvoker.IsSynchronous;
        }
    }

    public bool UserIsInRole(string role)
    {
        var winPrinc = new WindowsPrincipal(
                OperationContext.Current.ServiceSecurityContext.WindowsIdentity);
        return winPrinc.IsInRole(role);
    }
}
```

Of course, this example is a small representation of what should have been done in a real system. In fact, the **UserIsInRole** should not be hardcoded to use **WindowsPrincipal**. It should be injected to be able to test without having to use WindowsPrincipal. Also, the role variable may in fact not be exactly the name of the active directory (AD) group, so you may need to inject also a mechanism to translate the role used by the attribute to the AD group. Here is how to use the attribute over your WCF contract.

```
[ServiceContract]
public interface IMyEntityXYZ
{
    [OperationContract]
    [SecureOperation(Role = "Admin")]
    void Action(DTOXYZ[] xyz);
}
```

What I like is that you can set the security on the contract. It is simple for maintenance because the operation signature contains who has access to the method defined. It is also easy to test if you are using injection to create a stub method for the validation of the role.

# WCF The maximum message size quota for incoming messages (65536) has been exceeded.

Release Date: 08-Jul-13
Url: http://patrickdesjardins.com/blog/?post_type=post&p=2096

WCF The maximum message size quota for incoming messages (65536) has been exceeded. This is because the **MaxReceivedMessageSize** is set by default to 65536 and you are returning more than that. Most WCF Clients let you edit this property :

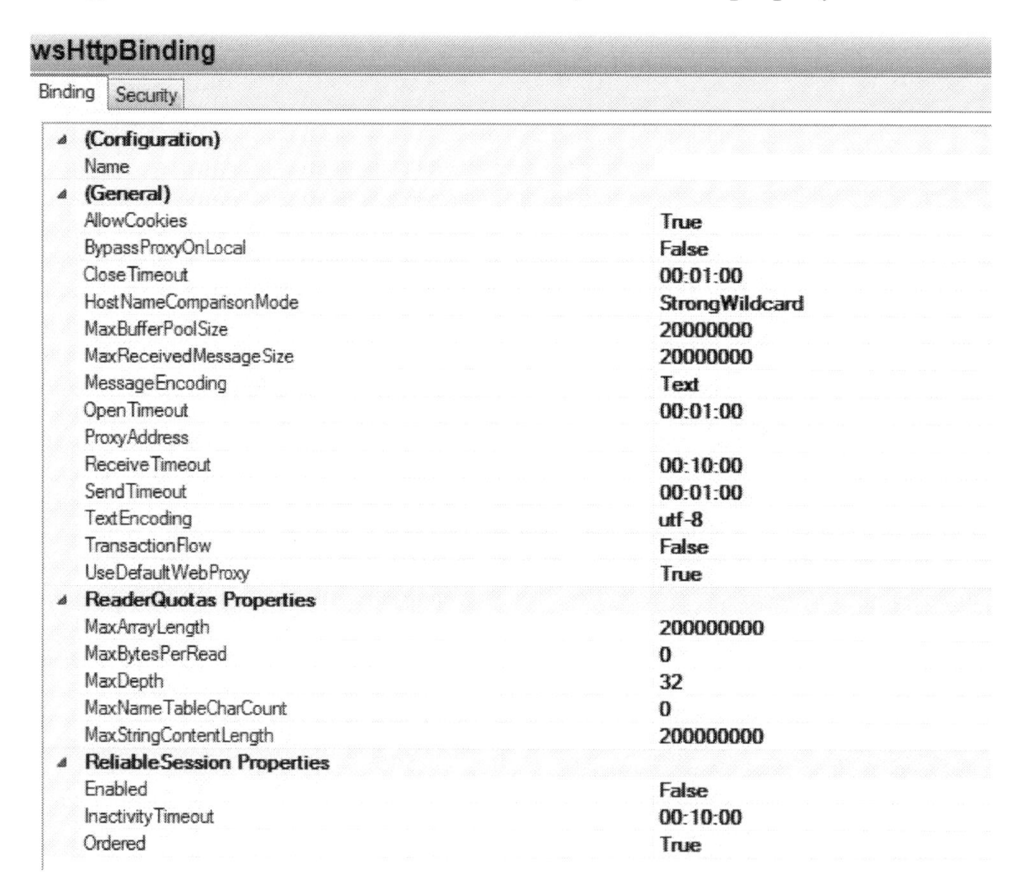


Even the WCFTestClient lets you edit the size. You just need to right click on **Config File**, then you select **Edit With SvcConfigEditor**.

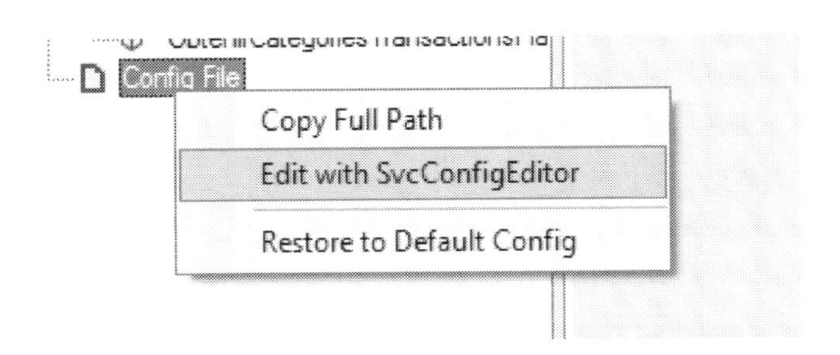


From here, you need to open the Bindings folder (of SvcConfiEditor) and change **MaxReceivedMessageSize** to something more related to the kind of size you are expecting to receive.

## WCF Data Services is the implementation of OData by Microsoft

Release Date: 18-Jul-13
Url: http://patrickdesjardins.com/blog/?post_type=post&p=2151

Several times a week I hear confusion concerning WCF services, WCF Data Services, ADO Data Service and OData. First of all, ADO Data Service is out. In fact, it is the old name for WCF Data Service which is also known as OData by Microsoft. WCF service focuses on contract while Data Service focuses more on the data. OData was invented by Microsoft but is not the implementation in .Net. It is the protocol which is open.

WCF Data Service is a type of service that provides information through a url. This is easily consumable because it requires only a web browser to execute a call, which can have filters, join between entities, and conditions. WCF Data Service uses the entity-relationship conventions of the Entity Data Model to expose resources as sets of entities that are related by associations. Not only can you get information the way you want but you can also update entity and insert.

WCF Data Service lets you use two well-known semantic structures, which are Atom (XML) and JSON. Both of these protocols are RestFul. That mean that when a call is executed, the life cycle ends once the data is sent back to the consumer.

To create a WCF Data Service, simply create a class that inherits from DataService. It's a generic class so you will have to specify a DataContext type. To use this class, you need to reference the dll : **System.Data.Services**.

```
public partial class MyService : DataService<MyDbContext>
{
```

```
    //...
}
```

You will have to also specify which entities are allowed to be accessed in InitializeService.

```
public static void InitializeService(DataServiceConfiguration config)
{
   //...
}
```

The simplicity lets you add this service in a later stage of your project. It is even more true if your project is already using Entity Framework because OData is a tightly coupled Entity Framework way to handle entity. It is very easy to create a WCF Data Service with Entity Framework because of the Data Model that both share.

OData is between the consumer and the source; the consumer could be a simple web browser and the source a .Net application or SQL Azure server. This is very powerful because you can make a mobile application that uses the same service as a web site or a winform. Even more, you can create on different web browsers (Internet Explorer, FireFox, Chrome) or different mobile platforms (Android, IPhone, Windows Phone) with the same WCF Data Service.

The OData protocol lets you send more than only a GET request. A GET http request will only give you the possibility to receive data. In case you want to delete data, a DELETE http request would be required. POST is used to insert, PUT to update. The protocol uses string and not a reference, this is why XML and JSON are used. It also respects the concept of not being tied to the server by being RestFul. So, in short, an SQL table (rows) is converted into Entity Set (entity) which is converted to a collection of entries (entry).

WCF Data Services also supports data models that are based on common language runtime (CLR) objects that return an instance of the **IQueryable** interface.

# OData Query syntax

Release Date: 25-Jul-13
Url: http://patrickdesjardins.com/blog/?post_type=post&p=2163

If you have set up WCF Data Service, you can now query your service with the OData syntax. If you are using Entity Framework, you will see a lot of similarity between Entity Framework and this string syntax. OData works with http request which is based on URL. Every query statement needs to be passed by this URL. Here is a list of all possible statements that can be used together as Entity Framework or as an SQL statement.

## OData ordering keyword: orderby

If you request one of your entity sets, you may want to order the result. To be able to order, you will have to user **orderby** with = and the property of the entity. If you need multiple properties in your ordering, simply separate them with a comma (,). Here are two examples.

```
http://yourwebsite/YourService.svc/YourEntitiesSet?$orderby=OneOfYourProperty
http://yourwebsite/YourService.svc/YourEntitiesSet?$orderby=OneOfYourProperty,ASec
ondProperty
```

## OData getting a limited amount of data keyword: top

This is the same keyword as in SQL Server or Entity Framework. This lets the consumer specify to the WCF Data Service the maximum results the consumer receives. It can be a specific number, or less, or none. Here is an example.

```
http://yourwebsite/YourService.svc/YourEntitiesSet?$top=10
```

## OData paging result keyword: skip

You can do paging with OData. For example, if you want to have a list that displays 10 elements per page, you could request the WCF Data Service to get the first 10 entities and then ask for the next 10 entities when the user requests the next page. This can be done with the previous keyword **top** to get the 10 entities but to get which group of 10, we need to use the new keyword **skip**. If you want to have the third page of 10 elements, we will need to use skip with the value 20 and the top at 10. This can be translated to: "I want the third page of 10 elements." The value of skip is 20 because we have 10 elements per page. One page means we display 10, two pages means we display 20. The third page skips those 20 pages and displays the next 10. This is specified with the top keyword.

```
http://yourwebsite/YourService.svc/YourEntitiesSet?$skip=20&$top=10
```

## Condition with OData by the filter keyword

In SQL, we would use the keyword **where** and the keyword **and** if we have multiple conditions. It's the same thing with Entity Framework. But, with OData, the keyword is not **where**. The keyword is **filter**.

```
http://yourwebsite/YourService.svc/YourEntitiesSet?$filter=YourProperty
equal('Test')
```

OData contains several keywords to compare:
http://go.microsoft.com/fwlink/?LinkId=186972

## Joining entity with the keyword expand

Entity Framework gives the keyword **include** which adds a reference to another entity or a list of entities. You need to specify the name of the property and it will be loaded in the foreign key that defines the relationship in the database. With OData, the keyword is **expand**.

```
http://yourwebsite/YourService.svc/YourEntitiesSet?$expand=YourPropertyThatLinkToA
nOtherEntity
```

## Selecting specific properties of an entity with the OData keyword select

This is exactly the same as SQL and Entity. As you can see since the beginning of this article, a lot of keywords in OData are the same with Entity and SQL. This is a strong positive point that reduces the learning curve. The **select** keyword gives you the posibility of not returning all the entity information but only the specific property.

```
http://yourwebsite/YourService.svc/YourEntitiesSet?$select=Property1,Property2
```

# WCF Inspector for logging

Release Date: 21-Nov-13
Url: http://patrickdesjardins.com/blog/?post_type=post&p=2222

We have already talked about how to log every call of your WCF service with a custom factory for all your WCF services. This is a good way to log or to verify access to all your service methods. The main point was to create a factory which is called every call. Once it is generated, it creates a new service behavior for which it needs to have a new operation behavior and invoker.

This time, the solution to log every method called is by using inspector. An inspector is a filter that is executed before and after a request is executed. First of all, this solution works by configuring in the web.config a behavior. An entry to system.serviceModel > extensions > behaviorExtensions needs to be added and will be used to system.serviceModel > endpointBehaviors > behavior.

Here is an example of the web.config:

```
<system.serviceModel>
    <extensions>
          <behaviorExtensions>
              <add name="myLogBehavior"
```

```
                    type="MyServiceA.LogFileBehaviorExtensionElement, MyServiceA"
/>
            </behaviorExtensions>
        </extensions>
...
 <services>
      <service name="MyServiceA.Service1">
        <endpoint address=""
                  behaviorConfiguration="behavior1"
                  binding="wsHttpBinding"
                  bindingConfiguration=""
                  contract="MyServiceA.IService1" />
      </service>
    </services>
    <behaviors>
      <endpointBehaviors>
          <behavior name="behavior1">
              <myLogBehavior logFileName="c:\log.txt" />
          </behavior>
      </endpointBehaviors>

...
```

Three parts are important. The first one is the extension that defines the behavior extension. This allows us to create a configuration outside the code that is defined inside the web.config. A name is specified that is referred to later inside the web.config, and the second attribute is the name of the extension inside the code. In the example above, the code displays a LogFileBehaviorExtensionElement that is inside the MyServiceA namespace. The second part is the service's endpoint itself. This is where we specify the contract, the binding and also the behaviorConfiguration. This behavior configuration leads us to the third important part which is the behavior that we have created. The third part is the endpointBehaviors where it specifies the behavior. In the example, it's named "behavior1" which is referenced inside the endpoint. Inside this third part, the myLogBehavior defines a parameter which is the file log name.

The next step is to create the behavior extension element inside the code.

```
public class LogFileBehaviorExtensionElement : BehaviorExtensionElement
{
    [ConfigurationProperty("logFileName")]
    public string LogFileName
    {
        get
        {
            return (string)base["logFileName"];
        }
        set
```

```
        {
            base["logFileName"] = value;
        }
    }

    protected override object CreateBehavior()
    {
        return new LogOutputBehavior(this.LogFileName);
    }

    public override Type BehaviorType
    {
        get
        {
            return typeof(LogOutputBehavior);
        }
    }
}
```

As you can see, this contains a configuration property which is the attribute of the file name defined in the web.config. It also creates the behavior. The next class to create is the endpoint behavior. This is where we add the inspector to the endpoint. This means that every method of the service will have the inspector hooked to it. If it's not the desired behavior, it's also possible to hook an inspector with a custom attribute.

```
public class LogOutputBehavior : IEndpointBehavior
{
    private string logFileName;
    public LogOutputBehavior(string logFileName)
    {
        this.logFileName = logFileName;
    }

    public void AddBindingParameters(ServiceEndpoint endpoint
                            , BindingParameterCollection bindingParameters)
    {
    }

    public void ApplyClientBehavior(ServiceEndpoint endpoint
                                    , ClientRuntime clientRuntime)
    {

    }

    public void ApplyDispatchBehavior(ServiceEndpoint endpoint
                                , EndpointDispatcher endpointDispatcher)
    {
```

```
        LogOutputMessageInspector inspector = new
LogOutputMessageInspector(this.logFileName);
        endpointDispatcher.DispatchRuntime.MessageInspectors.Add(inspector);
    }

    public void Validate(ServiceEndpoint endpoint)
    {
    }
}
```

The behavior creates the inspector.

```
public class LogOutputMessageInspector : IDispatchMessageInspector
{
    private string logFileName;
    public LogOutputMessageInspector(string logFileName)
    {
        this.logFileName = logFileName;
    }
    public object AfterReceiveRequest(ref Message request, IClientChannel channel
                                    , InstanceContext instanceContext)
    {
        MessageBuffer buffer = request.CreateBufferedCopy(Int32.MaxValue);
        request = buffer.CreateMessage();
        File.AppendAllText(this.logFileName, "[" + DateTime.Now + "] Request : "
                                            + request.ToString());
        return null;
    }
    public void BeforeSendReply(ref Message reply, object correlationState)
    {
        MessageBuffer buffer = reply.CreateBufferedCopy(Int32.MaxValue);
        reply = buffer.CreateMessage();
        File.AppendAllText(this.logFileName, "[" + DateTime.Now + "] Reply : "
                                            + reply.ToString());
    }

}
```

This is the inspector! We have the **AfterReceiveRequest** that is called just before the method of the controller is entered, and the **BeforeSendReply** that is called after the method is called. This allows you to create an entry in the log and to know the starting and ending time of the call. You can also have access to the message sent. This is in Soap format. Here is an example:

```
<s:Envelope xmlns:a="http://www.w3.org/2005/08/addressing"
xmlns:s="http://www.w3.org/2003/05/soap-envelope">
  <s:Header>
```

```
    <a:Action
s:mustUnderstand="1">http://tempuri.org/IService1/GetDataResponse</a:Action>
    <a:RelatesTo>urn:uuid:af68f512-6948-4c2f-b0a8-36cbd9799ebf</a:RelatesTo>
  </s:Header>
  <s:Body>
    <GetDataResponse xmlns="http://tempuri.org/">
      <GetDataResult>You entered: 0</GetDataResult>
    </GetDataResponse>
  </s:Body>
</s:Envelope>
```

You have all the information you want. In reality, you would like to parse this xml to get the method name which is inside the envelope>header>action or by using the Message property Headers, and use the Action property to get the method called. It's also possible to get HttpRequest information if the endpoint is an http one.

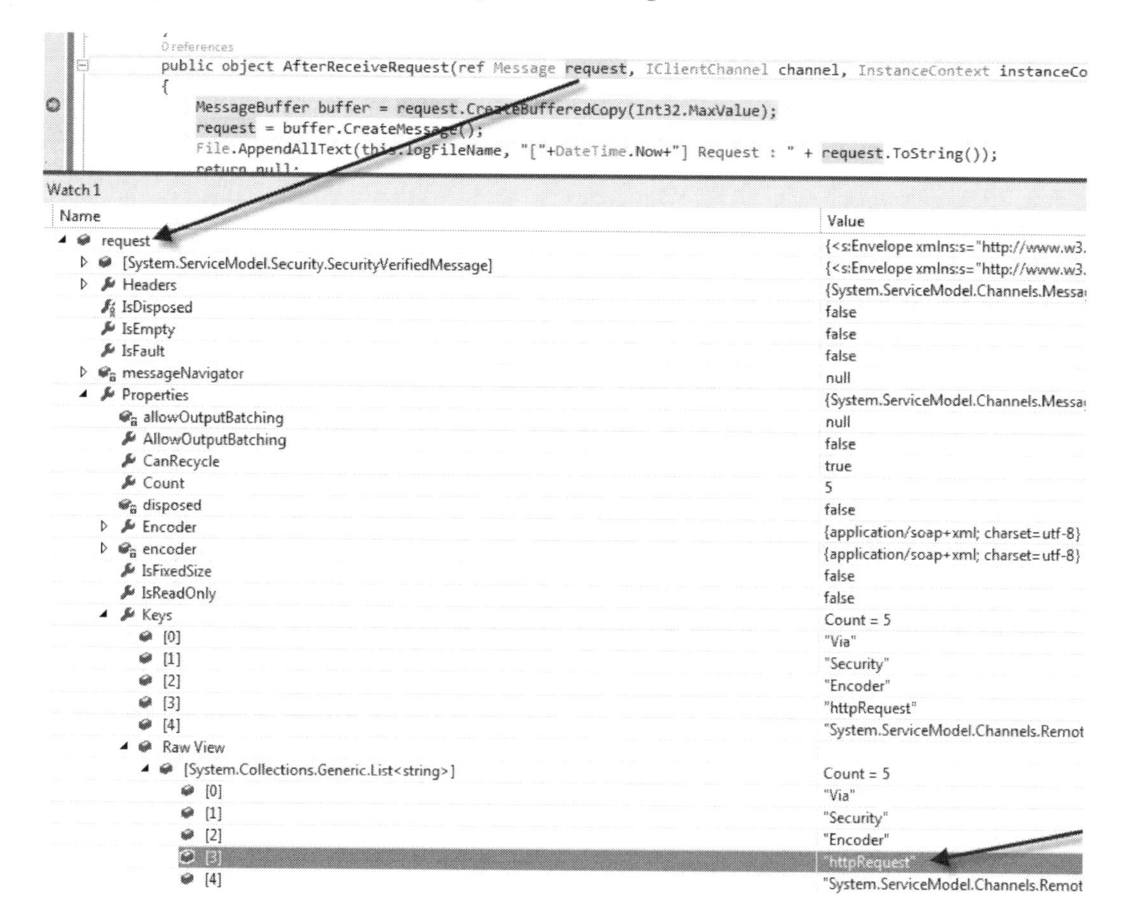


This is it for WCF inspector.

# Using Transaction with WCF Services

Release Date: 20-Dec-13
Url: http://patrickdesjardins.com/blog/?post_type=post&p=2219

If you need to call two different WCF services and be sure that both are successful before committing, you need to use transaction. This will require that both service's operation contains the attribute **TransactionFlow** with the option to **Allowed**. Many other options could have been possible. **NotAllowed** is when you do not want to be part of the transaction, which is the default value. **Allowed** allows participation in a transaction if the client specifies in his code a transaction scope. Finally, **Mandatory** forces that the operation is called within a transaction scope.

```
[ServiceContract]
public interface IServiceContractOne
{
    [OperationContract]
    [TransactionFlow(TransactionFlowOption.Allowed)]
    void Method1();
}
```

The next step is the implementation of this contract, the method *Method1* that has the **TransactionFlow** attribute. It needs to have the attribute **OperationBehavior** in the implementation. The method of the contract has an operation behavior that tells that it is required to be inside a transaction scope.

```
[OperationBehavior(TransactionScopeRequired = true)]
public void Method1()
{
    //Entity Framework here
}
```

The next step is to configure the web.config. It needs to have for the binding the attribute transactionflow set to true.

```
<configuration>
  <system.serviceModel>
     <bindings>
        <wsHttpBinding>
           <binding name="MyBinding" transactionFlow="true" />
        </wsHttpBinding>
...
...
```

Once the binding is created, you need to use this binding.

```
<configuration>
 <system.serviceModel>
    <services>
      <service name="MyServiceA.Service1">
        <endpoint address=""
                  behaviorConfiguration="behavior1"
                  binding="wsHttpBinding"
                  bindingConfiguration="MyBinding"
                  contract="MyServiceA.IService1" />
...
...
```

I have chosen **wshttpbinding** because to use a transaction you need to use a WS-Atomic Transaction or OleTransactions protocol. Finally, you can test the transaction by having an application that uses the two services (or more) that you created with the contract that has transaction score required.

```
using (var scope = new TransactionScope(TransactionScopeOption.RequiresNew))
{
   try
   {
      var obj = new ServiceReference1.Service1();
      obj.Method1();
      var obj1 = new ServiceReference2.Service1();
      obj1.Method1();
      ts.Complete(); //Commit everything!
   }
   catch (Exception ex)
   {
      ts.Dispose();
   }
}
```

If any exception occurs during the scope of the transaction, everything is rolled back. You can add additional information to the service that has the method with transaction mandatory or allowed. It is done with **ServiceBehavior**. You can specify the transaction timeout and also the transaction isolation level. The timeout is a time that you allow for the service to be executed. The isolation level is the same as when you use transaction without services. It tells how to lock the information during the transaction. By default, it is serializable which blocks everything to be changed. It is the most protective and also the worst in term of performance. I will not discuss every type of isolation level but some allow you to insert new data while others allow you to simply change everything. You have to figure out which one is the correct one for your needs. Do not forget to add a **System.Transaction** reference into your project if you do want to use transaction.

```
[ServiceBehavior(TransactionIsolationLevel=System.Transactions.IsolationLevel.Seri
alizable, TransactionTimeout="00:00:30")]
```

# WCF and data contract versioning

Release Date: 10-Mar-14
Url: http://patrickdesjardins.com/blog/?post_type=post&p=3385

Windows Communication Foundation (WCF) versioning has two different flavors. The first one works with **strict schema** and the second one works with **lossless schema**. The lossless schema are supported because elements are marked as optional by default. Adding a new data member is replacing this element with null if not provided. This is also known as Lax Versioning.

Working with strict schema forces you to have a data contract created with a custom namespace. This namespace should illustrate the version of the data member and the operation contract should reflect this change by altering the use of this new version. This is closely tied to the management of changes in the service contract. Microsoft recommended that you explicitly specify a name and namespace for the service contract and an action for each operation. This requires you to change the default "http://tempuri.org" and to specify that your namespace can contain a version number or the publish date. This can be done easily by using the attribute DataContract that you have to use to specify to WCF the classes to be used. This time, specify the name and the namespace. For example:

```
[DataContract(Name = "Entity", Namespace =
"http://YourWebsite/YourServices/2014/03/09/Entity")]
public class EntityV1
{
}

[DataContract(Name = "Entity", Namespace =
"http://YourWebsite/YourServices/2014/03/10/Entity")]
public class EntityV2
{
}
```

Over time, you will create new versions of your data. You can create as many versions as you want with different class names and with the same contract name if they have a unique namespace.

Most of the time, strict schema are not required. Having extra elements sent is not harmful. What must not be changed often is the name of the contract and the namespace name. This could result in having an older client not be able to reach the server. If the version of the operation changes by adding a field and the client does not provide this field, WCF will set the default value to the missing parameter. In the other case, if the client is sending more than required, WCF will ignore it. However, your entity must inherit from **IExtensibleDataObject** to handle round-tripping. This enables storing additional information into a property. It allows sending the object passed to the WCF back to the client without any loss. Otherwise, it is not used and the WCF service does not crash.

Having the attribute **IsRequired** not set helps maintainability or should be left at its default value. The point is to be able to add a new data member and still have an older version, that does not have this member, able to use the service. If the member is not required and if the client does not send the member to the service, WCF will use the default value. If it is not possible to have NULL or zero (for numeric value), then using *OnDesizalizingAttribute* should provide a default value. For example, you could generate a new Guid if nothing is sent for a Guid type instead of letting the Guid be Null.

## Asp.Net Web Api Getting 401unauthorized code

Release Date: 20-May-14
Url: http://patrickdesjardins.com/blog/?post_type=post&p=3486

If you are creating a brand new Web API and try to execute a POST query with Web API, you might receive a 401 status code from the request. This might be because the security of your service is not set correctly. Open the Web API project (hit F4 when with the project selected from the Solution Explorer).

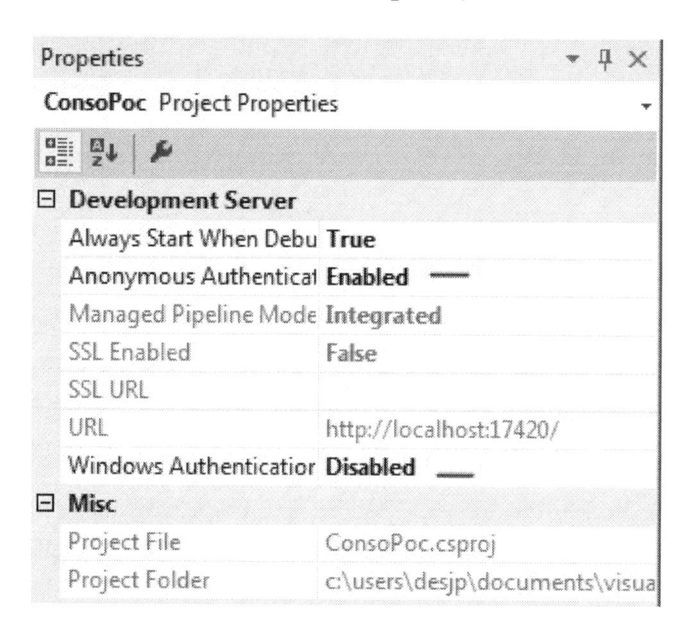

The second thing that you have to ensure is that you are requesting a JSON call. This means that you must have in the request header the **content-type** set to JSON .

```
User-Agent: Fiddler
Host: localhost:17420
Content-Length: 16
Content-Type: application/json
```

For example, running a post on an action that takes a single string requires Fiddler to have the Request Header set with the previous four lines and the request body of the string desired. For example "This is a test."

```
public void Post([FromBody]string value){}
```

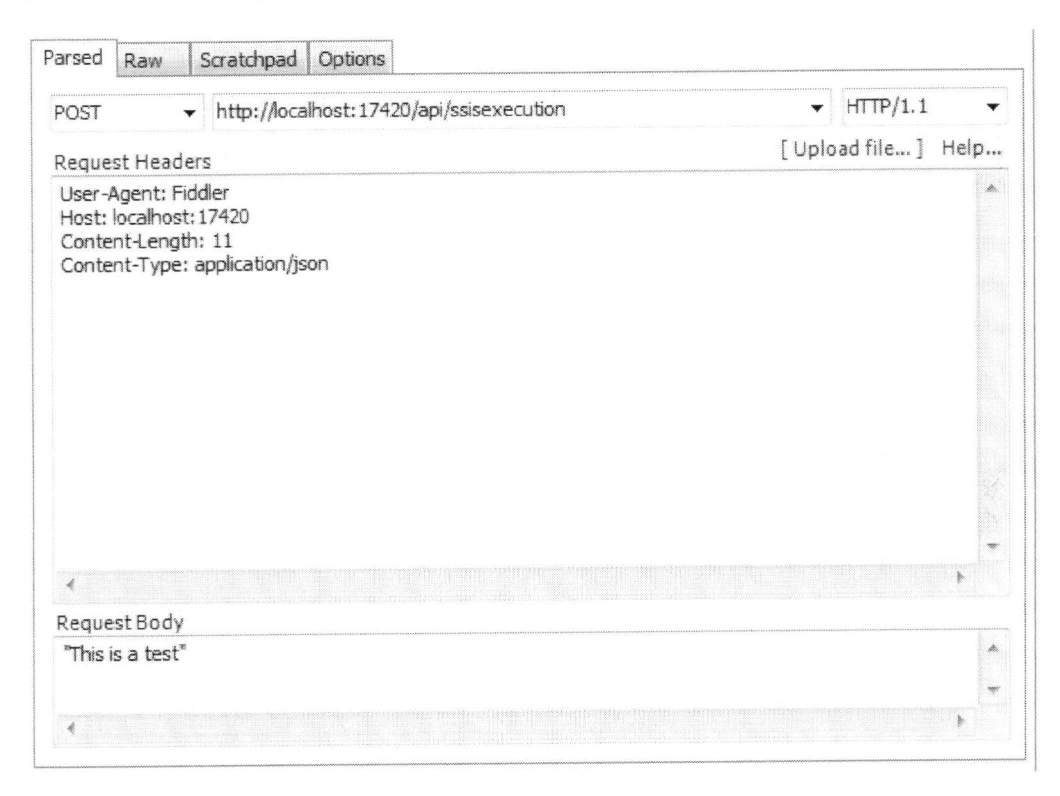


For a more exhaustive test, you can send an object. This requires you to use the JSON syntax. The Web API Controller also requires having the class defined and the parameter to use this class.

```
public void Post([FromBody]DTOExecutionParameters value)
{
}
```

```
public class DTOExecutionParameters
{
    public string  NameTask { get; set; }
    public string  ParameterName { get; set; }
}
```

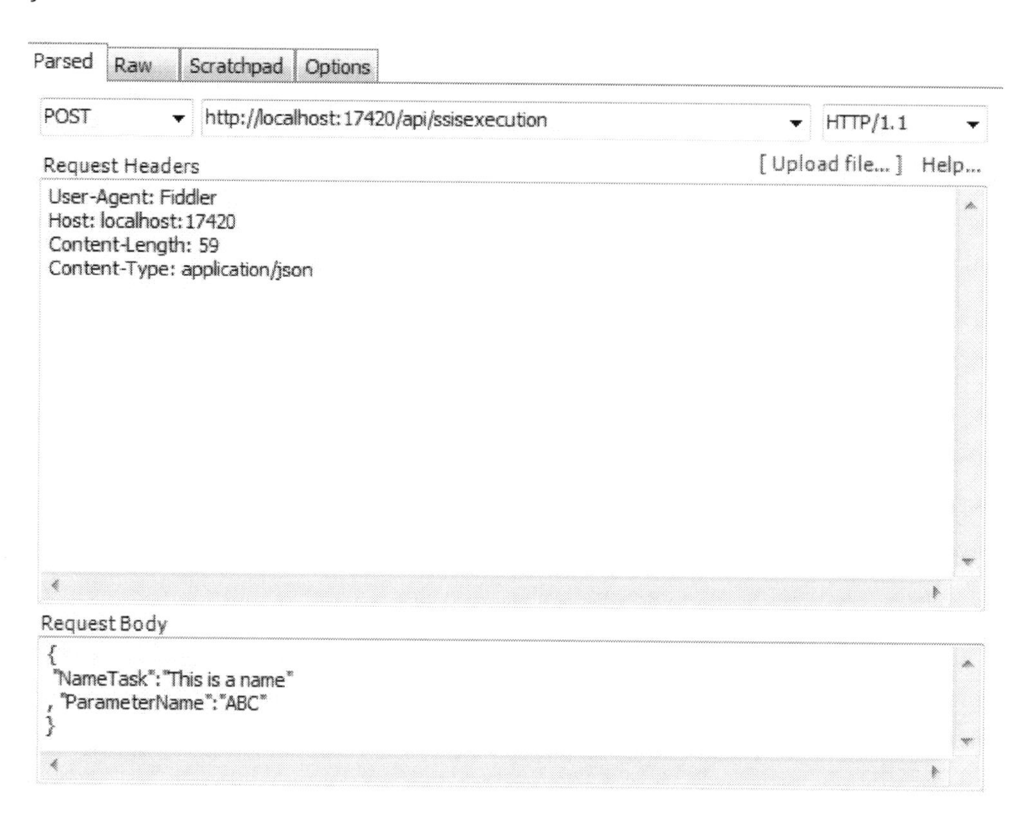


This request has the status 200 and if you set a breakpoint in Visual Studio you can see the values.

```
public void Post([FromBody]DTOExecutionParameters value)
{
}
```

value {ConsoPoc.Controllers.DTOExecut
NameTask "This is a name"
ParameterName "ABC"

•

# ABOUT THE AUTHOR

Patrick Desjardins has been working since 2014 for Microsoft as a Software Developer Engineer in the cloud and services team. He is a Microsoft Most Valuable Professional (MVP) in Asp.Net for two consecutive years, 2013 and 2014. He has studied software engineering and he is known for his analysis, resourcefulness, and abilities to find effective solutions quickly. Since his early professional career, his focus has always been to keep up to date in order to provide quality services to meet customers' needs. Patrick is a professional who has a well-developed work ethic and who has the desire to perform both in quality and timeliness. His area of interest is Web development, which he embraced since the early 2000s. For many years Patrick has continued to train daily in new technologies and apply all theories learned to various projects. Patrick is a huge fan of Microsoft technologies' .Net which he used to develop professionally since 2004. By contrast, since 2002 he developed in PHP many projects that make him someone with multiple perspectives on how the web can be developed. His main focus is to help people to embrace Microsoft technology in an enterprise environment. He is a strong believer in Asp.Net MVC and Entity Framework to help create quality websites for professionals that follow good standards with Html5, CSS3 and design patterns.

.Net Knowledge book

This book is a melting pot of several articles about Asp.Net MVC, Entity Framework, JavaScript, CSS, C# and SQL. They are scenarios that happen in the everyday work of developers who use these technologies. They are divided into short articles that are easy to understand. This book is ideal for anyone with intermediate to advanced knowledge of Microsoft web stack who wants to learn more about how to deal with practical cases. This book includes articles written during 2013 and 2014. It is volume 2 of a series of books that focus on real software developing problems. I strongly believe that the content of this book is a must for anyone who works with Microsoft Asp.Net in enterprise.

Here are some subjects discussed in the book:

Asp.Net MVC EditorTemplate, RouteData, OnActionExecuting, Web Api, Currency Template, Binding Attributes, Url Localization, Security, Complex Binding with Abstract Type, Multiple Actions per Form, Validation with ViewModel and Model. Entity Framework with Value Object, Disconnect Graph, Migration Tool, Database Initialization, DbContext, Complex Type and References, Unit of Work Pattern, Loading Recursive Structure, Validations, Detached Object, Tracing, Delete Object and ObjectStateManager, Identity Framework. Webservice logs, SvcUtil, WebTestClient, OData. Git Basic Commands for .Net Developer.

About the author:

Patrick Desjardins is working since 2014 for Microsoft as a Software Developer Engineer in the cloud and services team. He is a Microsoft Most Valuable Professional (MVP) in Asp.Net for two consecutive years, 2013 and 2014. He has studied software engineering and he is known for his analysis, resourcefulness and abilities to find effective solutions quickly. Since his early professional career, his focus has always been to keep up to date in order to provide quality services to meet customers' needs. Patrick is a professional who has a well-developed work ethic and who has the desire to perform both in quality and timeliness. His area of interest is Web development, which he has embraced since the early 2000s. For many years Patrick has continued to train daily in new technologies and put all theories learned into practice in various projects.